002384886

Co

D1565457

A MOST UNCERTAIN CRUSADE

A MOST UNCERTAIN CRUSADE

THE UNITED STATES,
THE UNITED NATIONS,
AND HUMAN RIGHTS,
1941–1953

ROWLAND BRUCKEN

NIU PRESS
DEKALB, IL

© 2014 by Northern Illinois University Press
Published by the Northern Illinois University Press, DeKalb, Illinois 60115
Manufactured in the United States using acid-free paper
Design by Shaun Allshouse

Library of Congress Cataloging-in-Publication Data

Brucken, Rowland.
 A most uncertain crusade : the United States, the United Nations, and human rights, 1941-1953 /
Rowland Brucken.
    pages cm
  Includes bibliographical references and index.
  ISBN 978-0-87580-471-2 (hardback) — ISBN 978-1-60909-091-3 (e-book)
  1. Human rights—United States—History—20th century. 2. United Nations—General Assembly—
Universal Declaration of Human Rights. 3. United States—Politics and government. I. Title.
  JC599.U5B75 2013
  341.4'809044—dc23
                                  2013024503

To Lisa, My True Love, who rekindled The Dream

To my Mother, Father, and Grandmother, who lived the principles

of honor, honesty, integrity, and stewardship

To Katherine, Grace, and Caroline, with my love and aspiration for them

to inhabit a peaceable world resting on the enjoyment of a full,

rich range of human liberty by all peoples

Contents

Acknowledgments

I am indebted to many people who have helped me academically, personally, and spiritually during the ten years it took to research and write this book.

My academic advisors at The Ohio State University, Dr. Michael Hogan and Dr. Peter Hahn, read chapter drafts of my dissertation and offered much constructive criticism. Dr. Carol Anderson helped me to place events within the Civil Rights Movement in broader perspective and sharpened my critique. Itai Sneh, Richard Wiggers, and Diane Hill are examples of why the historical study of American human rights policy has a bright future. Others scholars who have offered criticism and insights include Michael Cren, Ted Mearns, Jr., Cathal Nolan, Richard Falk, Bryan Young, Andrew Moravcsik, Gary Woodard, Joseph Cofield, and William Schabas. I am grateful for the feedback provided by two anonymous manuscript reviewers as well. I owe a tremendous debt of gratitude to my editors, Mark Heineke, Marlyn Miller, and Susan Bean, who expertly guided me through the publication process and offered insightful suggestions.

To Dr. Amy Sayward and Bruce Karhoff, graduate school colleagues at The Ohio State University, I owe a very personal debt: the discovery of how scholars can push each other to excel.

Norwich University generously awarded me a Charles A. Dana Fellowship and a semester-long sabbatical to complete this work, and I am most appreciative of the support. I also received a research fellowship over the summer of 2008 to do archival work for part of this book with Michael Self, who graduated from Norwich and who has a bright future ahead of him in the law enforcement field.

Over the last twenty-five years, friends and colleagues in Amnesty International have inspired me to fight passionately for those ideals I chose to study here. The tireless advocacy, creative thinking, and passionate commitment of Nancy Bothne, Michael Heflin, Simeon Mawanza, Tiseke Kasambala Dr. Hugo Adam Bedau, Dr. Mike Radelet, Sister Donna Schneweis, Jim Lyle, Dr. Elizabeth Dreyfuss, Ilona Kelly, James Graham, and Sarah Hager will all speak through the writings of historians who document the domestic and foreign work of the modern Human Rights Movement. Human rights defenders in Zimbabwe, some of whom I have come to know personally, have witnessed and endured the suffering and persecution that come from governmental oppression and neglect. I want to particularly mention Arnold Tsunga, Magadonga Mahlangu, Jenny Williams, and Teresa Dangwa; their struggle for human dignity must also be our struggle if the promises contained in the documents cited in this book are to have any resonance in the real world.

My parents, Robert and Lois Brucken, have guided and supported me in surprising, emerging ways. In addition to their love and prodding to finish this work, my late mother's lifelong devotion to volunteerism and my father's skillful dedication to the practice of law have educated me in small and large ways to think about the world outside of my suburban childhood home.

And finally, I must recognize the great novelist Alan Paton, whose lyrically profound novel of human suffering, *Cry, the Beloved Country*, first pointed me toward the study of contemporary human rights.

I dedicate this work to Lisa—my wife, best friend, and teacher—and to my inspirational daughters—Katherine, Grace, and Caroline.

A MOST UNCERTAIN CRUSADE

Introduction

The Origins of a Crusade

AS THE CHRISTMAS-TIME CHILL of the 1948 winter descended upon the city of Chicago, a middle-aged man with spectacles and a high forehead, looking appropriately professorial, addressed the annual meeting of the American Political Science Association. James Simsarian, a State Department liaison to the American delegation at the United Nations, delivered a summary of recent United Nations work in the field of human rights. He began with the most recent accomplishment: the unanimous approval of a Universal Declaration of Human Rights, which he described as "a common standard of achievement for all peoples and all nations." He spent much of the remainder of his address lambasting the Soviet Union for its attempts to delay and sabotage the document. Citing the numerous (and unsuccessful) amendments the Soviet delegation had offered to allow governments to ban Fascist speech and enact restrictions on other freedoms, Simsarian pronounced the duty of the United States to "make it clear time and time again to the totalitarian states that countries with free people cannot compromise with the principles of human rights and fundamental freedoms." He did admit, though, that his own nation was "far from perfect," but as its own human rights record improved, the country could provide leadership at the United Nations on principles such as the rule of law, individual liberties, economic freedoms, and impartial justice. The best way to attain this goal was to head the effort to draft a precedent-setting binding international bill of individual rights.[1]

Within five years, Simsarian's optimistic narrative lay in tatters. Upon taking office in 1953, President Dwight Eisenhower and Secretary of State John Foster Dulles withdrew the country from further involvement in drafting human rights treaties. "We do not ourselves look upon a treaty as the means which we would now select as the proper and most effective way to spread throughout the world the goals of human liberty," Dulles wrote to Eisenhower in 1953. The main cause for the policy shift lay not with Soviet obstructionist amendments to those treaties, but with domestic fears of what those binding agreements could do to rectify America's "less than perfect" human rights record. Worried that treaties would enforce the principles of freedom, liberty, and equality at home, Eisenhower and Dulles halted American efforts on a covenant partially in order to protect Jim Crow segregation in the South. The change in policy cannot, however, be understood solely by examining domestic and foreign events in the years following World War II. Such an endeavor would merely affirm Simsarian's rhetoric of the United States as a traditional crusader for human rights, applaud the Universal Declaration as an American-inspired victory, and criticize Eisenhower and Dulles for unprincipled, unnecessary, and reactionary unilateralism.[2]

An alternative interpretation, which examines the dilemmas and paradoxes confronted by State Department officials and non-governmental associations during World War II, views the human rights advocacy by the United States as flawed and conservative in nature from the start, the Universal Declaration as its logical and ambivalent handiwork, and Eisenhower's skepticism as overlapping that of Presidents Franklin D. Roosevelt and Harry S. Truman. This longer view more accurately situates and illuminates the role of human rights issues in American diplomacy, for it allows an examination of how consistently policymakers of both political parties used soaring national ideals to unify and give purpose to foreign policy during World War II and the Cold War, while allowing other prioritized domestic and foreign matters to weaken actual human rights commitments. Such consistent expediency had human costs, though, in prolonging racial discrimination in the United States and in helping to postpone human rights accountability in the larger world for decades. The irony of the United States abandoning a global cause that it once championed in theory in order to commit human rights abuses at home, moreover, is not rooted only in the recent past. In the opening years of a new century, the administration of George W. Bush embraced this contradictory policy in the war against Islamic fundamentalism by rhetorically promoting democratization abroad while employing torture, indefinite incommunicado detention without trial, and prejudiced military commissions in direct contravention of international legal norms, including the Geneva Conventions and the Convention Against Torture. This work will trace the genesis of such dualistic and unilateralist policies within the volatile, fluid, and transformative atmosphere of World War II.

The American catalytic role in defining and implementing a post–World War II global order premised upon the international protection of specific human rights is the subject of this book. President Franklin D. Roosevelt, believing that peace could occur only if governments granted political, economic, and social rights to their citizens, made the promotion of human rights a major Allied war aim. The Atlantic Charter and the Declaration by the United Nations, whose contents Roosevelt did much to shape, proclaimed that the Allies were fighting to guarantee religious liberty, freedom of speech, self-government, and economic security to peoples worldwide. As wartime crises mounted, State Department planners initially sought assistance in translating these goals into postwar policy from private organizations, including the Commission to Study the Organization of Peace and the Federal Council of Churches.

Roosevelt, though, soon turned down plans prepared by the State Department and private agencies to have a postwar international peacekeeping body enforce human rights standards. This was partially due to objections from British Prime Minister Winston Churchill, Soviet Premier Joseph Stalin, and key members of Congress, who worried that human rights oversight impinged on national sovereignty. Also, by 1943, Roosevelt had decided to create a postwar organization that relied on the Big Three to keep peace primarily through military co-operation rather than broad political and social reform. His plan to create a successor to the League of Nations, which he submitted to the Allies at the 1944 Dumbarton Oaks Conference, omitted any responsibility by the body itself or member nations to protect human rights. Only strong objections from domestic organizations and Latin American nations forced Roosevelt and the State Department to accept amendments, though with strong qualifications attached to protect national sovereignty. At the San Francisco Conference, which approved the U.N. Charter, the Allied powers reluctantly allowed the body to "promote universal respect for, and observance of, human rights and fundamental freedoms for all" through the creation of a human rights commission. To prevent a recurrence of the Holocaust and other wartime atrocities, U.N. members promptly assigned the body to draft the first globally applicable bill of rights in world history.[3]

Eleanor Roosevelt, the American delegate to the U.N. Commission on Human Rights (UNCHR), followed a very conservative human rights policy at the United Nations. This strategy required the careful pursuit of two contradictory goals: helping U.N. members with a diverse array of religions, cultures, political systems, and economies to agree upon the content and enforcement of meaningful agreements, while incorporating weak implementation schemes and insisting upon using the language of existing American constitutional jurisprudence. Both latter positions, Truman and State Department lawyers privately agreed, would prevent human rights agreements from invalidating Jim Crow laws and enhance the chances of Senate ratification. The resulting non-binding Universal Declaration of Human Rights, the conservatively worded and flawed Genocide Convention, and early versions of a covenant limited to political and civil rights and barren of meaningful enforcement schemes demonstrated the success of American diplomats in achieving their political and diplomatic goals.

By the early 1950s, though, foreign and domestic forces began to challenge the narrow assumptions that had guided American human rights policy. A growing bloc of non-aligned, underdeveloped former colonies led by India called for the inclusion in the covenant of economic guarantees and the right of all peoples to self-determination. Concurrently, isolationist-oriented anti-Communists, led by Senator John Bricker (R-OH) and the American Bar Association (ABA), claimed that U.N. human rights treaties would repeal parts of the U.S. Constitution, invalidate segregation ordinances, and promote socialism domestically and globally. Their strident and legally questionable claims nonetheless persuaded the Senate to postpone ratification of the Genocide Convention and to propose a series of constitutional amendments to limit the president's foreign affairs powers and the domestic impact of treaties. To prevent these proposals from hamstringing the general foreign affairs powers of the executive branch, incoming President Dwight Eisenhower withdrew from the U.N. treaty-writing process and began a propaganda campaign against Communist-bloc oppression. Eisenhower thus returned American human rights policy to its World War II rhetorical roots. Similar to Franklin Roosevelt's Four Freedoms speech and the Atlantic Charter, Eisenhower employed vague human rights pronouncements, unsupported by binding commitments, to unify the nation in the face of an external threat. I employ three themes that are deeply rooted in history to explain this result: the notion of American human rights exceptionalism, the tension between advocating for external human rights oversight while brandishing the shield of national sovereignty, and the often influential activism by non-governmental organizations (NGOs) to prod a reluctant government into taking meaningful action.

Prior to World War II, international law and diplomacy recognized, with few exceptions, that governments had sovereign control over peoples under their rule; heads of state could treat their citizens as they saw fit.

The United States, by 1941, was in a unique position to lead a partial revolt against this tradition. A nation born of rebellion against tyranny, its constitution included a revolutionary list of political and social limitations on governmental power that theoretically safeguarded individual freedom and personal liberty. American presidents throughout the nineteenth century had declared a right and duty to spread those treasured republican values across the continent (the philosophy of "Manifest Destiny") and overseas (the doctrine of ideological imperialism). Although this rhetoric of "human rights" still sounds progressive and even modern, policymakers often employed it, as during the Spanish-American War, to justify white supremacy, jingoism, and the oppression of racial and ethnic minorities both at home and in U.S. colonies. Senator Albert Beveridge (R-IN), a leading imperialist during the Spanish-American War, articulated the beliefs of many before and after him on the United States' exceptional and unique humanitarian role in the world. He wrote,

> God has not been preparing the English-speaking and Teutonic peoples for a thousand years for nothing but vain and idle self-contemplation and self-admiration. No! He has made us the master organizers of the world to establish a system where chaos reigns. And of all our race He has marked the American people as His chosen nation to finally lead to a regeneration of the world. This is the divine mission of America. . . . We are trustees of the world's progress, guardians of its righteous peace.[4]

This missionary drive, married to belief in the superiority and replicative quality of American democracy, provided a justification for interventions around the world in the nineteenth and twentieth centuries.[5]

President Woodrow Wilson, determined to prevent a resurrection of the European killing fields after World War I, expanded upon this evangelical tradition in his Fourteen Points. Using the unprecedented military and economic leverage the nation possessed, he strove mightily to create a world body that would prevent war while expanding the United States' power to influence global events. Wilson's combination of idealism and realism was new in American diplomacy; historian Thomas Knock called his vision "progressive internationalism"; Walter Russell Meade simply termed it "Wilsonianism." Wilson sought above all to sustain domestic support for an internationalist foreign policy by portraying the country as a self-denying, humanitarian-oriented seeker of peace, protector of the oppressed, and supporter of international law. At the Versailles Peace Conference, he tried to institutionalize a respect for the human rights of European minorities within the League of Nations. His efforts failed, though, as the Senate refused to join the League partially due to concerns that it would meddle in America's internal affairs. The debate between those who embraced international human rights activism and their opponents would be renewed once Fascist and Communist dictators launched wars of conquest, and the Senate again became the focal point for its resolution.[6]

Starting in the nineteenth century, American and European non-governmental organizations began to challenge the notion that national sovereignty prevented intervention by external actors on human rights issues. Their inspiration devolved from Enlightenment conceptions of natural rights, the inhuman treatment of vulnerable populations, and a religious duty to help the oppressed. Due to pressure from NGOs such as the British and Foreign Anti-Slavery Society, the American Committee for Armenian and Syrian Relief, and the International Red Cross, European, Middle Eastern, American, and African nations banned the slave trade, agreed to care for the wounded in battle, and permitted humanitarian intervention on behalf of persecuted ethnic or religious minorities.[7] Concurrently, economic upheaval generated by the Industrial Revolution spawned a transnational movement by NGOs to protect workers from economic exploitation. The writings of Karl Marx and Friedrich Engels exposed the poor and dangerous working conditions, low wages, long hours, and abuse of women and children in American and European factories. Their call for a global revolution by workers advanced the reforms of more moderate groups, such as the Salvation Army and the Young Men's (and Women's) Christian Association. NGOs also lobbied for universal women's suffrage, the fair treatment of indigenous peoples in colonies, and economic assistance for newly freed slaves.[8]

As the twentieth century dawned, these efforts, coupled with the outbreak of horribly destructive wars and the fear of Communism, caused governments in the United States and Europe to undertake precedent-setting human rights commitments. Fearful that people around a war-torn world would heed Vladimir Lenin's call for Communist revolution, they signed conventions to protect workers from the worst excesses of capitalism. The formation of the International Labor Organization in the wake of World War I, which soon drafted dozens of treaties on work hours, worker's compensation, and trade union rights, foreshadowed a post–World War II movement to guarantee economic and social rights by multilateral covenants.[9] At the Paris Peace Conference, the Allies redrew the map of Europe by carving culturally heterogeneous states out of the Ottoman and Austro-Hungarian empires. Cognizant that the per-

secution of ethnic minorities had led to war, and appalled by the genocide of Armenians by the Ottoman Turks, the victors penned a series of
minorities treaties with the vanquished Central Powers, the Baltic States,
and nations in central and southern Europe. Each required signatories to
protect the cultural and economic rights of racial, ethnic, and religious
minorities and guaranteed everyone equality before the law. They empowered the League of Nations to discuss and act upon petitions from
victims of alleged treaty violations.[10]

Wilson and other Allied leaders, though, refused to apply these human
rights standards to non-Europeans or even to their own citizens. Ignoring
the lobbying at Versailles by representatives from Southeast Asia, India,
Armenia, and the Middle East, they declined to grant independence or
protections to non-white peoples. In fact, the peace conference further
entrenched the colonial system by giving the colonies of defeated nations
to the Allies as mandates. The victors even opposed recognizing the principle of racial equality in the Treaty of Versailles. Japan, the only non-white
power invited to the peace conference, advocated tirelessly for its inclusion. Wilson, a white supremacist who knew such an addition would cause
turmoil in the racially segregated United States, used unusual procedural
tactics to defeat the motion. The issue would not vanish, though, for as the
American scholar and political activist W.E.B. Du Bois stated so prophetically in 1900, "The problem of the twentieth century is the problem of the
color-line . . . the relation of the darker to the lighter races of men in Asia
and Africa, in America and the islands of the sea."[11]

The advent of the League of Nations and the International Labor Organization inspired an interwar generation of NGOs to argue for the global
enforcement of political, economic, and social guarantees. As the Wom-
en's International League for Peace and Freedom fought for suffrage and
reproductive rights, Du Bois's Pan-African Association promoted self-
determination, and the Comintern attempted to spread Communism.
René Cassin, Alejandro Alvarez, and Wellington Koo, all of whom later
became architects of human rights activism by the United Nations, worked
with the Institut de Droit International, the Académie Diplomatique Inter-
nationale, and the Ligue pour la Défense des Droits de l'Homme to publish soon-forgotten drafts of an international bill of rights. The publicity
generated by these efforts induced individuals and NGOs to file hundreds
of petitions before the League of Nations. Working in co-operation with
NGOs, league bodies such as the Mandates Commission, the Advisory
Committee on the Suppression of Traffic in Women and Children, and the
Minorities Committees also oversaw and even attempted to regulate to an

unprecedented degree the relationship between national governments and disadvantaged peoples under their control. All of these efforts, though, made little headway as governments around the world refused to allow international institutions, even those to whom they belonged, to dictate how they had to treat their own citizens or colonial subjects.[12]

Within the United States, the Great Depression contributed to a nascent domestic civil rights movement in contrasting ways. President Franklin D. Roosevelt embraced cries for economic justice through governmental action in his victorious 1932 campaign and subsequent New Deal. FDR's reforms inspired labor and civil rights groups to launch unprecedented organizing drives to place their causes before national audiences. After another world war, they would merge this reformist impulse with the crusading tradition of American diplomacy by advocating for a strong successor to the League of Nations with the power to enforce human rights guarantees globally, including within the United States. This latter piece was critical: if Congress and the federal courts would not use constitutional promises and processes to improve conditions in the workplace and dismantle Jim Crow, perhaps a binding international bill of rights would be their long-sought salvation. Conversely, the Great Depression also further entrenched segregation. Lynchings continued, and racially based miscarriages of justice such as the Scottsboro Affair received much media attention, while many New Deal reforms ironically made living conditions for African Americans worse. In response to both trends, the United States Supreme Court haltingly began to establish national standards of due process based on the Fourteenth Amendment that increasingly upset states' rights–minded politicians. The latter interpreted a resurgence of federal authority in the human rights field as unconstitutional and dangerous to traditions of white supremacy. Their critiques laid the theoretical basis for a postwar insurrection against the ratification of human rights treaties by Congress and the enforcement of such measures by the federal judiciary.[13]

Although the coming of World War II derailed temporarily the further development of international human rights law, it also reaffirmed the conviction that peace could not exist if governments could hide behind the walls of national sovereignty and domestic jurisdiction to practice the worst forms of torture, murder, and oppression. But once again, the leaders of NGOs had to convince skeptical Allied leaders, including Roosevelt, that support for human rights must consist of more than rhetorical sound bites. Documenting their renewed advocacy for a binding bill of rights enforced under the aegis of the United Nations forms one part of this work. The reluctance of wartime and postwar Allied leaders to agree upon the need for meaningful human rights oversight by the United Nations forms a second theme. For Presidents Roosevelt, Truman, and Eisenhower, this opposition sprang from an exceptionalist, but ironic, belief that only American conceptions of human rights, namely the political and civil rights enshrined in the Constitution, had global resonance. Once Communist and underdeveloped nations, however, embraced an unfamiliar list of economic and social guarantees and the right of self-determination in binding human rights treaties, the United States retreated from participating in U.N. discussions. The story behind this retrenchment comprises a third theme in the book's later chapters.

This work is organized both chronologically and thematically. I introduce the Roosevelt administration's two-pronged approach to human rights in chapters 1 and 2: the issuing of grand statements of humanitarian war aims such as the Four Freedoms and the Atlantic Charter, and the preparation of early proposals for a postwar community of nations that lacked reference to such principles. The omission of human rights responsibilities given to a League of Nations successor disappointed domestic lobbying groups, which began to lobby the State Department. In chapter 3, I describe the often contentious wartime human rights trialogue undertaken by the Roosevelt administration, American allies, and domestic non-governmental organizations that culminated in the drafting of the United Nations Charter. As the result of compromise and tenacious advocacy by NGOs, the charter allowed the United Nations to "promote" human rights, but it also contained a clause banning interference in the internal affairs of nations. The question in 1945, then, was which article the United States delegation would identify as controlling.

Had confidential American records been available to the public, the answer would have been clear. Chapter 4 will analyze conservative American proposals for a human rights commission and a non-binding declaration of rights that would paradoxically protect national sovereignty, the racial status quo, and Allied colonial rule over peoples of color. The Truman administration, looking toward the 1948 presidential election, had to mend fences with important Democratic Party groups, such as civil rights activists and labor unions, while rejecting their plans for a powerful United Nations and a binding international bill of rights. One temporary answer, found in chapter 5, was to complete first a covenant that would ban a practice Truman deemed unlikely to ever occur in the United States: genocide. Yet even in undertaking this seemingly non-controversial task, he ran into a buzz saw of opposition. The American Bar Association and conservative

Democrats objected to the convention on states' rights and constitutional grounds. Their campaign against ratification generated the core arguments used against subsequent human rights treaties. The final chapter brings the twin conflicts to a head, as Truman waged battles at the United Nations for a weak and pliant binding covenant against progressive counterproposals, while fighting reactionary forces at home that were energized by the Senate's refusal to consider the Genocide Convention. The pulling out of the treaty drafting process by the Eisenhower administration merely provided a denouement to what Truman probably would have done had he been elected to another term in office.

Unable to find consensus at the United Nations or at home for a treaty that could ironically sanction human rights abuses at home and overseas, abandoning what the United States had started during World War II seemed like the only acceptable course of action to Eisenhower. The results would be tragic abroad and still apparent at home. With the nation committed to forming a weak human rights commission, the body would founder in obscurity and incompetence for almost 60 years before being replaced with the equally powerless Human Rights Council in 2006. The Genocide Convention, entering into force without American ratification in 1951, failed to create the political will and institutions necessary to deter or stop occurrences of genocide for the remainder of the twentieth century. At home, senatorial skepticism of human rights treaties placed the United States virtually alone among nations for its refusal to ratify human rights instruments, or, in the case of the Genocide Convention, to pass them only decades later with substantial reservations. If there is an uplifting lesson to learn from this narrative, it is the importance of civil society groups, in America and abroad, for exerting pressure on governments to respect human rights and respond to massive violations. Their activism in the face of repeated U.N. inaction to atrocities influenced Secretary-General Kofi Annan to articulate a doctrine entitled "The Responsibility to Protect" (R2P). He called upon all nations in 2006 to

> embrace the "responsibility to protect" as a basis for collective action against genocide, ethnic cleansing and crimes against humanity, and agree to act on this responsibility, recognizing that this responsibility lies first and foremost with each individual State, whose duty it is to protect its population, but that if national authorities are unwilling or unable to protect their citizens, then the responsibility shifts to the international community to use diplomatic, humanitarian and other methods to help protect civilian populations, and

that if such methods appear insufficient the Security Council may out of necessity decide to take action under the Charter, including enforcement action, if so required.[14]

Whether the "responsibility to protect" doctrine will force a change in the behavior of nations, including that of the United States, depends in part on whether nations choose to learn from their lamentable and tragic past refusals to protect.

CHAPTER 1

Defining a Crusade, 1941–1943

ON JANUARY 6, 1941, President Franklin D. Roosevelt delivered a somber State of the Union address to a concerned Congress that had witnessed Nazi Germany's conquest of most of Western Europe and Japan's occupation of Indochina and parts of China. Ever the careful politician, Roosevelt wanted to rally the public behind expanded aid to Great Britain without fueling isolationist sentiments that such assistance would ignite war with Germany. He turned to the rhetorical language of freedom to achieve his twin goals. "At no previous time," he warned, "has American security been as seriously threatened from without as it is today. The democratic way of life is at this moment being directly assailed in every part of the world [. . .] assailed either by arms or by secret spreading of poisonous propaganda." Only by actively resisting aggression, Roosevelt declared, could the United States help to construct a postwar world based upon the "cooperation of free countries, working together in a friendly, civilized society." Peace and global collaboration would come as national governments granted their citizens what Roosevelt called the Four Freedoms: freedom of speech and religion, and freedom from want and fear. "Freedom," he concluded, "means the supremacy of human rights everywhere." Four days later, Democratic leaders in Congress introduced the Lend-Lease Act as H.R. 1776, further strengthening the connection between mobilizing the nation's resources and ensuring the survival of endangered democratic principles.[1]

In his 1941 State of the Union address, Roosevelt clearly embraced for the first time what would become one of the central war aims of the United

States: to construct a peaceful, prosperous world order founded upon the revolutionary concept that governments must guarantee their citizens certain fundamental civil, political, and economic rights. Such a vision could unite the public behind the unprecedented mobilization needed to advance the war effort while making such future sacrifices unnecessary. If governments were bound to respect human rights, the emergence of charismatic, militaristic dictators who war against domestic opponents as a prelude to launching invasions against foreign enemies could be prevented. In wartime speeches and proclamations such as the Atlantic Charter and the Declaration by the United Nations, he encouraged other Allied countries and Americans to accept his bold but imprecise vision. To flesh out the president's ideas, Secretary of State Cordell Hull charged specialists in international law with drafting a bill of rights that would forever prevent mass human rights violations like those committed by the Axis powers. After several years of delay caused by a staff shortage, a lack of resources, and a growing rivalry between Secretary of State Hull and Undersecretary of State Sumner Welles, they generated a list of political and civil rights that nations should grant to their citizens accompanied by two enforcement proposals.

Opposition from other Allied leaders, disagreements within the State Department, and the emergence of more pressing postwar issues, however, led Hull and Roosevelt to set aside these human rights proposals. Roosevelt's own keen, sensitive political barometer, which periodically altered his commitment to such ideals in order to forge pragmatic compromises at home and abroad, is partially to blame. His State of the Union vision, describing a lasting peace based upon Wilsonian objectives and safeguarded by expanded American support for nations then under siege, exemplified his use of bold words in the service of more limited goals. Learning from his World War I predecessor, he knew that European and domestic opposition could derail expansive efforts to make human rights a cornerstone of the postwar order. His cautious instincts dovetailed with the sensitivities of State Department legal advisors, who had few precedents to consult and many questions to answer within this still new field of international law. The policy vacuum caused by this uncertainty, though, provided the opportunity for religious, legal, and academic lobbyists to translate Roosevelt's rhetoric into their own proposals for the protection of economic, political, and social rights. They circulated their plans in Washington, only to be ignored for three years by the administration for the same diplomatic, legal, and political reasons that had prevented Roosevelt from embracing the State Department's own preliminary work. As a consequence, these non-governmental organizations increasingly identified a credibility gap between Roosevelt's words and official postwar planning statements, a contradiction that soon bred frustration and anger as Allied plans to create a new world order began to take shape at wartime summit meetings.

The Roosevelt administration, in co-operation with non-governmental organizations, began wrestling with postwar human rights objectives a full two years before the United States formally entered World War II. Two days after Germany's invasion of Poland, the president declared, "It seems to me clear, even at the outbreak of this war, that the influence of America should be consistent in seeking for humanity a final peace which will eliminate, as far as it is possible to do so, the continued use of force between nations." Heeding these words, Secretary of State Hull began to assemble committees to explore how the nation could fulfill FDR's vision. He appointed Russian émigré Leo Pasvolsky, an economist with the Brookings Institution and special assistant to Hull since 1934, as his main advisor on postwar planning. Pasvolsky, whose first career in journalism involved reporting from the Versailles Peace Conference, became the secretary of state's closest advisor and a tenacious advocate for a worthy successor to the League of Nations. Historian Stephen Schlesinger described him as "the perfect public servant for Hull, endowed with a sharp analytical talent, a non-confrontational but principled personality, a library-like mind on global issues, a faith in free trade, and a passion to remain invisible." In the waning days of 1939, Hull approved Pasvolsky's recommendation to form a "committee on problems of peace and reconstruction," the first postwar planning entity created within the State Department. The group, drawn from economists, lawyers, and businessmen from within the department, did not survive for long. With German armies quickly conquering Western Europe in May and June of 1940, Hull and Pasvolsky reoriented planning to more immediate problems, including what might happen if Great Britain capitulated to Germany or Nazi subversion spread into the Western Hemisphere. The committee did set two key precedents for its successors, though. Hull and Pasvolsky learned, firstly, that effective and sustainable deliberations required assigning the immediate and long-term problems to separate agencies. Secondly, rejecting the outsourcing of long-range planning to independent scholars, as President Wilson had done by appointing members of "The Inquiry" as his contingency planners for peace during World War I, Hull tried to keep such activities within the State Department. Doing so proved difficult, however, as the unprecedented resources and technical expertise needed far outpaced the 1,000 permanent employees and $3 million budget that he commanded.

Not until the summer of 1941 did Hull believe he had the time and could spare employees with the necessary expertise to create a successor to the committee.[2]

By then, the secretary of state had changed his mind and decided to use foreign policy experts from the private sector to bolster his own staff on long-range planning committees. In early September 1939, Walter H. Mallory, the executive director of the Council on Foreign Relations, and Hamilton Fish Armstrong, the editor of the organization's journal, *Foreign Affairs*, offered to prepare policy studies for use by the State Department. The council, formed in 1921 partially from remnants of "The Inquiry," had been a lonely but prominent haven for internationalists during the interwar years.[3] Seeking to serve as "The Inquiry's" successor and armed with a $350,000 grant from the Rockefeller Foundation, the War and Peace Studies project eventually submitted 700 reports to the State Department over the next six years. An early product, "Basic American Interests," foreshadowed in general terms various postwar United Nations trade, environmental, and health agencies that would attempt to raise living standards, mediate diplomatic disputes, and promote democratic governance. To advance the latter cause, the report advocated "adherence to an international charter of human rights" containing articles on freedom of religion, speech, press, and assembly, and a commitment to racial equality. Such a document could undergird "the progressive development of a world order designed to promote economic progress, social justice, and cultural freedom for all national groups, races, and classes willing to accept their proper responsibilities as members of the world community." This report of July 1941 was the first to recommend a universal bill of human rights, an idea soon picked up by other domestic lobbying groups and State Department staffers.[4]

Another band from the defunct League of Nations Association also showed their internationalist credentials and subject expertise by sketching the importance of transnational human rights norms in fostering peace. The Commission to Study the Organization of Peace, led by the League's past president, Columbia professor James T. Shotwell, and its executive director, Clark Eichelberger, was formed in 1939 by 50 intellectuals who saw the advent of war as a second chance to press for a Wilsonian peace. Members included John Foster Dulles, soon an influential lobbyist for the Federal Council of Churches, and Dean Virginia Gildersleeve of Barnard College, a delegate to the 1945 conference that created the United Nations. Their first report of November 1940, signed by at least 16 members who soon began to advise the State Department on postwar planning, advanced the key thesis that an enduring peace could only exist if nations abdicated partial sovereignty to an international peacekeeping organ and granted unspecified human and cultural rights to their citizens. "The destruction of civil liberties anywhere," the report asserted as Axis armies crossed frontiers on three continents, "creates danger of war." In trying to resurrect human rights principles that had failed only 20 years earlier, these groups knew that a skeptical public and cautious administration in Washington, already uncertain about how to react to aggression overseas, would greet such recommendations warily. Pasvolsky's deputy, Harley Notter, declared curtly in his official State Department history of postwar planning, "The Department did not, however, give directives or special support to any of these groups." While Secretary Hull's agreement with these studies led him to invite their authors to serve on department planning agencies, this was done with no fanfare, and he made sure that all written collaboration was marked confidential. He and President Roosevelt were not about to ignite a debate over the parameters of future American foreign policy as war began to engulf Europe. They soon recognized, though, the political uses to which vague commitments to human rights might bring.[5]

The sudden defeat of France in June 1940 provided the first opportunity for Roosevelt to employ such rhetoric in order to justify aiding beleaguered Great Britain. British Prime Minister Winston Churchill, having barely defeated the Luftwaffe in skies over London but facing German U-boats in vital shipping lanes, appealed for American war materiel. In late 1940, he sent what he described as "one of the most important [letters] I ever wrote," which defined in stark terms how the war looked from 10 Downing Street. "The decision for 1941," Churchill predicted, "lies upon the seas. . . . We may fall by the way," he warned, if the country continued to lack the necessary shipping to move troops and supplies to confront German and Italian armies. Roosevelt, relieved and emboldened by his election to an unprecedented third term in office, replied with the Lend-Lease program. He anticipated that isolationists, buttressed by polls showing that four out of five Americans opposed a declaration of war, would frame his proposal as an excuse to become a combatant. While the Treasury Department drafted an actual bill for Congress, the president attempted to frame the terms of debate in two public speeches. In a Fireside Chat on December 29, 1940, Roosevelt proclaimed that "never before since Jamestown and Plymouth Rock has our American civilization been in such danger as now." To keep war away from American shores required arming Great Britain, which in turn necessitated transforming the United States into "the great arsenal of democracy."[6] One week later, he stood in the well of Congress and declared the importance of fighting for the Four Freedoms. Congress handily approved H.R. 1776. Roosevelt had successfully promoted wartime mobilization under the guise of protecting human rights as a crucial national interest without generating a crippling political backlash.

The progress of the war, though, soon demanded more than speeches to the American public, as German armies raced across the Russian frontier in the summer of 1941. Roosevelt sent troops to Iceland, authorized expanded naval patrols in the Atlantic, embargoed oil exports to Tokyo, and sought a personal meeting with Churchill. The reasons for the meeting were several, including a desire to discuss forging closer ties with Britain. In addition, Roosevelt wanted to forestall any deals that Stalin and Churchill, signatories to a military alliance in July, might cut over postwar spheres of influence that could provoke an isolationist surge at home. Roosevelt also, as he told Welles, hoped that the meeting could "hold out hope to the enslaved peoples of the world. The English-speaking democracies both stood for principles of freedom and justice. They should jointly bind themselves now to establish at the conclusion of the war a new world order based upon these principles." One way to accomplish all three aims would be to issue a joint declaration of war aims that built upon the political freedoms and economic guarantees envisioned in the Four Freedoms. Churchill, hoping for expanded American aid, readily accepted the invitation to talk, and the two met in secrecy at sea, shuttling between the USS *Augusta* and the HMS *Prince of Wales* in Placentia Bay off of Argentia, Newfoundland. As the midday sun broke through the clouds on Saturday, August 9, conversations began between the two leaders, one leading a belligerent nation under siege, the other maneuvering his nation closer to war by championing a new, humane world order that only a decisive victory over Fascism could make possible.[7]

The resulting Atlantic Charter contained a series of inspiring but compromised ideals whose postwar application would befuddle policymakers and political activists for years to come. After preliminary talks between Undersecretary of State Welles and his British counterpart, Sir Alexander Cadogan, demonstrated American free trade displeasure with England's restrictive Imperial Preference System, Roosevelt tactically asked Churchill to craft a working draft. Working that night in his stateroom with Cadogan, the prime minister eagerly complied, stating later, "I am glad it should be on the record that the substance and spirit of what came to be called the 'Atlantic Charter' was in its first draft a British production cast in my own words." Replying to Roosevelt's concerns that Great Britain and the Soviet Union would make secret deals, Churchill's wording eschewed any political gains for his nation and promised that any territorial alterations must obtain the consent of those directly affected. He also called upon both nations to defend the rights of self-determination and free speech and to create an "effective" international organization that would protect the sovereignty of all states. Finally, employing vague phraseology that would not undermine Britain's closed-door economic empire, he declared a commitment to "a fair and equitable distribution of essential produce not only within their territorial jurisdiction but between the nations of the world."[8]

Roosevelt and Welles, whose presence at the meeting further marginalized Hull as the president's diplomatic confidante, objected to both the implicit acceptance of England's preferential trade system and the explicit reference to a powerful international organization. Both men firmly believed that autarkic empires had contributed to both world wars and the Great Depression, as nations responded to economic calamity by using military tools to gain the vital resources that free trade could not. They also worried that any reference to a League of Nations successor would stir up an isolationist hornet's nest at home. Churchill complained mightily when he read the amended draft, which endorsed the principle of trade "without discrimination and on equal terms" and omitted any reference to a global peacekeeping institution. Accepting both, he declared, would go against public opinion and have an adverse effect on morale in his war-scarred country. Moreover, he took advantage of FDR's desire for a joint statement by asserting his need to consult the Commonwealth regarding the proposed trade language, a process that would take a minimum of seven days. Given that Churchill planned to depart on the twelfth, FDR accepted Churchill's economic position over Welles's strenuous objections, but he stood firm on omitting any mention of an international peacekeeping agency. On Tuesday, August 12, after adding references to international labor standards and social security, Churchill and Roosevelt approved the document and parted company in the afternoon. The summit had produced a commitment by Great Britain and the United States to link the struggle against Fascism with a determination to promote political and economic justice for all peoples. Neither leader enthusiastically embraced the work, though for opposite reasons. Churchill sailed home disappointed that the United States was no closer to entering the war. Roosevelt worried that the statement was too much of a commitment by a technically neutral country. His anxiety grew with the news that the House of Representatives had approved an extension of the draft by only a single vote.[9]

The American and British governments on August 14 released the Atlantic Charter with a muted enthusiasm that generated little excitement among their citizens. The dry voice of Deputy Prime Minister Clement Attlee first announced over the radio that both nations promised to promote self-government for the world's peoples, foster international economic cooperation by gradually collapsing trade barriers, and construct a "wider and permanent system of general security" to prevent another world war. The lack of any specific promises by Washington to enter the conflict sowed disillusionment throughout Britain. Writer H. V. Morton, an eyewitness to the Atlantic conference, reported afterward, "I have since been told that in clubs, and places where men gathered to hear the broadcast, faces grew long with disappointment as Mr. Attlee proceeded, and the exciting rumors set about by Mr. Churchill's Atlantic journey were all deflated in an atmosphere of anti-climax." Cadogan described the British public as having "a feeling of being let down when they were presented with a piece of paper." It fell to Churchill to try to inflate the document's importance as a strong warning to the Axis and as something of a blueprint for a future peace. In his first British Broadcasting Corporation (BBC) broadcast after returning home, he emphasized the preamble's statement that bound Washington and London to undertake the "final destruction of Nazi tyranny" as close to a declaration of war. In a speech two weeks later before the House of Commons, he promised that the charter would be a "milestone or monument which needs only the stroke of victory to become a permanent part of the history of human progress." Yet Churchill soon found himself on the defensive as indigenous leaders in British colonies such as India began to invoke the charter's self-determination clauses. The prime minister fervently disagreed, maintaining that the clause applied only to lands under Axis and possibly Soviet domination.[10]

Roosevelt had the opposite challenge as Churchill, which was paradoxically to minimize the significance of a document he had wanted badly in the first place. Given that isolationists would resurrect jaundiced World War I memories of secret diplomacy and entangling alliances, he admitted only the symbolic nature of the compact and stressed that no side deals had been made on entering the war. As the *Chicago Tribune* screamed, "Pact Pushes U.S. Near War; F.D.R. Alliance with Churchill Rocks Capital," others with isolationist sympathies skeptically wondered what else, besides a vague list of pious principles, had necessitated a summit meeting with Great Britain. The president, following the razor-thin vote in the House on the draft, did not want to fan such flames of doubt and anxiety. After the presidential yacht *Potomac* had landed in Rockland, Maine, on

August 16, he blandly told reporters clamoring for news that the charter comprised "an interchange of views relating to the present and future" and that its issuance brought the nation no closer to war. His official message to Congress made public five days later meekly framed the charter as "a goal which is worth while for our type of civilization to seek." Senator Alben Barkley, the Democratic leader in the Senate, similarly downplayed the pact as "just a statement of policy," although his influential Republican colleague, Robert Taft, angrily predicted that "Historians will regard it as a British-American military alliance." The American public similarly held schizophrenic views, as polls after the Argentia conference showed that three-quarters of Americans both supported Roosevelt's diplomacy and opposed a declaration of war. As a statement to galvanize the public behind a war against Fascism, Roosevelt's gambit had failed. If he also hoped he could contain the application of those words to American postwar planning, nascent pressure at home and abroad to make the Atlantic Charter a touchstone for revolutionary human rights planning would soon surprise him.[11]

Roosevelt and Churchill, soon joined by Stalin, were too pragmatic, independent, and experienced in diplomacy to feel bound literally by what they considered a simple statement of common beliefs. The two Western democratic leaders, avid readers of history who had held governmental posts during the First World War, learned that foreign policy based upon idealistic principles was bound to provoke popular disillusionment in the wake of peace conference compromises. The national interest was still primary, a point that had to be repeated through denials that the charter's ideals were the literal clay from which a postwar world would spring. Churchill pointedly reassured the House of Commons on September 9 that the document's language on trade and self-determination would not force a dismantling of the Imperial Preference System or the British Empire. After endorsing the charter at an Inter-Allied Meeting in London on September 24, Soviet Ambassador Ivan Maisky relayed his own doubts about the charter's postwar application, contending that the "practical application of these principles will necessarily adapt itself to the circumstances, needs, and historic peculiarities of particular countries." Indeed, the conspiracy-sensitive Stalin informed British Foreign Secretary Anthony Eden two months later that he believed the document served as a warning to his nation as much as to the Axis powers. Roosevelt's own half-hearted endorsement only reinforced the reserved, routine coverage given the document by the American media and public. A January 1942 Gallup poll revealed that only 7 percent of respondents could cite even one of the declaration's eight points and only a quarter could even recall the statement itself. Nevertheless, the Atlantic Charter was a significant marker in the history of U.S. human rights policy, for it marked Roosevelt's first attempt to obtain international recognition of his Four Freedoms.[12]

The Atlantic Charter's publication became a catalyst for bureaucratic expansion and consequent turf wars that made Rooseveltian postwar planning chaotic, improvisational, and halting. State Department officials immediately recognized that additional resources and expertise were needed for its exegesis as the first multilateral statement of war aims. This concern, however, competed with FDR's expansion of Atlantic convoy protection, the commencement of Lend-Lease aid to the Soviet Union, stalled diplomacy with Japan, and the sending of reinforcements to Pacific outposts, all of which placed the nation closer to war in the fall of 1941. The State Department's first effort at comprehensive study only underscored how ill-prepared it was to plan for the future. The release of the Atlantic Charter caused the department to circulate a flurry of proposals to expand its research capabilities, hire new staff, and undertake a thorough study of the short-term and long-term commitments implied in the document. To avoid bureaucratic inertia and delay, Leo Pasvolsky drafted the first of several reorganization plans that centralized planning within the State Department. "While it is thus clear that many departments and agencies of the Government should participate fully in the work of formulating an effective program of foreign policy designed to implement the principles expressed in the eight points of the Roosevelt-Churchill agreement," he explained to Hull, "it is equally clear that the task involved logically requires that leadership in the preparation of such a program should be exercised, under the President, by the Department of State, or, more specifically, by the Secretary of State." He proposed to lodge all such work in an Advisory Committee on Post-War Foreign Policy, comprised only of State Department officers, with personnel from other cabinet departments, such as Treasury, Commerce, and Agriculture, invited to sit only on various subcommittees. Though Hull, Welles, and Roosevelt discussed these suggestions, increasing confrontation with the Japanese diverted their attention.[13]

The surprise Japanese strike against Pearl Harbor catapulted the United States into World War II and allowed Roosevelt more freedom to define overtly the core principles around which he and the other Allied leaders would forge a postwar order. Only one week after Congress had endorsed Roosevelt's call to arms, Secretary of State Hull saw a chance to build upon the Atlantic Charter. He desired to craft an Allied consensus on postwar aims well before the war ended, thereby avoiding President Woodrow Wilson's bitter clashes with the other victorious powers at the Versailles Peace Conference. Such a statement, to Hull, would "bind [the Allies] together until victory and would commit them to the basic principles that we upheld." The accord obligated the signatories to adhere to the Atlantic Charter, to use all of their resources to defeat the Axis, and to make no separate peace. On December 19, Hull sent the draft to Roosevelt, who shared it with a visiting Churchill a week later. Roosevelt, responding to a discrepancy between the Four Freedoms and the Atlantic Charter, subsequently added a reference to freedom of religion. The amendment forced Roosevelt to reassure skeptical Soviet Ambassador Maxim Litvinov by convincing the diplomat that the term encompassed the right to hold atheistic beliefs. In its final form, the Declaration by the United Nations (whose name came to Roosevelt in such a burst of inspiration that he had interrupted Churchill's White House bath) asserted that "complete victory . . . is essential to defend life, liberty, independence, and religious freedom, and to preserve human rights and justice in their own lands as well as in other lands." In a key rhetorical shift, the reference to "human rights" rather than the more vague term "freedoms," implied that, whatever its content, the term applied to all individuals and could become legally justiciable.[14]

In a brief but memorable ceremony on New Year's Day, Churchill, Litvinov, and Chinese Foreign Minister Tse-Vung Soong gathered in Roosevelt's White House study to initial the Declaration. Satisfying Roosevelt's twin desires to have the "Big Four" sign first while also cementing a large anti-Axis coalition, 26 other countries or governments-in-exile did the same the following day at the State Department. Although the document was not a binding treaty, and although the peace aims were relegated to a preamble, Secretary of State Hull declared on January 2 that the declaration was "living proof that law-abiding and peace-loving nations can unite . . . to preserve liberty and justice and the fundamental values of mankind." Roosevelt termed it a "declaration of solidarity" in his State of the Union address four days later. Referring to the Axis powers, he announced, "They know that victory for us means victory for freedom. They know that victory for us means victory for the institution of democracy [—] the ideal of the family, the simple principles of common decency and humanity. They know that victory for us means victory for religion. And they could not tolerate that." He then summed up America's wartime objectives by invoking the Four Freedoms, which he had unveiled a year earlier before Congress, though this time he ended with a ringing injunction that "only total victory can reward the champions of tolerance and decency and freedom and faith." With his nation now at war and a general Allied agreement on war aims obtained, the president now delegated the harder tasks of defining and executing his human rights commitments to the State Department.[15]

The department, though, remained ill-prepared to launch such a grand research project. Responding to the Japanese occupation of Allied territories in the Pacific and Germany's renewed offensive against the Soviet Union still took precedence over conducting long-range planning in the allocation of staff and resources. In early February 1942, Leo Pasvolsky complained to Undersecretary Welles that he needed "a material enlargement" of staff and budgets to provide research studies and specialized expertise for the newly formed Advisory Committee on Post-War Foreign Policy. Its task, formalized after Roosevelt had approved its creation in the waning days of 1941, was to "translate into a program of specific policies and measures the broad principles enunciated in the Atlantic Declaration and in [the president's] other pronouncements on post-war policy." In Hull's regular absences due to chronic illness, Sumner Welles chaired the group, whose members included Pasvolsky, Norman Davis, and Hamilton Fish Armstrong, respectively the head of the Council on Foreign Relations and editor of the group's journal *Foreign Affairs*, and the department's Legal Advisor Green Hackworth. When the Advisory Committee convened in mid-February, Undersecretary Welles made a point to tell members that their recommendations would go directly to Roosevelt through Hull. Subcommittees, staffed by representatives from Congress, labor unions, and the State, War, Navy, Treasury, and Commerce departments, began meeting immediately. Three months after Pearl Harbor, the State Department had finally created a core staff of experts drawn from public and private life to plan for the postwar era. Pasvolsky aide Harley Notter described the daunting task ahead:

> The Advisory Committee carried on its work under circumstances in fundamental contrast to those prevailing during the earlier organization for consideration of postwar problems. The nature of American participation in the creation of the international order after hostilities no longer gave rise to questions concerning the influence that a neutral United States could or should exert. We, as a principal power among the victors, would share the heavy responsibility of all the victors in determining the character of the postwar world; we would participate in the war settlements; we would decisively influence the nature of any organization of international peace to follow. The opportunity[,] in recognition of the imperative need [. . .] to build a just and enduring peace would assuredly be forthcoming.

With these fundamentals clear, but with every question of what, how, when, and where unanswered, the necessity to prepare as fully and wisely as humanly possible was unmistakable. Though the war would be long, the preparation for peace would also need much time.[16]

Concurrent with this start of sustained governmental planning in which some of their members participated, visionary interest groups established the international protection of human rights as a postwar cornerstone. The Federal Council of Churches, representing 25 Protestant denominations with more than 25 million members, created the Commission to Study the Bases of a Just and Durable Peace as a deliberative and lobbying arm. The commission began to draft a comprehensive bill of political, economic, and social rights and a plan for a transnational peacekeeping body. John Foster Dulles chaired the commission, which gave itself the task "to lay now the spiritual foundations for a better world after the war." Dulles was a natural choice given his background as an international finance lawyer who had advised President Wilson at the Versailles Peace Conference. As a devout Presbyterian, Dulles believed that lasting peace must have Christian views of fellowship, economic justice, and human rights as its foundation and an international body to safeguard it. The Atlantic Charter's omission of such a body caused the commission, in Dulles's own words, to lament that "the Declaration seems to reflect primarily the conception of the old sovereignty system. In the absence of mechanisms creating rights on a basis of equality, there would probably result an Anglo-Saxon military and economic hegemony whose self-interest would be bound to the maintenance of the *status quo*." Though members disagreed on whether their proposed "international federation for peace" could employ force to carry out its decisions, a majority believed that moral suasion would be enough for nations to respect opinions of the world body.[17]

By February, enough research had been accomplished for the Federal Council of Churches to hold a referendum on 13 "Guiding Principles" for the postwar world order. The proposals had been drafted the previous fall by the group's leadership, most importantly by Dulles, and it fell to the gathering of four hundred Protestant clergy and lay activists in Delaware, Ohio, to discuss and ratify them. Encapsulating all of Roosevelt's Four Freedoms in a single paragraph, the ninth principle explained,

We believe the right of all men to pursue work of their own choosing and to enjoy security from want and oppression is not limited by race, color, or creed. The rights and liberties of racial and religious minorities in all lands should be recognized and safeguarded. Freedom of religious worship, of speech and assembly, of the press, and of scientific inquiry and teaching are fundamental to human development and in keeping with the moral order.[18]

Other articles called for disarmament, autonomy for colonial peoples, free trade, and delegating some measure of national sovereignty to an "international government." The delegates enthusiastically endorsed this Wilsonian program. The Federal Council had now received a mandate to press with holy fervor for the creation of a postwar order with the protection of civil and economic rights, with a world parliament of sorts as its centerpiece.[19]

Two other efforts exemplify similar bold thinking, which soon caused the more cautious Roosevelt some consternation. A study group organized by the Council on Foreign Relations, half of whose members soon joined State Department planning bodies, proposed the first plan to invest the enforcement of human rights in a peacekeeping body. Its March 1942 report stated that a neo–League of Nations should "encourag[e], in every feasible way, adherence to a charter of individual rights" that specifically included freedoms of speech, religion, press, association, "creative art," and "scientific inquiry." Under the leadership of James T. Shotwell and Clark Eichelberger, the Commission to Study the Organization of Peace likewise began to spell out a general vision for the world after war. In mid-February, the group decided to craft a "blueprint of the future on the basis of the Atlantic Charter and United Nations," which would include a detailed study of how the international community would protect human rights. When Eichelberger informed FDR of the group's efforts, though, the president ordered a non-committal reply that reflected his own uncertain and unclear perceptions: "Tell him I would like to see him some day and for heaven's sake not to do anything specific at this time . . . as things are changing every day." This mild rebuke was a harbinger of the disagreement between Roosevelt and non-governmental advisors over the scope of acceptable reforms and the pace of their implementation.[20]

As the Axis armies rolled across the Soviet Union, Asia, and northern Africa during the first half of 1942, two of Roosevelt's most liberal aides followed his advice and enlisted vague human rights ideals to exhort the nation to war without making peacetime commitments. On May 8 in New York City, Vice President Henry Wallace delivered a rousing, nearly apocalyptic appeal before the Free World Association, a year-old creation of the League of Nations Association comprised of American peace groups and exiles from occupied Europe. To Wallace, the war was a fight between "a slave world and a free world," and it was only the latest display of a "people's revolution" fought by those who had sought to obtain and defend economic and political freedom since biblical times. "The people, in their millennial and revolutionary march toward manifesting here on earth the dignity that is in every human soul, hold as their credo the Four Freedoms," Wallace thundered, and victory by the "common man" in this struggle was as inevitable as the defeat of the Axis. The address was translated into 20 languages, and so many Americans and foreigners asked for copies that the White House ordered a mass printing and free distribution. In an only slightly more restrained Memorial Day address at Arlington National Cemetery, Undersecretary of State Welles called for an end to imperialism and the creation of a world organization equipped with international police power. He asserted, "The right of a people to their freedom must be recognized, as the civilized world long since recognized the right of an individual to his personal freedom. The principles of the Atlantic Charter must be guaranteed to the world as a whole . . . in all oceans and in all continents." These potentially radical statements in a populist tone provided further evidence of the marginalization of the more conservative Hull, who had neither read nor approved either speech in advance.[21]

Despite generating internal State Department rivalry, the president saw two advantages of such bold pronouncements: to test the waters of public opinion about the future role of the nation in world affairs and to fill the information vacuum created by his insistence on secrecy regarding actual postwar plans. Roosevelt himself gave away no details of his long-term diplomatic thinking when he chose Flag Day to repeat the main theme of his State of the Union message to Congress 18 months before. Speaking four days before meeting with Prime Minister Churchill at the White House to discuss the first deployment of American troops to either Europe or North Africa, he explained why fighting for freedom was so important: "The four freedoms of common humanity are as much elements of man's needs as air and sunlight, bread and salt. Deprive him of all these freedoms and he dies; deprive him of a part of them and a part of him withers. Give them to him in full and abundant measure and he will cross the threshold of a new age, the greatest age of man." He concluded with an ambiguous and evasive prayer for a victory over tyrants that would "cleanse the world of oppression."[22]

The president's refusal to clarify his own human rights vision caused subordinates to fight one another to fill the policy vacuum. The resonant tone and scorching rhetoric used in public by Wallace and Welles, coupled with their protocol violations in private, unnerved and incensed the more conservative Hull, who began to draft meticulously his first major wartime speech. Employing members of the Advisory Committee on Post-War Foreign Policy over a period of five weeks to comb through every word of five complete drafts, Hull sought to outline precisely his own idea of the postwar world. The final product, "The War and Human Freedom," received Roosevelt's rather tepid endorsement as "a very able and conclusive summary of the present world situation" at a press conference two days before its delivery. On July 23, to a worldwide radio audience, Hull's plodding monotone laboriously described the unfolding of the conflict and painted the carnage as a struggle between principles. The Axis plan for world order, founded upon the physical and spiritual enslavement of subject peoples, was being implemented by mass murder, rape, starvation, and torture, "the most thorough-going bondage the world has ever seen." As defenders of liberty, justice, and economic opportunity, the Allies, and Americans in particular, were now part of a long and glorious struggle. Once they had won the war, the central task would be to rebuild the political, economic, and spiritual foundations necessary for those principles to blossom. Hull also gave no details on how to do this, implying only that some kind of informal international collaboration must occur. The speech was filled with clichés ("The manifold tasks that lie ahead will not be accomplished overnight"), the obvious ("We, Americans, are fighting today because we have been attacked"), and uncertain verbiage ("There must be international co-operative action to set up the mechanisms which can thus insure peace"). What is often overlooked is how much Hull's speech reflected Roosevelt's own uncertain thinking thus far; while both he and Hull believed in creating an international peacekeeping organization, they did not know how much power, and in what areas, to invest it with. The address also highlighted the growing philosophical differences and power struggle between Hull and Welles, who was closer to Roosevelt personally but whose independent streak made it increasingly clear that he and Hull could not work together.[23]

In response to the heightened public focus on human freedoms, the State Department's enlarged postwar planning apparatus began framing the text of an international bill of rights as the best way to implement the commitments of the Atlantic Charter and the Declaration by the United Nations. The task fell to the Subcommittee on Political Problems, a subsidiary of the Advisory Committee on Post-War Foreign Policy, whose broad mandate was to "consider the problems of formal reestablishment of peace, national sovereignty, international organization, and pacific settlement of disputes." Chaired by Welles, its 11 members included Council on Foreign Relations members Hamilton Fish Armstrong and Norman Davis, Roosevelt diplomatic advisor Benjamin Cohen, State Department Legal Advisor Green Hackworth, and Assistant Secretary of State Adolf Berle, Jr. At its second meeting in mid-March, the body identified a bill of rights as one of many important issues for likely international discussion during the war, in the initial period after the signing of an armistice, and following the creation of an international organization. Feeling no doubt overcome by the complexity and enormity of its charge, members delegated the discussion of a preliminary multilateral bill of rights three months later to Hackworth, Berle, Cohen, and Armstrong, all of whom would comprise the nucleus behind the administration's first specific human rights proposals.[24]

All four men had substantial expertise in international law, and all except Armstrong would extensively participate in State Department human rights planning for the next decade. Green Hackworth, whose thirty-year Foggy Bottom career started in 1916 as a law clerk, became its chief legal officer in 1931. He would resign the position in 1946 to become the first American judge on the International Court of Justice. Adolf Berle, Jr., a graduate of Harvard Law School and founding partner of a New York City firm specializing in corporate law, belonged to Roosevelt's "Brain Trust" before his appointment to the State Department in 1938. A graduate of Harvard Law School one year before Berle and a fellow member of Roosevelt's inner circle during the New Deal, Cohen had advised the president on Lend-Lease and other pre–Pearl Harbor foreign aid programs before transitioning to the Office of War Mobilization as its chief counsel. Three basic tenets dominated their work, which was without precedent in existing international law. First, recent history had informed them that nations that deprived their citizens of basic human freedoms faced a heightened risk of civil war and aggressive behavior in the international arena. They believed, therefore, that a transnational bill of rights enforced by an external agency might dissipate internal conflict before it posed a threat to international peace and security. Second, they supported the codification of such human rights norms in binding multilateral treaties, not simply in inspirational declarations such as the Atlantic Charter. Finally, they believed that the American Bill of Rights, a charter of specific civil and political (but not economic or social) rights, should serve as a template for choosing which guarantees to include.

It fell to State Department lawyer Durward Sandifer, a soft-spoken, dry-humored Columbia Law School graduate, to sketch a preliminary bill of rights that Cohen, Berle, Hackworth, and Armstrong would then revise.

Sandifer, who became Eleanor Roosevelt's close advisor at the United Nations, had spent the 1930s working for Hackworth before Pasvolsky personally asked him to undertake postwar planning research. Lacking any guidance on the scope, content, and enforcement of a list of rights, Sandifer felt free to make three conservative suppositions. Backing away from an international set of guarantees, he proposed merely to insert a list of rights into the constitutions of postwar European states. He derived its content by distilling provisions from European and American constitutions and historic texts such as the 1689 English Bill of Rights. By using such a documentary set, half of the 21 proposed articles defined due process procedures for individuals charged with criminal offenses, such as provisions for public, speedy, and fair trials and prohibitions on ex post facto laws, unwarranted searches and seizures, excessive bail, and cruel and unusual punishments. Other protections guarded the rights to assemble, worship, attend public school, pursue an occupation, express an opinion, own property, and attain "equal security of life, liberty and property without regard to origin, nationality, sex, language, race, political convictions or religious beliefs." Finally, Sandifer relied primarily on national courts to apply these constitutional provisions, though he cautiously recognized that some sort of regional or global authority might serve as an appellate court of last resort. The entire issue of implementation, he prophetically concluded, though with understatement, "presents an exceedingly difficult and complex problem."[25]

Sandifer's draft, completed in late July 1942, generated some enthusiasm among the members of the Subcommittee on Political Problems. After a week of review, the group reported its agreement with Sandifer on emplacing bills of rights within state constitutions. However, noting that "international enforcement of such rights [—] a restriction on sovereignty [—] is considered unacceptable," its members flatly rejected granting any supranational court or commission the power to review decisions made by national judiciaries. Deciding that further study was needed on what guarantees to include, the subcommittee created an ad hoc group consisting of Hackworth as chair, Berle, Cohen, and Armstrong joined by two additional members. James Shotwell, a veteran of Wilson's "Inquiry," a critical voice behind the creation of the International Labor Organization, and a history professor at Columbia, brought extensive knowledge about the League of Nations to the table. The director of the Cleveland-based Council on Foreign Affairs, Brooks Emeny, was a Princeton-educated diplomacy specialist who had transformed the organization into a model of citizen learning and activism focused on foreign relations using neighborhood and school-based discussion groups. On August 21, 1942, a year after the issuance of the Atlantic Charter, the group began its painstaking legal deliberations on Sandifer's work. Given the offensives by Allied armies in the Pacific and North Africa, a consensus emerged that the group should discuss a bill of rights for use in occupied nations only first. This topic largely occupied the subcommittee's two-hour weekly meetings for the next four months, and its work, mostly ignored by historians, marked a watershed in State Department wartime human rights planning.[26]

After Notter and Sandifer had disseminated background material on international law and a broad collection of historical documents relating to human rights, Hackworth, Cohen, Emeny, Shotwell, Notter, and Sandifer convened in the expansive Department of State Building at Seventeenth Street and Pennsylvania Avenue. The group quickly reached a consensus on the basic content of a bill of rights, though two major disagreements about terminology dominated discussions over the next three months. The technical problem of how to define basic legal precepts that would dovetail with terms already employed in the neophyte field of international human rights law, as well as within the discordant legal codes and languages of nations that embraced Roman civil law and Anglo-Saxon common law, led to abstract philosophical exchanges. Examples included whether an individual could be detained for up to two months without charge (which was allowed in Continental European civil law codes) and how to translate terms such as "due process of law" and "habeas corpus" into French and Spanish. The exact syntax that would both define a right *and* permissible derogations from it, such as in the interests of national security or public welfare, provided the second linguistic challenge. To overcome these twin challenges, the participants decided early on to borrow language from the first eight amendments to the U.S. Constitution, which they believed were paradoxically both specific and elastic enough to command global acceptance. The committee members assumed that the Constitution's provisions, modified by 150 years of American jurisprudence, provided the world's most complete and beneficial list of individual freedoms. As would become clear later, adopting them as the basis for a global bill of rights would ironically safeguard American human rights violations, for state and federal courts had already protected them with such constitutional verbiage.

These twin dilemmas would continuously bedevil all drafters of an international bill of rights, whether American or not, and so it is worth examining the context in which they first occurred. It took a mere ten minutes at the second meeting of Hackworth's group on October 1 for these dual problems to appear. With Sandifer's draft as the basis for discussion, the lawyers broke out into argument over the first article, whose two clauses stated,

> 1. Personal liberty is inviolable.
> 2. Restrictions or deprivations of personal liberty shall be imposed only upon the basis of laws which are in conflict with the rights guaranteed by this constitution.[27]

Sandifer had taken the language from the 1789 French Declaration of the Rights of Man, which to these Americans raised interpretive difficulties. Shotwell, believing the two clauses contradicted each other, opined that, given the revolutionary forces wracking France, the word "inviolable" meant that personal liberty should not be suppressed through the use of violence. Hackworth and Cohen discussed whether the permitted restrictions could be limitless (which would necessitate keeping "deprivation" in the article), and if that was so, whether the first clause had any real meaning anyway. Notter and Emeny wondered if personal liberty was a right to be "granted" or "restored" rather than "imposed," bringing retorts from Cohen that legal rights are neither, as they intrinsically belong to and are thus asserted by individuals. Emeny interjected that the French language had no word for Cohen's "rights," to which Cohen replied with favoring *loi* over *droit* (with *recht* thrown in as the German equivalent) as the closest synonym. Debate over article one ceased when Hackworth and Cohen favored using "declaration" over "constitution" in the second clause as a more appropriate term for a bill of rights that would be up to individual nations to enforce rather than the document have the force of binding international law. Committee members must have realized, if they had not already, that efficiency, brevity, and dispatch would not be hallmarks of their work.[28]

During many hours of deliberation in its October gatherings, the group struggled to balance brevity with substance and universal principles with acceptable derogations. The committee dissected each clause of Sandifer's draft, a process that expanded the number of articles and their length in order to narrow their scope. A familiar pattern soon developed: with the most complicated of articles, members proposed exceptions and restrictions not embodied in the text, forcing Sandifer to expand upon his original wording to sharpen its meaning. He was sometimes unsuccessful. An article on search warrants and pretrial detention doubled in length to describe the maximum time a person could be held without charge or hearing, and the remedies for those who were detained in violation of these constraints. New articles to protect minority schools and languages, ban slavery, and guarantee access to social security, workplace safety, housing, and medical care further lengthened the document. The committee's minutes record few internal disagreements, though, on other articles lifted almost verbatim from the American Constitution, such as bans on ex post facto laws, cruel and unusual punishment, excessive bail, double jeopardy, and self-incrimination. As Secretary Sandifer recorded once the committee had examined the ex post facto prohibition, "Mr. Hackworth said that this article embodied good American law, and it was agreed to without discussion." Discussions were not always tidy on familiar guarantees, particularly articles that had to include a basic right and a summary of precedents, mostly from American law, that had reasonably restricted their free exercise. This intricate task often led to clumsy and emasculating results, such as a clause allowing governments to censor speech in the interests of "public decency, good morals, and public security." It remained to be seen if other nations with discordant legal, political, economic, and cultural systems would accept this America-centered code of international law.[29]

The most contentious debates revolved around whether an international body would enforce the enumerated rights. Sandifer allowed for individual appeals from a nation's highest court to an international tribunal, which had the discretionary power to accept or ignore such pleadings. The tribunal's powers were almost unlimited: it could invalidate national laws, award monetary and property damages to individuals, and order the release of those unjustly imprisoned. This was an exceptional, breathtaking departure from existing international law, which had firmly allowed only national courts to judge the legality of criminal statutes and individual convictions. Only Emeny defended Sandifer's work; the others undoubtedly remembered the isolationist backlash that had resulted in the Senate rejecting Roosevelt's bid to join the World Court seven years earlier. They also doubted that any American government would favor granting citizens the right to an extranational appeal to challenge state or federal judicial proceedings. Acceding to such a procedure, moreover, would probably require amending the Constitution. Cohen, agreeing that the bill of rights should be binding on nations but opposing an international court, borrowed a lesson from American jurisprudence. He advocated inserting a clause similar to Article IV of the Constitution, which would proclaim the bill of rights part of the "supreme law of the land" for all signatories. If interpretational disagreements by judges of multiple nations arose, an international court could render a general decision and kick it back to national courts for application. This strategy would allow for the gradual development of a uniform code of rights, similar to what the U.S. Supreme Court had done by making decisions on individual state laws that were nonetheless binding on all states with similar statutes. Committee members, uncertain over whether a postwar international court would even exist, rejected Cohen's plan and omitted all implementation schemes from the draft for now.[30]

Ironically, after the thorough review, members of Hackworth's committee were more disappointed with their twenty-eight-page annotated draft than with the original seven-page bill drafted by Sandifer. The document's length, technical language, qualifications, and lack of enforcement provisions detracted from the inspirational, authoritative, and clear language that Shotwell and Cohen in particular desired. Some members worried about the inclusion of economic and social provisions that lacked an established place in the canon of international law. Paradoxically, though, this lack of judicial precedent led the group to offer few amendments to Sandifer's original clauses on the rights to engage in business, work in safe conditions, receive adequate health care, and own property. Remaining as short, simple statements, they could provide a model for revisions to the rest of the document. They also, more importantly, demonstrated the State Department's commitment to defining the economic components of the Four Freedoms and the Atlantic Charter. In late October, the stymied committee decided to start over and prepare a shorter, cleaner draft.[31]

Having produced a long and in places unwieldy document, the group of six now embraced a process of redaction to produce a general code of minimum rights. The shift resulted in a change in framework: members wrote the first draft with an eye toward reforming, expanding, and improving human rights practices internationally. Now they turned their eyes internally, deciding that they did not want their work potentially to alter the domestic legal status quo. Instead, they employed the same minimalist reasoning: though the rights identified had to command worldwide acceptance, domestic politics, personal experience, and America-centered thought demanded that they conform to existing United States constitutional principles. When a contradiction arose between existing American law and progressive human rights standards, the former usually won out due to fears that the latter would invalidate state and federal laws condoning racial, ethnic, or sexual inequality. Having adopted this consensus, members constricted their work to protect laws prohibiting property ownership by Chinese and Japanese aliens on the West Coast and statutes discriminating against African Americans in employment and education.

They accomplished this task by adopting a general article declaring that "All persons shall enjoy equality before the law, and equal rights with respect to life, liberty, property, and employment shall not be denied." The article's Fourteenth Amendment phrasing, according to the U.S. Supreme Court in *Plessy v. Ferguson*, nonetheless affirmed the right of states to pass Jim Crow and alien land laws.[32]

The revised draft comprised only nine articles of American constitutional distillation. The minutes taken contain no observations on the irony of limiting an international bill of rights to permit domestic racial discrimination. Nor do they record the paradox of constructing a document that would inspire worldwide adoption despite consisting of language lifted from the First, Fourth, Fifth, Sixth, Eighth, and Fourteenth Amendments to the American Constitution. Although Notter had completed a detailed analysis of transnational implementation possibilities, the drafting group, after a very short exchange, decided after all to adopt Cohen's language taken from Article IV of the U.S. Constitution. It would therefore be only up to the courts of each nation to interpret and enforce the broad guarantees, which were supposed to "constitute a part of the supreme or fundamental law of each state." Thus severed from any international enforcement power, the document only amounted to a declarative statement of goals that would purposefully have only minimal impact on human rights abuses in the United States. Its simplistic formula defined in large measure American policy for the next decade.[33]

As the half-dozen specialists tilled only somewhat new legal ground through the fall of 1942, they sought assurance and advice from outside experts. In early November, the State Department sent Sandifer to Philadelphia for a conference of the American Law Institute to learn about the organization's construction of an international bill of rights. The group, founded in 1923 by legal Progressives including former President William Howard Taft and ex-Secretaries of State Charles Evans Hughes and Elihu Root, sought to simplify and standardize the common law to make it more coherent and predictable. Toward this end, a majority of the 18 law professors and former diplomats in attendance favored a bill enumerating only those basic civil and political limitations on governmental action that many national constitutions already contained. Sandifer noted that a minority at the gathering, though, viewed such a list "with considerable scorn as the traditional eighteenth and nineteenth century liberal conception of human rights." Remembering the Great Depression and inspired by Roosevelt's Four Freedoms and Henry Wallace's "Common Man" vision, the dissenters sought to mandate the governmental provision of adequate food, clothing, shelter, and medical care to all persons. The majority objected to this departure from existing international law, calling such a list too abstract for nations to grant, and courts to enforce, with any precision. The group navigated the impasse by drawing up a list of basic civil rights within six months, assigning the minority to study economic and social guarantees and, at Sandifer's urging, sending periodic progress reports to the State Department. Sandifer left the meeting encouraged by the quality of debate, but he presciently worried that the "fundamental cleavage of opinion" over the two categories would be a hallmark of future domestic and international deliberation.[34]

Hackworth's group, emboldened by most of Sandifer's agreeable conference report, devoted only three more meetings to simplifying and synthesizing its draft bill of rights with existing domestic law. Its half-dozen members approved the document on December 10, 1942, a date that six years later for other reasons became International Human Rights Day. The final version contained 16 articles that tried to balance individual guarantees with acceptable qualifications for reasons of national security, public morals, and levels of economic development. The document contained familiar language on free speech, assembly, and religion, equality before the law, due process of law, and procedural protections for those charged with a crime. In a banal summary of its work on economic and social rights, the group affirmed that governments had a general responsibility to provide "minimum standards of economic, social, and cultural well-being as the resources of the country, effectively used, are capable of sustaining." Enforcement was solely placed in the hands of national courts and legislatures. After four months of study, the final product differed little from Sandifer's original proposal. Guided by a conservative set of assumptions in an America-centered framework, the outcome could hardly have been otherwise. As the only code of human rights formulated by the State Department during World War II, it would soon be pressed into service by American diplomats at upcoming international conferences that created a successor to the League of Nations and the world's first non-binding code of human rights.[35]

Chairman Hackworth forwarded the bill of rights to the parent Subcommittee on Political Problems, which skeptically took up the topic for the first and only time in June 1943. Undersecretary of State Sumner Welles set the tone by declaring, in Secretary Notter's words, that "he could not foresee this Government's ever agreeing to enter into any international obligation which would let other governments determine what its relationship with its citizens should be." He favored placing a list of basic rights in the charter of an international peacekeeping organization; acceding nations would have to give a non-binding promise to uphold them. When Representative Charles Eaton (R-NJ) asked Welles whether, through such a list, "we would ask all nations to adopt the American Bill of Rights . . . Mr. Welles replied that that would substantially be the case." A trilateral consensus now solidified: to gain American approval, any charter of human rights should consist only of familiar civil and political rights, be non-binding or leave enforcement up to a nation's own judicial system, and not invalidate any human rights violations presently occurring in the United States. The bill of rights now joined other policy contingencies in State Departmental confidential files ready for dusting off when needed.[36]

By late 1942, with battlefield momentum beginning to favor the Allies in the Pacific and North Africa, State Department planners turned to a much larger and critical component of their postwar plans: an improved successor to the League of Nations. The debate over human rights now shifted from detailed discussions of individual guarantees to larger political questions of national sovereignty, the appropriateness of *any* international oversight of a nation's human rights record, and the connections between peace, economic development, and the rule of law. A nexus of timing, topical necessity, and personnel explain this change. Roosevelt, who strongly supported the creation of some kind of postwar body, needed concrete proposals for summit meetings with other Allied leaders scheduled for the summer and fall of 1943. Any draft bill of rights, therefore, could not exist in isolation but now had to dovetail with the rather limited principles, organization, and powers that Washington wanted to grant to an international organization. Roosevelt's favoring of national sovereignty for personal and political reasons over any sort of powerful world parliament also spelled doom for any expansive, binding, and internationally enforced bill of rights. Hull and Welles, who also weighed in on postwar planning, also used their influence to ensure that State Department planners respected the president's beliefs when creating proposals for a League of Nations successor. With cautious work already done by Hackworth's committee, they did not need to apply any pressure to dilute their department's human rights proposals.

Given the complex and important task at hand, Hull created in the summer of 1942 the Special Subcommittee on International Organization, headed by Welles, and including Hackworth, Cohen, Notter, and Shotwell, plus Hamilton Fish Armstrong from the Council on Foreign Relations and Pasvolsky. Clark Eichelberger of the Commission to Study the Organization of Peace also attended most of the meetings. After studying the charters of the League of Nations and the International Labor Organization, the body began to piece together a constitution for a new international organization that would establish and maintain world peace with greater success than its predecessor. Following almost four dozen Saturday morning meetings in his office, Welles passed on the committee's work to Roosevelt one month before he and Churchill met at Quebec in August 1943.[37]

The Special Subcommittee authored the first official U.S. plan for what would become the United Nations Charter, and its inclusion of human rights authority illustrated a brief marriage of the topics. Their proposal was based on a "provisional outline" prepared by James Shotwell. The chair of the Commission to Study the Organization of Peace, who was concurrently helping to edit Sandifer's bill in Hackworth's committee, included the protection of human rights as a responsibility of the international body. His short preamble asserted that the United Nations, "having subscribed to a common program of human rights, [must] undertake to establish the instrumentalities by which peace and human rights may be secured." After approving this wording, the subcommittee wrote the remainder of a "Draft Constitution of International Organization." The lengthy and complicated plan, written in technical verbiage, called for an executive council of 11 nations, including permanent members Great Britain, China, the United States, and the Soviet Union, to have the authority to dispatch military force if at least six members (including three of the Big Four, collectively called the "Executive Committee") agreed. The other seven council members would come from five regional bodies that would set "neighborhood" police policy subject to review by the council. Issues of "social security, economic stability, general well-being and peace throughout the world" fell to the dryly named Bureau of Technical Services, which operated at the council's direction. Due to his growing personal and professional dislike of Welles and the plan's emphasis on regional blocs rather than a truly universal scheme, Secretary of State Hull refused to forward the document to Roosevelt. Welles, though, characteristically bypassed the secretary and briefed Roosevelt personally on its contents. Although the president favored Welles's quasi-regional approach and grant of special status to the Big Four, he took no official action on the proposal. The document's preamble, nonetheless, demonstrated continuing but cautious State Department support for making the protection of human rights an international responsibility, though without any actual international oversight.[38]

Hull retaliated against Welles by suspending the special subcommittee's work, creating a hand-picked body to generate another charter, and engineering Welles's firing. Desiring a much simpler and shorter blueprint for presentation at the upcoming inter-Allied Quadrant Conference in Quebec, Hull tapped the State Department's research arm in the summer of 1943. The "Staff Charter of the United Nations" emerged from an informal, ten-member drafting group that quickly generated an outline in early August 1943. The Big Four would exercise predominant power in the seven-member Executive Council, where they each possessed an absolute veto on most matters. The three non-permanent members were elected by all nations rather than drawn from regional blocs. Reflecting Hull's desire for a world parliament, membership in the General Conference, the main policymaking organ, was open to all states. Technical economic, scientific, health, and education agencies were linked directly to this body instead of being autonomous specialized bodies as under the Draft Constitution. After accepting this replacement for the Draft Constitution as the Quebec gathering approached, Hull engineered Welles's forced resignation. An embarrassing *New York Times* column provided the pretext. Written by Hull's close friend Arthur Krock, it blamed Welles and Roosevelt for disorder, dissention, and impairing the chain of command within the State Department. Roosevelt, knowing that Hull had also circulated rumors about Welles's past indiscreet homosexual behavior, reluctantly concluded that he needed Hull's influence with Southern senators skeptical of joining an international organization. Welles resigned on August 16, the same day Hull and Roosevelt left for the Quebec Conference. It was the only wartime summit they ever attended together.[39]

The Staff Charter they brought along did contain the most explicit connection yet between an international peacekeeping body and the protection of human rights. Lengthy internal debate by the charter's drafters centered on whether to include the subject merely in a preambular clause, as with the Draft Constitution, or in a substantive clause. Favoring the latter, the group drafted a stand-alone article under which member nations "agree to give legislative effect" to a "Declaration of Human Rights." Lacking time and expertise to draft the declaration itself, the committee simply appended the draft bill of rights done by Hackworth's group after favorably remarking that it "follows the American Constitution closely." The article's overall purpose was, as stated by commentary on the provision, "to facilitate the attainment of the Four Freedoms by all persons, and to prevent internal unrest and international tension arising from violations of individual rights." As an integral part of the Staff Charter, its drafters assumed that all states wanting to join the organization would correct any human rights shortcomings before applying for membership. The line connecting this simple provision to the vague human rights language of the future United Nations Charter would not be a direct one, but the article's approval by Hull and Roosevelt suggests that they considered it politically and legally acceptable for confidential discussion with Allied leaders.[40]

The key to understanding their approval lay in the article's language on enforcement, which was even weaker than that proposed by Hackworth's team and designed specifically to protect American-style racial discrimination. Alternatives considered, such as requiring states to amend their constitutions, allowing individuals to sue their nations before international courts, or making a bill of rights the "supreme law" of each state, were deemed politically unacceptable or too compromising of national sovereignty. Instead, individual nations would, as a prerequisite for membership in the body, "agree to give legislative effect" to a future human rights declaration and use their own "administrative and judicial authorities" as enforcement vehicles. The sole requirement was that such implementation be accomplished "without discrimination as to nationality, language, race, political opinion, or religious belief." As Congress had made no moves to pass civil rights laws, and as the federal courts had already ruled that "separate but equal" state segregation statutes did not violate the non-discrimination clauses of the U.S. Constitution, the Staff Charter posed no threat to Jim Crow's survival. As the group plainly concluded in its commentary, the promise to apply human rights in an egalitarian manner "will not interfere with the laws of some of our states for the segregation of races." As a final check, the United States, as one of the permanent members of the Executive Council, could veto any troublesome human rights agreements that the organization's technical agencies might draft.[41]

Due partially to the completion of the Staff Charter a mere four days earlier, Roosevelt did not formally discuss it with Churchill at the Quebec Conference that convened on August 17, 1943. Most of their conversations instead revolved around immediate war plans, from timetables for invasions of Italy and France to the formation of a joint Southeast Asia Command. Roosevelt knew that serious differences existed between himself and Churchill on the structure of a postwar organization: Churchill favored decision-making confined exclusively to the Big Three (though he now reluctantly added China), and he saw little need for any formal body beyond separate regional councils. The British leader would also, FDR believed, reject any international human rights obligations, including any external oversight of colonies, for his nation's empire. Given this chasm, the inability of Soviet leader Joseph Stalin to attend the meeting, and the fear of a backlash from congressional isolationists if they viewed the Staff Charter as a fait accompli, Roosevelt talked only in generalizations about a peacekeeping organ. He and Churchill did approve a cautious statement, accepted by China and the Soviet Union later in the year at the Cairo and Teheran conferences that "recogniz[ed] the necessity of establishing at the earliest practicable date a general international organization . . . for the maintenance of international peace and security."[42]

Even as they pigeonholed the Draft Constitution and the Staff Charter, both of which only indirectly placed the protection of human rights under the aegis of an international peacekeeping organization, Roosevelt and his secretary of state continued to embrace human rights rhetoric. In a national radio address, Roosevelt marked the first anniversary of the Declaration by the United Nations by outlining three goals that lay ahead: achieving a decisive military victory over the Axis, employing diplomacy to prevent future warfare, and obtaining international co-operation so that "mankind may enjoy in peace and in freedom the unprecedented blessings which Divine Providence through the progress of civilization has put within our reach." Following the August 1943 Quebec Conference, Hull delivered a foreign policy address over the nation's airwaves. As a typical Hull speech, marked by uninspiring clichés ("Each nation should maintain a stable government"), a moderate tone, and predictable content, it was not an impressive effort. After reviewing the improving Allied military situation in the Mediterranean, he affirmed American support of self-determination for "qualified" peoples only, the sovereign equality of nations, the peaceful settlement of transnational disputes, free trade, and transnational co-operation based upon a common regard for "liberty, equality, justice, morality, and the law." These non-committal generalities were uttered purely for exhortation and inspiration, a means to persuade the American public to sacrifice for a war that did not touch the American mainland. Yet in making these broad statements of policy, Roosevelt and Hull created rising expectations about the postwar world and America's mission within it. Veterans' groups, labor unions, religious denominations, and think tanks began forging their own recommendations, and they would soon look to the Roosevelt administration for affirmation, guidance, and concrete policies. For now, though, the secrecy surrounding governmental human rights policymaking prevented them from facing disappointment.[43]

Such bland assertions did not translate easily into policy anyway, and so once again lacking direction from on high, the State Department's mid-level technicians cautiously wrapped up their research. Human rights discussions continued to be led by Notter and Sandifer under the direction of Pasvolsky, who now commanded hundreds of researchers. Throughout the summer of 1943, they translated previous State Department work on human rights issues into briefings that advanced multiple policy choices with analysis of the strengths and faults of each. Turning first to protecting human rights, they sketched familiar arguments over whether an international treaty or national constitutions would be more politically acceptable, legally enforceable, and philosophically likely to create stability and peace. A second summary discussed the timing and jurisdiction of such guarantees: whether the Allies should enforce a bill of rights in occupied areas before or after a peace settlement, and if it should then apply to all sovereign states and their colonies, only sovereign states, or only some sovereign states such as the defeated Axis powers. The abstracts contained no policy prescriptions, only a list of possibilities, but their compilation was important nonetheless as it marked the completion of basic research on human rights issues. It fell to Roosevelt to choose among the options advanced, or, as was often his approach to diplomacy, to come up with his own initiatives.[44]

By late 1943, battlefield advances, impending summit meetings among the Big Four leaders at Teheran and Moscow, and domestic political pressure forced the finalization of briefing books on the general duties and structure of an international peacekeeping organization. Victories at Kursk and Kharkov on the Eastern Front, in the Solomon Islands of the Pacific Ocean, and in North Africa showed momentum passing inexorably to the Allies. Stalin pushed for a meeting with Roosevelt and Churchill to discuss opening a second front in Europe to relieve pressure on his armies, and the two Western leaders sought Stalin's views on an international security organization. Roosevelt worried that historical Russian xenophobia or Stalin's demand for an absolute veto would forestall any agreement. Domestically, cognizant of President Woodrow Wilson's failed fight with the Senate over the League of Nations, the president carefully maneuvered to obtain bipartisan support for American entry into its successor. With his encouragement, over 90 percent of both houses of Congress endorsed non-binding resolutions favoring the creation of a collective security organ, sponsored by Senators Tom Connally (D-TX) and Representative J. William Fulbright (D-AR). The president was now reflecting, rather than presaging, public acceptance of this radical departure from isolationism. His administration's speeches, press releases, and radio addresses had borne fruit: according to a September National Opinion Research Center poll, four of every five Americans thought the United States should join a "union of nations." Now Roosevelt was almost ready to discuss its details.

First, though, he sought the domestic leverage, diplomatic confirmation, and political momentum that an Allied endorsement of a League of Nations successor would bring.[45]

Given the emerging domestic consensus, Roosevelt thought the time was right to seek a concurrence of the Big Three when Hull traveled to a conference in Moscow in the last two weeks of October. Although Roosevelt's own vision for such a body was unclear, containing internal contradictions over the role and powers of small and large states, he desired only a general assent by Great Britain and the Soviet Union. Hull, emerging from under Welles's shadow as the nation's second diplomat behind Roosevelt, delivered. The final communiqué stated rather tentatively that the four main allies, China included, "recognize the necessity of establishing at the earliest practicable date a general international organization, based on the principle of the sovereign equality of all peace-loving states, and open to membership by all such states, large and small, for the maintenance of international peace and security." Roosevelt had gingerly engineered congressional and foreign acceptance of a key part of his postwar vision. The congressional resolutions and the Moscow Conference Declaration of Four Nations on General Security now provided catalysts for planning and public opinion mobilization by both the State Department and nongovernmental organizations.[46]

At times co-operative and at others competitive, the State Department, international law specialists, and foreign policy activists such as Clark Eichelberger and John Foster Dulles sketched out more detailed plans for the peacekeeping body and appealed for grassroots support. This interchange marked a new phase in wartime planning. Having read the Atlantic Charter and listened carefully to speeches by Roosevelt administration officials, progressives such as Dulles and Eichelberger now sought to advance plans predicated on making the observance of human rights an international issue. While details differed, their collective work laid the basis for increasingly sophisticated plans by State Department experts, international law specialists in academia and private practice, leaders of think tanks, and religious luminaries. Their work, at times confined to scholarly peers, politically connected activists, or the general public, placed the Roosevelt administration in a difficult chicken-and-egg position. While the president sought out advice from allies overseas, members of Congress, and domestic interest groups, they in turn wanted him to reveal his positions too. But he knew that if he did so, he risked alienating foreign and domestic supporters. His solution, carefully honed throughout the New Deal, was to ignore, obfuscate, feign agreement, and find compromise. He utilized all of these tactics toward those even in his administration who wanted to internationalize the postwar oversight of human rights.

Dulles and Eichelberger in particular began a sustained advocacy campaign to ensure that the peacekeeping organ had a greater measure of human rights jurisdiction than the still-confidential Staff Charter and Draft Constitution. Eichelberger and his Commission to Study the Organization of Peace pleaded for a United Nations equipped to handle a growing list of postwar economic and social challenges. During the summer of 1943, the National Broadcasting Company (NBC), in conjunction with the think tank, sponsored 13 radio programs on Allied war aims. Several expounded upon Roosevelt's Four Freedoms, including programs entitled "Food and Health in the Future" and "Justice and Human Rights," which reached at least 4 million Americans. The commission also wrote a study guide, *Winning the War on the Spiritual Front*. Distributed to rural parts of the country that could not receive the radio programs, the booklets facilitated a network of grassroots discussion groups meeting nationwide during the second week of August. The publication argued for a postwar world based upon law, justice, and economic co-operation, and it closed with a call for citizens to lobby lawmakers in Washington. The commission further refined its vision in a November 1943 report entitled "Fundamentals of the International Organization." The study recommended creating an international air force, arms reduction treaties, and a tribunal to judge disputes between nations. Worried, though, that the Moscow Declaration only referred to security issues, the document concluded by citing the need for an international entity to "provide means through international law for safeguarding essential human rights." Many of the one hundred signatories, including influential academics, intellectuals, lawyers, and business leaders, soon tenaciously lobbied the State Department to convert that recommendation into policy.[47]

Echoing that sentiment, John Foster Dulles and the Commission to Study the Bases of a Just and Durable Peace likewise endorsed the call for the creation of a body with peacekeeping, economic, and humanitarian responsibilities. Infused with a Christian ethos of justice, fairness, compassion, and the protection of those economically and politically marginalized, the commission circulated a collection of essays by prominent religious leaders. Princeton Theological Seminary President John A. MacKay enunciated the theme of the volume. The churches, he said, "must proclaim the enduring moral principles by which human plans are constantly to be tested." The fixed moral compass pointed toward a peace in which nations solved conflicts by adjudication, satisfied human wants through transnational co-operation, and behaved according to a code of Judeo-Christian ethics. Dulles's own contribution envisioned a nation of Christians who launched a crusade for humankind by lobbying their political leaders to ensure that the final peace contained a solid moral underpinning. His organization sketched more specific content in its March 1943 "Statement of Political Proposi- tions." The first five principles called for international co-operation to con- trol the use of force, to protect dependent peoples, and to harmonize na- tional economic and financial policies. The sixth tenet called for a postwar peace that "must establish, in principle, and seek to achieve in practice, the right of individuals everywhere to religious and intellectual liberty." To ensure President Roosevelt read the declaration, Dulles discussed it in person with him at the White House.[48]

Separate from the public lobbying by advocacy groups, lawyers shared technical knowledge through scholarly articles and offered their personal advice to the State Department on human rights issues. University of Iowa Law Professor Percy Bordwell was one of the first in his field to send President Roosevelt his suggestions. Bordwell outlined a "Constitution for the United Nations" that leaned very heavily on the American Consti- tution to create a three-branch union of nations. The division of powers between a world assembly and national governments under Bordwell's plan would be similar to that spelled out in the U.S. Constitution be- tween the federal and state governments, though with added protections for national sovereignty and colonial empires. He included the complete Bill of Rights to safeguard individuals worldwide against actions by the assembly, omitting only the guarantees that were inapplicable (such as Eighteenth and Twenty-First Amendments on Prohibition). He postu- lated that these provisions would underlie a global confederation similar to Clarence Streit's famous proposal in *Union Now*. Appealing to his- tory, Bordwell concluded that as the American Constitution had main- tained domestic tranquility, the rule of law, and individual freedom for 150 years, "There is no reason why a Constitution modeled on it should not do the same thing for the world." Roosevelt responded that he took "much pleasure" in reading this "very interesting" article. Bordwell did not know that State Department planners had reached the same basic America-centered constitutional conclusion.[49]

International Law Professor Quincy Wright made a more substantial contribution in an April 1943 article printed in *International Concilia- tion*, a publication of the Carnegie Endowment for International Peace. Wright's piece surveyed the human rights promises made by Roosevelt and the United Nations, the gradual evolution of international law, and the increasing interdependence of nations in order to argue the necessity of protecting basic individual rights. Those rights could be deduced, he claimed, from studying the natural rights theory of Enlightenment philosophers like John Locke, national bills of rights, international law, and recent Allied pronouncements such as the Atlantic Charter. He distilled from these sources a list of primarily civil, political, and property rights that had found widespread acceptance in theory, if not in practice. To ensure that nations adhered to those principles in the postwar era, Wright proposed four enforcement schemes: diplomatic channels, national legislation, and international courts that would either adjudicate disputes between states or receive petitions from individuals. The last point was crucial, for he argued that the Atlantic Charter, the Four Freedoms, and Wallace's "Common Man" speech all defined a new relationship between the individual and the world. This was an exceedingly fortuitous development, for as Wright noted in sweeping language, "Recognition that the individual is a subject of international law . . . has become in the modern world an essential condition of an effective world public opinion, of a living international law, of social and political stability and of human welfare and progress." His article served as the basis for the most important human rights report of the Commission to Study the Organization of Peace, and Wright himself became a leading rights champion at the San Francisco Conference that created the United Nations.[50]

The American Law Institute added its collective voice to the growing domestic consensus for an international bill of rights. Following the divisive organizational meeting that Sandifer had attended in November 1942, five subcommittees of the Institute's Bill of Rights Project began considering specific personal, property, procedural, social, and political rights. By the spring of 1943, each one had prepared a basic proposal accompanied by extensive technical commentary. Sandifer traveled to Philadelphia again in May 1943 to observe and summarize the progress. He reported back to the State Department that although the lawyers had made few final decisions, they did broadly agree to include basic personal freedoms, such as of religion and speech (with a vocal minority favoring a ban on hate speech), and to add requirements that nations provide basic living standards for their people. Many, though, voiced skepticism about adding pledges of employment, education, and social security due to definitional (what is "acceptable" schooling?) and enforcement obstacles. Others questioned guarantees of democratic governance to all peoples by enshrining the rights to vote, petition one's officials, and run for office. Such provisions would surely involve, a majority feared, an international body interfering too much in the internal affairs of nations. It was a pre-scient worry that had also bothered the State Department's own lawyers due to domestic racist statutes, and both groups of drafters responded by postponing the thorny discussion entirely.[51]

As the summer of 1943 progressed, bureaucratic disorganization and internal upheaval left the State Department in poor shape to respond to these pleas by legal scholars and human rights activists. The paralysis was unfortunate given the increasing need to finalize plans for an international peacekeeping body as an Allied victory grew closer. Upcoming confer-ences at Cairo and Teheran of the Big Four Allied leaders, for which the department had to undertake detailed planning on a host of military, eco-nomic, political, and social matters, exacerbated the administrative confu-sion. Funding and staffing levels were clearly inadequate given the broad range of problems and contingencies that demanded study. Adding to the inertia, the departure of Sumner Welles left the department without a skilled top-level administrator and Roosevelt without a close confidante inside Foggy Bottom.[52]

To meet these new challenges and opportunities, Hull thoroughly re-organized the State Department's entire postwar planning procedure. On July 12, 1943, he abolished the Advisory Committee on Post-War Foreign Policy and all of its subcommittees. In their place, Hull unofficially or-ganized a senior advisory body, the Informal Agenda Group. Its mem-bers, including Pasvolsky, Notter, Cohen, and Hackworth, met weekly in Pasvolsky's office to outline plans for an international organization after scanning policy summaries (including the Staff Charter) prepared by mid-level technicians. The Agenda Group became the nucleus of the American delegation to the first conference devoted to organizing a successor to the League of Nations: the 1944 Dumbarton Oaks Conference. One conse-quence of this restructuring on wartime planning was the marginalization of topics, such as human rights, that were not deemed of immediate mili-tary and political significance in creating an international organization. The Informal Agenda Group preferred to focus on planning a successor to the League of Nations that was simple, easily acceptable to the other Allies, and could enforce peace by primarily military means in a postwar world. By accepting such a focus and directing the work of the body, Hull pushed aside the controversial problems of defining, implementing, and enforcing a bill of rights. He also suspected that Britain and the Soviet Union, not to mention Roosevelt, would have little interest in these issues, a conclusion soon proven correct by the scope of discussion at Dumbarton Oaks.[53]

By late 1943, three paradoxes marked human rights discussions within the Roosevelt administration. While Roosevelt and Hull had issued the Four Freedoms, the Atlantic Charter, and the Declaration by the United Nations to mobilize public support for the war and expanded postwar commitments, they privately ignored proposals that allowed an international organization to implement or even simply promote the human rights principles contained in those statements. This policy determination occurred despite increased planning by State Department bureaucrats, legal scholars, and private organizations that had generated and lobbied for specific human rights proposals. The State Department's bill of rights, moreover, designed to appeal to a global audience, essentially plagiarized from the U.S. Constitution and added language that accepted and protected the nation's own systemic abuses against Asian Americans (over 100,000 of whom lay waiting in internment camps) and African Americans. Even this conservative work was forgotten. Bureaucratic and personal divisions within the State Department, British and Soviet skepticism given their own violations, and Roosevelt's own predilection for an international organization that would keep the peace through political and military action by the Big Four all mitigated against domestic and diplomatic adoption of any human rights proposal.

Roosevelt had succeeded, though, in lining up national and international support for creating a successor to the League of Nations. The Connally and Fulbright resolutions and the Moscow Declaration committed the United States to participate in the planning for an international peacekeeping organization. This was no small achievement given substantial public distaste for entanglements overseas prior to the start of World War II and the debacle at home over the League of Nations at the conclusion of the last global conflagration. This consensus came at a cost, which was the postponement of detail and silence over human rights. Hull's Informal Agenda Group, the British and Soviet governments, and President Roosevelt himself soon decided to delay high-level human rights discussions until late 1944. But in rejecting the human rights initiatives of State Department postwar planning bodies and private organizations, Roosevelt laid the foundation for a powerful domestic backlash that forced him to reorient completely U.S. human rights policy within the year.

CHAPTER 2

Implementing a Vision, 1943–1945

AFTER SECURING AGREEMENT among the Big Four in the Moscow Declaration to establish an international peacekeeping organization, the administration of Franklin D. Roosevelt spent the next eight months in deep planning for its creation. The final provisions of the United Nations Charter, signed by almost 50 nations on June 26, 1945, reflected inter-Allied bargaining, Roosevelt's own strong predilections, and pressure from American lobbying groups. The major discussions within the Roosevelt administration and with its wartime partners at the Dumbarton Oaks and San Francisco conferences barely touched upon human rights. Presidents Roosevelt and Harry S. Truman, Secretary of State Cordell Hull and his heir, Edward Stettinius, and even State Department planning agencies that had discussed human rights issues in the past, now focused on the procedural and security mechanisms by which the United Nations would come into existence and exercise its authority to prevent a third world war. British Prime Minister Winston Churchill and Soviet Premier Joseph Stalin seconded this focus, and they joined with Roosevelt in trying to harmonize a vision of collective security with the maintenance of their own national sovereignty, regional spheres of influence, and unilateral freedom of action. Given the emphasis on security matters, all proposals for a global bill of rights took on secondary importance to Roosevelt, met with indifference from Churchill, and generated opposition from Stalin. State Department documents pertaining to human rights extrapolation and enforcement lay unused inside the briefing books of American diplomats.

It remained for Latin American and Asian nations, whose populations had known foreign domination, and American religious, academic, and legal organizations to press for giving the international body the responsibility to define and protect human rights worldwide. The tenacious lobbying done by American organizations before the San Francisco Conference helped to persuade the Truman administration to support the inclusion of human rights references in the United Nations Charter. Their efforts were aided by the gruesome discoveries made at Nazi concentration camps, which generated an impulse to prevent such abuses from happening again. Truman and the State Department then convinced the British and Soviet delegates at the San Francisco Conference, largely by arguing that having the body merely promote human rights through a human rights commission would grant the United Nations no real power in that arena. The human rights clauses of the U.N. Charter, despite their substantial limitations, are a tribute to the lobbying of American activists who understood that a postwar peace could not last unless governments recognized the universality of basic human rights. Whether the charter's actual provisions would engender this vision was a question for the future.

American planning for an international organization took on renewed importance by early December 1943 due to the Teheran Conference, the successful prosecution of the war, and a reorganization of the State Department. At their first ever meeting, the leaders of the United States, Great Britain, and the Soviet Union spent four days in Teheran discussing a second front in Europe, the future of Germany, and a Soviet declaration of war against Japan. In addition to these military concerns, topics related to self-determination, the postwar prosecution of war criminals, and a League of Nations successor also appeared on the agenda. Roosevelt, looking to win an unprecedented fourth term in 1944, worried aloud that the 1940 Soviet incorporation of the Baltic States of Estonia, Latvia, and Lithuania would make Republican voters out of those with ethnic ties to those occupied areas. Stalin objected, telling Roosevelt that Americans "should be informed and some propaganda work should be done," so that they would recognize Moscow's suzerainty over the region. The exchange showed Roosevelt that the Atlantic Charter's call for peoples worldwide to determine their own political futures did not have much appeal to the Russian leader. Over dinner one night, Stalin angered Churchill's legal and moral sensibilities by off-handedly calling for the summary execution of 50,000 German officers. When Roosevelt playfully noted that the number ought to be reduced by a thousand, the British prime minister strode away

in anger. Both of these issues showed that the leading Allied powers substantially disagreed on major issues with human rights implications. On
the complex and evolving plans for a United Nations, though, there would
be even greater lines of division.[1]

Roosevelt shared his evolving concept of a United Nations at Teheran
with Stalin, a vision that combined elements of the Draft Constitution,
Staff Charter, and his own thinking. The president's vision looked to a
global plenary of nations that would discuss common issues; an executive
council, comprised of the Big Four and a half-dozen other nations that
would consider economic and social topics including, presumably, human
rights; and a peacekeeping body, composed exclusively of the Big Four,
that could employ military force against real or potential aggressors. To
facilitate Stalin's approval, Roosevelt stressed the latter component, promised that decisions of the executive council would not be binding on any
nation, and asserted that only the peacekeeping body could approve of
the use of military force. Although the final communiqué generally stated
that the participants "seek the co-operation and active participation of all
nations, large and small, whose peoples in heart and mind are dedicated,
as are our own peoples, to the elimination of tyranny and slavery, oppression and intolerance," Roosevelt's plan did little to promote such steps. The
president's presentation showed how little he felt bound by State Department proposals; he was willing to alter them based on his own predilections and what he thought would be acceptable to the Soviets in particular.
It also allowed him to capture the initiative, for the governments of Stalin
and Churchill had thus far given little formal study to the structure and
functions of an international legislature.[2]

Instead of making the world safe for democracy as President Woodrow
Wilson had promised, Roosevelt told Congress in his 1944 State of the
Union address a month later that his postwar vision revolved around "the
one supreme objective for the future, for all the United Nations, [which]
can be summed up in one word: Security." Even his call for a "second bill
of rights," which would graft guarantees of employment, adequate food
and housing, and medical care onto the list of familiar civil and political
rights, pointedly applied to American citizens only. His call for the realization of the Four Freedoms at home only further contrasted with his
growing conservatism on the transnational enforcement of human rights.
In his conversations at Teheran with Stalin, Roosevelt had proposed, in
part, what he thought the Soviet leader wanted to hear. The emphasis on
spheres of influence and national sovereignty did not bode well for those
who wanted a body invested with the worldwide power to protect indi-

vidual freedoms. Roosevelt's commitment to fulfilling a broad range of guarantees domestically, though, gave activists hope that, if they could bring pressure to bear on him, Roosevelt would broaden his plans for an international organization.[3]

The discussions at Teheran did inspire Roosevelt to take a renewed interest in plans for an international organization. On December 21, the president asked Hull for the latest State Department version, which Hull forwarded eight days later. Informally entitled the "Outline Plan," the document had been prepared on short notice by Hull's Informal Political Agenda Group (the renamed Informal Agenda Group), whose members now served as Hull's main advisors on postwar matters. The group, guided by the Draft Constitution, Staff Charter, and policy summaries prepared by Pasvolsky's researchers prior to the Moscow Conference, presented an ambitious plan. The blueprint called for an Executive Council of the Big Four and possibly other nations to mediate security crises, a General Assembly of all members to promote international co-operation, an international court of justice, and technical agencies to facilitate co-ordination on economic and social concerns. The plan emphasized the need to stop future wars through unified military action by Britain, the United States, China, and the Soviet Union. Although its authors included Cohen and Hackworth, who had participated in drafting the State Department's bill of rights, the final product presumably but not explicitly relegated future human rights discussions to "an agency for co-operation in . . . social activities, and such other agencies as may be found necessary." This was not an endorsement of an institution with broad humanitarian powers, but rather vague language that reflected Roosevelt's refusal to decide how he wanted to proceed in this area.[4]

The exclusion of economic and social duties, including specific human rights provisions, generated some objections within the Informal Political Agenda Group. Law Professor Quincy Wright, one of the nation's leading human rights scholars, led the charge. Noting that the authors of the Staff Charter had rejected the idea of a human rights commission as "politically unacceptable," Wright proposed instead an impartial and independent commission of jurists that could accept petitions from aggrieved individuals. Norman Padelford, a coauthor of the Staff Charter, dismissed Wright's suggestion as premature and invasive of sovereignty. The Agenda Group was also divided on whether to invest the international security organization with other economic and social responsibilities. Pasvolsky and Cohen favored doing so, pointing out that disconsolate living conditions, such as those experienced during the recent depression, could fuel wars of aggression. James Dunn, an attendee at the Dumbarton Oaks and San Francisco conferences, responded that a body tasked with non-security functions could become a nascent world government or "super-state," which Americans had soundly rejected after World War I. In the interest of consensus, the group adopted Dunn's minimalist view of a security organization. Hull agreed, stating in a December 29 cover letter to Roosevelt that the plan rested on one critical assumption: concurrence among the Big Four and with smaller nations would maintain global peace. Roosevelt approved the Outline Plan on February 3, 1944. He then asked Hull to begin conversations with London and Moscow in anticipation of a summer summit. The continued progress of Allied armies, as shown by costly wins at Anzio, Leningrad, and Kwajalein Atoll, meant that the postwar period was not so long in the future.[5]

Continued deadlock within the Informal Political Agenda Group forced its members to postpone permanently all discussion on a bill of rights and include only a token reference to human rights in its revised charter for an international security organization. Ruth Russell, a Pasvolsky assistant and author of a significant work of scholarship on the history of the United Nations, explained the decision as due to a lack of time and the controversial nature of the subject. Avoiding further discussion of a bill of rights yielded the double advantage of sidestepping inter-Allied debate over its content and application and shelving the thorny question of implementation that had previously divided State Department planners. The group decided to grant the General Assembly, the plenary body, the tepid ability to "promote the observance of basic human rights in accordance with declarations of principles or undertakings agreed upon" by its members. Dunn dismissed the article as "good propaganda," adding with apparent relief given the fractured debates with his colleagues that "no one could possibly object to the provision as now worded, but . . . one also could not get enthusiastic about it." Pasvolsky agreed, calling the statement "useful," but concluding that it "did not mean anything." The majority again rejected a motion to create a human rights commission and decided against referring to human rights as one of the general purposes and principles of the body. By March 15, the Agenda Group had completed its final draft. Its emaciated human rights language just about guaranteed that the entire subject would be an afterthought at the upcoming Dumbarton Oaks Conference, the first summit meeting of the Big Four devoted exclusively to framing a successor to the League of Nations.[6]

By the spring of 1944, the American public, members of Congress, and the leaders of Great Britain and the Soviet Union were all clamoring for details on Roosevelt's plans for a transnational peacekeeping body. Roosevelt and Hull, keenly aware that further delay might arouse the same feelings of mistrust, bitterness, and disillusionment shared between the victorious Allies and among U.S. senators after World War I, felt bound to share the parts that they believed would be minimally controversial. Hull consequently emphasized the body's security functions and downplayed its minimal human rights obligations. In a March 21, 1944, press release issued upon returning from a Florida vacation, he all but vetoed the promotion of human rights within a U.N. framework. The Atlantic Charter's promises of self-government, Hull declared in words that must have pleased Churchill, applied only to "qualified" peoples who showed "a decent respect to the opinions of mankind." Moreover, the principles of non-intervention and national sovereignty, which Hull explained as the "bases of the foreign policy of the United States," would severely limit any human rights jurisdiction given to an international organization. Hull's conservatism on human rights issues also sprang from his desire to offer a streamlined outline for a United Nations, to support ongoing talks with sovereignty-conscious congressmen, and to reassure security-conscious allies. One consequence was that colonial powers and American white supremacists did not need to fear investigation, condemnation, or invalidation of their repressive systems. In his first public speech three weeks later on plans for an international peacekeeping organ, Hull again prioritized security issues. He only briefly and dismissively mentioned human rights, describing the Atlantic Charter as a statement of common principles that did not apply literally to the postwar world.[7]

Beginning in late March, Hull briefed key members of the Senate on State Department plans for an international organization. The most important discussions involved a tripartisan "Committee of Eight" senators that included Tom Connally (D-TX), Walter George (D-GA), Robert M. La Follette, Jr. (Progressive-WI), and Arthur Vandenberg (R-MI). Half of the group had belonged to the dismantled Advisory Committee on Post-War Foreign Policy and all had strongly supported the 1943 Connally Resolution in favor of joining a peacekeeping body. Their main concerns, similar to those expressed by dissenting senators aligned with Henry Cabot Lodge (R-MA) after the First World War, were to protect American freedom of action in foreign policy after the war and prevent domestic interference by a supranational body. Vandenberg approved of the Outline Plan because, as he wrote in his diary, it was "so conservative from a nationalist standpoint" and was "virtually based in a four-power alliance." The senators recognized that the United States' possession of a veto also safeguarded sovereignty. The senatorial opposition to an international organization interfering in the domestic affairs of the country provided an additional argument for omitting human rights responsibilities from the lists of general principles and powers. Above all, Hull and Roosevelt wanted to avoid the long, bitter, and unsuccessful fight waged by President Woodrow Wilson to obtain Senate approval of the League of Nations Covenant. With the Senate's Republican and Democratic leaders now briefed and on board, Hull felt comfortable exchanging proposals with Churchill and Stalin, though Roosevelt characteristically held off final approval until early July.[8]

Hull confirmed that Great Britain and the Soviet Union had no desire to grant an international organization the power to define or enforce human rights norms. In February, Acting Secretary of State Edward Stettinius asked Churchill and Stalin to forward their plans for an international security body as soon as possible. The British government, though, could not agree on even a general proposal until mid-1944 due to differences between Churchill, who favored three regional peacekeeping bodies for Asia, Europe, and the Western Hemisphere, and the Foreign Office, which endorsed a single institution. The prime minister's own skepticism of long-range planning also delayed a reply. In final form, it sketched a Rooseveltian vision of a World Assembly of member states, a World Council of the Big Four and several other nations, an International Court of Justice, and a Secretariat. The memo relegated social and economic issues to specialized agencies answerable to the council and secretariat. It was clear that Churchill did not endorse any action by the body in the field of human rights. "To guard and enlarge the freedom of man by institutions for the removal of social wrongs" was the closest the proposal came to identifying a humanitarian role, though the language used spoke more to providing emergency food aid and combating transnational drug trafficking. The British, fearing any meddling in the affairs of their far-flung empire and having experienced waves of Luftwaffe attacks followed by near invasion, were far more concerned about the military aspects of postwar security and opposed discussing the protection of human rights in connection with the United Nations.[9]

Stalin, preoccupied with routing Axis forces from his territory and therefore focused solely on the obligations of an international body to keep the peace, strongly wanted to strip the future body of any economic and social responsibilities. Although the Soviet Union had done little planning prior to the Dumbarton Oaks Conference, Stalin had an unadorned vision that did not require detailed proposals: he wanted a simply organized, uni-focused security body in which he could veto all decisions contrary to Soviet interests. In concrete terms, he demanded an organization that would contain any future German militarism through a council of the Big Four (France included) that could authorize collective diplomatic, economic, financial, and military punishments. Any extraneous economic and social functions granted to the United Nations could only dilute the primacy of security issues in Stalin's mind. Not until August 12 did the Soviet government issue a proposal, which declared that the body would "devote itself wholly to the object of preserving the general peace and security of nations." The plan weakly added that collaboration within the economic and social spheres could occur in one or several *separate* transnational bodies. "It will be possible to begin to discuss and work out such questions later, when it will be deemed necessary," the proposal indefinitely and abstractly concluded.[10]

Human rights lobbying by private groups began slowly and haltingly in the months prior to Dumbarton Oaks due to internal divisions and lowered expectations. In February, the American Law Institute's Committee of Advisors submitted a bill of rights to the institute's governing council. Comprised of 18 articles that combined parts of the American Bill of Rights with guarantees of adequate food and housing, social security, and safe working conditions, the document incorporated the suggestions of lawyers from several continents. The council, though, unanimously refused to endorse the statement, probably due to previously expressed objections to including economic and social rights. In July, a group of 16 leading supporters of a world parliament, led by Harvard Law Professor Manley O. Hudson and including Shotwell, Eichelberger, and Wright, drafted a charter for a "General International Organization." The proposal, similar to that advanced by the State Department, outlined an assembly of all nations, a smaller council, and specialized agencies to "promote the general welfare." Under the latter heading, the charter called on all nations to treat their citizens "in a manner that will not violate the dictates of humanity and justice." The document lacked any provisions for a bill of rights, human rights commission, or transnational enforcement. Its authors, many of whom were veterans of State Department planning committees, knew that Roosevelt and Hull objected to such measures on political and sovereignty grounds. Still, the language used was more specific than in the Draft Constitution, the Staff Charter, or the Informal Political Agenda Group's proposal.[11]

Even the Commission to Study the Organization of Peace diluted its previously far-reaching human rights proposals in the interest of protecting national sovereignty. In May, the agency issued the most detailed report done by anyone thus far, in or out of government, on how to define and protect human rights in the postwar era. Declaring "how easily the step has been taken from internal oppression to external aggression, from the burning of books and houses of worship to the burning of cities," the commission asserted that "international concern for human rights goes to the heart of realistic measures for wiping out aggressive war." The report advocated the immediate convening of a United Nations Conference on Human Rights with delegates from nations and respected human rights groups. The convention would establish a permanent and independent Commission on Human Rights to draft general bills of political, civil, and economic rights, investigate human rights violations, and receive petitions from individual victims of abuse. Membership would be limited to impartial legal experts. In rather tortuous language, though, the authors concluded that "the enforcement of human rights must necessarily remain a national matter," despite observing that "we cannot rely simply on the uninspired disposition of each nation." Under such limitations, the human rights commission could only fulfill its mission if countries under investigation granted permission. This was a questionable assumption at best. Nonetheless, one hundred members signed on to its conclusions, including Shotwell, Wright, Eichelberger, future San Francisco Conference delegate Virginia Gildersleeve, who was dean of Barnard College, and Walter Kotschnig, who soon joined the State Department as an international human rights law specialist.[12]

Given conservative State Department human rights proposals and the absence of domestic and foreign demand for countervailing provisions, the final confidential American plan for Dumbarton Oaks contained only one vague reference to the issue. Largely based on the Outline Plan of the Informal Political Agenda Group, the document called for an eleven-member Security Council (with veto power by the Big Four) to tackle security questions, a plenary General Assembly to discuss all other issues, an International Court of Justice, and an economic and social council subject to the authority of the assembly. Three years of State Department discussions on how human rights fit into the postwar world concluded by allowing the General Assembly to "initiate studies and make recommendations for the promotion of the observance of basic human rights in accordance with principles and undertakings agreed upon by the states members of the international organization." It remained to be seen to what extent, if at all, nations would agree to measures that limited their own sovereignty. The pessimistic answer lay in words that narrowly tailored the body's duties as promotional in nature.

There would be no investigations, condemnations, or legal judgments made against governments.[13]

As Dumbarton Oaks approached, Hull and Roosevelt confirmed the marginalization of human rights by omitting the topic from their public statements while assuring Americans that the United Nations would not meddle in domestic matters. In a May 30 press conference, Roosevelt rambled,

> We have an objective today, and that is to join with other nations of the world . . . oh . . . not in a way that they would decide whether . . . some other nation would decide whether we were to build a new dam on the Conestoga Creek, but for general . . . general world peace in setting up some machinery of talking things over with other nations, without taking away the independence of the United States in any shape, manner, or form, or destroying . . . what's the other word? . . . the *integrity* of the United States in any shape, manner, or form." (emphasis in the original)[14]

As students of history, Roosevelt and Hull knew that questions of sovereignty and domestic jurisdiction had led to a senatorial backlash against ratifying the League of Nations, and both men were determined to draw distinctions between the past and the present. Regretting that the League had "got[ten] dreadfully involved in American politics, instead of being regarded as a nonpartisan subject," the president did not want any human rights language to raise the ire of segregationist Southern Democrats and isolationist Republicans in the Senate. He would succeed where Woodrow Wilson had failed by constructing a bipartisan consensus, backed up by substantial public opinion, to forge precedent-setting ties between the United States and the rest of the world. No longer would the Western Hemisphere be the only American sphere of influence; the current war taught Roosevelt that the nation's vital interests lay scattered across the globe. Joining and maintaining a leading role in a global diplomatic body would allow the United States to pursue and protect its newfound standing as a global superpower.[15]

Up to the eve of the Dumbarton Oaks conversations, Roosevelt worried whether the meeting would actually occur. Hull had transmitted the proposal that all but omitted human rights to China, Britain, and the Soviet Union on July 18, and invited them to begin talks on it as soon as feasible. Stalin issued a technical objection to the participation of Chiang Kai-Shek (as China had declared war against Japan but the U.S.S.R. had not), and thus it would be inappropriate for Stalin to discuss Pacific strategy. Roosevelt engineered a compromise that postponed Chiang's attendance until after Stalin had left the conference. The Soviet leader agreed but then attempted to limit discussion only to the security functions of the organization, which he assumed were primal. Roosevelt gently persuaded him to relent, for he did not want the meeting to repeat the inter-Allied rancor that had marred the Versailles Peace Conference after World War I. He knew that the four nations were wary allies, having maintained an alliance despite serious disagreements about wartime strategy and postwar concerns. With a consensus reached on the gathering's purpose, the State Department arranged for the use of Dumbarton Oaks, the estate formerly owned by Ambassador Robert Woods Bliss that now belonged to Harvard University. The Georgian nineteenth-century mansion and ten acres of elaborately landscaped gardens lay less than three miles from the White House. Due to the dangers of traveling long distances in wartime and viewing the meeting as relatively unimportant (a message reinforced by the State Department, which declined extensive press coverage due to the topic's sensitive nature), the Big Three did not send their leaders or top foreign policy officials. The Soviet Union dispatched Andrei Gromyko, its young ambassador in Washington, while Foreign Office Undersecretary Alexander Cadogan represented the British government. Though Secretary of State Hull initially had offered to lead the U.S. delegation, these lesser appointments prompted him to send Stettinius instead.[16]

Although the American delegates possessed briefing books on human rights topics including the State Department's bill of rights and related background material, they showed no interest in defending or disseminating them. Some historians, such as Robert Hilderbrand, Townsend Hoopes, and Douglas Brinkley, have argued that the U.S. delegation fought for the inclusion of strong human rights planks over ultimately successful British and Soviet opposition. Yet a closer look at the historical record reveals that the official American position before and during the conference had never favored a strong human rights plank, and that what emerged from the conference was an even weaker reference than the original American draft text possessed. After attempting to prevent any discussion on human rights, Stettinius proposed a vague and awkward statement, withdrew it, and finally accepted an impotent reference buried deep inside the conference's final product. His indecision reflected Roosevelt's and Hull's refusal to grant substantive jurisdiction over human rights to a transnational organization while concurrently employing vague human rights appeals to stir up popular support for the United Nations. Therefore, the American delegation lobbied primarily to safeguard national sovereignty, focus on defining the body's security functions, and marginalize consideration of economic and social matters.[17]

From the beginning of the talks, the American delegation wavered on whether even to support their own proposal's creation of an economic and social council. On the conference's first day, Stettinius told a relieved Gromyko that the entire subject was "debatable." Over the next three days, Roosevelt and his chief of staff, Admiral William D. Leahy, approved instructions that allowed the General Assembly to create bodies that *might* include an economic and social commission. According to Stettinius, Leahy did not want any "social uplift frills" attached to the organization, as "the real job of the organization [was] to prevent war." Stettinius presented this revised position in an August 25 meeting with Cadogan and Gromyko, though he stated that it was "merely a suggestion" and that he had "an open mind on the whole subject." The Soviet delegate strongly objected to forming any subsidiary bodies for economic and social issues, remarking that the one reason for the League of Nations' failure was that three-quarters of the issues it took up were extraneous, non-security items. Hull reminded Gromyko that economic and social crises had often led to international conflict, with the Great Depression's contribution to the ongoing war serving as one example. The resulting impasse between Stettinius and Gromyko delayed any further consideration. Within a few days, though, after Gromyko had received new instructions from Moscow, the Soviet Union conceded in principle to include an Economic and Social Council (ECOSOC) under the umbrella of the United Nations. Now the delegates could discuss what specific issues might fall under ECOSOC's domain, including human rights.[18]

By early September, the three nations had hashed out most of the security functions of the organization except for two major stumbling blocks: the Soviets demanded 16 votes in the General Assembly, one for each of their republics, and unfettered veto power in the Security Council, even if they were a party to the issue in question. Roosevelt made clear his opposition to both measures, as they would grant Moscow a disproportionate share of power and paralyze the council's ability to solve great-power tensions, which had led to the death of the League of Nations. Roosevelt also informed Gromyko that "we could never accept [the General Assembly proposal and] this might ruin the chance of getting an international organization approved by the United States Senate and accepted publicly in this country." The president also worried that some senators might demand an absolute veto for the United States as a check on intervention by the organization in America's internal affairs. The Soviets left Dumbarton

Oaks with both issues unresolved, and the whole task of creating a postwar peacekeeping agency lay in doubt. In this pessimistic diplomatic atmosphere, Stettinius was not about to confront Gromyko on human rights issues that both men already considered secondary in importance.[19]

The first human rights proposal, appended to a list of general U.N. principles, came from the Americans, though its awkwardness and lack of support from even its authors made its existence brief. On September 7, Benjamin Cohen, Roosevelt's personal representative, drafted a clause that the delegation approved two days later. "The international organization should refrain from intervention in the internal affairs of any state," his amendment began, for each state had the responsibility to ensure that domestic affairs "do not endanger international peace and security and, to this end, to respect the human rights and fundamental freedoms of all its people." The Americans submitted the amendment, as delegate Isaiah Bowman noted, in order to "appease" domestic groups that wanted a complete international bill of rights inserted into the charter. This rather clumsy statement, which Stettinius introduced apologetically to his British and Soviet counterparts as a "last-minute thought," unevenly reconciled international responsibility with national sovereignty; in a conflict, the latter would prevail, as Pasvolsky tried to reassure Cadogan and Gromyko. The two foreign ministers approved of the first clause, which Cohen had added to assuage congressional critics and prohibit foreign action against America's own Jim Crow laws. Both dissented from the second half, with Cadogan worrying about intrusions into national sovereignty and Gromyko arguing that, in Stettinius's words, human rights concerns were "not germane to the main tasks of an international security organization." A week later, Stettinius offered to withdraw the amendment if a compromise was not forthcoming.[20]

The climax of the human rights debate at Dumbarton Oaks provides a glimpse of what might have been accomplished had the United States insisted on challenging from the start the obstructionist views of Cadogan and Gromyko. Stettinius at first felt even less like defending his unwieldy amendment after the Soviets appended to it a ban on admitting "fascist states and states of a fascist type" to the organization on September 19. After Stettinius reported that only with this addition would the Soviets accept their amendment, the delegation reluctantly voted to oppose the entire article over strong objections by Cohen and Bowman. Undeterred, Bowman that afternoon sketched a proposal to have the economic and social council "promote respect for fundamental rights and human freedoms." Knowing that the Soviets and British would dissent but wanting to include at least *some* mention of human rights *somewhere*, Stettinius offered three places in which to place the reference: in the sections on general principles, General Assembly functions, and ECOSOC responsibilities. Stettinius then turned to subtle blackmail. If Cadogan and Gromyko refused to choose, the American threatened to place human rights on a list (that he slyly stated would become public) of outstanding topics, leaving all three governments open to criticism by a bewildered public that wondered why the Allies could not agree to incorporate such an important issue into the charter. Cadogan and Gromyko, taken aback, repeated their previous objections but agreed to cable their governments for further instructions.[21]

During the next week, the American delegation lobbied for the inclusion of a general, inconspicuous human rights clause somewhere in the outline for an international organization. Stettinius took a list of unresolved topics that included human rights to Roosevelt on September 21. He expressed his own disappointment about the impasse to the president, and he added that the delegates would "press the matter as hard as we know how" to get some minimum concession. Roosevelt, according to the secretary, was also discontented but "gratified" to learn about the delegation's aggressive stand. The lobbying paid off, for a week later Cadogan and Gromyko agreed to allow ECOSOC, but not the more visible assembly, to "promote respect for human rights and fundamental freedoms." On the very same day, the Big Three added a paragraph prohibiting the entire organization from intervening in matters that under international law fell within the domestic jurisdiction of nations. The timing was not coincidental, as Cadogan and Gromyko had refused to have the organization's purposes or powers include the promotion of human rights, which might then challenge their rigid conceptions of sovereignty. They believed it best to bury human rights within an insignificant and subsidiary ECOSOC. The deadlock had broken with no time to spare, as the Soviet delegation left Dumbarton Oaks the following day.[22]

The result was complicity among the leading Allies in the marginalization of human rights as a subject for action by the new security-focused "United Nations." Following the conclusion of a short second phase of talks attended by American, British, and Chinese delegates, the Big Four published on October 9 the "Proposals for the Establishment of a General International Organization." The document allowed for weaker human rights responsibilities than those in the initial American proposal of July 18. The duty to promote human rights now lay solely with the eighteen-member Economic and Social Council and not the General Assembly, which consisted of all member nations. The verb "promote" was carefully chosen, as it did not imply that the council could define what constituted a "human right" or enforce such a finding. The body also lacked the power to criticize or sanction nations that committed abuses. In fact, the charter stated that the council took its orders from the General Assembly, and so any action taken by the council would have to obtain the assembly's approval. The delegates also relegated the description of ECOSOC to chapter 9 of the proposals and omitted the body from a list of the organization's major committees. The United Nations' purposes lacked any reference to human rights, referring instead to the maintenance of peace, security, and co-operation on unnamed economic and social issues. No wonder Roosevelt, according to Stettinius, was "gratified" by the final result: vague, circumscribed by the domestic jurisdiction clause, and uncoupled from any implementation machinery, the human rights plank, he thought, was not and would not become controversial. Its inclusion in the document was nonetheless necessary, for he hoped it would rally support from NGOs and Americans in general just as vague human rights appeals had in his administration's key wartime speeches.[23]

Over the next six months, though, an extraordinary public debate erupted, as individuals, groups, and nations not invited to the conference criticized the inattention and indifference given to human rights issues. The Roosevelt administration ironically encouraged and even facilitated an open discussion on all issues, believing that such input could forge a lasting domestic consensus behind the transnational charter, something that had evaporated in the months after World War I. The roots of this public education campaign began with the formation of the State Department's Division of Public Liaison in 1944. The twin goals of the division were to educate the public about critical issues of foreign policy and to solicit their input through polls, media surveys, and public comment. Before the diplomats had adjourned at Dumbarton Oaks, the office had prepared a memo on "Certain Proposals for Public Education on Dumbarton Results." The effort called for the publication and distribution of thousands of copies of the conference's proposal, State Department briefings of non-governmental organizations, and off-the-record meetings with key leaders of civil society groups. The memo asserted that "these groups need two things from the Department of State (a) encouragement and (b) background guidance." The former came from nearly three hundred speeches given by department officials in the six months following Dumbarton Oaks. The latter came in the form of 2 million copies of a brochure, *Questions and Answers on the Dumbarton Oaks Proposals*.[24]

Acting Secretary of State Stettinius, who took over Foggy Bottom after the 1944 presidential election as diabetes, tuberculosis, and Roosevelt's disdain had all taken a toll on Hull's health, led many of the briefings. He had been a businessman who rose quickly through the ranks at General Motors and U.S. Steel before taking the reins of the Lend-Lease program. Stettinius perfected a natural gift for public relations through a quick smile, dashing good looks, extroverted nature, and conciliatory character. He now had to sell the United Nations to the American people, Congress, and foreign leaders, and the charter's human rights provisions provided one marketing item that he used almost immediately. In late October, after receiving an honorary law degree from New York University, he asserted blandly that the U.N. Charter was designed to advance the historical and worldwide struggle for human freedoms. He did not anticipate what would happen in the coming months. The feedback from many religious, civil rights, and internationalist groups was not thankful or congratulatory in nature. Instead, he faced criticism for achieving too little in the area of human rights at Dumbarton Oaks. These individual voices, which soon morphed into a sustained and concerted campaign, demanded adding the protection of human rights to the lists of purposes and principles of the organization, endorsed the creation of a human rights commission, and favored attaching a bill of rights as an integral part of the charter. Stettinius soon found himself losing control of the public relations drive that he himself had confidently launched.[25]

The Commission to Study the Organization of Peace, under Clark Eichelberger's steady leadership, once again led the charge for stronger human rights enforcement by the United Nations. Educator William Allan Neilson, the chair of the group's executive committee, had briefed Hull in person on the commission's detailed human rights report issued in May. Neilson, Dr. Quincy Wright, and two others shared the report with Dumbarton Oaks delegate Edwin Wilson in mid-October. Also in mid-October, the commission released the third edition of a booklet for study in the nation's high schools. Entitled *Toward Greater Freedom*, the text asked students to memorize the basic points of the Four Freedoms, the Atlantic Charter, and the purposes of the Dumbarton Oaks Proposals. The booklet even challenged students to think of ways American political leaders could apply those humanitarian ideals domestically to issues of race relations and immigration. Eichelberger himself led the "Educational Campaign on Dumbarton Oaks Proposals," which included radio spots, comic strips, informational brochures, advertisements, and meetings with dozens of NGOs. Informally named the "second chance" campaign, referring to the lost opportunity to join the League of Nations, the drive included the heads of the National Peace Conference, League of Nations Association, Church Peace Union, and General Federation of Women's Clubs. This joining together of secular and religious groups presaged the formation of a dedicated grassroots movement whose members would demand that the Dumbarton Oaks Proposals respond to the political, economic, and social needs of individuals and not just concerns of sovereignty-conscious nation-states.[26]

Elite lawyers and academics with a specialty in international law buttressed the campaign with technical expertise and access to influential policymakers, especially mid-level State Department planners. Progressive lawyers such as William Draper Lewis and Quincy Wright welcomed the opportunity to revolutionize international law by making it possible for individuals anywhere in the world to claim rights under the protection of a transnational agency. Lewis was the founder and director of the American Law Institute, known mostly for its influential restatements of American common law. Political scientist Wright was perhaps the nation's foremost expert in international law and conflict. In mid-December, Harvard law professor and judge of the Permanent Court of International Justice Manley O. Hudson forwarded to Stettinius a critique of the Dumbarton Oaks plan by Eichelberger, Shotwell, and Wright. Although the trio endorsed the overall thrust of the plan, they concluded that it "slighted" the topic of human rights. The error could be corrected by adding the promotion of human rights to the lists of the General Assembly's purposes and responsibilities. Lewis informed State Department lawyer Sandifer on December 27 that he would distribute nationally the American Law Institute's 1944 Bill of Rights. He inserted a preface by John Ellingsworth of Americans United for World Organization, the largest coalition of internationalist-oriented groups. The only way to obtain popular support for the United Nations, Ellingsworth stated, would be to give the body a real chance to improve the lives of ordinary citizens around the globe, such as by enforcing a bill of rights. Sandifer responded favorably to Lewis, though he was quick to add the State Department took no official position on the enclosed list of individual guarantees.[27]

Jewish, Catholic, and Protestant leaders, horrified by the growing revelations of Nazi atrocities and seeking to prevent another world war, lobbied for the international protection of human rights as a postwar moral imperative. The American Jewish Committee, a politically connected group formed in the wake of Russian pogroms in 1906, invited Roosevelt to sign a "Declaration of Human Rights." More of a policy statement than a bill of rights, the document argued that a new world order emerging out of the horrors of "Hitlerism" had to recognize as a cornerstone the inherent dignity of all individuals. The group's president, former New York State Supreme Court Justice Joseph Proskauer, asked Stettinius to call an international conference to adopt an enforceable international bill of rights so that "no plea of sovereignty shall ever again be allowed to permit any nation to deprive those within its borders of the fundamental rights." The nation's Catholic bishops released a commentary that rejected "power politics" based on spheres of influence, balances of power, and the use of force to settle disagreements. Instead, a durable and lasting peace could only take root if a democratic community of nations existed that would respect the "innate rights of men, families, and minority groups in their civil and religious life." The Commission on a Just and Durable Peace, a subsidiary of the Federal Council of Churches, held a national conference in Cleveland on the U.N. proposals in mid-January. John Foster Dulles, the group's leader, obtained promises from 34 Protestant denominations to lobby for nine changes, including a reference in the charter to a Commission on Human Rights and Fundamental Freedoms that would formulate a binding bill of rights.[28]

Foreign peoples excluded from Dumbarton Oaks also joined the growing chorus for granting the United Nations stronger and more specific human rights powers. Carlton Hayes, U.S. ambassador to Spain, reported that the Spanish press had been critical of the plan for reasons that included the omission of principles embodied in the Atlantic Charter. Belgian Foreign Minister Paul-Henri Spaak lamented that the principle of self-determination was absent as well. The Inter-American Juridical Committee, formed in 1906 to promote the progressive hemispheric codification of international law, issued its own recommendations in early December. Declaring that "the time has come when it must be formally proclaimed that the community of nations has rights in its own name," the legal experts meeting in Rio de Janeiro called upon the U.N. General Assembly to generate a bill of rights that all member nations would pledge to uphold. The committee also proposed to add the protection of human rights to the list of the United Nations' principles. Latin American governments, born of struggle against colonial rule and burdened greatly by the recent global depression, also began to prepare formal responses to Dumbarton Oaks. Many of their amendments formally submitted to the upcoming San Francisco Conference suggested incorporating human rights protections into the charter's chapters on purposes, principles, and powers. In addition, Cuba and Panama proposed inserting entire bills of individual rights and duties into the document, while Ecuador's offering instructed the General Assembly to draft such a statement as soon as feasible.[29]

In response to these formal and informal conversations, the State Department began preliminary studies on augmenting the human rights components of the Dumbarton Oaks plan. In late October, Alice McDiarmid, the human rights specialist who had assisted in crafting the 1942 bill of rights, completed a review of American wartime commitments to promote human rights. Beginning with the Four Freedoms speech, the Atlantic Charter, and the Declaration by the United Nations, she concluded that President Roosevelt had made the promotion of human rights a major war aim. Yet fulfilling this promise would be tricky because "the promotion of human rights in the peace settlement involves steering a course between undue interference with the internal affairs of states and absolute noninterference which might permit flagrant abuses of individual rights." She proposed that the Allies now draft a binding code of rights for incorporation into national constitutions and municipal laws and make the acceptance of such a code a precondition for United Nations membership. This would once again leave it up to states themselves to decide if and how to implement such a code. The scheme would concurrently grant the United Nations limited jurisdiction by allowing it to receive and investigate complaints of abuses. This conservative but unprecedented power was necessary, McDiarmid argued, given the connection between human rights violations and war, as "the infringement of individual rights may threaten the maintenance of peace and security either by producing tensions within or between states or by enabling states to insulate their citizens from world opinion and lead them on an aggressive course." Other colleagues studied whether to make explicit the creation of a human rights commission under the Economic and Social Council's purview and to allow the General Assembly, ECOSOC's parent body, to promote human rights by drafting international agreements.[30]

By late 1944, this review had yielded preliminary proposals that might have pleased many of the lawyers, religious leaders, and human rights activists who had started to lobby for human rights amendments. It was not a precipitous time to undertake substantive work, as Hull was increasingly ill and wanted to resign, but Roosevelt insisted on keeping him in place until after the November election. His replacement, Edward Stettinius, became preoccupied with another reorganization of the entire bureaucracy as the department struggled to transfer personnel away from short-term wartime planning and assign them to long-term peace-building. In this confusing environment, Sandifer had met with several colleagues to discuss possible human rights amendments. They tentatively endorsed adding a human rights commission under ECOSOC's purview and agreed to explore how best to increase the general visibility of human rights within the proposals. But who would take up these changes with Roosevelt and Stettinius? Under the new bureaucracy, Pasvolsky remained the point person for suggesting revisions to the United Nations Charter, but Durward Sandifer, who reported to Pasvolsky, was in charge of all issues involved in creating a peacekeeping organization. To streamline the policymaking process and prevent redundancy, an informal group entitled "Mr. Pasvolsky's Committee" met every other day in early 1945 to review issues left over from Dumbarton Oaks. Consisting of Pasvolsky, Notter, and Sandifer, among others, the temporary co-ordinating body discussed suggestions on how to increase the human rights obligations of U.N. members. Their output would depend upon the amount of political pressure placed on their superiors by foreign governments and domestic civic organizations.[31]

As these behind-the-scenes developments transpired in the wake of an ongoing and delicate public relations campaign on the charter, Roosevelt committed a careless blunder. At a December 19 press conference, he ad-libbed that no one had actually signed the Atlantic Charter, implying that therefore he was under no obligation to uphold its principles. In a literal sense, the president was correct that neither he nor Prime Minister Winston Churchill had actually initialed a statement at their summit meeting in Placentia Bay. The document was only an unsigned press release sent out via wireless radio. The outcry over the president's perceived dismissiveness was immediate. Senator Arthur Vandenberg (R-MI) asserted that regardless of the existence of a formal document, Roosevelt "wrote the Atlantic Charter into the hearts of the American people and into the hopes of the conquered peoples of the earth." "Mr. Roosevelt ponders the charter and remarks, 'a mere memorandum,'" decried the *Chicago Tribune*. The *New York Times* pointed out that FDR's comments provided "a windfall for scoffers and cynics," to which the *Christian Century* added that "no slippery words can disguise the fact that another great betrayal is under way." Although Roosevelt issued a mild endorsement of the document at his next press conference and in his 1945 State of the Union speech, the damage was done. In a time of growing public backlash, his slip-up illuminated an emerging political reality: The most influential objections to joining the United Nations no longer came from those who felt the Dumbarton Oaks Proposals committed the nation to doing too much abroad; rather they came from those who believed they allowed the United States to not do enough. The former represented the dusty past; the latter those who thought the fiery cast of war must ignite a new order based on justice, true democracy, and economic co-operation facilitated by a powerful United Nations.[32]

President Roosevelt's uncertainty over the Atlantic Charter's significance likely sprang from events unfolding in Europe and Asia. On the Eastern Front, Joseph Stalin's Red Army had liberated almost all of Russian territory captured by the Axis, forced Bulgaria and Romania to surrender, and advanced into Poland, Czechoslovakia, and Hungary. Disagreements between the Soviet-supported Lublin Committee of National Liberation and a Polish Government-in-Exile in London brought to the forefront the principle of self-determination and how it might be applied in Eastern Europe. With Japanese forces retreating to coastal China, on islands immediately adjacent to Japan itself, and out of northern Burma, the future of liberated European colonies in Southeast Asia now appeared. Would the clauses in the Atlantic Charter on self-determination and the foreswearing of territorial gains prevent Great Britain, France, and other Western European states from reannexing areas in Southeast Asia? To these potential fault lines among the Allied powers must be added three issues unsettled at Dumbarton Oaks that impinged on the ideals of self-government and sovereignty embodied in the Atlantic Charter: the use of the veto in the Security Council, whether to allow nations that had yet to declare war on the Axis to join the United Nations, and arrangements for international trusteeships for dependent areas. Any progress on these issues would first have to come out of two inter-Allied conferences. One was a final big power conference in ransacked Livadia Palace on a devastated Russian peninsula; the other was a meeting of most of America's Latin neighbors in glamorous Chapultepec Castle perched on top of a Mexico City hill.

The Yalta Conference, the last meeting ever between Churchill, Roosevelt, and Stalin, did not directly address the downgrading of human rights issues in the United Nations Charter, but it did clear up major issues that allowed such a discussion to occur subsequently. The three Allied leaders discussed a postwar government of Poland, policies to follow toward a defeated Germany, and a Soviet declaration of war against Japan. They also had to complete some unfinished work on a successor to the League of Nations. The problem of limiting the Security Council veto by the major powers proved most intractable. Stalin demanded the absolute right to yield it, but Roosevelt refused, knowing that such a concentration of power might prevent smaller nations from wanting to join the United Nations. At Yalta, Roosevelt and Stalin worked out a compromise, whereby no country could use its veto to strike an issue from the Security Council's agenda, but any action authorizing the use of force would require big power unanimity. Roosevelt also reluctantly agreed to give Stalin, who worried about the preponderance of pro-Western votes in the United Nations, three votes in the General Assembly. Having resolved two potentially explosive outstanding issues from the Dumbarton Oaks talks, the Big Three agreed to convene a conference in San Francisco on April 25. The convention would solicit input from the world's anti-Fascist nations for charter revisions, and then have all countries in attendance formally vote on the rules for creating the United Nations Organization. With a deadline now set, the Roosevelt administration began proactively to draft amendments to the charter in light of expansive demands from allies in Latin America and domestic voices but yet tempered by anxieties over senatorial ratification.[33]

At a hemispheric gathering in Mexico City, Roosevelt and his foreign policy advisors found that 18 Latin American neighbors did not share their indifference toward the international protection of human rights. The State Department had responded favorably to the increasing desire by its southern allies for a conference, the first since 1938, to discuss regional security issues, how to raise living standards, and the Dumbarton Oaks Proposals. The American delegation wanted to firm up support for the United Nations in advance of the San Francisco Conference. To achieve this end, the State Department lobbied half a dozen Latin American nations to declare war against the Axis and thus be eligible to attend the gathering. For America's southern neighbors, who felt slighted at the lack of prior consultation on a world body, the meeting was a chance to comment for the first time. This desire placed the United States in a potentially awkward position. If the conference proposed any changes to the U.N. Charter, the United States could not endorse them without the concurrence of Great Britain, the Soviet Union, and China. Yet Washington could hardly demand an up or down vote on the plan as it stood and expect hemispheric nations to attend and support the document in San Francisco. There was no time to mediate these issues before the meeting convened, as Stettinius flew directly to Mexico City from Yalta, and so they would have to be settled in Mexico's ancient capital instead.

Stettinius led a delegation to the Inter-American Conference on Problems of War and Peace that met from February 21 to March 8. He also chaired the U.N. committee that proposed seven alterations in the name of all conference participants except his own; he abstained due to the absence of Great Britain, China, and the Soviet Union. The changes included generically "amplifying and making more specific" the United Nations' purposes and principles and increasing the powers of the General

Assembly relative to those of the Security Council, suggestions that could encompass stronger human rights provisions. Many delegations also advanced explicit human rights amendments to the charter, and Cuba even submitted a lengthy "Declaration of the International Duties and Rights of the Individual." The conference voted to send Cuba's initiative to all nations invited to the San Francisco Conference. The gathering also made three other topical decisions. The plenary passed a Nicaraguan resolution calling upon all Latin American governments to affirm the principles of the Atlantic Charter and a Haitian condemnation of all forms of racial discrimination. In a precedent-setting act, the assembly empowered the Inter-American Juridical Committee, a body tasked with the codification of regional law, to draft a binding code of individual liberties. Three years later, the newly constituted Organization of American States approved the world's first multilateral statement of general human rights, the American Declaration of the Rights and Duties of Man. Its passage mirrored similar work by the United Nations that bore fruit the same year with the Universal Declaration of Human Rights.[34]

Other nations that were not invited to Dumbarton Oaks sent human rights–related comments to the State Department, and most fit into two categories: adding the promotion of human rights to the United Nations' lists of purposes and principles and attaching a bill of rights to the U.N. Charter. The first group included Polish and Danish proposals to append the Atlantic Charter to the document and Norway's desire to refer to the 1942 U.N. Declaration's call to "defend life, liberty, independence and religious freedom and to preserve human rights and justice." It also included suggestions on promoting "human welfare in all lands" (Australia), "respect for human rights and fundamental freedoms" (Egypt and New Zealand), and "racial equality" (the Philippines). Bolivia, Cuba, Uruguay, and Mexico, fresh from the Mexico City Conference, stressed again the need to annex a bill of rights to the U.N. constitution. Yet warning shots concurrently arose from states that officially practiced caste or racial discrimination. India obliquely worried that "if too much stress were laid on human rights, difficulties might ensue and demands might be made by new minorities." The South African ambassador in Washington stated his personal opposition "to placing too much emphasis upon such vague issues as human rights." These would not be isolated voices in the wilderness, as Washington would soon have to decide whether to put human rights commitments ahead of safeguarding domestic white supremacy.[35]

Cognizant that the San Francisco Conference was fast approaching, influential lawyers and politicians who favored the transnational oversight of human rights began a final, furious lobbying effort. In mid-January, Professor Quincy Wright notified the State Department of his desire to append a human rights declaration to the charter. The department's legal advisors also considered comments from Jacob Robinson, a Lithuanian who had fled Soviet occupation and later became a prosecutorial advisor at Nuremberg as the start to an illustrious legal career. He recommended authorizing the Security Council, General Assembly, or ECOSOC to investigate, advise, and intervene to "safeguard human rights and fundamental freedoms." William Draper Lewis of the American Law Institute forwarded to the president a copy of his group's bill of rights, which Stephen Early, Roosevelt's secretary, personally handed to him. Former Democratic presidential candidate John W. Davis read a statement over the Columbia Broadcasting System (CBS) radio network on February 4 that endorsed the creation of a human rights commission. The announcement, prepared by the Commission to Study the Organization of Peace, was signed by 150 lawyers, academics, and political activists. On March 9, Americans United for World Organization, a coalition of six grassroots-based internationalist groups, sent Roosevelt a summary of revisions that included the incorporation of a "Commission on Human Rights and Fundamental Freedoms" and the need to add a bill of rights. The group also distributed a concise list of political, civil, and economic rights, along with commentary, that an international all-star cast of lawyers had drafted. The authors included former Panamanian leader Ricardo Alfaro, French Law Professor Henri Laugier, and C. Wilfred Jenks of Great Britain, all of whom would take on leading roles in the U.N. human rights bureaucracy. Even Roosevelt's predecessor, Herbert Hoover, published several "Hoover Amendments" to the charter that began with the creation of a human rights commission to promote the "political rights of men and nations."[36]

Non-governmental organizations that had participated in the State Department's public education campaign began to unite in order to define and fight for human rights amendments to the charter. The nation's Catholic bishops issued a joint statement with the Protestant Federal Council of Churches in Christ asserting that a stable peace could not take root simply if nations feared war; what was needed was the "recognition of an international moral obligation" to assist individuals who were oppressed, impoverished, and battle-scarred. The National Council of Negro Women added to the list all people of color whose rights to "the democratic principles of liberty, equality, justice, and the essential dignity of man" demanded universal recognition and application. Organizations that favored the insertion of a bill of rights in the charter included the Friends Committee on National Legislation, the World Jewish Congress, the American Jewish Committee, and the Catholic Association for International Peace. In order to bring about a semblance of order, consensus, and prioritization to these submissions, the planning committee of the "Second Chance Campaign" assigned Chairman Clark Eichelberger and Janet Evans, the executive director of the National Peace Conference, to craft an initial statement of demands. Their letter, signed by over 40 religious and secular groups, went to Secretary of State Stettinius on April 6. The first of six recommendations called for the United Nations to create a commission of human rights under ECOSOC's supervision and to include an international bill of rights. As important as the specific recommendations was the advocacy by a variety of recognized and respected organizations that represented millions of citizens.[37]

The Roosevelt administration responded cautiously to the growing chorus of dissent with circumspect public speeches and non-committal private statements that nonetheless showed an emerging policy shift. On January 22, Henry Villard, chief of the African Affairs division, gave one of the few State Department addresses that touched upon ECOSOC's human rights duties, but he did so with skepticism. Proclaiming that "the true progress of mankind is gauged by the advances in the realization of human rights," he nonetheless warned of a difficult road ahead as diverse nations struggled to define what constituted human rights and how to enforce them. Roosevelt responded favorably to an American Jewish Committee plan to create a human rights commission, and he intimated in a White House meeting that he would refer obliquely to a bill of rights in his opening speech at the San Francisco Conference, an address he would not live to deliver. The State Department even explained in one of its four *Foreign Affairs Outlines*, of which over 330,000 copies circulated nationwide, that unnamed "leading citizens of several countries" wanted the United Nations to draft a bill of rights to guarantee freedom of religion, freedom of speech, and legal protections for defendants in criminal proceedings. After making hundreds of speeches all over the country, holding off-the-record conferences with NGOs, and collecting statistical data on public opinion, it was becoming clear to Stettinius and Roosevelt that buttressing the human rights provision of the charter would be necessary. In order to obtain crucial support from domestic activists, it now became a question of how to craft amendments that would not anger Southern Democratic segregationists and gain the assent of the Soviet Union and Great Britain.[38]

This realization hit State Department planners as well, and they began to craft carefully worded amendments to the Dumbarton Oaks Proposals.

Observing that "widespread demand for the observance of the rights and freedoms of the individual has arisen out of the horror aroused by Nazi abuses and the realization that contentment within states and understanding among peoples are essential to security and the harmonious relations on which peace depends," Alice McDiarmid recommended four changes. The first added the promotion of human rights to the charter's general list of U.N. purposes. The second would allow the General Assembly to make general human rights recommendations to members and develop a non-binding declaration of rights. The last two would specify the creation of a Commission on Human Rights and Fundamental Freedoms, staffed with independent and impartial experts rather than governmental representatives, who could initiate studies, formulate a binding bill of rights, and even receive petitions from individuals alleging human rights violations. The latter task, though, was an "ultimate" objective for the unforeseen future, as under no circumstances could the commission function as a supernational appellate court for challenging decisions made by a country's judicial bodies. The changes were "limited," as the proposal itself noted, given that nations in general were jealous of their sovereignty and would refuse to allow interference by the United Nations in their internal affairs. Still they invested the agency with unprecedented authority, if not actual power, to take up issues that were heretofore deemed appropriate only for discussion by the national governments directly affected.[39]

American human rights activists remained ignorant of these overtures until a few weeks before the San Francisco Conference, when they began to seek a way to influence directly the gathering's discussions. Once the Yalta communiqué set the date and location for the conference, Clark Eichelberger and the "Second Chance Campaign" made plans to attend. They struggled with how to balance the desire of two dozen organizations to send their own delegates with the need for a small "core committee" to plan strategy and seek meetings with key diplomats. Eichelberger wanted a steering group of a dozen people at most that included W.E.B. Du Bois (National Association for the Advancement of Colored People [NAACP]), James Shotwell (Carnegie Endowment for International Peace), Jane Evans (National Peace Conference), and Walter Van Kirk (Federal Churches of Christ), with himself as the chair. The State Department's Division of Public Liaison, sensing an opportunity to co-operate and perhaps co-opt dissenting NGOs, successfully proposed to Stettinius that he invite them to San Francisco as official advisors to the American delegation. Despite worries about how much influence they would actually possess, Stettinius announced on April 10 that representatives of 42 organizations had agreed to attend the conference as consultants to the U.S. delegation. It remained unclear up to the conference's opening plenary what roles and access they would have. The State Department agreed to provide copies of conference documents and arrange for meeting spaces, but it was left unknown how often the consultants would meet with Stettinius and his colleagues, and if such encounters would be mere briefings or back-and-forth exchanges on policy. The consultants were determined to express their constituents' views in a proactive and vocal way, though such pre-conference "warnings" to the State Department were met with silence.[40]

The State Department's first priority was to brief the eight official delegates who included influential Senators Arthur Vandenberg (R-MI) and Tom Connally (D-TX). The review began on March 13, when the group gathered in Washington, DC, for the first of 80 meetings over the next three months. One of the delegates' first tasks was to review the State Department's draft amendments, such as those written by McDiarmid, before passing them to Great Britain, China, and the Soviet Union for comment. On April 9, with little discussion, they inserted as a purpose of the United Nations, "to develop respect for human rights and fundamental freedoms" and to drop as redundant a similar addition to the list of the United Nations' fundamental principles. Two days later, the group agreed to allow the General Assembly to "foster the observance of human rights and fundamental freedoms." Only Senator Vandenberg sounded a note of caution, warning that the Senate would not join a body whose broad mandate would create a "world W.P.A. [Works Progress Administration]," a reference to a massive New Deal public works agency. The delegation could not reach a decision on adding a human rights commission. The results illustrated the U.S. government's continued reluctance to include any human rights machinery that might provoke debates over national sovereignty. Senator Robert Taft, a leading spokesperson for the conservative wing of the Republican Party, agreed on the proposals only if they "did not imply any intention to encroach upon the traditional systems of law in various countries or any interference with domestic politics." Vandenberg agreed, telling Stettinius that their position on granting the United Nations economic and social powers "should be pretty close to the zero line."[41] These comments of concern by two leading senators had an impact on the delegation, for the members could not reach any conclusions on amendments to ECOSOC's provisions prior to the start of the San Francisco Conference.

Other concerns, both historical and contemporary, mitigated against experimentation with a more expansive U.N. human rights program. The sudden death of President Roosevelt at the "Little White House" in

Warm Springs, Georgia, on April 12 upset preparations for the upcoming international gathering. A new leader, former Missouri Senator Harry S. Truman, now had to be briefed and prepared for one of the largest and most important conventions of nations that the modern world had ever witnessed. Within an hour of taking the oath of office, Truman announced that not only would the conference go ahead, but that American foreign policy toward it and the proposed charter would continue without interruption or alteration. Truman had largely been kept in the dark by Roosevelt about foreign policy during his four-month stint as vice president, so the new leader gave the reassurance without knowing exactly what he had embraced. Now he had to be caught up to speed with the opening plenary of the San Francisco Conference less than two weeks away.

His on-the-job education proved to be a trying experience marked by domestic and foreign distractions that demanded immediate attention. While Stettinius's revelation of the secret veto formula agreed to at Yalta, under which the big powers could not ban discussion of an issue to which they were parties, did not provoke much dissent, a related matter created a firestorm. On March 29, the *New York Herald-Tribune* published a front-page story on Stalin's demand for three votes in the General Assembly. Roosevelt and Stettinius tried to defuse the furor, arguing that the concession was only fair given the tremendous suffering that the Soviet Union had borne in the war. Meanwhile, President Truman quickly alienated his inherited secretary of state. Senator Tom Connally told Stettinius that Truman would replace him after the conference with James Byrnes, whom the president knew from his days in the Senate. Truman had little respect for the sunny Stettinius, admitting to an interviewer that "Stettinius was as dumb as they come." Truman tried to assure him nonetheless on the eve of his departure for California that he enjoyed the president's highest confidence. In addition to domestic crises, Truman also worried about Stalin's commitment. The Soviet leader had already announced that Ambassador Andrei Gromyko would lead his nation's delegation rather than Foreign Minister Vyacheslav Molotov, a signal that the Soviets had downgraded the meeting's importance. Three days before the gathering was to open, though, Molotov flew to Washington, DC, on his way to San Francisco. He and Truman had a stormy encounter about the makeup of a postwar Polish government. Molotov left angry with the issue unresolved, so Stettinius must have been relieved to see the Russian in the audience when he gave the opening address on April 25 in the War Memorial Opera House.[42]

The United Nations Conference on International Organization, convened with a war still raging on two continents, required enormous planning and resources. Lasting over nine weeks, the event involved some 850 delegates and advisors from 50 countries, over one thousand staffers, dozens of interpreters and security officials, and thousands of visitors and lobbyists. The total cost to the United States government came to over $2 million, some of which was spent on the over 500,000 pages of documents created and over three hundred vehicles (provided by the military) that the attendees used. Not all of the delegations had an equal say, of course, in creating a charter for a new United Nations. While head delegates from every nation sat on the Steering Committee, 14 of the most powerful sat on the Executive Committee that made all of the major decisions once a concurrence existed between the United States, the Soviet Union, Great Britain, and China. Below these bodies were the detail-oriented workhorse committees. Four general bodies examined pieces of the Dumbarton Oaks document with the assistance of 12 technical agencies. Within the American contingent, the official delegates met nightly, sometimes with representatives from the 42 consulting organizations, in Stettinius's penthouse atop the plush Fairmont Hotel. It was in this suite, where Stettinius also met with Molotov, British Foreign Secretary Anthony Eden, Wellington Koo, the Chinese ambassador to Great Britain, and Georges Bidault, the French foreign minister, that the United Nations Charter had its birth.[43]

The San Francisco Conference marked a watershed in the history of American wartime human rights policy and advocacy. The State Department now worked reluctantly, but steadily, to forge agreement. The final draft of the charter contained the promise to promote human rights in four places: among the U.N. principles, as one of the General Assembly's and ECOSOC's powers, and as the responsibility of a specific ECOSOC commission. The lobbying by consultants, the increasing knowledge of the Holocaust, pressure from mostly Latin American nations, and the concurrent passage of provisions protecting national sovereignty all contributed to the policy shift by the State Department. If, as Stettinius told the first plenary session, a measure of the conference's success would be the existence of multilateral co-operation "to foster respect for basic human rights," the U.S. delegation and its consultants had a catalytic role to play. One question, though, was whether Great Britain and the Soviet Union would agree to such amendments, which could undermine the former's colonial possessions and open the latter to criticism for its horrendous human rights record. Another unknown was the extent to which the United States' own civil rights shortcomings would lead its delegates to propose that the United Nations have only minimal human rights oversight authority. A look at the language already approved by Stettinius and his colleagues did not inspire much hope. Allowing the United Nations to "foster the observance of" and to "develop respect for" human rights was acceptable, but any phrases that implied a real grant of authority to the United Nations were not.[44]

The tug-of-war over the charter between the U.S. delegation and the 102 consultants began just as the conference convened. Those who gathered at the American delegation's headquarters in the Fairmont Hotel included individuals who had advocated for human rights protections throughout the war. Clark Eichelberger, Joseph Proskauer, James Shotwell, Henry Atkinson, Walter Van Kirk, O. Frederick Nolde, and W.E.B. Du Bois did not intend to take a passive role in their interactions with Stettinius. On April 26, the secretary of state tried to assuage their concerns by welcoming them and their ideas for charter revisions. "We want your assistance," he assured them, "we want your interest, we want your guidance, your counsel and advice. We are depending on it." Many consultants, though, grew increasingly skeptical that they would only be able to comment on decisions already made by the delegation. Although they met on average every other day with liaisons from the State Department, they did not have easy access to American delegates themselves. They had to send agenda items and questions through briefing officers first, and all sessions with the delegates and other State Department officials were off the record. To overcome the restrictions and raise their visibility, the consultants broke into four topical lobbying groups, one of which was devoted to expanding the United Nations' human rights responsibilities. They also decided, if necessary, to ask members around the country to contact U.S. delegates directly.[45]

Their fears of marginalization were confirmed on May 1 when delegate Virginia Gildersleeve cornered Eichelberger and revealed that her colleagues wanted the charter to focus on security issues at the expense of considering economic and social functions or a human rights commission. Dr. Gildersleeve, a pioneering English professor and dean of Barnard College in New York City, had long been a champion of women's rights in the fields of politics, education, and the work force. In response to her disclosure, that evening, Eichelberger, Shotwell, Proskauer, Nolde, Jacob Blaustein of the American Jewish Committee, and Margaret Olson from the American Association for the United Nations drafted an earnest letter to Stettinius signed by 21 of the consultants. They proposed four amendments: adding the obligation to respect human rights to the

United Nations' separate lists of general purposes and principles and to the General Assembly's powers, while also establishing a human rights commission. This has led some historians to credit the consultants with first proposing what would become all of the human rights additions to the charter. This is only half correct, as the delegation had already approved two of the proposed amendments, though the consultants could not have known that. The suggestions of a human rights commission and, in the section on principles, the duty of member states to protect "without discrimination such fundamental rights as freedom of religion, speech, assembly and communication, and to a fair trial under just laws," had not yet received official concurrence. The consultants concluded by warning Stettinius that "it would come as a grievous shock if the constitutional framework of the organization would fail to make adequate provision for the ultimate achievement of human rights and fundamental freedoms."[46]

The next two days seemed crucial for the consultants, who were still unaware of the substantial common ground they had with American officials. With a sense of desperation born of the uncertainty of success and an impending deadline for submitting amendments, Frederick Nolde, Joseph Proskauer, Walter White, and Clark Eichelberger met with Stettinius on May 2. Employing promises, flattery, and gentle threats, they tried to persuade him to accept the four human rights additions. Their organizational affiliations made them knowledgeable of public opinion, they argued, which would be thrilled at the presence or shocked at the absence of their charter amendments. Knowing their proposals would not likely have the unanimous support of other nations, they expressed faith in the delegation's lobbying skills. Proskauer implored the secretary of state to pressure resistant countries, for the American public would understand failure, but only if it was preceded by sincere attempts at persuading others. If stubborn opposition persisted, Eichelberger proposed the prioritization of the human rights commission, as its mere existence would allow for ongoing efforts to spread liberty around the world. The gathering applauded Stettinius after he reassured them that he believed in their suggestions "with all my heart." He then left the meeting in order to share their letter with the rest of the American delegation. The consultants immediately told their home offices to mobilize members on behalf of these provisions, and telegrams soon flooded the Fairmont Hotel.[47]

The resulting pressure from across the country was not needed to persuade U.S. delegates to support changes that were largely already agreed upon, but it may have raised their determination to succeed. Stettinius briefed his colleagues on the consultants' proposals on the same day, and he expressed his complete agreement with them. After Senators Connally and Vandenberg also endorsed the revisions and Bowman and Stettinius explained the consultants' resolve, the delegation approved the creation of a human rights commission under the authority of the Economic and Social Council. The discussion was mostly positive, though a few members commented on the danger of trying to list all bodies that the ECO-SOC might conceive. The delegation tabled, though, the other consultant amendment to the section on U.N. principles. Its members also opposed a Soviet addition to the list of U.N. principles that asked nations to promote "respect for human rights, in particular the right to work and the right to education and also fundamental freedoms for all without distinction as to race, language, religion or sex." It was both too broad and too incomplete. Isaiah Bowman cynically remarked that it contained everything "but the right to be assassinated," while Harold Stassen and Senators Arthur Vandenberg and Tom Connally worried that the text excluded other key liberties, such as the freedoms of religion, assembly, and access to information. This position was consistent with the State Department's previous opposition to including any specific guarantees in the charter as premature, including the lengthy bills of rights that Latin American governments had offered at the Mexico City Conference and that Panama and Cuba had submitted in San Francisco. There would be plenty of time later to hash those out and ensure their compliance with existing American law (and discriminatory American practice).[48]

That same night Stettinius introduced the three American revisions, two of which the delegation had originally drafted and one proffered by the consultants, to the foreign ministers of China, Great Britain, and the Soviet Union. Molotov at first insisted on including his list of rights, explaining that empty phrases were meaningless and that even a partial enumeration of freedoms would "represent a great advancement." Vandenberg, Connally, and Stettinius replied that the result would be the exclusion of equally important guarantees, and Molotov relented. With minimal discussion the Big Four agreed that the United Nations should promote and encourage "respect for human rights and fundamental freedoms" and that the General Assembly should "assist in the realization of human rights and basic freedoms for all, without distinction as to race, language, religion or sex." They also accepted a Soviet amendment that blandly called upon nations to respect the self-determination of peoples. The consensus ended over whether to add a reference to the Atlantic Charter, and after two hours of debate, the foreign ministers reached no

conclusion. The American senators strongly favored its inclusion, arguing that such a reference would increase the chances of congressional approval. The British and Soviets demurred. The latter position eventually
triumphed, but the Americans had achieved a victory of sorts. The charter's verbiage allowed the new institution to wield the carrot of supporting
human rights without any sticks that could enforce them or punish non-
compliant nations. Whether it signaled impotence, as Molotov assumed, the
gradual promotion and acceptance of human rights principles as Stettinius
believed, or an immediate commitment to remedy shortcomings as the consultants expected, it fell to U.N. members to debate in the future decades.[49]

Stettinius's proposal that the Economic and Social Council create a human rights commission provoked strong Soviet and British objections, but
this time, unlike at Dumbarton Oaks, postponing the question was not an
option. British delegate Clement Attlee and Molotov, suspicious of what
the body might undertake, responded that the charter should merely grant
ECOSOC the freedom to form any committees it wanted. To solve the impasse, the head delegates appointed a four-member drafting subcommittee of subordinates. The quickly drafted settlement allowed ECOSOC to
establish "such commissions as may be required for the performance of
the functions and the exercise of the powers entrusted to it." To placate
the Americans, the subcommittee proposed to stipulate ECOSOC's general responsibility "to make recommendations for promoting respect for
human rights and fundamental freedoms," but this merely repeated the
General Assembly's charge. Needing more to satisfy the consultants and
the authors of telegrams that continued to stream in, Stettinius decided
to fight for the more explicit commitment approved by his delegation. At
that evening's Big Four meeting he persuaded the other three nations to
allow ECOSOC to "set up commissions in the fields of economic activity, social activity, cultural activity, promotion of human rights, and any
other field within the competence of the Council." The other powers may
have agreed because the Human Rights Commission was one of many
ECOSOC bodies or perhaps they believed its powers were circumscribed
enough by the weak human rights language already emplaced in the charter. The long wartime struggle by U.S. non-governmental organizations
to create a League of Nations successor with some human rights powers
had now ended, and Stettinius quickly awarded credit to the consultants.
"I am sure that you recognize your own proposal," he added after reading
the amendment to them.[50]

The secretary of state, known for his affability and public relations skills,
employed both to fool the consultants and historians who subsequently

wrote about the San Francisco Conference on two counts. The first was the myth that if not for the consultants, the subject of human rights would have been as downgraded in the charter as it was in the Dumbarton Oaks agreement. The historical evidence shows this to be half true. Pressure applied by American NGOs *before* San Francisco helped to persuade the State Department to propose two amendments and to discuss adding a reference to a human rights commission. This was important given the willingness of the State Department to forsake the topic at Dumbarton Oaks. At the conference itself, the consultants' lobbying might have strengthened Stettinius's backbone, but it was not responsible for the final human rights provisions of the charter. Even the reference to a human rights commission was more a product of Big Four compromise than due to direct influence by the American NGO leaders. Stettinius, though, knew it would be good politics (even if bad history) to credit millions of Americans and their civic leaders with this triumph.

The second myth was that Stettinius truly believed that the human rights powers of the United Nations would allow it to become an effective force for spreading principles of democratic governance and individual rights. Stettinius popularized this theme by providing platitudes to the press and gratitude to the consultants. "I look forward confidently to the time when the Economic and Social Council will become one of the great institutions towards which all peoples will turn for hope and effective action," he told reporters at a May 5 press conference. To the consultants, he explained that they "could justly claim credit for getting a consideration of human rights into the Charter." One skeptic was not fooled. General Frank McCoy, president of the Foreign Policy Association, accused Stettinius of having "made no determined effort" to fight for human rights. As a soldier who had seen action in the Spanish-American War, served on the General Staff of the American Expeditionary Force in World War I, and commanded combat units for four decades, he had tired of wars caused and accompanied by atrocities. Given that the Big Four had approved a clause at Dumbarton Oaks preventing the United Nations from intervening "in matters which are essentially within the domestic jurisdiction of the State concerned," he worried that the doctrine of national sovereignty would trump all supernational attempts at human rights oversight. Stettinius replied with a good dose of realpolitik. "We have to have sovereignty and not get into the question of intervention and rights and freedoms of states," he told McCoy. While the ways in which the United Nations would balance the domestic jurisdiction and human rights clauses remained to be seen, past precedent and contemporary understanding between

Stettinius and his Allied colleagues tilted the scale sharply in favor of national sovereignty.[51]

Other evidence comes from the actions of Stettinius and his fellow delegates, who spent the rest of the conference trying to defeat more progressive human rights proposals. This was a tricky task to perform without seeming to undermine the very ideals that the victors had adopted as war aims and that had filled the hopes of war-weary Allied peoples. It also necessitated rejecting suggestions from smaller nations without inviting criticism of being overbearing and insensitive. The suggestions were many: Cuba and Panama strove to incorporate an actual bill of rights, Chile proposed to state boldly that human rights obligations superseded any competing claims of national sovereignty by governments, and Liberia wanted to allow the United Nations to investigate alleged human rights violations. Belgium, Norway, and China were disappointed with the sweeping protection of the domestic jurisdiction clause, arguing that it made U.N. human rights work practically impossible. They supported more liberal wording, exempting from U.N. action only measures as defined by international law that were "solely" within a nation's purview. As international law was organic and encompassed an increasing list of issues, it was clear that the influence of the United Nations would grow over time. This is exactly what the U.S. delegation, and future Secretary of State John Foster Dulles in particular, opposed. He told the smaller nations that the Big Four position, which would disallow U.N. action on matters "essentially" within state jurisdiction, was the price to pay for sprinkling references to human rights in the charter. The U.S. delegation then approved ECOSOC's functions and powers only on the condition "that nothing in the charter could be construed as authorizing intervention in the domestic affairs of any member state." None of these changes offered by the smaller nations made it into the charter due in part to U.S. opposition.[52]

The halfhearted support for (or, in Stettinius's own words, "not energetically promoting") the human rights amendments did not escape criticism. *U.S. News* chastised the unwillingness of the Big Four to give up any real measure of sovereignty while a series of editorials by the Scripps Howard News Service exposed the non-binding nature of the charter's human rights references. America's largest Jewish groups, appalled by growing evidence of the Holocaust, castigated the "vagueness" of the references and demanded that guarantees of individual liberty be "clearly and unequivocally" listed in the document. The widely disseminated critiques forced Stettinius to hold a press conference on May 15. Ironically, the delegation, especially Representative Sol Bloom, thought that the secretary's planned statement was too strong and pushed him to delete an affirmation that the human rights clauses applied equally to all minorities worldwide, including "to the Jewish people [and] to members of the Negro race." He did admit that the State Department opposed any attempt to draft a bill of rights now (as he expected the Human Rights Commission to do so later) and that the enforcement of the charter's human rights provisions depended solely upon voluntary international co-operation. The conference could only make a start in this area, though he believed it to be a "good and substantial beginning." The secretary strongly defended the specific proposals, predicting they "may well prove to be the most important of all the things we do here for peace and advancement of the peoples of the world." To dispel any cynicism, he promised that the United States would "work actively and tirelessly . . . through the International Organization—for peoples generally, toward the protection and promotion of these rights and freedoms." The press covered his speech widely.[53]

Betraying Stettinius's bold words, the delegation on May 16 agreed to oppose any further human rights stipulations and fight for a strong national sovereignty affirmation in the charter. For the rest of the conference, the secretary of state pursued three goals: gaining approval of the smaller nations for the four-power amendments, turning back a Soviet full employment proposal, and defeating the more expansive Latin American human rights provisions. The first task was the easiest, as simple power politics ensured that all three human rights references became part of the charter. The Americans also succeeded in the second, as no non-Communist support for Moscow's wording existed. ECOSOC's approved mission included only the governmental promotion, rather than achievement, of full employment.[54] Stettinius's promise that the Human Rights Commission would draft a bill of rights helped to mollify Latin American governments that wanted to add an enumerated list of guarantees. But to prevent any "misunderstanding" of the charter's human rights references, the State Department renewed its push for a concise and expansive domestic jurisdiction clause. Success came as the charter forbade the United Nations from intervening in matters "which are essentially within the domestic jurisdiction of any state." Stettinius connected this clause with ECOSOC explicitly in a May 28 radio broadcast, describing the United Nations as a compact of nations. Under this conception it was clear that nations retained substantial sovereignty. "I must emphasize, however," he stated to a nationwide listening audience, "that the Economic and Social Council is essentially a co-ordinating and recommendatory agency. It cannot interfere with the domestic affairs of any member nation."[55]

The San Francisco Conference adjourned on June 26 with an uplifting speech by the American president followed by an action that caused careful observers to doubt his sincerity. Compared to the accolades by politicians who spoke of the meeting as setting a precedent for international co-operation in the pursuit of peace, justice, the rule of law, and economic development, President Harry Truman's address was not particularly memorable. He did assert that if the charter had existed a few years earlier, perhaps World War II would have never begun. Looking to the future, he warned that the charter's words would be useless if nations did not respect them, because the world's war-weary peoples demanded fundamental diplomatic changes. One example he highlighted was an international bill of rights, which he predicted "will be as much a part of international life as our own Bill of Rights is a part of our Constitution." The very next day, Stettinius resigned as secretary of state. His replacement, former Representative, Senator (when he served as a mentor to Senator Truman), and Supreme Court Justice James F. Byrnes, was an unrepentant segregationist from South Carolina who had opposed anti-lynching bills, supported African American disenfranchisement, and demanded the prosecution of the NAACP in 1919 for advocating racial equality. "This is a white man's country, and will always remain a white man's country," Byrnes wrote to Attorney General A. Mitchell Palmer in support of the lawsuit. This might seem a curious choice for a president who had just asserted that respect for human rights was a cornerstone of the emerging postwar order. But the appointment was not strange if American policy continued to be grounded in rhetorical promises but minimal commitments, both at home and abroad. Byrnes was a good choice to shield the Southern racial caste system from any United Nations interference.[56]

The Senate believed any U.N. interference unlikely, for the body ratified the charter with only two dissenting votes after obtaining reassurances that, on human rights and other matters, national sovereignty provisions controlled. Byrnes' close advisor Pasvolsky, in testimony before the Senate, defused such worries at the outset, stating that "it was quite clear that the principle regarding domestic jurisdiction already inserted in the Charter would be governing." Senator Eugene Millikin (R-CO) was not satisfied. His probing of Pasvolsky on how to reconcile national sovereignty with ECOSOC's powers to promote human rights almost caused Vandenberg to rule him out of order. After he inquired of Pasvolsky whether a nation could deny admittance to U.N. investigators on a mission endorsed by the Security Council or the General Assembly, an exasperated Vandenberg adjourned the committee for a few hours. Before raising his gavel, though, he cryptically replied in the negative as long as the mission's members stayed within the terms of the charter and "behave[d] themselves." Only a few witnesses bothered to highlight the human rights provisions. John Foster Dulles, Clark Eichelberger, William Green of the American Federation of Labor, and Leo Cherne of Americans United for World Organization commented briefly on the necessity of observing them if a lasting peace were to emerge from the ashes of World War II. It was clear from their testimony as well as the words of Stettinius and Pasvolsky that the extent of any such observance was at the pleasure of individual governments.[57]

The delegates who had met inside the San Francisco Opera House on June 26 for the closing plenary session celebrated a document that gave the United Nations on paper unprecedented, though sharply circumscribed, authority to expand the nascent field of international human rights law. Beyond including vague promises to promote and respect human rights, the charter authorized a three-tier system for their gradual realization. The Human Rights Commission, the Economic and Social Council, and the General Assembly, in ascending order, had the responsibility to promote respect for human rights worldwide. The Security Council could also intervene in crises that threatened international peace. Yet the ability of these agencies to act was circumscribed by a sovereignty clause that left them in reality powerless unless United Nations members assented to their initiatives. The degree to which this assent would be forthcoming was, of course, unknown in mid-1945. Future delegations would have to establish an agreeable agenda for the nascent Human Rights Commission that fulfilled the U.N. mandate to promote a respect for human rights guarantees while gaining the voluntary support of sovereignty-conscious countries. Given the history of charter negotiations, it should have seemed clear to a careful contemporary observer that the world's major powers were unlikely to sponsor bold initiatives in a field that involved sacrificing any real control over how their governments treated their own citizens.

American wartime human rights policy encouraged and reinforced this conservative thinking. Not all of the pressure for limiting human rights initiatives and language emanated from Washington, DC, though, for sovereignty-conscious senators joined with America's Allied partners in objecting to strong international oversight of any nation's human rights practices. For Moscow, this position was a reflection of traditional xenophobia, a historical record marked by repeated foreign invasions, and massive violations committed against real or perceived enemies of the state. Great Britain, as a colonial power, opposed any external review of its policies toward indigenous peoples on principle. Within the Senate, which would have to ratify any agreement that allowed the United States to join an international peacekeeping organization, a prewar isolationist bloc still existed that defended its 150-year refusal to enter into entangling foreign alliances and its even longer tradition of maintaining white supremacy. The Roosevelt and Truman administrations made a conscious decision not to challenge these limitations and not to embrace a more activist human rights policy. American non-governmental organizations opposed this decision. What united groups of lawyers, religious leaders, civil rights activists, and internationalist-oriented academics was the assertion that the unprecedented death and destruction that modern wars caused meant that some national freedom of action had to be sacrificed to a supernational body. Thus they advocated for a reduction in armaments, a global parliament that would have to approve of the use of force, progressive economic development programs to eradicate poverty, and protections of individual rights. These activists passionately believed that the acquisition of these rights would force governments to respond to the dictates of public opinion, which would prevent civil wars, revolutions, and the rise of aggressive dictators who might declare war against their own people and those of neighboring lands.[58]

The San Francisco Conference saw a discussion between the leaders of the major Allied powers and these non-governmental organizations. It was not a dialogue carried out on an equal plane, of course, because it was ultimately up to Moscow, London, and Washington to support a new world order based upon the internationalization of human rights norms if each saw doing so as in their national interest. The main powers were willing to grant some degree of legitimacy to the postwar vision of the consultants, which they had in fact helped to define, inspire, and encourage with wartime statements such as the Atlantic Charter and Declaration by the United Nations. The resulting inclusion, however reluctant and vague, of human rights principles in the U.N. Charter marked a departure in international law. What remained to be seen, though, was whether the words would help to launch a real departure in how governments around the world treated their citizens in practice. The wild card was the position of the United States and its new leader, President Harry Truman. As the world's only economic, military, and political superpower, his government occupied a position partially similar to Woodrow Wilson's coming into the Versailles Peace Conference. As in 1919, progressive Americans, conquered peoples, and liberals from within America's allies now looked to a Southern-born reformer who had made a reputation for independent thought and action to help create a parliament of nations that would banish war, set colonial peoples free, and bring about improved living conditions for ordinary individuals across the globe. Whether the ending would be similar, involving a compromised peace, a disillusioned network of grassroots activists, a potentially revolutionary system of human rights protections overseen by a world legislature that foundered on the shoals of national sovereignty, and the world teetering on the brink of another armed catastrophe . . . well, that remained for prophets to predict and governments to try to prevent.

CHAPTER 3

A Conservative Revolution Begins, 1945–1948

A MONTH AFTER SENATE RATIFICATION of the United Nations Charter, P. Bernard Young, Jr., the editor of the *Norfolk Journal and Guide*, an African American newspaper in Norfolk, Virginia, telegraphed President Truman. He endorsed Truman's call for free elections in Bulgaria, but asked if the president's comments applied to the disenfranchisement of blacks in the American South. "This newspaper is concerned," Young said, "lest our allies and other peoples whom we have liberated increasingly doubt the sincerity of our leaders who advocate a democratic way of life for them but refuse to make it a reality in this country." The hypocrisy identified by Young would haunt Truman's effort to lead the construction of the United Nations' human rights machinery and to draft the world's first international declaration of rights. Translating Roosevelt's soaring rhetoric into the legalistic, formal prose of multilateral agreements proved difficult because State Department legal experts had to satisfy several contradictory political demands. They had to produce a list of human rights and a plan for their implementation that would inspire Americans and their allies to fight the Cold War while preventing domestic human rights activists from using their work to challenge the denial of such rights to African Americans and Asian Americans. Their work also had to incorporate American legal norms in order to satisfy a growing number of domestic critics while gaining the approval of nations with vastly different legal traditions and political agendas. The stakes were high, for the nation's credibility and claims of moral superiority as the guardian of human rights were put to the test as the Cold War dawned.[1]

To solve this dilemma, Truman and his diplomatic advisors proposed to continue Roosevelt's use of symbolic and tentative diplomacy. The Truman administration would attempt to persuade other Western governments to draft a list of familiar-sounding civil and political rights, adding only vague economic and social promises. They would seek a non-binding declaration that could not overturn domestic law, and they would try to contain attempts by American civil rights groups to have the United Nations investigate allegations of domestic human rights abuses. After accomplishing these restrictive goals, moreover, they would trumpet the resulting document before a global audience as a triumphal accomplishment. The 1948 Universal Declaration of Human Rights is a paper monument to their success. The major consequences, though, would be an increasingly emasculated U.N. human rights program, strained relations with key African American leaders at home and with allies in the United Nations Commission on Human Rights (UNCHR), and damage to U.S. credibility on human rights issues abroad. Ironically, therefore, the price paid by Truman included accepting, for the most part, continued human rights violations at home summarized by the names of Jim Crow and Joseph McCarthy.

"The ratification of the Charter of the United Nations by the Senate is not so much an end as a beginning," telegraphed Clark Eichelberger to President Truman on July 30, 1945. He understood that the U.N. Charter provided only a blueprint and a mandate, not detailed procedures, for how the new organization should carry out its overall responsibilities. The process of generating these specifics began the day after the San Francisco Conference ended, when conferees formed the U.N. Preparatory Commission. A fourteen-member Executive Committee (which included the United States) drafted policies for the full Preparatory Commission to approve. With this machinery in place, the State Department could no longer postpone discussion of the United Nations' specific human rights structures and powers. Immediately following senatorial ratification of the charter, Alice McDiarmid and Harley Notter, joined by a few other lawyers, began to sketch the possible responsibilities and structures of the charter-authorized Human Rights Commission. The Executive Committee was due to convene for its first session in mid-August in London's historic Church House at Westminster, and Edward Stettinius, the former secretary of state and the head U.S. delegate to the conference, needed position papers.[2]

When measured against the conservative bent of Second World War policies, the State Department's earliest postwar proposal for protecting human rights worldwide was quite progressive. McDiarmid, who was second only to Sandifer in human rights expertise in the State Department, outlined a bold proposal. She called for a dozen-member human rights commission composed of experts chosen by the Economic and Social Council "on the basis of their competence and prestige in the field of human rights" in consultation with non-governmental organizations. Aided by a technical staff, commissioners could undertake efforts to increase public awareness of human rights issues, raise international standards, and "check discrimination and other abuses." McDiarmid suggested that the commission's mandate included formulating human rights conventions, sending investigators to troubled lands, and examining complaints submitted by aggrieved victims of human rights abuses. All of these activities, she carefully noted, were circumscribed by the charter's ban on interfering in the domestic jurisdiction of states, but the body could still report to ECOSOC "serious violations of human rights, which seemed likely to impair the general welfare or constitute a threat to the peace." By calling for an energetic, independent body of technical experts that could send investigators into crisis countries and discuss grievances filed by individuals, McDiarmid presented an outline that could, if accepted, have radically reoriented U.S. policy and U.N. human rights capabilities.[3]

Stettinius and his State Department advisors, reverting to form, rejected two of McDiarmid's key provisions. Notter led the charge from Washington, warning in a memo that the "treacherous" petition provision could allow persecuted racial minorities in the United States and abroad to ask the United Nations for redress. He also sought language that would protect national sovereignty by having the Human Rights Commission merely call attention to instances of unequal treatment. The American delegation to the Preparatory Commission agreed with Notter and shelved McDiarmid's discrimination, petition, and investigation components. In addition, Stettinius successfully lobbied for the appointment of commissioners by member governments. In the sterile words of a State Department briefing book, such delegates would add "realism and responsibility to the recommendations and improve the prospects for implementation by governments." The danger, though, was that members would not be impartial, independent, and objective. Their nationalist, political, and diplomatic biases could sanitize and even obstruct the commission's work.[4]

The full Preparatory Commission's final report, completed in late December with the participation of 51 nations that had ratified the U.N. Charter, did contain other American proposals authored by McDiarmid. The body could, at the request of the ECOSOC or the General Assembly, undertake studies to draft an international bill of rights, make recommendations to prevent racial, sexual, or religious discrimination, suggest measures to protect minorities, and examine other human rights issues "considered likely to impair the general welfare or friendly relations among nations." In all of these activities, though, it would be bound by the charter's non-intervention clause. In response to sovereignty-conscious Soviet objections, Stettinius willingly made the political nature of Human Rights Commission appointments even more explicit. The Preparatory Commission, in its final report of December 23, called for a body of "highly qualified governmental representatives" whose decisions, their report obliquely stated, were more likely to find favor with national governments. The rejection of individual petitions and independent committee membership provided early evidence of the State Department's preoccupation with safeguarding national sovereignty. With procedures and agendas for the General Assembly and ECOSOC complete, delegates prepared to convene the United Nations in a new year, the first in almost a decade marked by the absence of major armed conflict somewhere in the world.[5]

One representative in particular gazed upon the opening session of the General Assembly with a characteristic mixture of anticipation and self-doubt. The recently widowed Eleanor Roosevelt had reluctantly accepted President Truman's offer to become a delegate to the United Nations. The decision was sound politics: the appointment was a memorial to her late husband, a reward for her own long-standing Democratic Party activism, and a stratagem designed to cement progressive support for the Truman administration. The choice proved brilliant in retrospect for Truman. Although not a lawyer and instinctively bored by the intricacies of legal writing, Roosevelt possessed a tremendous capacity to learn and the patience and diplomatic tact needed to explain U.S. human rights policy while also serving as chair of the U.N. Commission on Human Rights. Her appointment brought instant credibility to the department's human rights program from internationalist groups who knew of her work against prewar isolationism, her efforts on behalf of wartime refugees, and her support for postwar peace with the Soviet Union. Roosevelt also channeled to the president political support from African Americans, who both remembered her husband and her own work against segregation, disenfranchisement, and poverty. Appointed by the delegation to sit on the UNCHR, Roosevelt presided over its deliberations for four years, gaining the respect of its members for her dedication, modesty, and composure. Her willingness to take the position, though, meant she had to balance the conflicting goals of U.S. human rights policy, even when doing so deviated from her own views and those of her liberal activist friends.[6]

At the time, though, both Roosevelt and Truman knew that the appointment was a gamble. Taking the position would require a moderation of the independent streak that had sometimes led her to criticize publicly her deceased husband's positions. President Truman nominated her despite her total inexperience in international diplomacy, perhaps believing that, in a foreign environment, she would then become malleable and fall back uncritically on her State Department advisors. Nonetheless, his move brought criticism from diplomatic veterans Senator Arthur Vandenberg and John Foster Dulles and white supremacists such as Senator Theodore G. Bilbo (D-MS). Although she decided to accept Truman's offer and open a new chapter of her post–White House life, she acknowledged that her first reaction was, "Oh no! It would be impossible! How could I be a delegate to help organize the United Nations when I have no background or experience in international meetings?" She soon departed on the *Queen Elizabeth* for London and learned that her assignment would be to a committee whose jurisdiction encompassed educational, cultural, and humanitarian issues. As the renovated troop carrier steamed across the Atlantic, Roosevelt digested eagerly a large pile of position papers that she nonetheless found dull and oftentimes incomprehensible reading.[7]

Also on her mind was a flood of letters she had received just before departure from organizations committed to continuing their watchdog role over policymaking at the United Nations. Given her longtime connections to domestic reform groups, activists considered her a trustworthy friend and fellow advocate for an independent and impartial human rights commission. Lutheran minister Frederick Nolde of the Joint Committee on Religious Liberty (a lobbying arm of the Federal Council of Churches) forwarded a memo he had sent to the State Department in November. The Human Rights Commission should draft a declaration or a binding international bill of rights as soon as possible, he proposed. Given this sensitive, precedent-setting, and vitally important work that lay ahead, he asserted that the body must contain "men and women whose record in national and international life commands the confidence of the world." In a handwritten addition, he scrawled, "The prayers and good wishes of our people go with you as you proceed to undertake your important work at London." The NAACP's Walter White also asked her to push for a bill of rights. He believed that Roosevelt, who had joined the NAACP's board of directors six months earlier, would become a strategic asset in advancing the group's goals at the United Nations.[8]

The position papers that Eleanor Roosevelt reviewed on her voyage dictated a strategy of containment and process control that had prevented the adoption of a bill of rights at the San Francisco Conference. Given that the charter explicitly called for the creation of a human rights commission, Harley Notter tried to anticipate what issues would be on its agenda. By late November, he had referred to "strong pressure for rapid preparation of a bill of rights," an urgency that came from domestic groups and other nations on the Preparatory Commission. He worried that the Truman administration would be caught unprepared should the assembly itself decide to consider a bill of rights. His uncertainty and concern grew as the General Assembly convened for its first session in London. As at San Francisco, Panama introduced a "Declaration on Fundamental Human Rights and Freedoms," and Cuba submitted a 22-article list of political, economic, and social guarantees. After determined lobbying by the United States, the assembly sent both documents to the Human Rights Commission for discussion. As the latter did not yet exist, the assembly then established an 18-nation ECOSOC and under it, a "nuclear" or temporary human rights commission (UNCHR) of nine members that would first draft its own terms of reference, membership structure, and agenda before considering any substantive proposals. Roosevelt came away from the gathering with confidence and a close bond with Durward Sandifer, her chief State Department advisor and friend for the next seven years.[9]

The decision to have the "nuclear" UNCHR itself decide on membership qualifications renewed the debate between the State Department and human rights lobbying groups. The debate over whether members should represent their governments or serve independently was really a struggle to influence the UNCHR's work. Alice McDiarmid continued her lonely struggle for independent experts, and this time she was joined by James Hendrick, soon to be appointed to the human rights body. They identified a need for persons with varied expertise, renowned ability, and "progressive points of view" who would not represent any nation but "the principal races, religions, and linguistic groups of the world." Durward Sandifer agreed, telling Roosevelt that members should serve as experts rather than as spokespersons. Letters from Joseph Proskauer and William Ransom, leaders of the American Jewish Committee and the American Bar Association's Committee on Peace and Law through United Nations, also endorsed the idea of independent members on the Human Rights Commission in order to have the best minds possible draft a bill of rights. These organizations had learned from their wartime lobbying: the State Department would only listen to them if they had institutionalized access to policymakers. The chances of this continuing, they believed, were greater if officials did not owe primary allegiance to governments.[10]

Other State Department officials responded that since governments ultimately had to approve the commission's work, it was impractical and even dangerous to rely on independent delegates. Notter led the opposition. In response to Hendrick's memo, he scribbled in the margin, "For good work, yes, but for effective recommendations, no." John Ross, a Notter subordinate, called Hendrick's proposal a "two-faced approach" because the department would be responsible for briefing U.S. delegates who could then reject any advice offered. Governmental representation, he concluded, meant "a far better chance" of American approval of the body's work. At stake in this debate was a decision far more important than just how members would be chosen. The real issue was whether the commission would be governed by real-world politics and the strategic interests of its members, or whether it would be a technocratic body of experts whose impartiality and moral authority might persuade governments to enact its recommendations. In the end, though, the governmental appointees on ECOSOC voted to support a Soviet proposal to have countries represented on the UNCHR. Behind the vote lay a concern that unaccountable commissioners would meddle in the internal affairs of states. As this concern only grew once the commission began working, the State Department soon appreciated the wisdom of siding with the Soviets on this issue. After the first General Assembly adjourned, Roosevelt sailed home to become the inaugural American delegate to the UNCHR.[11]

The nuclear UNCHR convened on April 29 at Hunter College in New York City in an atmosphere marked by escalating Cold War tensions. Disagreements over German reparations and the presence of Soviet troops in Iran alarmed Western officials. In response, State Department Soviet specialist George Kennan penned his famous "Long Telegram," which called for the containment of Communism. In early March, former British Prime Minister Winston Churchill famously declared the existence of an "iron curtain" falling across the European continent, separating allies of the Soviet Union and those of the United States. In this tense atmosphere marked by charges from Washington that Stalin was subverting the principles of freedom and self-determination and counter-charges that the United States sought to create an informal, exploitative capitalist empire, Roosevelt was elected chair of the nuclear commission. It was not an auspicious first meeting, as only six of the nine members bothered to attend, and halfway through the session a new Soviet delegate arrived and announced that he was not bound by the voting record of his predecessor. Roosevelt's hope that commission members would be "able to do much to help the United Nations achieve its primary objective of keeping the peace of the world by helping human beings to live together happily and contentedly" would be sorely tested as Cold War rivalries spilled over into UNCHR meetings.[12] After disposing of the contentious membership issue, the delegates in the UNCHR and ECOSOC quickly agreed on the full Human Rights Commission's structure, mandate, and program of work. The body would consist of 18 members elected to three-year terms. Its broad mandate included submitting to the ECOSOC proposals for a bill of rights, recommendations for the protection of minorities and the prevention of discrimination, and decisions regarding "any matters within the field of human rights likely to impair the general welfare of friendly relations among nations." Once established as a full commission, the body's first priority would be to draft a bill of rights. Roosevelt and the State Department were pleased with these results, for they corresponded closely to their own proposals. They even accepted the liberal mandate, believing, as ECOSOC delegate John G. Winant underscored in his brief to Secretary of State James Byrnes, that the U.N. Charter prohibited the commission from infringing upon national sovereignty. The government-appointed delegates would no doubt serve as dutiful enforcers of this principle.[13]

The first test to the UNCHR's restricted jurisdiction arose just a month after the nuclear Human Rights Commission issued its report. In late May, the National Negro Congress (NNC) held its tenth annual conference in Detroit under the banner "Death Blow to Jim Crow." Founded in 1936 out of ideological and strategic disputes with the more conservative National Association for the Advancement of Colored People, the NNC soon also split with the Communist Party USA over the latter's doctrine of prioritizing the war against Fascism at the expense of fighting for domestic racial equality. During World War II, the NNC had called for the issuance by President Roosevelt of a Pacific Charter, which would explicitly commit the federal government to granting the Four Freedoms to people of color around the world. These hopes were quickly dashed. The NNC was greatly disappointed by the U.N. Charter's strong domestic jurisdiction clause. After a series of postwar high-profile murders and assaults on African Americans, some of them returning veterans, the NNC decried the Truman administration's refusal to file federal criminal charges. The appointment of white supremacist James Byrnes as secretary of state seemed to foreclose the possibility that Washington would embrace any transnational human rights platform that might alter the domestic racist status quo. With channels of redress blocked, the NNC itself took the fight for racial equality to the United Nations.[14]

The thousand delegates at the Detroit convention approved the NNC's initiative to forward a damning petition to ECOSOC entitled "The Oppression of the Negro: The Facts" by historian and NNC Executive Board member Herbert Aptheker. The report statistically documented occupational, income, housing, educational, and legal discrimination nationwide against African Americans. It decried the atmosphere of grinding poverty that forced 70 percent of African Americans to live without electricity and indoor plumbing. Given the wide spending gap by states on black and white schools, gaining an education was not an available method for achieving upward class mobility. Suffrage restrictions prevented the application of political pressure on local, state, and federal officials to ameliorate such conditions. A cocktail of grandfather clauses, poll taxes, literacy tests, and other procedures resulted in less than a third of Southern African Americans voting in the 1944 presidential race (compared to 62% for the rest of the electorate). The report concluded with a stirring declaration that "the cancer of racism has spread its poison throughout the life of America. Its throttling and killing effect upon the people of the entire nation—North and South, Negro and white—grows more fearful and more anachronistic with the passing of each hour." Citing the U.N. Charter, the NNC asked the Human Rights Commission to make recommendations for "the elimination of political, economic, and social discrimination against Negroes in the United States of America."[15]

On June 6, 1946, Max Yergan, the NNC's leader, personally presented the petition to UNCHR administrative secretary Petrus Schmidt. Schmidt informed Yergan that as the ECOSOC had not yet outlined procedures for receiving petitions, he could only promise to forward the document to UNCHR chair Roosevelt and include it on a list of communications circulated to that body's members. He did offer Yergan the opportunity to provide more evidence of African American mistreatment in order to continue the dialogue, but Yergan and the NNC were unable to do so. Part of the reason was organizational; due to an emphasis on centralizing power within the national office, the congress soon lost the local affiliates and members needed to document acts of racist terror. The Communist affiliations of Yergan and others, coupled with the emergence of the Red Scare, drove off potential members in black churches and trade unions, including the powerful Congress of Industrial Organizations. Lacking funds and victimized by a growing anti-Communist witch-hunt, Yergan became embittered by the NNC's collapse. He resigned a year later and, in a stunning about-face, became an informant for the FBI on Communism within the civil rights movement and an apologist for apartheid in South Africa.

Yet blaming the NNC's radicalism or its internal struggles for the petition's failure misses the fact that the purposefully underdeveloped U.N. machinery also prevented mainstream civil rights organizations from bringing complaints of racial discrimination to the UNCHR.[16]

Learning from the failures of the NNC effort, the NAACP counted on its anti-Communist purges, its grassroots membership, and the influence of Eleanor Roosevelt, a board member, to facilitate its efforts. In mid-September, Walter White and W.E.B. Du Bois, the secretary and director of special research for the NAACP respectively, decided to craft a more detailed report on racial discrimination for submission to the United Nations. As various authors drafted its parts, the NAACP leadership gave President Truman a chance to act by describing "an unprecedented wave of mob violence" committed against African American veterans with a "savagery equaled only at Buchenwald." They called upon Truman to have the Department of Justice prosecute the offenders and support a preventative anti-lynching bill. Independently but concurrently, Dr. Metz Lochard, the editor of the influential black newspaper *Chicago Defender*, requested a meeting on behalf of a group of prominent white and black citizens with Roosevelt and U.N. Secretary-General Trygve Lie. Not wanting to be affiliated with the NNC's earlier effort, he nonetheless wanted to follow up on Schmidt's willingness to receive additional evidence of American racial discrimination. Roosevelt declined the invitation. Citing her role as U.N. delegate that superseded her NAACP role, she encouraged Lochard to submit a written document to the Economic and Social Council. Her increasing distance from civil rights groups dovetailed nicely with the State Department's determination to keep domestic controversies from reaching the United Nations.[17]

The opposition to civil rights initiatives stemmed not only from sovereignty concerns and a fear of international embarrassment. The State Department's inability to appreciate the international consequences of America's own racist sins also grew out of the lack of African American personnel at Foggy Bottom. The agency was exceedingly hostile to the employment of African Americans except in menial positions and "special" assignments that necessitated a black face for symbolic reasons (such as serving as ministers to Haiti and Liberia). The first comprehensive survey of employment by race was completed in 1953 at the behest of civil rights activists A. Philip Randolph, Mary McLeod Bethune, and Walter White, among others. It found that there were only 55 African American Foreign Service officers out of 8,321 total State Department personnel abroad. Of the 6,700 State employees in Washington at the GS-7 level (the highest entry-level position) and above, only 15 were black, and few had any influence over United Nations policymaking. As a result of segregated employment practices, with policy decisions within the department made by an all-white cast largely drawn from elite Eastern schools, it is not surprising that proposals by the NNC and NAACP met with disdain or indifference. As historian Michael Krenn has noted, the department sought to "treat race and civil rights as propaganda issues, which, if given the proper treatment, would redound to America's favor or, perhaps more hoped for, simply go away."[18]

These efforts by private groups to petition the United Nations did indeed spawn strong attempts by the Truman administration to make future efforts invisible or fruitless. In preparation for the full UNCHR first session in January 1947, the State Department studied how to make sure that the United Nations had no power to act on any non-governmental petition brought before it. The issue was paramount: by the fall of 1946, there were a thousand communications on alleged human rights violations from civic organizations or various nationalities to the U.N. secretary-general. The U.N. Secretariat, unsure of what to do with these letters, informed UNCHR members they should find a solution. When it met as a full body for the first time in late January, Roosevelt joined the Soviet Union to pass a declaration of inaction. The commission voted to "recognize that it has no power to take *any* action in regard to *any* complaints concerning human rights," and instructed the secretary-general to compile a confidential list of communications received that UNCHR members could consult privately if desired. By passing a rule that permitted no exceptions, and blanketing the process with a cloak of secrecy, the commission missed a chance to publicize the most serious and systemic abuses. The passage of what became known as the "self-denying rule" marked another victory for American efforts to prevent the UNCHR's work from impinging on domestic sovereignty. It also made the UNCHR, in the words of John Humphrey, the head of the U.N. Secretariat's Human Rights Division, "probably the most elaborate wastepaper basket ever invented."[19]

The Truman administration concurrently maneuvered to forestall human rights activity by another U.N. body on a matter of racial discrimination. India sought to ameliorate the discriminatory treatment of its nationals in South Africa. Indians began emigrating to South Africa in the 1860s as indentured servants in the sugarcane fields and as traders. Now numbering over 300,000, they encountered intolerable racial oppression. Driven by its emergence from colonialism and the insulting experiences of independence leader Mohandas Gandhi, who had lived as a young man in South Africa, New Delhi reacted with alarm as the system of apartheid matured. In March 1946, the South African Parliament passed the Asiatic Land Tenure and Indian Representation Act, which prohibited Indian land and business ownership in white communities. After recalling its high commissioner from Pretoria in protest and declaring a trade embargo, the interim Indian government of Prime Minister Jawaharlal Nehru charged South Africa with violating the 1927 Cape Town Agreement. Under that treaty, India agreed to send laborers to whom South Africa promised full rights of citizenship. Nehru's complaint, filed in the General Assembly, cited the charter's human rights clauses and the threat of a breach of international peace in order to justify intervention by the world body. By taking this bold step, Nehru tried to force the United Nations to confront the conflict between the organization's human rights responsibilities and its domestic jurisdiction clause.[20]

During the fall 1946 General Assembly session, Pretoria responded to India's complaint by declaring the matter outside of the United Nations' authority. Privately, its U.N. representatives reminded the American delegation that "other nations" had racial problems that the assembly might discuss. Agreeing with the transparent inference, Senator Vandenberg, also serving as a U.N. delegate, privately remarked that little difference existed between "Indians in South Africa and Negroes in Alabama." Desiring to avoid a precedent-setting vote that would condemn an American non-Communist ally, the State Department tried first to limit discussion to whether existing bilateral treaty obligations had been broken and then to adjourn debate by asking the International Court of Justice for an advisory opinion. A coalition of Third World and Soviet bloc nations rejected both suggestions and approved in December a weakly worded resolution generally directing South Africa to observe its bilateral *and* U.N. Charter obligations. The United States voted against even this mild rebuke. The result was a partial victory for each side: the General Assembly ruled it could legislate in this situation, but it did so cautiously in a way that invited delay by South Africa.[21]

As the State Department fought to limit human rights oversight by the United Nations, Truman moved gradually to forestall the most serious abuses from recurring at home. Action on civil rights, which was another way of preventing United Nations intervention, could either help or hurt his party's standing. In the November 1946 congressional elections, the Democrats lost 54 seats in the House of Representatives and 11 in the Senate. Wanting to run for election in 1948 and saddled with a 32 percent approval rating, Truman had to act to prevent his diminishing support from evaporating. Clark Clifford, his closest political advisor, concluded that the electoral losses were "due in large part to the black vote [because African Americans] had slowly begun to return to the Republican Party, which seemed more amenable and sensitive to their demands." By proposing civil rights measures, Truman could hope to maintain crucial support from African Americans and co-opt civil rights initiatives from liberal Republicans. Taking Clifford's advice, he asked Congress to create a Fair Employment Practices Commission to hear allegations of job discrimination, promised to sign a federal anti-lynching bill, and announced that he would use available legal channels to punish murderers of African Americans in the South. His most notable achievement was the creation on December 5, 1946, of the President's Committee on Civil Rights, led by General Electric President Charles Wilson and Robert K. Carr, a scholar of civil liberties at Dartmouth College. Composed of private citizens from the fields of education, religion, law, labor, and industry, the committee's task was to discover how federal, state, and local governments could employ "more adequate and effective means and procedures for the protection of the civil rights of the people of the United States."[22]

In another effort to mollify civil rights groups, the Truman administration began haltingly to work on position papers for an international bill of rights. The likely inclusion of political, economic, and social guarantees necessitated the creation of a body drawn from agencies across the executive branch that were not used to working together. In August 1946, discussions began between the Federal Security Agency (FSA) and the Departments of State, Interior, Agriculture, Commerce, Justice, and Labor that together convened the Interdepartmental Committee on International Social Policy (ISP). Inauspiciously, the Labor and State departments clashed over the chairmanship, with the former privileging its participation in the International Labor Organization, while officials at Foggy Bottom refused to work under Labor's leadership. After a three-month turf war, the ISP met for the first time in late December under nominal State Department leadership and established five subcommittees, including one on Human Rights and the Status of Women (HRW). The HRW was led by Walter Kotschnig, a wartime refugee from Austria with a PhD in Political Science from the University of Kiel. He had fled to the United States in 1936, joined the State Department, and attended the Dumbarton Oaks and San Francisco conferences. He became one of the most familiar American representatives at the United Nations, attending 45 of 49 ECOSOC sessions until his retirement in 1971. Although HRW also had interagency representation, Kotschnig's leadership ensured that State's voice was primary on human rights issues.[23]

While the ISP lay in limbo, a State Department working group carried out the first substantive discussions of a postwar bill of rights. The group included three individuals who would play prominent roles in forging American human rights policy. Durward Sandifer, the secretary-general of the U.S. delegation to the San Francisco Conference and advisor to Roosevelt at the first General Assembly session, presided over the group's deliberations. He would serve as Roosevelt's favorite advisor at UNCHR meetings for the next five years. James Hendrick, who worked directly under Kotschnig in the Division of International Organization Affairs, was the main liaison between the State Department in Washington and Roosevelt and Sandifer at the United Nations in New York. Marjorie Whiteman, an advisor to the U.N. delegation, was a brilliant scholar of international law. A graduate of Yale Law School, she had worked under Legal Advisor Green Hackworth from 1929 to 1946, taking on the position of legal counsel to the U.N. delegation when Hackworth joined the World Court. In 1970, just before retiring, she published the fifteen-volume *Digest of International Law*, which solidified her credentials as a world-renowned expert on the law of nations. The trio set two precedents that would become cornerstones of American human rights policy. The group favored the completion of a non-binding General Assembly resolution that "should be sufficiently comprehensive and generous as to raise the hearts of people throughout the world" followed by work on an international convention of human rights. Yet enforcement of the convention should involve a minimal protocol, such as the simple receipt by the UNCHR of governmental compliance reports. Both policies privileged rhetorical aspirations over substantive commitment and, in the larger context, marked the continuation of wartime principles.[24]

This conservative American approach won initial acceptance by UNCHR members who lacked time, home government instructions, and a clear alternative proposal. Meeting for the first time in an abandoned Long Island, New York, airplane manufacturing facility on January 27, 1947, 16 delegates elected Roosevelt chair by acclamation, but any illusions of commission harmony engendered by the vote quickly vanished. The first fault line was philosophical. In drafting a bill, should the emphasis be on individual rights or on individual duties to the state and society? The former was grounded in Enlightenment principles of limited government, individual autonomy, and freedom of conscience. Communist ideals such as class unity, individual sacrifice, and obedience to party officials prioritized obligations to the larger community. Delegates Vladislav Ribnikar from

Yugoslavia and Valentin Tepliakov from the Soviet Union defended the latter vision, while rapporteur Charles Malik from Lebanon, René Cassin from France, and Chinese Vice Chair P. C. Chang spoke of the need to safeguard individual freedoms from state interference. The debate demonstrated that members came to the table with radically different politically or culturally ingrained assumptions about human rights and their practical application within a polity.[25]

Adding to the dust kicked up by this philosophical inquiry, an intense discussion began on what form an initial bill of rights should take. The U.N. Secretariat provided three possible models: a declaration in the form of a General Assembly resolution, an enforceable multilateral convention, or an amendment to the U.N. Charter that coupled membership to fulfilling a code of rights. The State Department informed Eleanor Roosevelt that any legally binding measures were not an "immediate, practical objective" due to their complex and controversial nature. Her push for a declaration met with opposition. Hansa Mehta, a fiery orator from India who had been repeatedly arrested for leading protests against British rule, strongly believed that a bill should become "an integral part of the Charter and a fundamental law of the United Nations." In response to Roosevelt's proposal, she "wondered whether the Commission should be satisfied with an academic discussion of a Bill of Rights or whether it wished to implement such a Bill." Australian Colonel William Roy Hodgson, a World War I Gallipoli veteran and former secretary of the Department of External Affairs, bluntly informed the delegates that he wanted to create a U.N. human rights court that would hear allegations of human rights abuses from individuals. They were a vocal minority, though. The UNCHR agreed to draft a "preliminary bill of rights" in the form of a General Assembly resolution.[26]

Having decided the format, the representatives engaged in power politics over who should do the initial drafting. Hodgson, who despaired of governmental representatives on the commission writing anything of substance and teeth, urged the job on the independent Secretariat, which could call upon outside experts to assist. British delegate Charles Dukes, a fifty-year member of the British Trades Union Congress and staunch Labor Party leader, agreed. Roosevelt, Cassin, and Malik led the successful charge to keep the drafting within their own personal purview with assistance from the Secretariat. After the vote, though, the agreement shattered when Tepliakov from the Soviet Union announced that he would vote against the recommendation. Having belatedly received instructions from Moscow, he criticized the small number of countries on the drafting committee. Roosevelt, upon hearing the objection, used her position as chair to nominate five other members, including the Soviet Union and Australia, while the addition of Chile, France, and Great Britain bolstered the number of American allies. The State Department now turned to influencing the bill's contents. James Hendrick, using words that echoed those of wartime State Department planners, stated plainly that "Our policy was to get a declaration which was a carbon copy of the American Declaration of Independence and Bill of Rights."[27]

As Hendrick, Whiteman, and Sandifer collaborated on a bill of rights, two events starkly exposed the problematic consequences of U.S. policy. On March 20, freshman Republican representatives from New York Robert Ross and David Potts introduced concurrent resolutions in Congress that asked the State Department to raise at the General Assembly the imprisonment of Yugoslav Archbishop Aloysius Stepinac. He had been convicted on charges of serving the Nazi puppet state of Croatia under its brutal wartime Ustaše Fascist government. Once Tito's Partisans defeated the hated Ustaše and created the nation of Yugoslavia, Stepinac was tried in 1946 for treason and sentenced in mid-October to 16 years of hard labor. The proposed legislation declared that Stepinac's trial "was a travesty on justice and offensive to the democratic ideals of freedom and fair play," thus violating the U.N. Charter. The Chair of the House Foreign Relations Committee, Charles Eaton (R-NJ), forwarded the resolutions to Secretary of State George Marshall for comment.[28]

The State Department might ignore or try to block attempts by the National Negro Congress and the government of India to place specific violations of human rights on the United Nations' agenda, but a move by the Republican-controlled coequal branch of government required more subtle obstructionism. Hendrick, Notter, and Kotschnig carefully argued, under Marshall's signature on June 11, 1947, that domestic jurisdictional boundaries found in Article 2(7) of the charter prevented any discussion of individual human rights cases. The reply omitted a major private concern of Notter: having the General Assembly act could backfire by allowing the Soviet bloc to charge the U.S. government with indifference toward "the cruelest forms of lynching." Marshall weakly promised the congressman that he would "seek a favorable opportunity through other means for making known its views in a manner which might be conducive to good results." This disgraceful episode, in which the State Department equated even the discussion of human rights abuses with a violation of Article 2(7), underscored the department's unwillingness to back any human rights initiatives that could have domestic repercussions.[29]

As State Department lawyers fought to keep Congress from investing the United Nations with human rights capabilities, they also had to thwart a similar attempt surprisingly from within the executive branch. In an attempt to bypass congressional opposition, President Truman charged the President's Committee on Civil Rights with exploring how federal, state, and local governments could better enforce existing anti-discrimination statutes. On April 24, the committee's executive secretary, Robert Carr, requested that Acting Secretary of State Dean Acheson outline any federal governmental obligations to protect domestic civil rights that derived from being a member of the United Nations. After ignoring several follow-up requests, Secretary Marshall finally directed State Department Legal Advisor Charles Fahy to respond two months later. The resulting fourteen-page memo evinced evasion and condescension. More than half of the reply consisted simply of quotations from the International Labor Organization's constitution, the Act of Chapultepec, and the U.N. Charter. Echoing Marshall's reply to Eaton, Fahy denied that any of these agreements placed *any* legal responsibility on *any* nation to promote human rights internally. As far as the State Department was concerned, the United Nations possessed no real human rights authority at all.[30]

The State Department adopted a two-track policy to ensure the continued enshrinement of these restrictive views as work began on a human rights declaration. Just six days after the UNCHR's first session adjourned in mid-February, Eleanor Roosevelt invited P. C. Chang, Charles Malik, and John Humphrey, who led the U.N. Secretariat's Human Rights Division, to her apartment for tea. She was anxious to start the drafting process, but she also knew from contentious committee meetings that any proposal was bound to meet with controversy. The group quickly decided to have Humphrey and his multinational secretariat prepare a version for consideration by the Drafting Committee when it convened in June. As a Canadian scholar of international law at McGill and a linguist fluent in French and English, Humphrey was certainly prepared to undertake the task. Concurrently, State Department lawyers busied themselves with articulating their own version that reflected the desire to protect U.S. sovereignty by supporting only the inclusion of rights already guaranteed by the Constitution. Just two weeks after the UNCHR's session ended, the State Department finished its proposal. The ten-article document incorporated whole phrases lifted from the U.S. Bill of Rights: "equal protection of the law," "probable cause" for search and seizures, and a ban on "cruel and inhuman punishments." It contained, in short, the basic elements of the First, Fourth, Fifth, Sixth, Eighth, Thirteenth, and Fourteenth Amendments with two additions: the right of peoples to self-government, and the freedom to find a job, receive a public education, and collect social security. It was virtually a carbon copy of the 1942 departmental draft, which showed how little the momentous changes of World War II had impacted diplomats at Foggy Bottom.[31]

Even this draft was too much for Harley Notter, who mounted a final effort to cease all work on an international bill of rights. Notter's Office of Special Political Affairs no longer labored on human rights proposals, and it was only by accident that he learned about the draft declaration. He had always doubted the utility of spending much time on a document few nations would execute, especially those committing the worst abuses. He warned that forging ahead would only increase cynicism toward the United Nations as an ineffective body and falsely raise the hopes of those living behind the Iron Curtain. "Accordingly," he concluded matter-of-factly, "I think that the U.N. should do something but not attempt very much," such as only asking nations to self-report on domestic efforts to promote and protect human rights. "We need to help [sic] the doers of good will stay down to earth in this field," he warned, and not give "a ready basis for supposing that real action anywhere would take place soon or in any substantial measure." Although the memo found wide circulation within the department, no one responded. Notter, who had been so active in participating and chronicling the creation of the United Nations, soon stopped participating in all human rights discussions. Ironically, Notter's opposition to enforceable human rights standards was completely in line with State Department policy; he differed with his colleagues, though, on whether a pious-sounding declaration would invite cynicism or celebration of the United Nations.[32]

Notter's skepticism would have increased substantially had he access to the long and complicated bill of rights submitted to UNCHR members. Humphrey completed his forty-eight-article draft by early May, spending at least one day a week away from the cacophony of his office in the old Sperry Gyroscope Company. Over a desk at the Lido Beach Hotel on Long Island, he created an outline that distilled ideas submitted by individuals such as H. G. Wells and Law Professor Hersch Lauterpacht, and NGOs including the American Law Institute, American Jewish Congress, and American Association for the United Nations (the former Commission to Study the Organization of Peace). The sources were, therefore, from English-speaking countries, which hardly reflected the national origins of most UNCHR members. Some articles articulated a right and an acceptable limitation: freedom of speech (with a duty to report news in a fair and impartial manner), a ban on slavery (but individuals could be forced to perform public service work), and freedom of assembly (though not to undermine other's freedoms). The draft also went beyond civil and political rights to include guaranteed access to education, social security, good working conditions, and adequate food and housing. Implementation was simple: individuals could petition their own governments and the United Nations because the rights "shall be deemed fundamental principles of international law and of the natural law of each of [the United Nations'] Member States. Their observance is therefore a matter of international law and it shall be within the jurisdiction of the United Nations to discuss any violation thereof."[33]

Meeting half a dozen times in May in a State Department conference room, the newly constituted Subcommittee on Human Rights and the Status of Women (HRW) led by Kotschnig examined in excruciating detail every article of the Secretariat's draft. In striving to fit the articles into existing American law, not all of their amendments were regressive. The group expanded prohibitions against unauthorized police searches, arbitrary detentions, and imprisonment for debt, attached a ban on inhumane prison conditions, deleted the duty to present news and information objectively, and added the rights of criminal defendants to bail and a speedy trial. The subcommittee did delete guarantees that were totally foreign in American law, including the rights to "resist oppression," acquire a nationality, and gain (rather than merely apply for) asylum. Its members refashioned other unfamiliar rights, such as to own property and be free from racial and sexual discrimination, into guarantees of due process and equal protection. The latter change was crucial, for the federal courts had already declared segregation laws in harmony with the Constitution's Fourteenth Amendment, so the proposed wording would not invalidate Jim Crow statutes. Using human rights terminology to sustain racial discrimination was not a tidy matter. Including an article defining the right to participate in government caused problems, because several states prohibited Native Americans from voting, and obstacles to African American suffrage were pernicious throughout the South.[34]

Parts of the Secretariat's draft forced HRW, on behalf of the federal government, for the first time to take an official position on the inclusion of economic and social rights. Domestic law did not recognize them, yet President Roosevelt had included them in his Four Freedoms, and preventing a repetition of Great Depression suffering meant giving governments more responsibility for enacting a social safety net. But how, HRW members wondered, could they support individualistic claims to food, housing, medical care, and other guarantees while also embracing a limited New Deal welfare state and a free-market economy? Moreover, what value would these rights have in nations whose governments were too poor to afford them in the first place? And how could one measure their fulfillment? What standards of housing and medical care did nations have to achieve? Thanks to a longer history of practice, these questions had been answered about civil and political rights through legal precedents and a formal structure of courts, prisons, and police.

The strategy chosen was to refashion the governmentally mandated guarantees into more vague promotional obligations. The Secretariat Draft had included the rights of individuals to obtain free primary public education, medical care, social security, "good food and housing," and "socially useful work." HRW members, recognizing the difficulties outlined above, sought to frame these guarantees as long-range goals that governments should strive to satisfy given variations in their available resources and economic ideologies. Subcommittee members also continued American opposition, dating back to the San Francisco Conference, to requiring governments to guarantee full employment. They remembered Truman's battle with Congress over the 1946 Employment Act, which forced the president to accept "maximum" rather than "full" employment as a public policy goal. The final draft approved by HRW included the duty of governments only to *promote* "full employment" as well as "adequate" levels of health care, food, housing, and education. Governments could use legislation or "other appropriate means" to meet these obligations, thus recognizing the private sector as a partner in meeting this international obligation. With these changes, the State Department hoped to avoid pious but meaningless promises of bountiful living standards for all as well as any implication that nations had to enforce these guarantees through essentially centrally planned economies.[35]

HRW members furthermore agreed to include egalitarian language and economic and social duties only if the declaration banned intervention by the United Nations or complaints to it by aggrieved individuals. Humphrey's draft specified that the United Nations had jurisdiction to discuss and act upon violations. This aroused the ire of the State Department, as the UNCHR had already decided to write a symbolic declaration of human rights first. The subcommittee replaced the clause with an emasculated provision that made the bill of rights a matter for "discussion or action by the United Nations in conformity with the Charter." As HRW frankly concluded after citing evidence from San Francisco Conference deliberations, "The charter imposes no duty to refrain from violations of human rights within the borders of a state." The message was clear: a declaration of human rights must have absolutely no force anywhere as a matter of law.[36] Having affirmed that consensus, Humphrey's article asserting the right of individuals to petition the United Nations for redress was also off the table. The State Department cited national sovereignty concerns and fears that Americans would file potentially embarrassing appeals to justify its vehement opposition. Somewhat disingenuously, the department also argued that since the UNCHR could not accept petitions (due to American opposition!), it did not want to "stimulate unwarranted hopes" of peoples worldwide by recognizing such a process. After failing to convince a majority in HRW to omit the section, Hendrick and Kotschnig reluctantly proposed an alternative. The United States would not acknowledge such a right but would endorse a simple clause preventing states from denying the right to petition. Such a negatively worded proposal would "remove the spotlight from the article which would encourage false hopes for the fulfillment of what will not (at least for the present) be fulfilled," HRW members dryly concluded, knowing anyway that UNCHR's procedural rules rendered such petitions unactionable and invisible the moment they crossed the U.N. bureaucracy.[37]

The UNCHR's Drafting Committee met at Lake Success, New York, from June 9 to June 25, and it proved to be a trying time for achieving consensus on how to proceed. The Truman Doctrine signified that Washington would challenge Communism's expansion in Turkey and Greece. The Marshall Plan and the merging of occupation zones in western Germany signaled the increasing division of Europe. The United Nations grappled with Arab-Jewish violence in Palestine and a civil war in China. These events created tension among Drafting Committee delegates including Soviet representative Vladimir Koretsky, Charles Malik of Lebanon (a spokesperson for the Arab League), P. C. Chang of China, and René Cassin, a French Jew and Zionist who had lost 29 relatives in the Holocaust. They clashed on the most important issue facing the eight-person body: whether to formulate a binding treaty or a simple declaration of principles. Geoffrey Wilson of Great Britain, desiring the former only, submitted a convention containing carefully drafted political and civil rights for consideration. Implementation would be done at the national level, though the treaty allowed the United Nations to expel members that violated the agreement. Ralph Harry from Australia, asserting that the British proposal "was not sufficient to assure to the peoples of the world that the bill of rights would be more than a declaration of principles," proposed an international court of human rights to hear from aggrieved individuals.

Roosevelt and the Soviet Union led the charge for a declaration. Koretsky, using words that could have come from Roosevelt, stated that any list of guarantees must not "be of such a nature as to interfere in the internal systems of various governments." To break the impasse, the committee diplomatically decided to submit texts of both and let the full UNCHR decide which to approve. The committee asked Cassin to forge a non-binding declaration in light of the Secretariat's proposal and comments from committee members. Roosevelt, Malik, and Wilson volunteered to discuss the contents of a covenant.[38]

Due to Roosevelt's determined lobbying, Cassin's effort as subsequently revised included most of the major changes proposed by the State Department. His proposed declaration also relied heavily on Humphrey's work, which was unsurprising given that he had only two days to write. The Drafting Committee had only one week in mid-June to discuss Cassin's work, but it made substantial alterations. Reflecting the novelty of economic and social rights, only seven of the 36 articles retained by the Drafting Committee fell into this category. Roosevelt agreed to their inclusion as the state had no responsibility to fulfill the rights to "adequate" health care, "socially useful work," social security, and safe working conditions, among other clauses. Committee members allowed states to determine their own asylum laws and transformed the non-discrimination proviso into an equal protection article. Roosevelt also successfully changed the right to petition the United Nations into a promise by governments that they would not interfere with citizens who chose to do so. "The U.S. views were accepted on virtually every point," Warren Austin, the head U.S. delegate to the United Nations, concluded. Secretary of State Marshall agreed, telling Roosevelt that the outcome was "a very real tribute to your ability as United States Representative and as Chairman."[39]

Having won the emasculating petition language in a future human rights declaration, State Department lawyers now saw a promising chance to vitiate ECOSOC's current ability to handle them. Their efforts ensured that the eighteen-nation ECOSOC ratified the strict "self-denying rule" that the UNCHR had passed in its January 1947 session. Knowing that even allies France and India opposed the inability of the commission to even discuss petitions as too restrictive, Kotschnig and O. Benjamin Gerig focused on prohibiting the commission from acting on them. Gerig wanted to make sure that the body "does not have the right to look into human rights in individual countries, for example, problems relating to the right of negros [sic] in this country." Marshall had Roosevelt lobby uncommitted ECOSOC members Uruguay and Egypt. With little opposition, on August 5, the ECOSOC passed Resolution 75(V). After approving the UNCHR's own recommendation that "the commission has no power to take any action in regard to any complaints," the ECO-SOC endorsed a clumsy process that required the Secretariat to compile confidential lists of petitions for the UNCHR's members. UNCHR members could examine the list and request the originals for further examination. That was it. The State Department victory came with some criticism though. James Frederick Green called its contents "exceedingly restrictive." The decision moved Hersch Lauterpacht, a renowned international lawyer, to find the UNCHR and ECOSOC guilty of emasculating "an obligation grounded in the Charter." Eerily similar to the infamous "gag rule" that had prevented congressional action on American anti-slavery petitions a century before, Resolution 75(V) tabled U.N. action on allegations of gross human rights abuses.[40]

ECOSOC's straitjacket did not stop domestic efforts to utilize the United Nations General Assembly to focus attention on overseas human rights violations. State Department officials had to weather renewed domestic pressure to bring Archbishop Aloysius Stepinac's imprisonment to the Assembly's attention. He had become, especially to Catholic groups, a martyr to religious freedom in a Communist state. Chapters of the Knights of Columbus called upon the Truman administration to sever all ties with Tito's Yugoslavia, while in White Plains, New York, construction workers broke ground on the Archbishop Stepinac High School. On July 20, 1947, an official with the San Francisco Archdiocese inquired as to what "other measures" Secretary of State Marshall had taken to help the archbishop as promised in the previous month's letter to Representative Eaton. The response must have been disappointing. In the ten months since the trial had ended, a State Department spokesperson replied, "no occasion has subsequently arisen which would permit the United States Government to take effective action in this matter." Yugoslavia regarded the case as an internal matter, the letter stated, omitting that American policy agreed with that assertion and courted Tito as a Balkan ally. Three months later, after receiving "thousands" of letters asking for action on behalf of the archbishop, Representative Robert Ross again requested that Marshall submit the case to the General Assembly. The department again demurred. The real reason for sidetracking public debate, Dean Rusk of the State Department's Office of U.N. Affairs told Legal Advisor Ernest Gross privately, was that such a discussion "would leave the United States vulnerable to similar charges against it by other states." The government stood by its assertion that the U.N. Charter "does not place a treaty obligation upon Members actually to observe specific human rights."[41]

As the State Department moved to muzzle discussion at the United Nations, it denied in public what it admitted hesitantly in private: that other nations were interested and offended by domestic racial discrimination to the degree that they might bring the controversy in the United Nations. Robert Carr, the secretary of the President's Committee on Civil Rights, wanted to know if America's "bad domestic record in the civil rights area" damaged its standing in the world. In private discussions on how to reply, State Department lawyers admitted that "the conduct of our foreign policy is handicapped by our record in the field of civil rights and racial discrimination." The department's own country specialists, though, refused to provide examples of criticism in the foreign press on the ground that any such reports existing must be manufactured by Communists to discredit the leader of the free world. Marshall concurred, telling Charles Wilson, the committee's co-chair, that much of the publicity was "inspired by political elements utilizing it as propaganda material to promote for themselves a political philosophy which almost completely denies the concept of civil rights as we know it." This distorted lens created "embarrassment out of proportion to the actual instances of violation" in the United States. It was truly a confusing letter, part confession and part denial. As Foggy Bottom concluded that any criticism of America's own human rights record was suspect, and thus there was no real evidence that Jim Crow harmed the nation's image abroad, it was not up to the former head of General Electric to question that judgment.[42]

To prove Marshall's point, Rusk appended a list of unclassified quotations from "communist or acknowledged left-wing organs" and classified transcripts of largely Soviet radio broadcasts monitored by the Central Intelligence Group, forerunner to the Central Intelligence Agency. The former included Soviet commentary on the banning of Paul Robeson from performing in Peoria, Illinois, and an analysis of the movie roles of "imbeciles or madmen" that African Americans were limited to playing in Hollywood. Carr became clearly frustrated at Marshall's evasiveness and Rusk's anecdotal evidence. He responded pointedly to Rusk, asserting that the commission's "unequivocal" position is that while it "believes that there is much distortion in foreign propaganda . . . it also believes that the American record is in many ways a bad one and the Committee is not attempting to minimize this condition." He wanted a confession that racism at home harmed American interests abroad and that therefore the way to improve the latter was to take strong action on the former. As the report was almost done, Carr proposed three alternatives: Marshall could write a new letter that dovetailed with the committee's finding, Carr could quote selectively from Marshall's letter to the commission, or Carr could insert a 1946 statement by Dean Acheson to the Fair Employment Practices Committee. The undersecretary of state back then had minced no words in stating that "The existence of discrimination against minority groups in this country has an adverse effect on our relations with other countries." Carr received no reply, so he unilaterally chose the third option.[43]

The committee's final report, *To Secure These Rights*, issued on October 29 to much publicity at home and abroad, consisted, in the words of lawyer Michael Gardner, of "176 pages of social dynamite." To ensure that every citizen enjoyed freedom from fear, the document called upon all three branches of the federal government to protect individual rights to personal security, citizenship, conscience and expression, and equal opportunity. The three dozen recommendations included banning the poll tax and criminalizing lynchings at the federal level, creating a civil rights division in the Justice Department, and outlawing restrictive covenants in real estate. To justify such controversial measures, the report made public the private concerns of the State Department. After detailing the economic, political, and judicial discrimination suffered by African Americans, the report declared that the repercussions of such mistreatment "echo from one end of the globe to the other." How, it asked, could U.S. diplomats demand free elections overseas if American citizens remain disenfranchised? Most controversially, the committee concluded that the U.N. Charter gave the federal government the jurisdiction and obligation to enact the committee's recommendations. Because the charter, as a treaty, was now "the supreme Law of the Land," Congress and the Truman administration could cite the duty of U.N. members to promote "respect for, and observance of, human rights and fundamental freedoms" as the statutory basis for passing civil rights laws. The committee had handed Truman the weapons needed to shoot down racial discrimination at home, but it remained to be seen whether he would pull the trigger, and if he did, whether he would cite America's international human rights obligations.[44]

Domestic civil rights activists refused to wait, and agreeing with Carr, they petitioned the United Nations for redress. Building on the work of the National Negro Congress, Walter White and W.E.B. Du Bois of the NAACP compiled an extensive report on the discriminatory treatment of African Americans across the country. Their goal was to use the organization's moderate image, anti-Communist credentials, and governmental contacts (all of which the NNC had lacked) to place the petition before the United Nations. Part history, part socio-economic study, and part legal treatise edited by Du Bois, *An Appeal to the World* was a powerful and detailed indictment that revealed the hypocrisy of the free world's leading nation. The qualitative and quantitative evidence contained in the report, Du Bois wrote in the introduction, "show[s] clearly that a discrimination practiced in the United States against her own citizens and to a large extent a contravention of her own laws, cannot be persisted in, without infringing upon the rights of peoples of the world and especially upon the ideas and work of the United Nations." Du Bois tasked Dr. Rayford Logan, a history professor at Howard University, to argue the United Nations' responsibility to accept the petition. Logan, unable to cite precedents that did not exist, fell back on the words of the charter, the UNCHR's terms of reference, and the debate over Indian nationals in South Africa. Unless the charter's human rights articles meant nothing at all, he concluded, Article 2(7) "must be liberally interpreted" to allow the United Nations to at least receive petitions from oppressed groups around the world. Du Bois and White then contacted U.N. Secretary-General Trygve Lie, every U.N. delegation, and NAACP board member Roosevelt to ask their assistance in bringing the document before the General Assembly.[45]

The State Department scrambled to prevent that from happening. Walter White contacted Roosevelt for help in making arrangements for a presentation ceremony to which he had invited 125 black and white Americans and the heads of every U.N. delegation. Her negative reply cited the fact that the petition had not come up through the proper channels, by which she meant as one of hundreds of anonymous and confidential reports sent from the Secretariat to a UNCHR powerless to act on them. After Lie told the NAACP to contact John Humphrey, the State Department warned Humphrey that "no good would come" of the petition. Retreating behind the walls of ECOSOC Resolution 75(V), he refused to accept the document and told Du Bois that only U.N. member states could place petitions on the General Assembly's agenda. A defiant Du Bois then leaked the petition to major newspapers, including the *New York Times*. The resulting interest of U.N. delegations ranging from Great Britain and India to the Soviet Union, Mexico, and Liberia forced Humphrey to retreat slightly. On October 23, Humphrey and Assistant Secretary-General Henri Laugier listened impassively as Du Bois implored them to act upon the document. "[The petition] is open and articulate and not designed for confidential concealment in your archives," he argued. Humphrey, still "afraid of the document" according to White, took it but countered with ECOSOC's instructions that it remain confidential. Although the media

publicity embarrassed the State Department, Resolution 75(V) had prevented U.N. action on the petition. The State Department's victory would
be total: the NAACP soon retreated from U.N. activity while Roosevelt,
who had privately threatened to resign from the NAACP's board due to
the petition, remained a hero to many African Americans who provided
the critical votes for Truman's election a year later.[46]

Despite these political and diplomatic victories, Marshall and his legal
advisors feared the political ramifications if the federal courts agreed with
Carr and rule that the charter's human rights clauses invalidated all inconsistent domestic laws. The day before Du Bois released the NAACP study to
the *New York Times*, former Undersecretary of State Dean Acheson argued
before the Supreme Court the unconstitutionality of California's 1913 Alien
Land Law. The statute, passed by the California legislature due to pressure
from white farmers worried about economic competition from Japanese
aliens, banned land ownership by those ineligible for citizenship. Japanese
nationals responded by buying land in the names of their American-born
children, who were U.S. citizens, but the legislature outlawed the practice
in 1920. Fourteen years later, Kajiro Oyama, a Japanese alien, bought six
acres of land in the name of his six-year-old American-born son Fred. They
owned the parcel for eight years until the Roosevelt administration's internment policy forced them to evacuate. With the land "abandoned," the
state of California moved to take it over, arguing that Fred's "purchase" was
a naked attempt to bypass the Alien Land Law. The petitioners' brief in
Oyama v. California and an amicus brief filed by the American Civil Liberties Union (ACLU) asserted that the statute was "a law which flaunts, for
all the world to see, a conflict with the [U.N.] Charter." One week after the
NAACP's petition, Acheson's presentation to the court, and the release of
To Secure These Rights, Attorney General Tom Clark publicly announced
that he would file an amicus brief in four cases adjudicating the constitutionality of restrictive covenants. This began a new strategy by the Truman
administration to participate as plaintiffs in civil rights cases. Clark's amicus briefs maintained that racist statutes were only obnoxious to the U.S.
Constitution, ignoring the U.N. Charter completely, and thus supporting
the State Department's innocuous reading of the latter document.[47]

Acting in tandem with Marshall and Clark, HRW members pored over
the UNCHR's Drafting Committee text of the human rights declaration
to ensure its domestic legal impotence too. Although Roosevelt and Marshall were generally pleased with the draft, several members thought it too
complex, unworkable, and lacking in inspirational appeal. By September 5,
after farming each article of the declaration out for study within the federal

bureaucracy, the resulting commentary grew to over 60 pages. Its authors wished to delete the unfamiliar clauses allowing individuals to resist oppression and the responsibility of governments to promote full employment. Most of the commentary, though, suggested stylistic revisions of almost every article proposed by the Drafting Committee to make them more general, and therefore less like actionable governmental commitments. The irony of conducting such a widespread, careful, and detailed study (with the second longest section dissecting the preamble) of a non-binding document that already contained substantial American language was not lost on Hendrick. "We could continue to discuss and make changes from now until Doomsday, as the people love to change their minds," he exasperatedly told his boss Kotschnig. Within a week of obtaining the HRW's approval to write a simpler text, he and two colleagues turned out a ten-article replacement that fit on a single page.[48]

The trio strove to encapsulate the thus far irreconcilable goal of obtaining world approval on a simply written, concise document informed by U.S. constitutional jurisprudence but containing no enforcement obligations. Their "short form" declaration approved in mid-November was, like the attempt nine months earlier that had drawn Notter's ire, mostly a restatement of the Bill of Rights and the Thirteenth and Fourteenth Amendments. As a non-binding document, they felt comfortable adding articles that permitted U.N. petitions (that the UNCHR could not publicly recognize or act upon anyway), prohibited racial discrimination, and included the rights to work, health care, social security, and education. Yet even these safeguards did not satisfy Acting Secretary of State Robert Lovett, who, after initially approving the short text and having it released to American and foreign newspapers, then demanded the excision of two preambular statements that hinted at state obligations but were actually quotations from the U.N. Charter itself. His last-minute intervention caused a firestorm, as the bill's drafters made the obvious assertion that "the United States should avoid language weaker than that of the Charter." Embarrassed, Lovett retreated. The entire incident created bad feelings between HRW's lawyers and Lovett, and it underscored yet again how sovereignty-conscious upper-echelon State Department officials had become.[49]

Although UNCHR members decided to discuss their own Drafting Committee's text rather than Kotschnig's short form at their December meeting in Geneva, Roosevelt's skillful lobbying still resulted in a declaration that fit within the close confines of State Department policy. Her objective was the same as Lovett's: to craft a list of human rights that would be inspirational and aspirational but not legally obligational upon governments. Roosevelt chaired an ad hoc working group tasked with revision, which included Cassin and a new, co-operative Soviet delegate, Alexander Bogomolov, whom John Humphrey remembered fondly for the alcohol-soaked parties he threw at the Hotel Richmonde. Roosevelt's instructions were quite clearly and candidly reflected in her opening speech to the full UNCHR. The United States, she announced, thought that the declaration should receive priority status, though it "should not be drawn up in such a way as to give the impression that Governments would have a contractual obligation to guarantee human rights."[50]

After nine meetings, Roosevelt's colleagues approved 33 articles that differed only slightly from the Drafting Committee's original work. The working group deleted the problematic right to resist oppression, and Roosevelt successfully lobbied against a Soviet amendment to ban miscegenation laws, which existed throughout the South. The body approved weakly worded U.S.-backed articles on property, work, and marriage that made all individual guarantees subject to statutory regulation by national governments, a position that the equally sovereignty-conscious Soviet bloc also endorsed. To further defend national prerogatives, the group approved Roosevelt's suggestion for a generic limitation clause that made all rights listed eligible for limitation "by the just requirements of the democratic State." The State Department's summary of the meeting was satisfactory: "From the standpoint of practice, as opposed to laws, the United States should be in a better position than almost any other country to show compliance with the standards set forth, with the single exception of problems relating to discrimination." There was little to be concerned about on that issue, though, as the draft incorporated the Fourteenth Amendment's equal protection clause that did not, according to the Supreme Court, invalidate Jim Crow legislation. Overall, to Roosevelt's satisfaction, the working group shortened the text and made it "readily understood by all peoples," thus making the entire document look less like a formal legal contract.[51]

The greatest source of tension in Geneva, the issue of implementation, pitted the American, Yugoslav, and Soviet representatives against the Australian, Indian, and Latin American delegates. Fearful that the United States would reject any legally enforceable human rights treaty, a majority in the ad hoc working group favored an article calling on states to "ensure [that] their law[s were] brought into, and maintained in, conformity with the principles of the present Declaration." Due to Roosevelt's determined opposition to what sounded like a back-door legal obligation, the full UNCHR agreed instead that state laws *should* conform to the vague human rights clauses in the U.N. Charter. Meeting separately from Roosevelt's editing team, an implementation working group, chaired by Hansa Mehta of India, proposed a radical overhaul of the U.N. human rights machinery. It called for the creation of an international court of human rights, a favorite proposal of Australian delegate William Roy Hodgson, and an Indian plan for U.N. receipt of petitions from aggrieved individuals. Bogomolov and Vladislav Ribnikar of Yugoslavia led the opposition charge on sovereignty grounds, with Roosevelt adding that she believed that the United Nations was "not yet in a position to take effective and comprehensive action upon petitions." The UNCHR took no action on the recommendations and simply forwarded them to the Economic and Social Council. With an acceptable declaration in the editing pipeline and implementation measures sidetracked for now, the State Department was pleased with Roosevelt's performance during the UNCHR's second session. President Truman congratulated Roosevelt just before Christmas on "the valiant fight" she had waged "on behalf of our ideals."[52]

The Supreme Court's final determination that the United Nations Charter created no internal human rights obligations also must have pleased the president. Appointments by Franklin Roosevelt and Truman had turned the court away from its embrace of states' rights and toward the dismantling of segregation due to contrary provisions only found in the Constitution. The first hint of the shift came in 1944, when the justices in *Smith v. Allwright* abolished the white primary. On January 19, 1948, the court adjudicated the constitutionality of California's Alien Land Law. Four of the nine justices published two concurring opinions adopting the petitioners' claim that the law violated the U.N. Charter and the Fourteenth Amendment. The opinion of Justices Frank Murphy and Wiley Rutledge did not mince words. Their brief concluded, "And so in origin, purpose, administration and effect, the Alien Land Law does violence to the high ideals of the Constitution of the United States and the Charter of the United Nations. It is an unhappy facsimile, a disheartening reminder, of the racial policy pursued by those forces of evil whose destruction recently necessitated a devastating war. It is racism in one of its most malignant forms." The opinion was so strident that several other justices, including Chief Justice Frederick Vinson and Justice William O. Douglas, worried the Soviets would circulate it to embarrass the United States, and they unsuccessfully pressured Murphy to revise it. Vinson, who wrote the lead opinion, strongly disagreed that the charter imparted any binding obligation, and he relied instead solely on the Fourteenth Amendment to invalidate the statute. NAACP lawyers, heartened by the decision, began an aggressive litigation strategy to dismantle Jim Crow but without any reference to the United Nations.[53]

The entire Supreme Court accepted the State Department's and Vinson's views on the irrelevance of the U.N. Charter in *Shelley v. Kramer*, an NAACP challenge to the constitutionality of restrictive covenants. The American Association for the United Nations (AAUN), in an amicus brief, forcefully argued that the charter's human rights clauses nullified the enforcement of such discriminatory contracts by federal and state governments. In response to this assertion, the recommendations of the President's Committee on Civil Rights, and pressure from Democratic liberals across the country, State Department lawyers James Hendrick, Ernest Gross, and Marjorie Whiteman worked with the Justice Department to prepare the administration's first amicus brief in a civil rights case. Prominently bearing Attorney General Tom Clark's name, their submission conceded only that racial discrimination embarrassed the United States abroad and was "inconsistent with the public policy of the United States." Hendrick and Whiteman also prepared the Solicitor General's office to answer any oral argument questions by the justices about the applicability of the charter. The message was clear: "The Articles of the Charter . . . are not interpreted by the Department of State as imposing a legal obligation to guarantee observance of specific human rights and fundamental freedoms without distinction as to race, sex, language or religion." The Supreme Court implicitly agreed, for its unanimous decision on May 3, 1948, relied only on the Fifth and Fourteenth Amendments to find state enforcement of restrictive covenants unconstitutional. The court was "thunderously silent," in the words of human rights lawyer Bert Lockwood, on claims raised by the AAUN. Between 1948 and 1955, the court consistently rejected claims of U.N. Charter violations in eight other civil rights cases.[54]

In the spring of 1948, the State Department renewed its drive to create a non-binding human rights declaration should that document too ever come before the justices. Legal and political considerations led officials to take divergent views on whether the Geneva draft declaration fulfilled this aim. Dean Rusk and Walter Kotschnig were troubled by the UNCHR's lengthy work, which by its specificity and references to state action might imply real obligations by signatories. They advocated reintroducing the department's short form in the Drafting Committee's May 1948 session, despite its previous rejection by the UNCHR in December. Roosevelt and Hendrick dissented, the latter observing that even allies in the UNCHR thought the United States "was trying to ram down the throats of other countries a declaration so devoid of substantive content as to be virtually meaningless." In a compromise, the HRW chose Hendrick and two other colleagues to revise the UNCHR's draft. The three suggested changing all mandatory language to declaratory phrases and to eliminate any mention of state action. Truman initialed their suggestions and sent them to the U.N. secretary-general in mid-April for delivery to UNCHR members. "It is inappropriate to state the rights in the Declaration in terms of governmental responsibility," his letter proclaimed. The declaration should only list goals to inspire peoples around the world. In a thinly veiled reply to critics of U.S. racial discrimination, Truman quoted President Abraham Lincoln, who had defended the authors of the Declaration of Independence and their statement that "all men are created equal." The phrase was not meant for literal application, Lincoln surmised. "[The Founders] meant simply to declare the *right*, so that the enforcement of it might follow as fast as circumstances permit."[55] It would be up to the United States government on its own accord, without foreign interference, to decide when that would be.

A second set of suggested revisions, made by HRW in confidential position papers for use by Roosevelt, aimed at even more emasculating changes. To banish the possibility that U.S. courts or the United Nations itself might find the declaration justiciable, Hendrick proposed to delete any governmental obligations to codify the enumerated rights or to allow individuals explicitly to petition the United Nations. He defended the desire to have the declaration mirror American laws, "which are thought to be a generally satisfactory standard with respect to human rights." This view did not command unanimous acceptance. Labor Department representative Thacher Winslow derided Hendrick for arguing that "international progress could be achieved merely by bringing the laws of other countries up to the level of U.S. laws." A majority agreed to a compromise: the U.N. petition clause would remain, an equal protection article would be added, and the obligation to change domestic laws would go. The emerging consensus favored a short list of general statements consistent with U.S. law, though the cost of failure if UNCHR members disagreed was still small. If the committee rejected these recommendations, American courts would have to demolish three barriers before using the declaration to challenge Jim Crow: the declaration's non-binding legal status as a General Assembly resolution, its conservative and vague language largely consistent with the U.S. Constitution, and its clause permitting governmental derogations according to the "protection by law of the freedom, general welfare and security of all."[56]

As the 1948 presidential campaign unfolded, Truman encountered additional reasons to avoid any controversy on the issue of civil rights. On

January 18, former Vice President Henry Wallace announced a Progressive Party bid for the presidency on a strongly anti-discrimination platform. Just two days later, the Mississippi legislature endorsed Governor Fielding J. Wright's plan to desert the Democratic Party if Truman and Congress embraced any civil rights initiatives. Facing the possibility of schisms by liberals and Dixiecrats, Truman turned to close aide Clark Clifford for advice. Clifford argued that African Americans, among other groups, held the balance of power in key states. "Real efforts (as distinguished from mere political gestures which are today thoroughly understood and strongly resented by sophisticated Negro leaders)" were needed to prevent their tilting Republican, he warned. Truman assented. A February 2 speech to Congress incorporated several recommendations from the President's Committee on Civil Rights, including the passage of bills to criminalize lynching and outlaw the poll tax. Southern Democrats reacted with shrill disapproval; influential Senator James Eastland (D-MS) threatened to leave the party altogether while Senator John Rankin (D-MS) called the *Shelley v. Kramer* decision the Soviet Union's "greatest victory." Truman retreated and refused to send actual legislation to Congress. Given this turmoil, few heard the first public statement opposing U.N. human rights intervention by the House of Delegates of the American Bar Association (ABA). Sovereignty-conscious, devoted to states' rights, and skeptical of international institutions, the ABA soon allied with Southern Democrats and Midwestern Republicans against Truman's work on the human rights declaration.[57]

Worried that the conservative backlash might focus on her United Nations work and its potential domestic impact, Roosevelt waged a hard-fought struggle to shorten the declaration and delete all language that hinted of legal commitment when the UNCHR's Drafting Committee met for a second and last time from May 3 to May 21, 1948. The pressure of ending on time, for the full UNCHR was due to meet on May 24, was only one barrier to a calm and efficient atmosphere for careful deliberation. Outside the interim U.N. headquarters in Lake Success, crises abounded. The Chinese Civil War distracted delegate T. Y. Wu, who was sitting in for P. C. Chang. Vice Chair Charles Malik lost sleep as Zionists announced the creation of Israel on May 14, setting off a regional war. Soviet unhappiness toward the West was demonstrated by the arrival of new delegate Alexei Pavlov, who unexpectedly announced that Moscow wished to scrap the draft declaration and start from scratch. He also gave hour-long harangues that tested the delegates' patience. UNCHR members nonetheless struggled to achieve a timely consensus. Four lawyers sat behind Roosevelt alone, quickly handing her notes before committee votes. Though the committee did not complete an examination of the entire declaration, it did to her delight insert vaguely aspirational language throughout (e.g., "everyone has the right to . . .") to reinforce the work's legal impotence.[58]

With the four members of the Communist bloc outnumbered, the 18 delegates at the third full UNCHR session ratified a non-binding document with few substantive changes. The commission standardized the declaration's language, added a preamble passage proposed by Roosevelt that blandly and harmlessly characterized the document as a "common standard of achievement," and deleted the call for nations to harmonize their own laws with the declaration's contents.[59] The amendments did not go unchallenged. Alexei Pavlov's numerous attempts to make the enforcement of civil and political rights completely and explicitly up to states failed as Western and Latin American delegates asserted that they would make the document utterly meaningless. The Soviet bloc then tried to embarrass the West by mandating state action as the primary means for individuals to secure economic and social rights. Its members argued that merely stating that everyone has a right to work, for example, meant nothing without clarifying the means by which individuals could actually obtain a job. In a major defeat for the Communists, who had centrally planned economies, the majority of nations with relatively free markets, led by England, India, and the United States, omitted all specific obligations by nations to fulfill economic and social rights, which now comprised just six of the 28 articles. The articles now merely stated that individuals possessed the rights (but without any remedies) to food, clothing, housing, a basic education, medical care, property, social security, rest and leisure, and employment opportunities.[60]

Overall, the UNCHR approved more than 80 percent of almost 50 recommendations offered by Roosevelt. The State Department had almost completed its quest for an inspiring but ultimately hollow list of basic human needs, and now it was up for the General Assembly to discuss. "Americans will find in the *Declaration* a good many things with which they are very familiar," Roosevelt reassured in a press release following the UNCHR's unanimous approval of the document (with the four Communist states abstaining). "A good deal of good, sound American tradition and law are wrapped up in it." Even Hendrick wondered if it was a truly international document. While such a result might have led to disapproval by other nations, the declaration's non-binding character and its intrinsic value as the first international human rights code combined to ensure its passage. Roosevelt tried to mitigate one of the central contradictions in

American policy by articulating the importance of her commission's work. Her press release predicted that "The Declaration, upon its approval, will become a document of moral force in the world. But it will not be legally binding upon any government."[61]

With the UNCHR united behind a favorable declaration, the State Department could now take the offensive against domestic and foreign critics of its policy of emasculation. The State Department used Roosevelt to scuttle W.E.B. Du Bois's final attempt to place the NAACP's *An Appeal to the World* before the 1948 General Assembly. The State Department offered the NAACP a consultant's spot in the upcoming General Assembly discussion of the declaration, and Executive Secretary Walter White agreed to attend. This move opened a chasm between the two men. White and a majority of the organization's board of directors had agreed to shelve the petition in favor of trying to influence the United Nations' declaration deliberations. Du Bois, infuriated that his colleagues supported what he believed to be a meaningless statement of rights, fought back. On June 30, Roosevelt told Du Bois that the State Department would not place the petition before the General Assembly as "no good could come from such a discussion," which would only embarrass Washington. Du Bois refused to give in, announcing that "one or two other nations" might be interested in submitting the document. He then sent a missive to the NAACP's board (and to the *New York Times*) that castigated Roosevelt as a major obstacle to the attainment of racial equality and excoriated White. In response, White engineered Du Bois's firing from the NAACP after four decades of service. With his nemesis gone, White now allied the NAACP with the State Department and the "positive work of the Human Rights Commission and the Declaration on Human Rights." The two-year effort to expose at the United Nations the entrenched racism in the "land of the free" ended in a maelstrom of internal bickering that almost drove the NAACP to financial ruin.[62]

The State Department concurrently tried to expose the hypocrisy of the Soviet Union, which in the UNCHR's last session had often stridently compared its human rights record favorably to those of Western nations. The specific issue was the right of Soviet nationals who married foreigners to emigrate. In mid-February 1947, Moscow decreed that such persons could no longer leave the country. Those affected included 350 Soviet wives and 65 Soviet husbands of American citizens and the Soviet wife of the son of the Chilean ambassador to Moscow. In its eagerness to censure Moscow for this practice, the United States now argued that the ECOSOC and the General Assembly *could* condemn nations for violating Articles 55 and 56 of the U.N. Charter. Chile asked the ECOSOC to deplore in principle all emigration restrictions placed on the spouses of foreigners as violations of diplomatic protocol and the general right of individuals to marry and reside with whomever they chose. Pavlov countered by not only proclaiming that Article 2(7) prohibited the United Nations from action, but also by seeking to expand the debate to encompass "the racial practice [of some nations] of prohibiting mixed marriages between persons who are subjects of the same State." Knowing that 30 states had miscegenation laws, U.S. delegate Willard Thorp had to tread carefully. After weakly rebutting that all U.N. action infringed on national sovereignty to some degree, he joined the Western bloc to defeat Pavlov's proposal. The resolution adopted by the ECOSOC on August 23 still deplored legislative obstacles to mixed marriages but condemned only spousal emigration restrictions. The United States had, for the first time, argued that a nation's domestic human rights record might be reviewed and judged by the United Nations. Cold War expediency lay behind the shift; it was not a precedent Washington sought to build upon in the future.[63]

Diplomatic cynicism also lay behind the Truman administration's effort to enlist Roosevelt's international prestige and liberal credentials to embarrass Moscow. Roosevelt's colleagues suggested that she deliver a major speech on human rights once the General Assembly convened in Paris. Harley Notter, from the Office of United Nations Affairs, wanted the address to "blast the ground from under the whole Soviet position" on issues including human rights. "I think," he continued, "we should take full initiative at last and compel the Soviets to be on the defensive." Rusk agreed and sent a detailed outline to Roosevelt, who wrote her own speech and added two divergent points. The first stated her sympathy for the Russian people, who "have more opportunity for advancement and greater security" than in any previous era and who would eventually, after losing a justified fear of foreigners, embrace those human rights "useful to them." She also frankly stated American shortcomings, "recogniz[ing] that our minorities have not yet achieved the full rights which this [Declaration] will make the essential rights of every human being." Notter opposed both additions, which muddled the contrasting "concepts of free nations and the concepts of totalitarian police states" that he sought to emphasize. Sandifer also objected to both addenda, describing the first as "inaccurate" grist for the Soviet propaganda mill and the second as erroneous because "in large areas of our country discrimination has already been practically eliminated." Roosevelt agreed to delete her first proposal, and she altered the second to describe Americans as having "some problems of discrimination but we find steady progress being made in the solution of these problems." The result was, as John Humphrey stated afterward, "a speech that had obviously been written by the State Department and ninety percent of which was devoted to an attack against the U.S.S.R."[64]

Roosevelt's address, delivered on September 28 at the Sorbonne before a large crowd, clearly showed the influence of Rusk, Notter, and Sandifer. More than half of her address compared the existence of freedom in the United States, which she defined as the fulfillment of political and civil rights, with its denial in the Soviet Union. The critical struggle of this age, predicted Roosevelt, would be between the "forces of reaction, retreat, and retrogression" and those of "democracy, freedom, and human rights." The Soviets celebrated their free press, labor unions, and equal status of citizens, but lurking behind those claims were censorship, government control, and the rule of the few over the many. "We must not be deluded by the efforts of the forces of reaction to prostitute the great words of our free tradition and thereby to confuse the struggle," she asserted. It was the duty of the United Nations, she proudly proclaimed, "to hold fast to the heritage of freedom won by the struggle of its peoples; it must help us to pass it on to generations to come." Roosevelt herself might have thought little about the address in retrospect, for she included no mention of it in her autobiography. The world's major newspapers, including the *Washington Post*, the *New York Times*, *Le Monde*, and the *London Times* did not bother to print a transcript. One nation commented on it, though. Writing in an official publication, a Soviet journalist informed his countrymen that the speech betrayed "a senile weakness for loquacity of Eleanor Roosevelt [which] has recently been combined with [an] anti-Soviet itch."[65]

In an attempt to ensure that these confrontational themes captured the world's attention, George Marshall had also addressed the General Assembly two days after it convened in Paris. In a speech entitled "No Compromise on Essential Freedoms," he provided the strongest public statement yet for the internationalization of human rights. The human rights declaration was of utmost importance, he proclaimed, because

> It is not only fundamentally wrong that millions of men and women live in daily terror of secret police, subject to seizure, imprisonment, or forced labor without just cause and without fair trial, but these wrongs have repercussions in the community of nations. Governments which systematically disregard the rights of their own people are not likely to respect the rights of other nations and other people and are likely to seek their objectives by coercion and force in the international field.[66]

Therefore, he implored the delegates gathered in the French capital liberated from Nazi domination only four years before, to "approve by an overwhelming majority the Declaration of Human Rights as a standard of conduct for all; let us, as Members of the United Nations, conscious of our own shortcomings and imperfections, join our effort in good faith to live up to this high standard." Whether or not such rhetoric was designed to isolate the Soviet Union in order to promote full-throttled support for a non-binding bill of rights in the United States and beyond, Marshall's and Roosevelt's speeches showed a new Cold War lens through which American policymakers now viewed human rights policymaking.[67]

The State Department's celebration of the declaration, though, caught the critical attention of the American Bar Association, which increasingly viewed U.N. human rights work as engendering, rather than obstructing, the spread of Soviet Communism. On September 7, 1948, in Seattle, the ABA's House of Delegates approved a report by its Committee on Peace and Law through United Nations that called for a one-year delay in U.N. passage of the declaration. The postponement was necessary due to the declaration's confusing, non-technical language and the inclusion of economic and social rights. These faults led the body to assert that the declaration "should not be in any manner approved, accepted or promulgated by or on behalf of the Government of the United States." Fearing that federal courts would apply the declaration in unpredictable ways, as had almost happened with the charter in the *Oyama* decision, the resolution also mandated that Congress approve any list of U.N. guarantees before domestic courts could utilize them. Two weeks later, newly elected ABA President Frank Holman stridently characterized the declaration as part of a scheme to "promote state socialism, if not communism, throughout the world." Decrying the failure of the press and general public to recognize this plot, he announced that it was the "immediate and important duty of lawyers to study and analyze these proposals before it is too late."[68]

Holman decided to dedicate his one-year term to exposing the constitutional evils of U.N. human rights activity. In a warning to the California State Bar Association that found publication in the *American Bar Association Journal*, he castigated the lack of Western-trained lawyers serving on the UNCHR and denigrated the "missionary spirit on the part of social and economic reformers to establish throughout the world their social and economic ideas." The declaration would ironically weaken the American Bill of Rights, he claimed, as the federal government would use the declaration's vague articles to enhance its own power (at the expense of state and local governments) and strip away civil and political liberties from citizens. Holman renewed his call for lawyers to organize in opposition to the declaration and "[do] something more than complacently [sit] by while our heritage is undermined." The nation's largest legal association soon became the severest and most vocal critic of the United Nations' human rights work. Its voices would not cry out in the wilderness for long.[69]

Past and present State Department officials mobilized to rebut Holman's opinion that the toothless declaration was a socialist Trojan horse. Hendrick, no longer one of Roosevelt's advisors, received a copy of the ABA resolution from William Ransom, the chair of the Committee for Peace and Law through United Nations. His reply, made in a personal capacity, pointed out the difficulty in drafting a document acceptable to nations of vastly different legal, political, economic, and cultural systems. "It is easy enough for a group of lawyers in the crystal clear air of Seattle to conclude that a United Nations document is unsatisfactory," he noted. He lamented that the bar had sent no observers to the UNCHR nor invited anyone involved with the declaration's drafting to brief the House of Delegates. If either had happened, Hendrick prophesied, "the Association's conclusions would have been materially changed." The double irony of advocating that the United States join the Soviet bloc in opposing the declaration and have Congress give legislative sanction to a non-binding document did not escape Hendrick's replacement, James Simsarian, who privately chastised the ABA for fundamentally misunderstanding the declaration. Undeterred, Ransom and Holman continued pleading with Secretary of State Marshall to postpone any final action by the United Nations. Their pleas fell on deaf ears, though, and the relationship between the ABA and the State Department grew increasingly bitter.[70]

The Truman administration now found itself in a dangerous situation, navigating between ABA critics who believed the declaration would do too much and Soviet and European delegates who wanted to give it more teeth. State Department officials found out how difficult a task that would be by listening to two days of criticism in the United Nations' Economic and Social Council (ECOSOC). The Soviet bloc, led by Pavlov, predictably railed against the failure to stipulate governmental responsibility in fulfilling the enumerated economic and social rights. But even U.S. allies, such as France, Turkey, and the Netherlands, demanded that the declaration impose real obligations on U.N. members, and the Dutch even proposed sending it back to the UNCHR for the attachment of implementation provisions. Other nations, including Great Britain, wanted to postpone consideration until the UNCHR had completed work on a separate binding human rights covenant. On August 26, a unanimous ECOSOC sent the unamended declaration without a recommendation to the General Assembly. Turning aside all objections expressed in the ECOSOC, Roosevelt, Sandifer, and Simsarian now decided to lobby intensively for final passage of the declaration with minimal debate and no amendment in the assembly. To accomplish these goals, they joined the non-Communist members of the assembly to oppose an expected floodgate of proposed changes to the document and obtain final passage before the body adjourned for the holidays. Roosevelt even tried to gain ideas from Humphrey, an impartial member of the Secretariat, on how to limit debate.[71]

The General Assembly's Social, Humanitarian, and Cultural Committee began discussions of the declaration the day after Roosevelt's Sorbonne speech. Other conflicts, though, distracted key delegates that Americans were trying to unify behind the declaration. Charles Malik, the UNCHR's Lebanese rapporteur, presided over the committee's deliberations as his nation's forces fought in the first Arab-Israeli War. Chinese representative P. C. Chang, suffering from heart disease, saw his Kuomintang government in the final throes of collapse. His greatest contribution to the debate now was to reassure Islamic nations that the perceived Western-based rights to freedom of marriage and religion still allowed for traditional cultural practices. Hernan Santa Cruz of Chile, another UNCHR member, worried about a failed military coup by former president Carlos Ibanez. Santa Cruz proved instrumental in forestalling a move by other Latin American nations (and the Communist bloc) to postpone discussion. A long speech by Pavlov on racial discrimination in the United States and a move by Vladimir Dedijer of Yugoslavia to apply the declaration to European colonies did not sit well with Western nations, which replied by attacking the Soviet bloc for limiting civil and political freedoms. Such sparring took time; after four weeks, the committee had only approved three articles. "To some of us," Roosevelt wrote in her *My Day* syndicated newspaper column, "it looks almost impossible that the committee will get through any worth-while work at this session." The pace picked up only after Malik used a stopwatch to enforce a three-minute rule on motions and convened nighttime sessions.[72]

Although the committee's 59 members discussed the declaration in 86 long meetings between late September and early December, few revisions resulted, which pleased the State Department. The length of debate was partially due to discussion of over 170 unsuccessful amendments proposed by Western, Latin American and Soviet bloc nations and the committee's decision to examine the declaration almost word-by-word. Despite disappointment over the length of the debate, during most of which Roosevelt remained passive and silent, the State Department succeeded in omitting articles allowing U.N. petitions and granting the right to asylum. The only real American loss was its lone negative vote on the right to work provision. Finally, on December 7 at 3:00 a.m., the committee approved the human rights declaration with no dissenting votes and seven abstentions mostly from the Soviet bloc. Three days later, after defeating a Soviet bloc motion to postpone the poll, the full General Assembly passed the document by a similar vote.[73]

The General Assembly's approval of the Universal Declaration of Human Rights amounted to a milestone in world history. For the first time, nations around the world had agreed on a voluntary code of conduct toward their own citizens. "We stand today at the threshold of a great event both in the life of the United Nations and in the life of mankind," Roosevelt hopefully told the assembly. "This declaration may well become the international Magna Charta of all men everywhere." Carton de Wiart of Belgium also described the declaration as a foundational document, for in its "moral value and authority which is without precedent in the history of the world . . . there is the beginning of a system of international law." Both its content and legal status reflected substantial American influence, not the least a desire to prevent the United Nations from interfering in the internal affairs of the United States. Roosevelt, though, refused to be carried away by the rhetoric of the moment. While walking back to her hotel after the historic vote, she felt worn out and "wondered whether a mere statement of rights, without legal obligation, would inspire governments to see that these rights were observed." Her superiors agreed. The next logical step, according to James Simsarian, the Acting Chief of the Division of United Nations Economic and Social Affairs, was to draft a binding covenant of political and civil rights "typical of those included in the first nine amendments to the United States Constitution."[74]

As State Department lawyers pondered how to proceed, though, they began to realize that they had entered a legal cul-de-sac in discussions over the declaration, the charter, and human rights abuses in South Africa and the Communist bloc. How could they square a position that privileged sovereignty over U.N. human rights enforcement if the United States now supported formulating a covenant and international condemnation of Soviet bloc oppression? Crafting a non-binding list of "guarantees" only temporarily solved the internal contradiction embedded in U.S. human rights policy. The State Department had successfully insisted that the diverse membership of the UNCHR draft a statement of American constitutional rights that the United Nations and American courts were nevertheless not allowed to enforce within the United States. Yet that international consensus that had made the declaration possible was disappearing. France, Great Britain, India, and Australia, concerned that American moves to weaken the declaration masked a skepticism toward all binding human rights commitments, commenced pressing for a covenant that would permit individual petitions and some kind of U.N. enforcement. A growing number of non-aligned, underdeveloped nations began to criticize Washington for polarizing human rights debates along Cold War lines and for refusing to attach economic and social guarantees to the covenant. It was now up to Truman's State Department to discover a synthesis of progressive and reactionary domestic pressures, Cold War imperatives, and U.S. legal doctrines that could command acceptance within the changing balance of power blocs within the United Nations.

CHAPTER 4

Opposition at Home and at the United Nations, 1948–1951

THE PASSAGE OF THE UNIVERSAL Declaration of Human Rights marked the apex of American influence within the United Nations Commission for Human Rights (UNCHR). Immediately after approving the historic document, the General Assembly gave Eleanor Roosevelt a standing ovation. Herbert Evatt, its president, proclaimed, "It is particularly fitting that there should be present on this occasion the person who, with the assistance of many others, has played a leading role in the work, a person who has raised to greater heights even so great a name—Mrs. Roosevelt, the representative of the United States of America." This outpouring of gratitude, though, was partially deceptive, for serious divisions on what to do next lurked both inside and outside the U.N. meeting rooms. The decision by the UNCHR to complete the Universal Declaration had merely postponed a simmering debate between the United States and other commission members over the content and implementation of a binding human rights covenant. The delay also gave American neo-isolationist groups, which had just begun to draft and publicize criticisms of the declaration, time to mobilize opposition to any further State Department work. Led by the American Bar Association (ABA), this opposition soon allied with conservative Midwestern and Southern legislators to defeat any human rights agreement submitted for senatorial ratification. Progressive and liberal organizations, though, were not about to cede political ground to groups that wanted to roll back the U.N. human rights program. The Truman administration had the unenviable duty of trying to satisfy both constituencies in order to keep the Democratic Party unified, while persuading U.N. members that its timid and emasculating proposals would not, in fact, weaken the covenant.[1]

By late 1950, however, this strategy came under sustained attack in the United Nations and at home. A coalition of Communist and underdeveloped, non-aligned nations, which now constituted a majority in the Economic and Social Council (ECOSOC) and the General Assembly, voted to add economic guarantees, the right of self-determination, and detailed enforcement mechanisms to the covenant. Worried that any economic provisions would undermine a free-market economy and that recognizing the right to self-determination could inspire revolts against European colonial rule, the State Department unsuccessfully opposed both measures strenuously. These amendments nonetheless prompted a growing number of U.S. congressmen and private organizations to criticize the covenant. Senator John Bricker (R-OH) and the ABA urged the United States to reject all human rights treaties, predicting that they would spread Communism, overturn segregation laws, and create a strong national government at the expense of states' rights. By the end of Truman's term in office, it was uncertain whether these challenges would force a dramatic change in American human rights policy at the United Nations.

Eleanor Roosevelt and advisors James Simsarian and Durward Sandifer could have predicted these troubles. During debates over the U.N. Charter, the State Department had believed that the Senate would vehemently object to any direct U.N. oversight of America's human rights record. In July 1947, Roosevelt met with James Hendrick, from the Division of International Organization Affairs, and Warren Austin, a former two-term internationalist Republican senator from Vermont who was now the American ambassador to the United Nations. Roosevelt sounded Austin out about the chances of senatorial ratification of a human rights covenant. According to Hendrick, Austin predicted that "there would be certain elements from among the Southern contingent and the reactionaries from other parts of the country where very strong opposition to a convention would be met." Others in the State Department expressed similar uneasiness. Legal Advisor Charles Fahy and Harley Notter and Dean Rusk of the Office of Special Political Affairs worried about the impact of the covenant on American federalism. Since the enforcement of individual rights was largely the responsibility of state and local governments (as the Supreme Court had only recently begun federalizing, or "incorporating" the Bill of Rights), they worried that the covenant would cause a far-reaching transfer of power to Washington. Well in advance of criticisms by the American

Bar Association, the State Department had identified a potential danger that necessitated careful policymaking. The prescription would be to press for an agreement with familiar content, barriers to application in the United States, and emasculated enforcement provisions, the same principles that marked American wartime planning and debates over the Declaration of Human Rights.[2]

Given the presence of a bloc within the UNCHR that was determined to craft a binding treaty after completing the declaration, State Department lawyers began to delineate a cautious U.S. position in response. The department gave Roosevelt the green light to support a covenant under two conditions. The first was that the content must remain limited to familiar civil and political claims that American law already recognized.[3] The second prerequisite was the inclusion of a federal-state article modeled after a provision in the 1946 International Labor Organization (ILO) constitution. To prevent the assumption of too much power by the federal government in enforcing workplace issues traditionally in the domain of state law, the ILO charter directed that for a federal state such as the United States, the central government was responsible for implementing only what it was constitutionally permissible to do. For other matters, it had only the responsibility to promote adherence by state and local authorities. Absent such a state's rights affirmation, the Senate would likely reject a human rights treaty as constitutionally flawed or as a tool to eradicate white supremacy as defined by state and local statutes. The downside of such an inclusion, though, was that unitary nations, whose governments could ratify treaties binding the whole *polis*, might see the article as an escape clause by federal states to avoid implementing treaties in good faith. As the State Department privileged a system of oppressive racial discrimination above human rights treaty compliance, that criticism, soon articulated by even American allies in Europe, was correct.[4]

This embrace of a federal-state article to shield systemic racial discrimination would touch off a political firestorm in Congress and the United Nations, for interagency Subcommittee on Human Rights and the Status of Women (HRW) members did not think completely through the proposal's *political* implications. If they had, several contradictions would have become apparent. If they argued that a federal-state article was necessary to protect the constitutional and racial status quo, unitary nations would charge Washington with transparent hypocrisy. If the State Department tried to deflect such attacks by claiming that the article would make no difference in the United States' implementation obligations, unitary states might wonder why it was necessary in the first place and senators from Dixie would feel betrayed. These conservative senators would have confirmation that the covenant was in their minds an unconstitutional Trojan horse that would create a powerful central government, eliminate Jim Crow, and upset the system of federalism bounded by the Tenth Amendment. Whether the State Department and liberal lawmakers could respond effectively to these concerns and anxieties remained to be seen.

In addition to the federal-state clause, the HRW lawyers examined three other ways to minimize the legal impact of a human rights treaty. The first was to limit content to rights already guaranteed under the Constitution. In eight tersely worded articles, the HRW draft mentioned suffrage; freedoms of religion, assembly, and speech; and bans on arbitrary arrest, torture, cruel and inhuman punishment, slavery, and ex post facto laws. Second would be to insert the seemingly egalitarian language of *Plessy v. Ferguson*, which would nonetheless permit segregation in public facilities throughout the South. "All persons, without distinction as to race . . . are equal before the law, and are entitled to equal protection of the law," their proposal read, accompanied by the dryly ironic observation that "the United States delegation is not in position at present to consent that the phrase 'equal protection of the law' forbids such compulsory segregation." The third strategy was to oppose all intrusive enforcement schemes that gave the Security Council, the General Assembly, or any transnational court the explicit responsibility to judge a United Nations member for its human rights actions. Alleged violations could only be discussed confidentially in small subcommittees of the UNCHR that would mediate behind closed doors. The intent, then, was to issue a proposal that simply replicated and exported the American Bill of Rights as narrowly interpreted by the U.S. Supreme Court, so that human rights violations could continue in the land of the free unabated and unchallenged.[5]

Toward this end, Secretary of State Marshall, Undersecretary of State Robert Lovett, and Dean Rusk from the State Department above all did not want to allow any enforcement body to consider grievances from alleged individual victims of human rights violations. Fearing embarrassment and harm to America's image if their own citizens petitioned the United Nations for redress, they refused to compromise despite strong internal and foreign support for such petitions. The Secretariat's 1947 Bill of Rights and reports by a subcommittee of the UNCHR on implementation permitted petitions lodged by individuals and NGOs. Even HRW members disagreed with their superiors. After asserting that one lesson they learned from discussions over the declaration was that "the difficulty with the United Nations to date has not been that it went too far but that it did not go far enough [so that] inaction has proven to be a worse danger than action," the HRW approved on October 24 a British plan that admitted individual petitions. Rusk and Lovett had the final word, though. Just one month after the NAACP's unsuccessful U.N. petition had confirmed their fears about damage to America's image, they struck all pro-petition language from Roosevelt's position papers before the UNCHR convened in late 1947.[6]

The resulting first American covenant proposal, which was really a Bill of Rights facsimile, nonetheless met with strong opposition within the top ranks of the State Department, leading to an embarrassing incident that cost Roosevelt advisor James Hendrick his job. Acting Secretary of State Robert Lovett, a realist who opposed the drafting of human rights agreements as irrelevant and naïve, did not want the United States to take the initiative on the covenant at the UNCHR's Geneva session in December. Just two weeks before the committee convened, Lovett instructed Roosevelt to delete from the U.S. draft an article on the right of individuals to participate in their government directly or through secret ballot. He worried about objections from Southern senators whose states systemically disenfranchised African Americans. Roosevelt objected strongly to the deletion, though, thinking "it would seem strange for the American delegation, in view of the guarantees in our own Constitution." Lawyers in the State Department backed her up, and Lovett backed down. Yet Lovett soon changed his mind again and decided to pull the U.S. draft entirely. In Geneva, Hendrick received a call at 3:00 a.m. to "kill the covenant." Hendrick replied that it was too late, as he had already distributed copies to the Secretariat and the press. He was punished, in his eyes, with an immediate transfer to working on the Marshall Plan. The self-proclaimed leader of the free world had pulled its draft over the right to vote in free elections. Fortunately for Washington, given its diplomatic blunder, the UNCHR's session in Geneva made little headway on the covenant due to prioritizing the declaration.[7]

Despite his strong views, Lovett could not "kill" the covenant due to strong backing in the UNCHR and lobbying by Roosevelt. She briefed her Foggy Bottom advisors after the holiday season, reporting that the smaller nations on the UNCHR were vehemently opposed to a declaration-only plan that would be meaningless without a covenant to make those rights enforceable. In response to concerns over possible Senate objections to the covenant, Roosevelt replied that a public education campaign to generate substantial support for it was critical. The theme she proposed, though, was hardly persuasive: citizens must realize "that the subject of Human

Rights, which it has been accustomed to regard as a purely domestic issue, can no longer be so regarded because it has recently become an acute
international issue." At Hendrick's invitation, Roosevelt dined with Lovett
to mollify his obstructionism. After the meal, she proceeded to debate the
merits of the covenant with the undersecretary, but the conversation became so strained that Lovett almost kicked her out of Hendrick's house.
While officially the United States remained committed to drafting a covenant, Lovett would do all he could to obstruct, including hollowing out the
American positions that Roosevelt had to advocate at the United Nations.
Tenaciously successful resistance to articles on petitions, equal protection,
and enforcement measures demonstrated Lovett's effectiveness in shaping
the recommendations emanating from the interdepartmental Committee
on International Social Policy (ISP) and from HRW.[8]

Lovett found President Truman receptive to his campaign against allowing individuals to petition the United Nations for redress. The UNCHR
Working Group on Implementation, which had met in December 1947,
endorsed the right of individuals, groups, and states to allege violations
of the proposed covenant. The move forced the Truman administration
to confront a trilemma. The United States could not simply object to a
petition article, for such a move might cause UNCHR members to call
into question American support for any convention. This might then inspire a move to insert binding language into the unfinished declaration.
Truman could simply oppose a UNCHR-drafted covenant in general, but
that would make the nation's commitment to human rights seem hollow. Or he could initial a list of guarantees that the Senate would likely
reject. Lovett in particular worried about appeals to the United Nations
by unsuccessful parties in anti-discrimination lawsuits before the federal
courts. Most in HRW agreed with him, noting that his scenario "is to invite defeat of the entire covenant" in the Senate. The Interior Department
dissented, arguing the obvious point that states could not be counted on
to report their own violations or those of their allies. Faced with internal
division, hoping to avoid international criticism, and citing the need to
"preserve the integrity of domestic jurisdiction," Truman initialed a secret statement that rejected petitions except by state parties that explicitly
agreed to allow them.[9]

Buoyed by the president's decision, Lovett continued his emasculation
crusade by scuttling a non-discrimination article. The opportunity arose
over the right of individuals to participate in government, a provision that
would mandate the enfranchisement of African Americans in the South.
Its existence deeply divided ISP members. Harry Weiss from the Labor

Department described suffrage as "a foundation of the U.S. form of government," and his agency asserted that governments faced no pressure to respect human rights if their citizens could not vote. When Hendrick warned that it was "inconceivable that the U.S. Senate would accept a covenant which included such a provision," Daniel Goldy from the Interior Department replied that its inclusion would be "good ammunition for selling the Covenant to the U.S. Senate since such a provision might furnish a peg in the UN on which to hang complaints" of Soviet persecution of dissidents. Others in ISP reminded Goldy that the Soviets would not be the only targets, for only 610,000 out of 5 million eligible African Americans in the South were registered to cast ballots. Moreover, the federal government would be found in violation for prohibiting blacks from voting in the District of Columbia. Lovett settled the impasse. He concluded that Roosevelt should not introduce such an article due to "the present situation in certain States in the U.S. and the present situation in the District of Columbia," and she should oppose its inclusion unless unilateral American opposition would be "embarrassing" in the UNCHR.[10]

Domestic political considerations and the unexpected ruling of four Supreme Court justices in the *Oyama* case that the U.N. Charter created human rights obligations on the federal government drove Lovett and Truman to change the entire covenant into a second non-binding human rights declaration. Any hint that a U.N. body could investigate, issue binding recommendations, or issue shaming judgments was completely unacceptable on legal and political grounds. They believed that enforcement began and ended with state and national laws, a position reinforced by their reading of Article 2(7) of the U.N. Charter, which would control in any event over a covenant implementation plan. They reached a consensus that the covenant should "not expand the authority of the United Nations in the human rights field." Further diluting the treaty, the two men approved a general limitation clause that allowed countries to restrict all rights in order to preserve "peace, order, security, or the promotion of the general welfare." With Lovett's and Truman's approval, the State Department forwarded these "minimum positions" to other UNCHR members in advance of the body's spring 1948 session.[11]

Far from being satisfied with a legally impotent human rights agreement that would safeguard domestic racial discrimination, the Truman administration looked for yet additional protections. In response to the *Oyama* decision, the Justice Department proposed another defense of inconsistent federal and state laws: a non-self-executing article. Under U.S. law, the federal judiciary examined a treaty's contents and the intent of its drafters to ascertain if the courts could enforce the treaty directly (making it self-executing) or if they must wait until Congress had incorporated the treaty into federal statutes (making it non-self-executing). To avoid any misinterpretation, as they worried had almost happened in *Oyama*, the Justice Department's draft article categorically stated that without implementing legislation, "no provision of the covenant shall render invalid . . . law in effect." Worried that the negative language would lead to charges that the United States was trying to avoid enforcement, ISP altered the proposal to state that any rights not already recognized in a nation's legal code would be following the passage of "appropriate legislation." Although some ISP members worried that any delay by Congress might cause "serious embarrassment," they understood the political advantages and legal reassurance such a clause might provide senators in ratification debates.[12]

Due to the presence of the United States (with Roosevelt as chair), Great Britain, France, Lebanon, China, and Chile on the eight-nation UNCHR Drafting Committee, most of the State Department's proposals for the covenant found a receptive audience. After meeting two dozen times at Lake Success in early May, the body approved unanimously a federal-state article and a non-discrimination clause that would not invalidate "separate but equal" segregation statutes. The convention also omitted the right to participate in government, much to Washington's relief. Although the group did not insert an explicit non-self-executing article, it did append a footnote stating that "the Drafting Committee agree[d] . . . that the Covenant is not self-operative." The only defeat came from strong British, Australian, and Chilean objections to a general limitation clause, which they interpreted as a giant loophole for nations to evade compliance. Instead, the committee appended to each article all of the exemptions proposed by U.N. members, which made for awkward reading. For example, given the 25 grounds listed under which governments could restrict freedom of information, it was not clear whether the covenant's purpose was to proclaim a right or to spell out how governments could deny it. Work on the covenant stopped for the rest of 1948 as the full UNCHR concentrated on putting the Declaration of Human Rights in final form.[13]

The drafting group's work on a binding treaty ironically inspired the State Department to formulate yet another way to escape the covenant's jurisdiction. The impetus was the introduction of enforcement schemes, none of which Foggy Bottom supported. The Australian plan to create a court of human rights was an unacceptable violation of national sovereignty and an unconstitutional mechanism for appeals of Supreme Court decisions. A French plan to have the General Assembly elect a special commission to hear complaints from individuals and NGOs constituted "a degree of intervention in matters deemed essentially domestic which the United States is unable to accept at this time." The State Department needed a credible but far more toothless alternative. Just two days before the UNCHR adjourned, in time to get credit without having to defend it, China and the United States jointly introduced a proposal that allowed for covenant signatories to file complaints before a body created by other parties to the treaty. If mediation did not work between the body and the alleged violator, the complaining state could sue in the International Court of Justice (ICJ). For the United States, this had little meaning, as Washington recognized the jurisdiction of the ICJ only on a case-by-case basis and not in "disputes with regard to matters which are essentially within the domestic jurisdiction of the United States of America *as determined by the United States of America.*" The State Department felt confident that the United States could sign a human rights covenant with these inclusions without controversy or delay.[14]

That feeling evaporated quickly once a very influential group of lawyers condemned any human rights treaty as unconstitutional and paradoxically dangerous to freedom. Founded in 1878, the American Bar Association was dominated by small-town, intensely conservative lawyers. The political bias existed partly due to a profession that prejudiced precedent and rarely supported challenges to the legal status quo. It also survived due to a lily-white composition. A membership form that required the disclosure of an applicant's race (a rule affirmed by the House of Delegates in 1949) all but disqualified African Americans and other minorities from joining; only 13 of 41,000 members in 1949 were black. In that same year, at its annual meeting in St. Louis, the House of Delegates debated a move to strike the de facto race requirement. A resolution, sponsored by New Jersey lawyer Adrian Unger, would have eliminated the race question on applications to join. The proposal fell on a voice vote after the chair of the rules committee told the delegates that "Negroes are now admitted to the ABA, and we believe that we have a complete right to know who is seeking admission." Not until a year later did the ABA appoint the first African American to serve on one of its numerous committees, and it would not be until 1957 that the Board of Governors officially revised its membership form, concluding that the race inquiry "served no useful purpose." The move came three months after the Harlem Bar Association called upon attorneys not to join the ABA due to its application being "an insult to the dignity of being a lawyer." Largely parochial and isolationist in principle, members, who knew about governmental affairs as much as, in the words of a past ABA president, "a titmouse knows the gestations of an elephant," chose representatives to the House of Delegates, the group's official policymaking arm. In 1948, that body showed its conservative credentials by calling for the registration of all Communists, the public exposure of any elected official who "pandered" to Communists for votes, and (until it overrode the vote the next day), the expulsion from the ABA of all who refused to take an anti-Communist loyalty oath.[15]

The House of Delegates chose Utah-born Frank Holman to lead this crusade as its annually elected president. Holman, a Rhodes scholar with a law degree from Oxford, had settled in Seattle and specialized in tax law. During the war, he chaired the Enemy Alien Hearing Board for the Western District of Washington, deciding whether citizens of Axis nations should be interned or set free. He was, in his own words, an "enthusiastic supporter" of the United Nations Charter, given that he believed that the Security Council veto and Article 2(7) protected the United States should the United Nations act as a "World Government." Yet by 1948, as a member of the ABA's Committee on Peace and Law through United Nations, he had become concerned about the actions of the human rights commission. During his one-year term as president, he became an energetic and polemical speaker, traveling widely and garnering much newspaper coverage. He continued this crusade for the next decade, visiting every state, publishing over 150 articles and pamphlets, and spending over $30,000 of his own money. His message was simple: the United Nations sought to use human rights agreements to decrease national sovereignty and create a tyrannical world government. The liberal Truman administration was either an active partner wanting to use such treaties to eliminate states' rights or an ignorant dupe of a Communist conspiracy emanating from the United Nations' Lake Success, New York, headquarters.[16]

Holman's criticisms became a catalyst for action by the American Bar Association even as the State Department moved to mend the growing rift. In February 1948, the House of Delegates passed its first resolution on the topic, opposing a court of human rights and any enforcement process that allowed individual or group petitions to U.N. agencies. Seven months later, the ABA pronounced the covenant unacceptable and asked its Special Committee on Peace and Law through United Nations to undertake ongoing analyses of future U.N. work on the treaty. It fell to James Simsarian to reply, and he strove to emphasize the common ground existing between the ABA and the State Department. Neither group approved of the covenant in its present form. He enclosed the emasculated United States-China enforcement proposal as a token of State's commitment to

U.N. non-interference and opposition to individual petitions, and he welcomed further discussion with the organization. His conciliatory tone did lead to more moderate views by the ABA's leadership. An editorial in the *American Bar Association Journal* reminded readers, using gentle words, that "deep interest in and devotion to human rights do not, however, compel a conviction that of necessity they should be summarily and inclusively dealt with by international action." Simsarian's rejoinder was correct, as agreement existed to protect states' rights and white supremacy from U.N. intrusion. The ability to maintain a working relationship with the ABA, though, depended on other nations on the human rights commission accepting these goals as well.[17]

Although Roosevelt predicted that passage of the human rights declaration would allow nations "to move on with new courage and inspiration" to complete and ratify a treaty, the new composition of the Senate called into doubt whether those words applied to the United States. The Democratic Party's gain of nine seats, which allowed it to retake control of the chamber, ironically did not bode well for the Truman administration's covenant policy. Included in the freshman class were legislators who opposed the U.N. human rights program, including Democrats Guy Gillette (IA) and J. Allen Frear (DE), while diehard isolationists such as James Eastland (D-MS), Kenneth Wherry (R-NE), and A. Willis Robertson (D-VA) were reelected handily. Yet at the same time, increased Cold War tensions might persuade these legislators to revisit their anti-covenant position. Communist coups in Eastern Europe had focused renewed attention on human rights repression. If the Truman administration could sell the covenant to the public as a measure to spotlight Communist governments' human rights shortcomings, perhaps the Senate would go along. Truman described this tyranny in his 1949 inaugural address as "subject[ing] the individual to arrest without lawful cause, punishment without trial, and forced labor as the chattel of the state. [These governments decree] what information he shall receive, what art he shall produce, what leaders he shall follow, and what thoughts he shall think." If framed as a Cold War weapon, perhaps senators from the South and West would ratify a treaty that could embarrass and condemn America's ideological enemies in an international forum.[18]

Any hope for this strategy immediately ran into contrasting opinions from conservative and liberal opponents, with the State Department caught in the crossfire. The American Bar Association's shift from a skeptical wait-and-see policy to outright hostility occurred after Secretary of State Marshall rebuffed the House of Delegates' request to postpone

American acceptance of the declaration until after Congress had given its assent. One month after U.N. adoption of the Universal Declaration, the ABA unanimously censured the State Department for hastily support- ing the proclamation and demanded that "sufficient time should be ac- corded to the lawyers and peoples of this and other Member Nations to study the text" of any covenant. In calling for "full public consideration and discussion," the statement urged a postponement of any General As- sembly approval until 1950. During the winter and spring of 1949, the Peace and Law through United Nations Committee facilitated 25 regional ABA meetings attended by hundreds of judges, lawyers, and law profes- sors, who discussed the legal and constitutional issues raised by drafts of the covenant. President Frank Holman devoted his column in the March issue of the *ABA Journal* to outlining his worries that the treaty would cede national sovereignty, create a world government, and override the Bill of Rights. Subsequent attacks on the treaty by Holman and others were so strident that it appeared to some that the ABA had "fallen into the hands of a lot of crotchety old men approaching senility [who] have little to no knowledge of international law and a general hostility to the whole pro- gram of the [State] Department."[19]

As the ABA mobilized against the covenant, State Department lawyers had to beat back attempts by the Interior and Justice departments to add even more controversial provisions before the UNCHR met in April. Ar- thur Goldschmidt, the Interior Department's delegate to the Committee on International Social Policy (ISP), wanted the treaty to apply automat- ically to all dependent territories of signatory nations. Such a position, Sandifer and Simsarian knew, would upset Great Britain, the Netherlands, and France, causing the Western alliance to fall into a disunited "Soviet trap." The ISP agreed, approving only a weak fallback position that called upon nations "to take as soon as possible the steps necessary" to apply the treaty to their colonies. Goldschmidt also strongly supported the right of individuals to petition the United Nations for redress of alleged covenant violations. Simsarian replied that Truman had shot down a similar plan a year earlier as impractical, and he added that its inclusion would make it "difficult, if not impossible, to get the approval of the Senate and thus would jeopardize the entire Covenant."[20]

State Department acceptance of these limitations only fueled the desire by covenant opponents for more concessions. In admitting the proposition that domestic law needed override protection from the covenant, Foggy Bottom was forced to argue why solutions proposed by the ABA to achieve the same ends to this problem were nonetheless unneeded. The Justice Department's

Assistant Solicitor General George Washington advanced an ABA proposal to allow Congress itself to determine which parts of the covenant the federal and state governments respectively had to implement. If added to the treaty, he believed that the clause would buttress senatorial support, for the Senate itself would determine the covenant's application to America's system of federalism. He also endorsed an ABA suggestion that would mandate Congressional legislation to implement each individual covenant provision not already provided for in domestic law. Simsarian fumed. Such a process, he exclaimed, "would be so vast that Congress would probably never finish its job" and the resulting delay would embarrass the United States internationally. Legal Advisor Jack Tate questioned Washington's motives, stating that it was "well known that the American Bar Association doesn't want a covenant at all," and that Washington's amendment was no more than an ABA "blocking tactic." In the end, the State Department overrode Justice's objections, though new Secretary of State Dean Acheson had to intervene to ensure the outcome. Whether the State Department could continue to fend off the ABA depended on political calculations of its influence in the Senate.[21]

The strategy of emasculating U.N. human rights work presented an ironic problem, though, when Washington searched for a way to criticize the human rights records of Communist nations. American delegates had maintained that the U.N. Charter's promise to promote "universal respect for, and observance of, human rights and fundamental freedoms for all" required non-interference in nations' internal affairs. Having called the Universal Declaration of Human Rights only a "declaration of basic principles" and a "common standard of achievement," the State Department had no grounds for holding other nations accountable to its terms. Yet Truman and Secretary of State Acheson wanted to hold the Soviet bloc culpable for its poor human rights record. The catalyst for condemnation was a decision by the Hungarian government to arrest Archbishop Joseph Cardinal Mindszenty on charges of treason. The Communist government had earlier banned all religious orders, and the arrest of the highest-ranking Catholic official in the country was a further attempt to eradicate organized religion. After five weeks of torture, Mindszenty's trial began on February 3, 1949. Five days later, based on "confessions" he gave under duress, the cardinal received a lifelong prison sentence. An international outcry followed, and the U.S. Senate, under pressure from Catholic voters, quickly passed a resolution urging Secretary Acheson to condemn all Eastern European Communist governments for imprisoning and killing political and religious dissenters.

At the United Nations, the governments of Bolivia and Australia cited the U.N. Charter's human rights clauses to justify placing the issue on the agenda of the upcoming General Assembly.[22]

Although he knew that cosponsoring the resolution could gain support from conservative organizations such as the ABA, Acheson opposed setting a precedent for U.N. oversight of an alleged human rights violation. The Soviet bloc and non-aligned nations might then sponsor a resolution denouncing American racial discrimination. Besides, the State Department had consistently argued that the charter's Article 2(7) prevented the United Nations from addressing human rights abuses in specific nations. Acheson, though, found a way out of his dilemma. The secretary of state accused the governments of Bulgaria, Hungary, and Romania of violating World War II peace treaties, under which they promised to guarantee "the enjoyment of human rights and of the fundamental freedoms, including freedom of expression, of press and publication, of religious worship, of political opinion, and of public meeting." This move activated the treaties' dispute resolution process, with the first step being direct negotiations between the parties. If those failed, the Soviet, British, and American ambassadors in the three Eastern European countries would consult on what to do next.[23]

Acheson concurrently, but carefully, brought the topic before the United Nations. Two days after notifying the three Communist governments, he asked Warren Austin, the U.S. General Assembly delegate, to place the item on the body's agenda for discussion. Acheson carefully noted that the topic fell within the General Assembly's purview under Articles 34 and 35 of the charter, which allowed for any nation to bring to the body "any situation which might lead to international friction or give rise to a dispute." He deliberately did not invoke the human rights provisions (Articles 55 and 56) of the document, which the State Department interpreted as circumscribed anyway by Article 2(7). The gambit worked, as Austin convinced the delegates from Bolivia and Australia to frame the item as an interstate treaty dispute, and not an abridgement of the charter's human rights provisions.[24]

State Department General Counsel Ben Cohen continued the avoidance of precedents that could rebound against the United States. He prosecuted the indictment of Hungary and Bulgaria (Romania, for some reason, having been temporarily omitted) in the assembly's Special Political Committee. After the two countries categorically denied the charges and invoked Article 2(7) to stop further discussion, Cohen awkwardly asserted the committee's right to discuss and pass judgment on human rights violations. "Generally speaking," he explained, "no organ of the United Nations could impose corrective action in such [human rights–related] matters if there had been no breach of the peace or threat to international peace and if there was no treaty providing for such action." In this case, though, the commission of serious treaty violations allowed the General Assembly to debate the issue. Although the United States had argued the opposite view in regards to a treaty protecting Indian laborers in South Africa, Cohen did not look backward. He asked for the United Nations' endorsement of the dispute resolution processes as spelled out in the treaties. A week later, the full General Assembly passed a resolution, with only the Communist bloc dissenting, that expressed "deep concern at the grave accusations made against the Governments of Bulgaria and Hungary regarding the suppression of human rights and fundamental freedoms in those countries" in violation of their treaty obligations. It called upon Bulgaria and Hungary to co-operate with the peace treaty procedures for settling disputes. Cohen had affirmed the hollowness of the charter's human rights articles.[25]

Careful observers of the UNCHR's 1949 session could detect a subtle backlash against such hypocritical and cynical U.S. initiatives. With the human rights declaration approved and the covenant first on the UNCHR's agenda, the State Department could see what other countries thought of its push for an ineffectual treaty. It became apparent quickly that nations in the Middle East and East Asia, led by India, were prepared to pursue an independent path on human rights issues. In the General Assembly's vote to censure Hungary and Bulgaria, nine nations had abstained. Rejecting the bitter partisanship of the major powers, the leaders of these non-aligned nations embraced a common diplomatic front based on the ideals of self-determination, peaceful coexistence, and national sovereignty. The history of many of these states as colonial possessions that now sought independence and economic development bred support for U.N. human rights work, though in two ways that would create problems for the United States. In supporting rapid decolonization, the non-aligned bloc viewed the self-determination of peoples as a fundamental human right. Also, economic underdevelopment in the Middle East and Asia made leaders protective of their own valuable natural resources, such as oil, while it also encouraged them to press for the recognition of economic rights that they believed all governments owed to their citizens. It might seem paradoxical that countries with the least wealth wanted such guarantees until it is understood that these promises could provide leverage for development assistance from the First World. This embrace of independent economic nationalism, a call for a global redistribution of wealth, and identification with a strong state using centralized economic planning to guarantee a minimum standard of living provided little overlap with American policy principles.

The human rights commission's fifth session in May and June 1949, therefore, saw much maneuvering between Communist, non-Communist, and non-aligned nations. The Soviet Union and its allies made no secret of their objection to any covenant on sovereignty grounds. If there was to be a covenant, though, they and the non-aligned nations voting together might be able to add guarantees of self-determination and economic rights, much to the consternation of Washington. Several decisions reflected the fluid balance of power. After the body had elected Eleanor Roosevelt as chair, the U.S.S.R. predictably moved to strike all covenant implementation measures. Once that effort failed, the commission fractured over allowing individual and group petitions. Unwilling to go beyond State's 1948 mediation proposal, Roosevelt voted with Great Britain and the Soviet bloc to defeat, by one vote, a pro-petition resolution supported by the non-aligned nations of India and Lebanon. Foreshadowing another bitter debate, the Western bloc defeated by only one vote (with most non-aligned nations abstaining) a Soviet effort to attach economic and social rights to the covenant. The committee was unable to agree on whether the covenant should apply automatically to the colonies of signatories; it also deadlocked on the United States–sponsored federal-state article. It decided to send texts of both without a recommendation to member governments for study and comment.[26]

The UNCHR spent the rest of the spring polishing the list of civil and political rights from its 1948 draft. Roosevelt forcefully lobbied to add an open-ended general limitation clause that allowed derogations "reasonably necessary for the rights and freedoms of others or for national security or for the general welfare." When the British objected that such a clause would render the entire document meaningless, Roosevelt replied that inserting the over one hundred specific exceptions proposed by various governments "would give the impression that the limitations were being emphasized rather than the right itself." As the UNCHR waded through each article, though, she became satisfied enough with the article-specific exceptions to withdraw her overall limitation proposal, which had little support from other nations anyway. The UNCHR also unanimously approved the covenant's first non-self-executing article due to Roosevelt's repeated promise that its inclusion would "in no way lessen the obligation for any State to adopt legislative or other measures" to enforce the covenant within its territory. The commission agreed to continue working on the document when it reconvened in 1950, and it was now apparent that the non-aligned bloc held the balance of power for approving covenant amendments.[27]

This dynamic, repeated in other U.N. organs as well on other topics, worried the Truman administration, which began to see its Jim Crow edifice as an obstacle for alliances with the increasingly important non-aligned nations. The State Department grew concerned that segregation and racially motivated violence might make peoples of color around the world cynical and suspicious of American claims of moral and political leadership. Yet Congress, with Dixiecrats entrenched in key leadership positions, had bottled up President Truman's legislative initiatives drawn from *To Secure These Rights*. An initiative to outlaw the poll tax passed the House of Representatives in July 1949, but the Senate did not take it up due to John Stennis's (D-MS) influential seat on the Rules Committee. The House Judiciary Committee sat on a bill to make lynching a federal crime, as did the Senate's leadership once a proposal made it out of committee in June. Hearings on a permanent Fair Employment Practices Committee (FEPC) dragged on for months in the lower chamber, and Speaker Sam Rayburn (D-TX) stood determined to block any full House vote. If this political deadlock was to be broken, the State Department might have a key role to play. Its leaders were in a unique position to argue that delays in passing landmark civil rights legislation could hurt the United States in prosecuting the Cold War and influencing neutralist nations.

Anticipating the need for a change necessitated by Cold War geopolitics, the State Department took awkward and tentative steps to document and lobby for civil rights reforms at home. HRW members, recognizing that Soviet condemnation of U.S. racial discrimination might make inroads among non-aligned countries, had prepared a long and detailed statement for the 1949 UNCHR session. In the drive for equality, the statement flatly asserted, "We are well aware that there are many points at which we have not yet reached perfection. But our people are concerned about our inadequacies, and we try to correct them." The rest of the apology outlined statistical evidence documenting African American employment, entrepreneurial, political, and cultural achievements. The conclusion turned the focus against those nations that had attacked the United States by asking, "Why is it that the very countries that are criticizing the United States are not progressing in the expansion of human rights and fundamental freedoms in their own countries? We understand why, instead, they would wish to advertise and make much of our problems and to draw the shroud over their own." Two ironies marked this effort, though, betraying sloppy research practices. The main source of statistical evidence, the 1947 *Negro Year Book*, relied on numbers from the early 1940s. Washington was thus using outdated (and unfavorable, premobilization) figures to demonstrate postwar racial progress; the research staff could have included recent and more positive statistics from the President's Committee on Civil Rights. The second irony was that the only other source cited was a 1948 article by W.E.B. Du Bois, the very civil rights pioneer who had scandalized the State Department two years earlier by presenting the NAACP's petition to the United Nations Secretariat.[28]

The State Department's lawyers also tried to burnish America's overseas image by prodding the legislative and judicial branches to fight racial discrimination. Given that the 81st Congress was a hostile audience for President Truman's reforms, Legal Advisor Ernest Gross faced suspicion when explaining the damage that delay and obstructionism inflicted on the nation's image abroad. To a House committee holding hearings on the FEPC, Gross bluntly stated that the department was "frequently embarrassed by the apparent conflict between the principles of nondiscrimination and the protection of human rights . . . and instances of discrimination which occur in this country." His statement provided a vivid contrast to the vague and dismissive responses that the State Department had sent to the President's Committee on Civil Rights just two years earlier. In addition, its lawyers now assisted Attorney General J. Howard McGrath and Solicitor General Philip Perlman in filing amicus briefs in civil rights cases. The first example of this partnership, *Henderson v. United States*, tested segregation in interstate railroad dining cars. Segregation "has furnished material for hostile propaganda," Perlman wrote to the U.S. Supreme Court, and such laws "raised doubts about our sincerity even among friendly nations. . . . Our position and standing before the critical bar of world opinion are weakened if segregation not only is practiced in this country but also is condoned by federal law." The brief quoted condemnations of Jim Crow by Soviet and Polish delegates at the United Nations.[29]

Now on record as opposing segregation, Secretary of State Dean Acheson gained some moral high ground from which to continue the condemnation of Bulgaria, Hungary, and Romania for human rights violations. After the three nations refused to meet and denied Acheson's allegations by claiming a sovereign right to punish Fascists and enemies of "democracy," Undersecretary of State James Webb invoked the second stage of the treaty dispute resolution process. It required the creation of a commission for each nation, each staffed by an American, a delegate from the Communist nation involved, and a third chosen either by the two feuding parties or the U.N. Secretary-General. The bodies could issue binding judgments on all complaints, and appeals would go to the U.N. Security Council. After Webb announced that his government would "press for a full hearing" on human rights abuses behind the Iron Curtain, though, the Soviet Union refused to meet with American diplomats, and Romania, Hungary, and Bulgaria declined to appoint representatives to their peace treaty commissions.[30]

With the complaint procedures deadlocked, Secretary Acheson announced that he would return to the General Assembly to discuss what to do next. Benjamin Cohen once again took to the floor of the assembly's Special Political Committee for an impassioned speech. The three nations have "an avowed public policy to deny to the people the right freely to express views on political, cultural, scientific, and even religious matters, unless such expression is within the very narrow limits of conformity with current doctrines of a one-party regime responsible not to the people themselves but to the Communist high command." He reviewed the pattern of human rights violations that had occurred since he had last spoken and summarized the obstacles to fulfilling the dispute resolution process as outlined in the peace treaties. Cohen then asked the assembly to authorize an International Court of Justice advisory opinion on whether the commission could assess charges of human rights abuses absent representatives of the appellant nation. Cohen promised that the United States would accept as binding the ICJ advisory opinion. In response to Communist claims of American human rights abuses, including segregation, Cohen weakly declared that at least the United States was "not turning back the clock of human freedom." The Political Committee and the General Assembly both overwhelmingly approved the ICJ request.[31]

The State Department now worried about payback. The price for having non-aligned nations endorse the censure of Eastern Europe could be the inclusion of economic and social rights in a fully binding human rights covenant that allowed for individual and NGO petitions. The UNCHR had tabled a move to add economic and social guarantees under the condition that the body would discuss them at its 1950 session. Roosevelt, in her report to Secretary of State Dean Acheson that touched upon her husband's New Deal programs, commented that a treaty limited to civil and political rights "will not mean a great deal to people, not even in our own country because these rights have been proved to be of little value when not accompanied by some measure of economic and social rights." Acheson replied in a non-committal fashion, pointing out that the State Department recognized the "general significance" of economic and social guarantees.

It fell to HRW's members to thread a particularly narrow needle. Its members had to create minimum standards to satisfy the developing world, allow for their fulfillment by free-market economics, omit any responsibility of the First World to redistribute its wealth, and obtain the support of conservatives in Congress. HRW also had to decide whether to pass along the weak American enforcement proposal that relied on interstate mediation in the face of strong calls for petition mechanisms. Finally, given American Bar Association complaints, lobbying other nations to accept federal-state, non-self-executing, and weak non-discrimination provisions despite their prior criticism was a critically important task.[32]

The solution of a cafeteria approach to human rights treaties came about surprisingly easily. Roosevelt proposed to Acheson that the UNCHR place the petition, non-self-executing, federal-state, and non-discrimination articles in separate protocols that nations could accept or reject individually. Another optional protocol would mandate that colonial powers apply the covenant to their dependent territories. Steering these articles into appendices provided several political and legal advantages to the United States. The scheme could lead to UNCHR approval of the covenant quickly and with minimal disagreement in 1950. It would allow the United States to introduce specific proposals, thus allying the United States with the developing world, even if Washington itself had no plans to sign them. For example, the State Department would ascertain first if there was a majority vote in the UNCHR to delete all references to petitions. If there was not, Washington would introduce, either directly or through another government, its proposal for a petition system in a separate annex and reap either public or private credit. This ad hoc approach to treaty adoption would also permit the Senate to decide what pieces to approve in order to maintain the needed two-thirds majority vote for covenant ratification. On the larger issue of economic and social rights, which might be too important for some nations to place in an optional protocol, HRW members offered the possibility of their placement in a separate treaty.[33]

The State Department settled upon this strategy just in time to meet the most serious broadside yet fired by the nation's largest group of lawyers. Carl Rix, the chair of the ABA's Peace and Law Committee, prominent Milwaukee lawyer, and past ABA president, asserted that the covenant could recast the current balance of state and federal jurisdiction. If the United Nations and the federal government were ultimately responsible for enforcing civil and political rights, the existing sovereignty of nations and of the 48 states would diminish. Rix also speculated that federal courts would rule parts of the covenant self-executing, and thus allow unelected judges, under the Constitution's assertion that treaties "shall be the supreme law of the land," to invalidate any acts of Congress, state laws, and state constitutions found inconsistent with the treaty.[34]

He furthermore argued that a federal-state clause would be legally impotent due to the 1920 Supreme Court decision in *Missouri v. Holland*. President Woodrow Wilson and British Prime Minister David Lloyd George, concerned about the possible extermination of avian species that flew between the United States and Canada, signed a treaty in 1916 that imposed hunting restrictions, and Congress subsequently passed implementing legislation. The state of Missouri sued, citing the Tenth Amendment and the usurpation of federal authority into what had historically been within state purview. In *Missouri v. Holland*, though, a 7–2 majority upheld the statute, as made pursuant to the treaty, as a valid exercise of the Constitution's treaty-making powers. Rix's concern, then, was that any legislation passed by Congress to enforce a human rights covenant would be upheld under the *Missouri* precedent, even if a federal-state clause existed. "Leviathan," he wrote sarcastically in the *ABA Journal*, "with deep concern for the food supply of wild duck for a suffering people, blithely asserted that there is no limit in the United States to the treaty-making power and legislation enacted thereon unless it is prohibited by the Constitution." This trend, once unleashed by the United Nations, would overturn over one hundred years of constitutional precedents that gave the states almost exclusive jurisdiction in defining permissible criminal procedures, religious expression, and limits on speech, press, and assembly. Given these dour and dire possibilities, he hypothesized, only an amendment to the Constitution that made all treaties non-self-executing would safeguard the federalist status quo. His article proved to be a clarion call for a movement that itself would embrace a revolutionary new doctrine based upon severely limiting the foreign affairs powers of the national government.[35]

State Department lawyers scrambled awkwardly to reply to Rix's legal analysis. Marjorie Whiteman wrote to Eleanor Roosevelt that the contents of the covenant would not "supercede the rights of the state" and therefore the "dividing line between State and Federal jurisdiction would remain just where it is." This was true, she wrote, because human rights had never before been considered matters of international concern, and their insertion in a treaty would not (despite the *Missouri* precedent) make them so. It would be up to individual state legislatures to enforce the covenant, she argued, and the federal government would have "no way of compelling the States to take action to implement the Covenant." She and her colleagues at State backed a federal-state article only for political reasons, so that the

State Department could reassure "the Senate that the Covenant does not disturb States' rights." When brilliant University of Chicago political science professor Quincy Wright challenged Whiteman by asking why she would fight for a legally meaningless article, James Simsarian offered to defend what he called the "indispensible" federal-state provision. Whiteman, though, refused to approve the reply, and Legal Advisor Jack Tate warned that "we should not endeavor to argue the matter of federal and state jurisdiction with a man like Quincy Wright." She substituted a note blandly thanking Wright for an "interesting letter." The State Department and the ABA now ironically agreed that the federal-state article would be meaningless, but for different reasons. The ABA believed that the federal courts would ignore it, thus trampling states' rights. The State Department now believed it was unnecessary as a point of law, as federal courts would rule that the covenant did not alter the balance of state and federal jurisdiction despite Wright's persuasive analysis.[36]

Given the growing backlash against American policy at home and in the UNCHR, Durward Sandifer, Ernest Gross, and Dean Acheson carefully prepared the United States' covenant positions for the 1950 UNCHR session. A coalition of Western and developing nations had held together to pass the Universal Declaration of Human Rights and to condemn human rights violations in Eastern Europe. Whether the alliance would embrace American proposals for a covenant limited to civil and political rights, weak enforcement articles, and separate protocols for controversial items was uncertain.[37] One problem was the expected walkout of all delegates from the Soviet Union in protest of the U.N. seating of Taiwan as the legitimate representative of China. While Roosevelt no doubt breathed a sigh of relief that meetings would no longer be disrupted by long propaganda speeches, the United States lost two votes for keeping enforcement schemes weak and excluding petitions from NGOs and individuals. She expected tough opposition from the developing world, which held nine of the 16 remaining seats in the UNCHR, on the issue of including economic and social rights. Even usually reliable Great Britain was in revolt, believing that a non-self-executing article was unnecessary since, its delegates professed, nations should not ratify a treaty *unless and until* their domestic laws adapted to the treaty's requirements. Contending that it would be impossible to reform U.S. law before ratification, Acheson warned that such a view would prevent American accession to the covenant.[38]

The 1950 UNCHR session marked the climax of U.S. human rights influence over the covenant drafting process. The American-British enforcement plan, which allowed only states to bring charges before ad hoc human rights committees, received much criticism. France and several non-aligned nations attacked the committees' inability to issue binding recommendations or independently investigate alleged violations. Observers from the International League for the Rights of Man and World Jewish Congress faulted the omission of petitions. In a compromise that Roosevelt brokered, the UNCHR created a permanent Human Rights Committee of seven chosen by state parties to discuss complaints against covenant parties. The committee could only mediate and publish a report; it could not issue a binding ruling or send disputes to other U.N. bodies for action. Led by the United States and Western Europe, the UNCHR voted to allow the committee to receive petitions by NGOs and individuals only if their home countries had ratified a separate protocol. Having run out of time to consider economic and social rights, the UNCHR voted, with only two dissenting, to place them in a separate treaty in 1951. Before adjourning in mid-May, after two months of meetings, the UNCHR approved the covenant on civil and political rights. The only disappointment for Roosevelt was that members ran out of time to attach a federal-state clause. The decisions for two covenants and an optional protocol made it appear that she had persuaded neutral nations to embrace key American positions.[39]

Yet too many compromises engendered dissatisfaction, and few in the UNCHR or the Secretariat were happy with the draft treaty. Just two weeks into the UNCHR's session, evidence of frustration and polarization appeared. Angry that the "covenant was being ruined by the excessive prudence of Mrs. Roosevelt's State Department advisors," John Humphrey of the Secretariat's apolitical Human Rights Division crafted an unprecedented speech that castigated the weak implementation machinery, general limitation article, and the exclusion of economic and social rights. His assistant, Henri Laugier, gave the address to a group of NGOs. When Roosevelt heard about it, she publicly scolded him for "comprom[ising] the future of the covenant" and held a closed session of the UNCHR to punish the indiscretions of an ideally invisible and nonpartisan Secretariat advisor. Unexpectedly, though, delegates leaped to Laugier's defense. The incident added to existing bitter feelings between veteran UNCHR leaders Roosevelt and P. C. Chang, who opposed petitions, and René Cassin and Hansa Mehta, who favored them. The decision to approve a covenant of only civil and political rights due to time constraints opened fissures too. Even Roosevelt had become somewhat disillusioned, as she narrated in a *My Day* column after the Human Rights Commission had adjourned:

Some members of the Commission think that if the first Covenant does not cover as many rights and freedoms as the Declaration, then it will hurt the Declaration to have a first Covenant. They would prefer to let it die, or, string it along in the Human Rights Commission in order to keep it from the General Assembly, and finally, to the countries for ratification.

There are other members in the Commission, who, for one reason or another, have no desire ever to see a Covenant written. Anything that binds them legally would be very awkward. There is still another group who want a Covenant ultimately, but only when it reaches the perfection they desire. Until that time they think that the subject can be kept alive, and remain a source of interest to all sorts of people, even if nothing particular happens during the next year or two. This is the most difficult group for me to understand since, realistically, I know so well how easy it is for people to forget all about a subject which is not constantly in the news and brought to their attention.[40]

Roosevelt and the State Department soon encountered similar divisions among liberal human rights activists and reactionary lawyers and congressmen who all were displeased with the latest covenant draft coming out of Lake Success. The American Federation of Labor, the Catholic Association for International Peace, the American Jewish Committee, and the American Association for the United Nations (AAUN) all implored James Simsarian and Marjorie Whiteman to allow for individual petitions and complaints from NGOs. Rabbi Irving Miller of the American Jewish Congress warned that a covenant without the ability to petition would be "gravely defective and likely to remain largely ineffective." These and other organizations brought such pressure upon the State Department that Kotschnig, Sandifer, and Tate proposed a compromise: the State Department would not change its opposition to including the right to petition in the covenant, but it would support (though not propose) a General Assembly resolution asking the UNCHR to study the issue further. This brush-off did not satisfy some NGOs, which proceeded to lodge objections with the secretary-general. The International League for the Rights of Man, perhaps the oldest human rights organization in the United States, requested that the UNCHR add the right to make complaints "on the grounds that the right to petition is an elementary right of human beings and constitutes the very basis of any effective system of implementation." The World Jewish Congress pointed out that omitting petitions would be a "retrograde step in international law," as the League of Nations had accepted NGO submissions.[41]

At the same time, critics on the right who privileged state sovereignty over U.N. human rights intervention received a shocking jolt from a California state appeals court. On April 24, three judges unanimously struck down the 1920 Alien Property Initiative Act that banned the ownership of property in the state by Japanese aliens. Their ruling in *Sei Fujii v. California* did not rely on the American or Californian constitutions or any judicial precedent. Instead, the court struck down the law based on Article 17 of the Universal Declaration of Human Rights, on the understanding that the right to property guarantee was an elaboration of the U.N. Charter's human rights clauses. Therefore, the justices ruled, "clearly such a discrimination against a people of one race is contrary both to the letter and to the spirit of the Charter, which, as a treaty, is paramount to every law of every state in conflict with it. The Alien Land Law must therefore yield to the treaty as the superior authority." Reaction came quickly. *New York Times* Washington bureau chief Arthur Krock wondered if domestic courts could cite the charter to implement Truman's civil rights program. If he had known about the *Sei Fujii* decision in 1945, Senate Foreign Relations Committee Chair Tom Connally stated, he would have voted against charter ratification. Republican Representative Paul Shafer (R-MI) remarked to his colleagues: "Our sovereignty is too sacred to be lightly tossed away for a mess of international pottage." To Frank Holman, the lesson was that "blank check" human rights treaties could allow a foreigner to become president, overturn race-based immigration quotas, and change the federal government "from a republic to a socialistic and centralized state." The opposition had now turned angry, but its leaders stopped short of embracing Carl Rix's constitutional amendment to ban any domestic enforcement of human rights treaties.[42]

Roosevelt and her advisors, caught off-guard by *Sei Fujii* and its accompanying backlash, struggled to defend their work. Complicating this task, the Committee on International Social Policy (ISP) had disbanded due to poor attendance caused by most of its work falling to its subcommittees such as Human Rights and the Status of Women. With ISP's dissolution, though, the HRW stopped meeting too. While this allowed for a more efficient decision-making process as other Cabinet departments no longer participated in discussions, it also placed the entire policymaking burden on Acheson's staff in a time of political turmoil. The alleged spying of Alger Hiss and the persecution of the "China Hands" had already damaged the State Department's credibility in Congress. In an attempt to protect continued work on the covenant, James Simsarian and Walter Kotschnig suggested that the respected and admired Eleanor Roosevelt testify before a subcommittee of the Senate Foreign Relations Committee. Durward San-difer and Harley Notter rejected the suggestion, fearing Senator Connally's "adverse attitude" and entangling the covenant in the *Sei Fujii* backlash.[43]

Having rejected an overture to the Senate, the State Department turned to public statements and private legal analysis to silence its critics. James Simsarian penned an implicit reply to critics when he reviewed the 1950 UNCHR session for the *U.S. Department of State Bulletin*. He described the covenant as "limited to basic civil and political rights well-known in American tradition and law." He attached the weak American plan for in-terstate complaints and promised that the federal government would abide by the restrictions of a federal-state article even if it were omitted from the treaty. He explained, "Although the United States is not prepared to undertake all the obligations of the Covenant . . . [it will] undertake as many of the obligations of the covenant as are determined in accordance with the constitutional processes of the United States to be appropriate for federal action."

A second strategy was to overturn the basis of the *Sei Fujii* decision. After learning that the Justice Department planned to file an appellate amicus brief in the California Supreme Court, State Department Deputy Legal Advisor Jack Tate submitted a memo arguing for the non-self-executing nature of the charter and Universal Declaration. He argued that the U.S. delegation to the San Francisco Conference "never in the least contemplated that the provisions of the Charter would of them-selves be held by United States courts to invalidate any existing domestic legislation." One event gave Tate some hope. The U.S. Supreme Court de-cided three cases on segregation in graduate education, railroad dining cars, and law schools on June 5. None of the three decisions referenced the U.N. Charter or the Universal Declaration; they relied instead on the Fourteenth Amendment to overturn Jim Crow statutes. This was a dou-ble-edged sword, though, for the banning of white supremacist law was bound to agitate Southern Democrats and make them even more hostile to U.N. human rights activism.[44]

At this critical juncture in the domestic political battle, a coalition of Communist and developing nations in the Economic and Social Coun-cil caused the State Department a severe setback. Instead of sending the covenant draft to the General Assembly without comment, as the United States had proposed, a two-vote majority decided to undertake a discus-sion of "broad aspects" of the treaty for two weeks in July and August. American positions on controversial articles now came under fire. With general covenant dissatisfaction still running high, a majority in ECOSOC proposed that the full General Assembly set policy on five covenant issues: the general limitation article, implementation procedures, economic and social rights, and the federal-state and non-self-executing provisions. Roosevelt, Sandifer, and Simsarian agreed that a discussion of these principles would be disastrous, as the Western bloc was even more outvoted in the sixty-member assembly. The American position lost, though, and ECOSOC voted by a large margin on August 9 to ask the General Assembly for guidance. After only six of the 18 members in ECOSOC supported the UNCHR's lopsided vote to drop economic and social rights from a draft covenant, U.S. delegate John Cates darkly noted, "I am convinced that we must have a complete review of our whole position on the Covenant."[45]

The State Department had six weeks to prepare for what promised to be a bruising General Assembly gathering in Lake Success. On August 19, Washington contacted all of its embassies in non-Communist nations. Foreign Service officers were to discreetly lobby governments to support only a general discussion of the covenant, with no votes or resolutions taken by the assembly. On the advisory questions, governments were to be briefed on the basic positions of the United States: the State Department was "basically satisfactory" with the covenant as written, strongly favored adding a federal-state article, desired that economic and social rights go into a separate covenant, and embraced the implementation plan already in the treaty. Over the next few weeks, replies poured in from diplomatic outposts. The strongest agreement came from Taiwan and, tellingly, South Africa, which was in the process of institutionalizing its version of Jim Crow following the 1948 victory of the Nationalist Party. But even U.S. allies dissented. Great Britain and Denmark, while sympathetic to some of the American positions, did not think it helpful to avoid policy votes in the General Assembly. Absent a trail of votes, these governments believed, it would be impossible for the UNCHR to craft a treaty that would find approval in its parent body. Momentum in favor of a limited and innocuous human rights covenant along American lines was fast disappearing.[46]

The growing sense of alarm felt within the corridors of the Old Executive Office Building that housed the State Department had other roots as well in the summer of 1950. The start of the Korean War and the subsequent approval by President Truman of NSC-68, the Cold War blueprint for responding to Communist aggression, made American foreign policy more focused on military confrontation than diplomatic compromise. A growing domestic campaign against the Genocide Convention, then before the Senate, generated doubts about the ratification chances of the far broader covenant. Adding to the disillusionment was an International

Court of Justice advisory ruling on July 18 against the United States in its human rights dispute with Hungary, Bulgaria, and Romania. The peace treaty mediation system could not legally proceed, the ICJ decided, until all parties to the dispute had appointed the necessary three members. As the three Communist nations had refused to do so, valid commissions could not convene. The decision forced Acheson to stop using the World War II treaties to condemn human rights abuses. Backed into a corner, he now also cast off America's past reluctance to involve the General Assembly in judging a nation's human rights record. Acheson told the press, "These governments . . . should be made to feel the full weight of the condemnation of all free peoples which their actions provoke."[47]

The 1950 fourth session of the General Assembly, which passed resolutions on human rights in Eastern Europe, South Africa, and the covenant, marked a continuing decline in American human rights leadership. The session started well with quick action following the ICJ decision on Eastern Europe. Sandifer and Simsarian proposed that the assembly pass a censure resolution. In a blistering speech before the Ad Hoc Political Committee, Benjamin Cohen defended a censure resolution by proclaiming that the three Communist nations "have been as contemptuous of the General Assembly and of what its members have been striving to do in support of the principles of the Charter as they have been of the elementary principles of freedom of their own people." The United Nations' main body had, therefore, the "right and duty to condemn in no uncertain terms this default of the Bulgarian, Hungarian, and Romanian Governments and to expose their bad faith before world public opinion." On November 3, the assembly voted 40 to 5 with 12 abstentions to pass Resolution 385(V), which "condemned the willful refusal" of the three governments to carry out their treaty obligations and for acting "callously indifferent to the sentiments of the world community." James Frederick Green called the statement "one of the most unequivocal condemnations of a state ever made by an international organization," though its lack of reference to the United Nations' own human rights powers betrayed the weakness of that very international organization.[48]

Despite this "victory," the State Department failed to persuade the United Nations to move slowly against South Africa for its continued discrimination against Indian nationals. In May 1949, the assembly had invited India, Pakistan, and South Africa to hold a round table conference. Preliminary talks yielded a tentative agenda: South Africa wished to discuss a decrease in its Indian population, while India and Pakistan favored the removal of laws that discriminated against their nationals. Passage by Pretoria in June

1950 of the Group Areas Act, which prohibited non-whites from owning land and living in certain urban areas, dashed India's and Pakistan's hopes for productive talks. Indian Prime Minister Jawaharlal Nehru hoped the assembly would ask South Africa to rescind the law pending the start of trilateral discussions. The U.S. delegation knew that agreeing with Nehru would please the non-aligned bloc, in which India played a leading role and whose vote it coveted in the United Nations. Washington also saw the importance of backing an Asian state as the Cold War had expanded to the Korean peninsula. With China and the Soviet Union seeking political influence in the region, they would no doubt seize upon an American vote for apartheid as a valuable propaganda opportunity. Yet deserting South Africa, a staunch anti-Communist friend and supporter of American intervention in Korea, would cause other allies to wonder about American loyalty. Negotiations with Pretoria were also in a critical phase over buying uranium ore for U.S. nuclear stockpiles, which NSC-68 had singled out for massive enlargement. The key, then, was to use American influence "in the direction of avoiding extreme positions which would exacerbate the conflict without improving the lot of the Indian population in South Africa."[49]

How to accomplish this was another matter, as demonstrated in a long and tense U.S. delegation meeting on November 10. Henry Cabot Lodge, sensing an opportunity to take action on an issue "which symbolized our Achilles' heel before the world . . . [and] to overcome some of the grave disadvantages under which our country labored because of the civil rights question," agreed with India and refused to defend segregation. Cohen replied that Lodge "would be walking on hot coals" with that position. Having shepherded the condemnation of human rights violations in Eastern Europe through an assembly committee, Cohen warned that on the one hand, "we did not want the Indians to feel we were unsympathetic; on the other, we could not let the domestic jurisdiction issue get out of hand." John Foster Dulles, noting America's own segregationist record and Senate inaction on the Genocide Convention, remarked that "we could not be so righteous about this case." "We have a beam or two in our own eyes," Assistant Secretary of State John Hickerson added. The group reached an awkward compromise after Lodge steadfastly refused to vote for any resolution that did not explicitly condemn apartheid. The delegation would simply try to get the parties talking once again.[50]

The plan only partially worked, as the resolution passed by the Ad Hoc Political Committee included two problematic statements that antagonized South Africa. The first, located in the preamble, stated the rather obvious truth that the system of apartheid was based upon the principle of racial discrimination. Even more controversial was a clause calling upon South Africa to suspend enforcement of the Group Areas Act. Lodge had abstained in a vote on the preambular clause and had to be strong-armed to cast a negative vote on the latter component, but the delegation argued about whether to continue these positions in the full General Assembly plenary. Cohen now argued in favor of both, pointing out that the resolution nonetheless called for the resumption of talks, and they were unlikely to resume if the Group Areas Act remained in force anyway. An abstention or negative vote, moreover, might embolden Pretoria to reject any negotiations with India. Other delegates dissented, worrying that an affirmative vote would result in the loss of "our present constructive influence" on South Africa. On December 2, after voting unsuccessfully to strike a request to repeal the Group Areas Act, the delegation voted for a resolution as a whole that encouraged tripartite discussions under U.N. auspices if necessary. One reason for the vote: the Chinese military had just intervened in the Korean War, and the Truman administration desired the support of India more than ever.[51]

The emergence of a confident, independent, and unified block of non-aligned nations dealt the United States another blow by fulfilling Washington's fears over what would happen if the General Assembly held a debate on the covenant. In the starkest renunciation yet of American human rights policy, the assembly, led by the developing nations, voted to add economic and social rights to the covenant, affix a mandatory colonial clause, and affirm the right of all peoples to self-determination. An assembly committee narrowly adopted a Yugoslav amendment that reversed UNCHR's decision to draft two separate covenants, explaining that "the enjoyment of civic and political freedoms and of economic, social and cultural rights are interconnected and interdependent." The American position, that economic and social rights needed careful definitions, required unique implementation mechanisms, and could only find fulfillment gradually, sounded like excuses to avoid sharing the world's resources or assisting developing nations to combat poverty. Roosevelt had sounded defensive just prior to the vote when in responding to these sentiments, she declared, "It seemed scarcely necessary to point out the extent of United States support for efforts made to improve economic and social conditions in the present-day world." With Americans enjoying a per capita income 13 times greater than people living in the developing world, Roosevelt afterward worried that the vote signified growing anti-colonial and anti-capitalistic sentiment in developing countries, which she charged "have been largely visited for purposes of exploitation" by American businessmen. Accepting defeat, the U.S. delegation did not even speak before the assembly ratified the inclusion of economic and social rights along with civil and political guarantees in a single treaty by a four-to-one ratio.[52]

The backlash against the West continued in debates over the federal-state and territorial clauses. The assembly committee acrimoniously debated the federal-state article for two days, with Roosevelt arguing its necessity and the Soviet bloc, joined by some non-aligned nations such as Pakistan, India, and Iraq, declaring that it was really an escape clause. Due to a rare combination of American–West European unity and the decision to abstain by almost all non-aligned countries, the committee rejected a Soviet bloc amendment that would have forced federal states to implement the covenant throughout their countries. Instead, by a vote of 31 to 3 with 12 abstaining, the committee approved an American request for UNCHR to study an article that would secure "the maximum extension of the Covenant to the constituent units of federal states and meet the constitutional problems of federal states." Attempts by the U.S. delegation to repeat the voting pattern on a weak territorial article failed miserably. England and France demanded the right to implement the covenant as they saw fit in their colonies, which Roosevelt termed a "perfectly indefensible" position, while former colonial nations rejected the "go slow" approach of their ex-imperial rulers. The latter group also turned back an American compromise that would have metropolitan nations apply the covenant as soon as possible to their dependent areas. The committee instead asked, by a three-to-one margin, that obligated nations extend the treaty to all dependent territories immediately. The United States and colonial powers dissented. On December 4, the General Assembly plenary passed the federal-state and territorial compromises by large margins as well as a directive to place, either in the covenant or in separate protocols, mechanisms for the receipt of individual and NGO petitions.[53]

The most severe rebuke to the West occurred when the assembly asked the UNCHR to study "ways and means which would ensure the right of peoples and nations to self-determination." Introduced by Saudi Arabia and Afghanistan, supported by the Soviet and the non-aligned blocs, and resisted by the United States and every Western European nation, the resolution passed the assembly's Third Committee on a vote of 31 to 16. Its supporters claimed that self-government and sovereignty for peoples and nations were prerequisites to the enjoyment of all other human rights. Colonialism, as a form of slavery, kept individuals disenfranchised, economically exploited, and powerless in the face of laws and practices forced upon them by others. Moreover, the principle was hardly controversial in theory, as the U.N. Charter even mentioned it, though colonial nations believed it applied to existing nations only. Other opponents, such as Roosevelt, argued that not all peoples had a claim to self-government, for that position could fuel secessionist movements and civil wars. The State Department was not about to provide ammunition for decolonization, especially as its North Atlantic Treaty Organization (NATO) allies relied on overseas raw materials to rebuild their war-devastated economies. Roosevelt, though, also felt embarrassed to oppose the principle that had laid the legal basis for her country's independence. Even President Truman had recently endorsed it, telling the National Council of Negro Women, "We welcome the recognition of [self-determination] . . . and are deeply interested in the encouragement it has provided to the political aspirations of many peoples." The assembly easily passed the proposal by a 30 to 9 poll.[54]

Eleanor Roosevelt and James Green tried to identify the causes of these stunning defeats, finally settling on the new biases of a post-colonial bloc of nations. These Asian, Latin American, and Arab nations, led by India, Mexico, and Saudi Arabia, refused to take sides in the Cold War and chafed under Western economic and political imperialism. Green explained in the appropriately titled "Post-Mortem on the Third Committee" that debates in the General Assembly frequently had a trio of "obvious undertones: the colored peoples in opposition to the white, the newly independent countries against the administering powers, and the underdeveloped against the industrialized nations." He imperially castigated the immature, emotional, and irrational natures of delegates from small nations who "tend to free-wheel as individual experts and to be swayed by the oratory of their colleagues" rather than follow the lead of the United States. Roosevelt also stated in a letter to President Truman that "the race question has become a very vital one," explaining that nations in the Near East and Asia have known white people in two negative capacities: as colonial lords and as greedy businessmen. The existence of segregation and American support for South Africa and Israel did nothing to shed the stereotype of insensitive, prejudiced, and hypocritical whites who articulate humane principles while subverting them in practice. Given the Soviet Union's support for racial equality, economic and social rights, and decolonization, it was no wonder that many Third World delegates found common cause with Moscow. Neither Green nor Roosevelt offered specific solutions. Roosevelt thought that greater wisdom and empathy would go far toward moderating the suspicion nations had toward the United States, while Green recommended more flexible U.S. positions.[55]

The 1950 assembly votes, inaction on the Genocide Convention by the Senate Foreign Relations Committee, and a resurgent Republican Party also forced liberal domestic organizations to reevaluate a treaty-centered human rights policy. This was a significant reappraisal, for many had lobbied for U.N. oversight since before the San Francisco Conference. It had become clear that the political tide in the United Nations was turning against a covenant that the Senate would find acceptable. The Democratic Party had furthermore lost five upper-chamber seats in the fall elections, holding now just a one-seat majority. In this deteriorating environment, in late January 1951, the Carnegie Endowment for International Peace assembled the leaders of the American Bar Association, American Association for the United Nations, American Civil Liberties Union, National Association for the Advancement of Colored People, and other NGOs. State Department lawyers James Simsarian, Jack Tate, and Marjorie Whiteman also attended. The minutes reflected that "it became clear that there was strong, though not unanimous, sentiment in favor of shifting the emphasis . . . from a Covenant to other means of promoting human rights." The attendees found it impossible to navigate around a central dilemma: the covenant envisioned by the latest General Assembly was increasingly unlikely to obtain Senate approval. That left the United States delegation either participating in drafting a treaty the nation could not sign and thus opening Washington up to charges of hypocrisy, or withdrawing and losing credibility and influence as the leader of the free world.[56]

The American Association for the United Nations sought a way out by holding a follow-up conference in Chicago a month later. In preparation for the meeting, the group's Board of Directors endorsed continued work on a covenant of only civil and political rights, but there was also a call to turn away from U.N. activity. The gathering of over 90 labor, religious, women's, and human rights organizations ratified the AAUN's focus. While one resolution called for continued work on a covenant, delegates focused more on other ways of promoting human rights. They recommended the worldwide "practical application" of the Universal Declaration by the United Nations' specialized agencies. This global education campaign would "strike at the tyrannies of the police state, whether Communist or Fascist . . . and constitute one of the greatest hopes for human progress through the United Nations." Furthermore, they advocated that the United Nations promote its human rights work through press and radio outlets and on specific issues such as trade union rights and freedom for colonial peoples. Closer to home, the activists vowed to create the vibrant human rights culture necessary for acceptance of U.N. treaty drafting. The last item must have seemed nostalgic though, given the opposing political winds blowing outside the conference auditorium.[57]

This forbidding domestic and international landscape placed the Truman administration on the defensive in planning for the 1951 meeting of the Commission on Human Rights. Fearing a loss of support for the UNCHR's work by domestic NGOs and the Senate, Roosevelt and her advisors tried to revise policy and recapture the initiative. The internal debate on specifics was so long and intense that Sandifer, Green, Simsarian, and Tate could not submit any comments to the secretary-general before the UNCHR convened. They decided to offer minimal concessions. To assuage those who termed the federal-state provision an escape clause, the department appended a loose requirement that nations report on progress in enforcing the covenant. They now accepted the assembly's text of the territorial clause under which colonial nations had to apply the covenant to their dependent lands. More problematic was a cynical move by the Communist bloc to embrace the right of individuals to participate in government through free elections. The Senate, they knew, would reject a treaty that overturned the disenfranchisement of Southern blacks by poll taxes, literacy tests, and other methods. However, the lawyers knew it would damage the nation's image to oppose a provision so basic to democratic practice. So while the preferred position was to oppose its adoption, Roosevelt could "participate in the drafting of such an article to have its language as consistent as possible with American practice and constitutional principles."[58]

The State Department, given its stinging losses in the General Assembly, did revisit other policies, but the resulting symbolic changes could hardly have fooled anyone. For the very first time, its lawyers acceded to including economic and social principles, but not rights, in a single treaty. The single article was unsurprisingly heavily qualified and non-committal:

> Each state party undertakes to promote conditions of economic, social and cultural progress and development for a higher standard of life in larger freedom for all, with due regard to the organization and resources of the State; and to co-operate for effective international action in economic, social and cultural matters with organs of the United Nations.[59]

In a similar vein, the State Department continued to demand that any measures to allow individual or NGO petitions must be placed in separate protocols. Its lawyers also strenuously argued against adding the right of self-determination to the covenant. If a majority in the UNCHR nonetheless supported the ideal, Roosevelt could propose placing it in a non-binding UNCHR resolution, in the covenant's non-justiciable preamble, or in a meaningless clause under which nations would "promote the principle of self-determination of peoples in accordance with the provisions of the Charter of the United Nations."[60]

Given these embarrassingly restrictive proposals, it was just as well that the 1951 UNCHR session, the first without Eleanor Roosevelt as chair, was most notable for what did not happen. Its members had no time to revise articles on self-determination, civil and political rights, and the application of the covenant to dependent territories and federal states. Under the leadership of Charles Malik of Lebanon, the only agenda item completed was the drafting of a list of economic and social rights, and the ensuing debate demonstrated that the United States had not lost its influence completely. Soviet bloc delegates predictably identified national governments as the ultimate provider of minimum living standards. "The State shall ensure to everyone the right to work and to choice of profession," a sample article mandated, though Moscow also opposed any transnational oversight of those promises. The United States and its European and Latin American allies, which comprised a majority, objected to the proposals by citing their incompatibility with a free-market system and limited government. Instead, they viewed the economic and social provisions as objectives to be realized progressively through a combination of individual, business, and governmental action. In this polarized atmosphere, the Soviet bloc's emphasis on state enforcement lost dismally.[61]

In consultation with the International Labor Organization, the World Health Organization, and the U.N. Educational, Scientific, and Cultural Organization (UNESCO), the Human Rights Commission yielded a list of principles that did not displease Roosevelt and the State Department. The approved text differed hardly at all from the Universal Declaration, as the articles merely "recognized" the rights of individuals to have a safe workplace, gain "fair" remuneration, enjoy "adequate" housing, have access to the "highest standard of health" possible, and obtain an education, among other goals. On the question of enforcement, the UNCHR only asked nations to submit progress reports to the Economic and Social Council. The tension between the two Cold War protagonists was apparent throughout, with Russian delegate Platon Morozov often quoting statistics on poverty and unemployment in the United States to show the need for state action. Roosevelt responded by attacking Morozov's idealistically banal descriptions of living conditions in the workers' paradise he called his homeland. She did so by concentrating her fire on the lack of political freedoms in the

U.S.S.R. At one point the debate became personal. After Morozov repeatedly called James Simsarian, who was sitting in for Roosevelt, her "advisor," the American replied in a huff that he was actually sitting as a "duly accredited alternate" delegate to the commission.[62]

Despite the promotional language of the articles, their subordination to a federal-state clause, and the conservative implementation scheme attached, Acheson and Roosevelt were disappointed by their "sweeping scope and loose language" and their status nonetheless as "rights," which nations had to satisfy using "the maximum of their available resources." The United States was on the defensive for much of the five weeks. Acheson grew increasingly concerned because the length and level of detail of articles increased as the session proceeded, which he noted would "make ratification difficult." By the middle of May, Acheson was so "disturbed" by the commission's work that he authorized Roosevelt to abstain from voting on all of the new section. He and Roosevelt held out hope that the Economic and Social Council would reverse the assembly's decision and sanction the drafting of two distinct conventions. In a diplomatically worded letter to Secretary-General Trygve Lie, the State Department asserted that the entire section would "warrant careful re-examination upon further consideration of the draft covenant in the United Nations."[63]

After the UNCHR had adjourned, Roosevelt tried to explain her mixed verdict. "I think the great nations, but especially the United States, have got to understand that there is a feeling in the world of a desire to attain some kind of better standard of living, and they [sic] feel that particularly the United States has an obligation to make the plans and help them to carry them out to attain these standards," she began. She remarked that her colleagues from the developing world thought that her government cared not at all for peoples of colors worldwide and only sought to control them economically. So the inclusion of economic and social rights was a way to communicate the developing world's concerns and to inspire their citizens, even if such guarantees required long-term and complex solutions. As she wrote accurately and eloquently in a *My Day* column, "We must decide, that is, whether we can declare that a whole list of things which are not very precisely defined are 'rights' and then modify the actual declaration by explaining that these 'rights' can not [sic] be acquired except in certain ways which will take a long time to fulfill. This does not seem very satisfactory for the people involved, but a number of delegates feel that it will give people, in the great masses, high hopes for their future." But she recognized in a letter to Hickerson, "Now how we are going to explain all of this to the American Bar Association and Congress, I really do not know."[64]

The addition of economic and social rights and UNCHR inaction on other desired items left Roosevelt even more doubtful that the Senate would accede to the covenant. The Korean War stalemate and the firing of General Douglas MacArthur had emboldened conservatives in the Senate and sunk President Truman's public approval ratings. On April 24, as the UNCHR began discussing economic and social rights, Roosevelt wrote Truman that she thought "ratification of whatever is agreed upon is a distant hope." On the same day, in a *New York Times* article noting that the Senate Foreign Relations Committee had refused to pass the Genocide Convention, an anonymous lawyer stated, "You could not get a treaty incorporating our own Federal Bill of Rights ratified by the United States Government today." Roosevelt felt a bit beleaguered in Geneva. Looking around at her UNCHR colleagues, she thought that there were "a number of people who agree with a few of our own lawyers in the United States in feeling that no covenant can be written at this time." She resigned herself to the fact that the commission would not finish its work on the covenant, necessitating at least another UNCHR session in 1952. While relaxing during the summer at her house in Hyde Park, New York, Roosevelt began to receive more and more letters opposing American adoption of the covenant. In deciding how to reply, she had to recognize a central dilemma that had first emerged from the 1949 General Assembly: the United States was caught between the desires of underdeveloped nations and what the Senate would find politically and constitutionally acceptable. Her only reply was a non-answer. "It is unthinkable from my point of view that the United States should not co-operate in working on the first draft of a covenant on human rights which will apply to the world as a whole. But that will in no way mean that the United States is bound to accept anything that its own representatives in the Senate do not feel is right to accept when the final draft is submitted to them for ratification."[65]

Senator John Bricker (R-OH) was too impatient to await the arrival of the human rights covenant on his desk. He was a politician of some national standing, having run as Thomas Dewey's running mate in the 1944 presidential race. Dewey added him because of Bricker's successful three-term stint as Ohio's governor, during which he balanced the state's budget, rooted out political corruption, and reorganized state government to reduce bureaucracy. He also provided a conservative Midwestern alternative to Dewey's more liberal Eastern establishment ties. As the vice-presidential pick, he frequently criticized the New Deal and President Franklin Roosevelt's expansion of federal power, which Bricker called unconstitutional and dangerous to liberty. His often strident rhetoric made for popular media sound bites. Referring to Sidney Hillman of the Congress of Industrial Organizations and American Communist Party leader Earl Browder, he asserted during the campaign that "to all intents and purposes the great Democratic party has become the Hillman-Browder Communistic party with Franklin Roosevelt as its front." Though he and Dewey lost by a fair margin, he was not long out of politics. In 1946, the voters of Ohio elected him to the Senate by a wide margin. As an "Old Guard Republican," he consistently criticized the New Deal state, voiced distrust of the United Nations as a nascent world government, and favored aggressive prosecution of the Cold War at home and abroad. His support of Joseph McCarthy's crusade to ferret out Communists was unstinting, and he once famously told his Wisconsin colleague, "Joe, you're a dirty son of a bitch, but there are times when you've got to have a son of a bitch around, and this is one of them."[66]

On July 17, 1951, the state's rights crusader introduced a resolution calling for the United States to withdraw from the covenant drafting process. Such a drastic step was necessary, the proposal declared, because the covenant would "prejudice those rights of the American people which are now protected by the bill of rights of the Constitution of the United States." The "Covenant on Human Slavery," Bricker told the Senate, would seriously undermine the First Amendment in particular. He quoted from the document's general limitation clause to warn that the covenant would allow the federal government to punish those who spoke or published remarks that vaguely endangered "national security, public order, safety, health or morals." He feared that President Truman would utilize such an open-ended provision to stifle rising criticism of his failed foreign policies in China and Korea. Citing the cases of *Sei Fujii* and *Missouri v. Holland*, Bricker also concluded that the federal judiciary could now use the covenant to override the Tenth Amendment and continue the centralization of power in Washington. Laying the blame for all of these possible consequences at the feet of Franklin and Eleanor Roosevelt, he warned that "the Covenant on Human Rights is the instrument they are using for destroying freedom of the press in America." Within three days, Frank Holman and American Bar Association Committee on Peace and Law President Alfred Schweppe had congratulated Bricker on his "excellent" speech and offered their assistance in support of his resolution. Bricker told both of his larger plan: the non-binding resolution was only a temporary measure "to slow down the State Department in its mad pursuit for a World Bill of Rights." A permanent solution would require a constitutional amendment, similar to that first mentioned by Carl Rix, limiting the domestic impact of all treaties. The push for the "Bricker Amendment" had begun.[67]

To many in the State Department and on the Commission on Human Rights in 1948, the worldwide movement to draft a covenant of civil and political rights looked strong and cohesive. The Declaration of Human Rights and the Genocide Convention had received unanimous approval from the General Assembly. Commission members understood that the next agenda item would be to complete a covenant containing civil and political rights. With Eleanor Roosevelt at the helm, the State Department was confident that the UNCHR would accomplish the task at its 1950 session, and assembly approval would soon follow. Obstacles did exist, such as racial discrimination and segregation at home, but the State Department was confident that the worst such abuses were gradually disappearing and that they could rather cynically press for covenant clauses that would legally allow racial segregation to continue.

Within two years, though, the State Department was on the defensive over its support for a limited human rights covenant. Non-aligned nations that now comprised the balance of power in the General Assembly demanded the inclusion of economic and social guarantees and the right to self-determination. They also refused to include federal-state and non-self-executing clauses, despite repeated explanations by Washington of their constitutional necessity. These decisions, much to the growing alarm of Roosevelt and her advisors, began to fuel a growing domestic backlash led by Senator John Bricker and the American Bar Association that threatened to disrupt American participation in the very U.N. treaty-writing process that the United States had helped to launch. The timing of their opposition could scarcely have been worse from the State Department's point of view. With a nuclear Soviet Union carving out a sphere of influence in Eastern Europe, the fall of China to Communism, and the outbreak of the Korean War, policies that stressed universal values and compromise with foreign nations were bound to face suspicion. Human rights treaties, based upon voluntarily giving up some measure of sovereignty to the United Nations, seemed increasingly irrelevant and utopian in light of the military challenges of the Cold War. Unable to satisfy these criticisms and faced with an increasingly hostile U.N. majority, the State Department and domestic civil liberties groups began a shift away from prioritizing the treaty-making process to promote human rights. The ratification debate over the Genocide Convention accelerated this trend and foreshadowed an important struggle over whether the Senate or the State Department would define U.S. human rights policy at the United Nations.

CHAPTER 5

United Nations Success Breeds Failure at Home, 1945–1950

AS THE UNITED NATIONS COMMISSION on Human Rights (UNCHR) drafted the Universal Declaration of Human Rights and early versions of the covenant, other agencies pieced together the organization's first human rights treaty. Memories of the Holocaust and of other atrocities committed during World War II led member states to draft an agreement to punish those who tried to destroy religious, national, racial, or ethnic groups. The State Department consistently supported what would become the Convention on the Prevention and Punishment of the Crime of Genocide, and its U.N. delegation was very influential throughout the drafting process. As with the Universal Declaration and the covenants, American diplomats demanded that the Genocide Convention incorporate a conservative American jurisprudence that placed a premium on defending national sovereignty. Unlike with the covenant, though, the State Department successfully fought for language that limited the scope, application, and enforcement of the document in order to minimize any domestic legal obligations. The final draft, approved unanimously by the U.N. General Assembly on December 9, 1948, defined "genocide," declared its practice to be a violation of international law, and proposed that perpetrators be punished by national courts or by a special international tribunal. President Harry S. Truman submitted the Genocide Convention to the Senate for ratification, and he expected its quick approval.

Ironically, given the heavy American handprint on the Genocide Convention and the Truman administration's strong endorsement, the treaty never passed the Senate Foreign Relations Committee. A coalition of conservative Southern Democrats and isolationist-oriented Republicans, supported by the American Bar Association (ABA), interpreted the convention as a dangerous assault on the American Constitution and national sovereignty. Castigating the performance of America's U.N. delegation, Senators Tom Connally (D-TX), Walter George (D-GA), and Alexander Wiley (R-WI) denigrated the convention as Communist-inspired propaganda designed to eclipse the constitutional rights of states and individuals and make its citizens vulnerable to scurrilous charges of genocide. Their successful drive to bury the convention in the Foreign Relations Committee provided the inspiration, political experience, and language for a movement led by Senator John Bricker (R-OH) to restrict the ability of all treaties to invalidate domestic laws. Although Bricker's crusade failed, sympathetic lawyers, private organizations, and powerful senators forced President Dwight D. Eisenhower to abandon the Genocide Convention in 1953. As a result, the United States increasingly lost its leadership role in the U.N. human rights movement during the early Cold War years.

Genocide was by no means a new occurrence in world history, but the Holocaust and other wartime atrocities generated an unprecedented transnational movement to make it a violation of international law and punish its perpetrators. In the summer of 1944, Soviet troops approached Majdanek, a forced labor camp near Lublin, Poland. The Soviet advance occurred so rapidly that the German guards had little time to destroy the facility, leaving the gas chambers as evidence of the estimated 80,000 individuals who died there. In the coming weeks, the Red Army overran the extermination camps of Belzek, Sobibor, and Treblinka, whose crematoria had processed the remains of 1.5 million victims of the Nazi killing machine. American forces, a month before the end of the war in Europe, occupied Buchenwald, whose 20,000 survivors told of horrendous conditions that had killed 56,000 of their fellow prisoners. Across Europe, scenes of the dead, the dying, and the emaciated confronted Allied soldiers. On the other side of the world, Japanese atrocities, such as the Rape of Nanking, the Bataan Death March, and the murders of millions of civilians in occupied Southeast Asia, also evoked feelings of anger, disgust, and disbelief. A consensus quickly arose between President Franklin Roosevelt, Prime Minister Winston Churchill, and Premier Joseph Stalin that Axis leaders must be held accountable for committing crimes against humanity. Gathering information about atrocities and punishing their perpetrators would be a short-term and reactive response; what was also needed was a way to guard against such barbarity ever recurring. A group of Western-trained lawyers and diplomats soon seized upon the crafting of an international treaty to ban genocide.

The leader of this cause was Raphael Lemkin, a Polish lawyer residing in the United States, who lost 49 members of his family in the Holocaust. His experiences had uniquely prepared him to become one of the world's preeminent experts on mass killing. Years spent as a criminal prosecutor in Warsaw in the early 1930s provided him with the opportunity to help codify Poland's entire legal structure. He collaborated with Duke University Law Professor Malcolm McDermott to translate the work into English; McDermott later facilitated his escape from Europe following the German invasion of Poland. In 1933, Lemkin wrote a scholarly paper for the League of Nations on one of his personal interests, crimes he called "barbarity" and "vandalism" that amounted to the state-sponsored killing of a particular, specifically chosen group of people and the destruction of its cultural, religious, and economic underpinnings. The destruction of Armenian Christians under the late Ottoman Empire and the 1933 Simele Massacre, in which the government of Iraq murdered 3,000 Assyrians, made him realize that the world community needed the power to prosecute perpetrators of this uniquely horrible transgression. Arriving in the United States as a refugee in 1941, he joined the law faculty at Duke University. For the next three years he worked tirelessly on a book that exposed the capricious and repressive changes to the rule of law that German-allied administrators made in countries under Nazi domination. *Axis Rule in Occupied Europe*, published by the Carnegie Endowment for International Peace, became the touchstone for all future works about genocide. Ironically, Washington lawyer George Finch, who wrote in the forward that the book "is offered as a contribution toward the restoration of peace based upon justice," became a staunch opponent of Genocide Convention ratification by the United States.[1]

Lemkin coined the word "genocide" in *Axis Rule*, and defined it as "a co-ordinated plan of different actions aiming at the destruction of essential foundations of the life of national groups . . . and the actions involved are directed against individuals, not in their individual capacity, but as members of the national group." The term comprised an amalgam of the Greek word "*genos*," or "race," with the Latin "*cide*," or "killing." It is critical to understand, though, that Lemkin did not intend genocide to encompass only mass murder. As he wrote in *Axis Rule*,

> Generally speaking, genocide does not necessarily mean the immediate destruction of a nation, except when accomplished by mass killings of all members of a nation. It is intended rather to signify a co-ordinated plan of

different actions aiming at the destruction of essential foundations of the life of national groups, with the aim of annihilating the groups themselves. The objectives of such a plan would be disintegration of the political and social institutions, of culture, language, national feelings, religion, and the economic existence of national groups, and the destruction of the personal security, liberty, health, dignity, and even the lives of the individuals belonging to such groups.[2]

His study of ancient and modern history taught him that this process of annihilation occurred in two stages. In the first phase, the aggressor would attempt the destructive path laid out above, followed by a subsequent period during which it would impose its own culture, religion, and ways of living on a weakened and demoralized populace. As heartrending stories and photographs of liberated concentration camps began to appear in American newspapers as evidence of the first phase, Lemkin accepted an invitation to prosecute some of those responsible.[3]

Serving as an advisor to Supreme Court Justice Robert H. Jackson, the American chief counsel at Nuremberg for the prosecution of Nazi war criminals, demonstrated to Lemkin that a critical hole existed in international law. Of the 24 defendants, 19 were charged with crimes against humanity, defined in the International Military Tribunal's statute as "murder, extermination, enslavement, deportation, and other inhumane acts committed against any civilian population." Two problems arose with the definition. The first is that it did not give special significance to the mass persecution of a group because of a desire to see that group vanish from the face of the earth. Lemkin's own personal losses, coupled with his earlier efforts to criminalize "barbarity" and "vandalism," persuaded him that a unique offense of "genocide" needed recognition. The second shortcoming was a decision to prosecute only those crimes against humanity that the Nazi leadership had committed in connection to waging war. This prevented the tribunal from holding anyone accountable for the persecution of Jews and others in Germany before the Nazi invasion of Poland in September 1939. Thus, international law did not recognize the illegality of legislation or actions that resulted in violence directed against minority groups unless a proven tie existed with a transnational war. This fact prevented proactive intervention against governments that committed widespread "preparatory" acts before they launched genocidal campaigns; it would also allow nations to commit genocide if they did not raise arms against their neighbors. The experience made Lemkin "conscious of the great necessity of establishing a rule of international law which would make sure that 'revolting and horrible' acts committed by a government on its own citizens ... should in the future not go unpunished."[4]

Lemkin put his legal expertise to work when the first United Nations General Assembly convened in October 1946 at Lake Success, New York. He befriended delegates from Cuba, India, and Panama, who all agreed to sponsor a resolution on genocide penned by Lemkin himself. The document eloquently asserted that throughout history, "national, racial, ethnical, or religious groups have been destroyed, entirely or in part, and such crimes of genocide not only shocked the conscience of mankind but also resulted in great losses to humanity in the form of cultural and other contributions represented by these human groups." It decried the Nuremberg finding that genocides committed in times of peace did not rise to international legal violations, while pointing out that relatively lesser offenses such as piracy and trafficking in obscene publications did. To remedy this situation, the three governments called for the U.N. Economic and Social Council to study genocide with an eye toward making it an international crime. Lemkin knew that his crusade had just begun, and in a letter published in the *New York Times*, he argued, "it is now the task of the United Nations to see to it that the generous action of the three member states should be transferred into international law in order to prevent further onslaughts on civilization."[5]

One month later, the General Assembly's Sixth (Legal) Committee endorsed Lemkin's resolution and set out an agenda for future work. Written by State Department Legal Advisor Charles Fahy, the measure called upon the General Assembly to make the commission of genocide an international crime, ask nations to pass their own laws to punish offenders, and take "early action looking toward the preparation of a draft convention on the subject of genocide." On December 11, 1946, the General Assembly passed landmark Resolution 96(I) unanimously and without any debate. Much of the preamble contained Lemkin's original words, and the bill satisfied one of his key objectives by "affirm[ing] that genocide is a crime under international law which the civilized world condemns." Now what was needed was superstructure, namely a concise definition of genocide, a means to prosecute it, and a binding contract that committed nations to take proactive measures to prevent its occurrence. Lemkin's invented word had now become well known; it even served as an answer to a *New York Times* "Words in the News" quiz.[6]

The first sign that a treaty to prohibit genocide would generate disagreement between nations was ECOSOC's choice of author for a first draft. The council itself, consisting of 18 members, was too large of a body to undertake the duty itself, and its members spent two weeks discussing whether to give the task to the Secretariat or the Commission on Human Rights (UNCHR). The United States and its European allies wanted the topic referred to the UNCHR and the U.N. Commission on the Development of International Law and Its Codification, which was studying how to apply legal precedents created by the Nuremberg trials. With Eleanor Roosevelt as chair of the former group, and with the latter comprised of Western-oriented legal scholars, the State Department presumed it could influence the drafting process more than if autonomous civil servants in the Secretariat did the work. Lemkin and a majority of the ECOSOC nations, though, worried that the UNCHR's overloaded agenda, dominated by discussions of an international bill of human rights, would force a delay in completing a treaty. While Lemkin unsuccessfully lobbied State Department lawyers to change policy, a majority in ECOSOC asked the Secretariat to lead the drafting of a convention.[7]

The product of the Secretariat's Human Rights Division, which consulted with Lemkin, did indeed worry the State Department, as several provisions went beyond existing American law. Compared to Resolution 96(I), the draft expanded the types of protected groups, the acts against them that comprised genocide, and the responsibilities of treaty signatories to punish perpetrators. The document defined genocide as acts directed against "racial, national, linguistic, religious, or political groups" with the intent of destroying them "in whole or in part." The work prohibited a broad range of actions that might promote such destruction, including mass murder, withholding food, clothing, and medical care, restricting reproduction, and denying the opportunity to earn a living by confiscating property and terminating employment. Building upon Lemkin's concept of cultural genocide, the treaty barred the censoring of indigenous languages and the destruction of houses of worship, historical sites, and works of art. Individuals who committed these acts, either public officials or private individuals, could be charged with attempting to commit genocide, participating in "preparatory acts" such as studying how to execute genocide, engaging in "direct public incitement to genocide," and conspiring with others. Signatory nations took on three obligations: to make genocide a domestic criminal offense; to eradicate all propaganda that could "promote genocide, or tending to make it appear as a necessary, legitimate or excusable act"; and to either try or extradite suspects in custody. Offenders could therefore face a trial where the acts occurred, in any state that had custody of a suspect (called "universal jurisdiction"), or before an international tribunal.[8]

The release of the Secretariat's proposal reopened the debate over whether legal specialists or political delegates should review it. The Commission on the Development of International Law lacked enough competent personnel skilled in human rights law, and so it informed U.N. Secretary-General Trygve Lie that it could not offer an opinion. Lie called for comments on the draft by U.N. member governments, but few replied. The UNCHR, which had no scheduled meetings until late 1947 and whose leaders were presently involved in generating a bill of rights, was unavailable to edit the document. It was up to ECOSOC, therefore, to decide what to do when it convened in late July. This pause allowed the American delegation to study the draft, propose critical amendments, and seize the initiative in shaping what would become the Genocide Convention.[9]

While the Secretariat's draft lay in bureaucratic limbo, the State Department's Subcommittee on Human Rights and the Status of Women (HRW) excised several objectionable components by clarifying the definition of genocide and, unsurprisingly given similar policies on the human rights declaration and covenant, weakening its enforcement proposals. The subcommittee opposed listing specific criminal actions because no list could include every conceivable method of exterminating people. Instead, the document defined genocide simply as an attempt to annihilate a group. Reflecting Anglo-Saxon legal tradition, HRW explained that proving an intent to accomplish this aim was more important than focusing on the specific means utilized. The subcommittee also rejected the doctrine of universal jurisdiction. Nations might abuse the principle, HRW concluded, by using the convention to prosecute non-citizens on scurrilous grounds. Universal jurisdiction would also require every country to try those accused of genocide, extradite them to another country, or send them to an international court. This principle would conflict with a long-standing doctrine of international law under which treaties did not apply to non-parties. To address this shortcoming, HRW members gave the Security Council, on which the United States exercised veto power, the discretion to take "appropriate action" against any government that granted immunity to genocide suspects.[10]

As with the covenant, the State Department tried to balance its desire to press for amendments to harmonize the treaty with American law while avoiding charges of procrastination from the treaty's domestic and foreign advocates. Given the substantial number of critical comments on such a "new and complex subject," Foggy Bottom advocated that a body of legal specialists, perhaps the International Law Commission (ILC), conduct a thorough review before the General Assembly acted on the final version.

The ILC was a fifteen-member body of independent jurists that did not yet exist, for its statute lay before the General Assembly for approval. As the ILC thus existed only on paper, a delay of at least one year would be necessary if the ILC's input was desired. If the ILC was unable to provide commentary, the American proposal continued, ECOSOC should table the convention until January 1948 to give member governments more time to submit critiques. Lying behind this determination to employ the ILC was the belief that lawyers, many of them trained in Western law schools, would be more sympathetic to American amendments. The danger was, though, that this timetable would invite criticism by domestic and foreign treaty supporters who preferred immediate U.N. action on a very sensitive topic. One State lawyer worried that the United States would be "accused of burying the subject of genocide," while Harley Notter in the Office of Special Political Affairs predicted that postponing debate would bring "extreme difficulty . . . for us in the Economic and Social Council." A *New York Times* editorial expressed the hope that the United States would "not permit the issue to be shunted from committee to committee, but will press for the earliest possible decision," while the World Jewish Congress called for the "earliest possible action" by the United Nations to eradicate "this foul crime against humanity."[11]

The strategy of controlled delay failed at ECOSOC's July session. After U.S. delegate Leroy Stinebower moved to send the treaty to the International Law Commission, telling his fellow delegates that "the drawing up of a draft convention was . . . a complicated legal question" requiring at least three months to study the Secretariat's work, Norway, Chile, and Venezuela led the charge for an accelerated timetable. In a resolution passed on August 6, the council called upon nations to submit comments on the Secretariat's convention "as soon as possible," and it announced a desire to "proceed with the consideration of the subject as rapidly as possible." One month later, the General Assembly endorsed the need for quick review and asked its own Sixth (Legal) Committee to propose a work plan for completing the convention. The United States reluctantly supported the proposal, bowing to demands that, in HRW's words, the United Nations finish the project "before world opinion has forgotten the atrocities committed during the war." Having lost the process vote, Foggy Bottom lawyers turned to controlling the outcome.[12]

State Department Legal Advisor Ernest Gross and Dean Rusk from the Office of Special Political Affairs further sought to ground the Secretariat's draft in American law. Believing, as with the declaration and the covenant, that U.S. legal precedents offered the best guidance for an international human rights agreement, the two lawyers also did not want the treaty to alter any controversial domestic statutes, which might endanger Senate ratification. Therefore, they favored the protection of political groups only if genocide was understood to mean their physical destruction. Otherwise, they worried, governments might face charges for legitimately suppressing political activity, say by Communist movements, in the interest of national security. Their overall critique argued for a more limited definition of genocide than Lemkin and the Secretariat offered. Gross and Rusk omitted all references to cultural extermination, arguing that genocide "should be confined to those barbarous acts directed against individuals which form the basic concept of public opinion on this subject." Turning to the list of prohibited actions, they sought to circumscribe the ban on research and propaganda, as the broadly written articles were too far removed from the commission of an actual crime and might encroach upon the American constitutional right of free speech. The provisions could remain if they were limited to actions that presented "a clear and present danger" to others and were committed "under circumstances which may reasonably result" in genocide, which were concepts taken from the 1919 Supreme Court decision *Schenck v. United States*. Gross and Rusk retained only five criminal acts that they believed to be the most serious and significant: murder, the denial of minimal living standards, the practice of conducting mutilations or biological experiments, the prevention of reproduction, and the forcible transfer of children to non-members of the targeted group.[13]

Gross and Rusk proposed a mixture of national and international accountability, with a clear emphasis on the former for reasons of sovereignty. They opposed the troubling principle of universal jurisdiction, under which courts of the nation where genocide occurred would have primary responsibility to try individuals, but if that country refused or could not prosecute, then the courts of *any* other nation could indict, try, and punish alleged perpetrators. Gross and Rusk opposed this principle on three grounds. Nations where the crime took place should have the first chance to prosecute in any instance, they believed, and not the courts of a third-party state. They agreed with HRW that universal jurisdiction would wrongly place legal obligations on all nations to prosecute offenders in their territory, even if those countries had not ratified the Genocide Convention. Moreover, such a provision could be easily abused by giving states a blank check to prosecute resident aliens on charges of genocide "when the real purpose is political retribution." They did propose one uncontroversial exception: a nation could try individuals for crimes committed elsewhere if the country where they had taken place concurred. This first comprehensive position paper showed much overlap with thinking on the human rights covenant, namely minimal U.S. commitment to any internal legal changes, a desire to export American legal precedents, and rejection of intrusive international enforcement.[14]

Gross and Rusk then anticipated and responded forcefully to the two most influential arguments later raised by domestic opponents of the convention. As the crimes of murder, assault, kidnapping, and theft of property, among others envisioned by the convention, were historically prosecuted by state courts in the United States, the two lawyers were sensitive but agreeable to the fact that the treaty would make them into federal crimes when tied to genocide. Any states' rights or Tenth Amendment objections to this change, they believed, would fail due to Congress's constitutional right to "define and punish . . . Offenses against the Law of Nations" and the Constitution's Supremacy Clause, which declared treaties superior to inconsistent state laws. They also responded to the possibility that defenders of racial segregation in the Senate might fear the prosecution of lynch mobs on spurious charges of genocide. Gross and Rusk believed that any such move would fail, as those who participated in vigilantism did not have the prerequisite intent to destroy the whole African American race. Even if such intent could be proven, America's own state and federal courts would have primary jurisdiction in the matter. They concluded that "no possibility can be foreseen of the United States being held in violation of the treaty" by refusing to hand over violent racists to stand trial abroad.[15]

Armed with this substantial critique and suggestions for amendment, the U.S. delegate to ECOSOC, Charles Fahy, was ready to proceed on the treaty's merits, but he faced a bureaucratic logjam partially of Washington's own making. He still favored having the International Law Commission's experts revise the Secretariat's work, but the body had not yet formed. The Secretariat's draft lay before diplomats in ECOSOC, while the General Assembly had assigned its Legal Committee to come up with a work plan. Fahy had to work through a dilemma that involved recognizing public pressure for rapid signing of a convention, while granting legal specialists on the Sixth Committee and the International Law Commission the right to craft it. This strategy reflected the State Department's view that a ban on genocide was a legal issue with political implications. A majority of delegates on the Sixth Committee, including the Soviet Union, Great Britain, and Belgium, saw the topic as a political issue first, which persuaded them to leave the rewriting to governmental representatives in ECOSOC. Fahy, who decided not to "press our position" given the majority's wishes, voted in favor of Resolution 180(II). It was now exclusively up to ECOSOC to formulate a treaty to ban genocide within a year.[16]

Even after the General Assembly had twice affirmed ECOSOC's primary role, the State Department privately contradicted Fahy's words by continuing efforts to shift the drafting to a body of legal experts. HRW members confidentially concluded that formulating a genocide treaty was too complex and technical a task given the legal inexperience of ECOSOC's government-appointed members. The State Department's previous position of delegating the matter to the International Law Commission, though, was no longer feasible in light of Resolution 180(II) and the continued delay in creating the agency. The State Department instead proposed that ECOSOC ask the Secretariat's own lawyers to shorten and simplify its "very long and complex" draft with guidance from comments by member governments. Using informal contacts covertly, the advisors sought to steer the task to the Secretariat's Legal Department rather than the Human Rights Division that had formulated the problematic first draft. Once vetted by the Eleanor Roosevelt–led Human Rights Commission in the late spring of 1948, ECOSOC could discuss the improved version over the summer in anticipation of fall approval by the General Assembly. This strategy privileged the expertise of lawyers, promised to allow the United States to exercise disproportionate influence on the final product, and outlined a tight timeline to avoid any stalling charges from treaty advocates.[17]

Walter Kotschnig found some opposition when he introduced the plan in the ECOSOC in mid-February 1948, but the resulting changes placed Washington even more squarely in control of the drafting process. As the State Department specialist on international organizations, Kotschnig had a close and personal involvement with human rights violations. In the two years after Adolf Hitler became Germany's führer, the Austrian had assisted fleeing Germans as the head of the League of Nations' High Commission for Refugees from Germany. The Anschluss forced Kotschnig, a well-known critic of Hitler, to leave for the United States with his family, and he taught at Mount Holyoke and Smith colleges. He joined the State Department in 1944 and attended the Dumbarton Oaks and San Francisco conferences. Kotschnig proposed that the Secretariat rewrite the convention while considering comments by the four nations that had submitted them, which included the United States. The Human Rights Commission, ECOSOC, and the assembly would then revise the draft. In early March, ECOSOC approved most of Kotschnig's plan, but instead of the Secretariat taking the lead, the drafting would be done by a seven-nation committee on which the United States and allies from France, Venezuela, China, and

Lebanon comprised a majority. The bloc's cohesion showed at the onset when choosing a chair. After the Soviets nominated one of their diplomats, John Maktos, the assistant legal advisor in the Office of International Organization Affairs, called the State Department and "pointed out the increased difficulty of implementing our position regarding certain provisions we wanted incorporated in the convention, with the U.S.S.R. delegate as a presiding officer." He received permission to run, and he won the chairmanship of the Ad Hoc Committee on Genocide.[18]

Capitalizing on the favorable momentum, the State Department distributed its own version of a genocide treaty based on Rusk's and Gross's analysis before the committee convened on April 5. The growing desire for quick passage and the inclusion of controversial articles in the Secretariat's draft convinced Foggy Bottom lawyer Katherine Fite to place a premium on brevity and limited state responsibility and to postpone the thorny issue of enforcement. Fite, a graduate of Vassar College and Yale University Law School, had learned about human rights atrocities by helping Supreme Court Justice Robert Jackson prosecute the Nazi leadership at Nuremberg. Her three-article convention defined genocide narrowly as "the act of exterminating, or conspiring or attempting to exterminate a racial, national, religious, or political group," omitted any list of specific criminal charges or a reference to cultural genocide, and obviated the need to prove intent, all of which the Secretariat's draft contained. Enforcement would be accomplished through "a competent international tribunal or by a domestic tribunal designated by such international tribunal." This article left the creation of an international court up to the United Nations without implying an endorsement by the United States, and it explicitly rejected the principle of universal jurisdiction. Criminal responsibility only lay with state officials who permitted or condoned systemic genocidal acts, which would forestall the prosecution of state or federal officials for "sporadic lynching." Fite might have added this point following W.E.B. Du Bois's unsuccessful attempt to place a petition that detailed Southern lynchings on the UNCHR's agenda.[19]

During the 26 meetings of the Ad Hoc Committee on Genocide in Lake Success, New York, Chairman John Maktos strove to reconcile the contradiction between supporting a comprehensive international ban on genocide and safeguarding American sovereignty and constitutional protections. Tracking Fite's recommendation closely, Maktos accepted a Soviet effort to define genocide as only attempts at the physical "extermination of particular groups of the population on racial [and] national (religious) grounds," though he proposed adding "political groups" to reaffirm the language of General Assembly Resolution 96(I). Answering Soviet, Polish, and Venezuelan objections, Maktos asserted that the inclusion of political groups would not prevent states from legally combating partisan subversion if they employed non-genocidal means to restore order. Privately, he believed the amendment important so that the United States could use the treaty to criticize Soviet bloc suppression of non-Communist political parties. As the U.N. Ad Hoc Political Committee was about to censure Hungary, Romania, and Bulgaria for violating their World War II peace treaty, Maktos believed that a genocide convention could create a broader multilateral platform with which to censure the entire Soviet bloc. The support of China, France, and Lebanon gave him a one-vote majority to add the amendment.[20]

Due to a lack of precedents in American law and to protect the First Amendment's guarantee of free speech, Maktos opposed criminalizing cultural genocide and genocidal "propaganda." Going beyond acts of physical violence, he warned, risked the rejection of the convention by nations including his own that feared spurious charges, for "it would be child's play for any clever lawyer to find a large number of new definitions of genocide [and] it was precisely that profusion which had to be avoided." Such imprecision, he predicted, would also provoke ratification objections in the Senate from civil libertarians. The key to acting quickly and gaining a broad international and domestic consensus, Maktos believed, would be a simple "condemnation of physical genocide." A majority disagreed with his crabbed approach, believing that mass murder was often preceded by attempts to eliminate a targeted group's identity. As it was important to ban such steps and thereby prevent genocide, measures taken to suppress the oral or written expression of indigenous languages and the destruction of "libraries, museums, schools, historical monuments, places of worship, or other cultural institutions and objects of the group" were also prohibited. Maktos was at least relieved that the committee placed these provisions in a separate article, which would make it easier for governments to add qualifying reservations when ratifying the convention.[21]

Maktos also sought to beat back attempts to multiply the charges that national and extranational courts could prosecute, such as conspiracy, incitement, engaging in genocidal propaganda, and participation in "preparatory acts." The Soviets defined the latter as conducting research, producing equipment or materials, or issuing commands that would support the commission of genocide. The State Department had omitted a list of crimes from its draft because of the belief that doing so was unnecessary if genocide was equated only with mass murder. Moreover, American constitutional law recognized only conspiracy and incitement, Maktos declared, and the Bill of Rights protected the latter unless it presented a "clear and present danger" to public order. Maktos worried that penalizing the release of "propaganda" or the conduct of research into genocide would unconstitutionally limit the First Amendment rights of Americans to freedoms of speech and the press. He repeatedly tried to eliminate the references to propaganda, preparatory acts, and incitement, or failing that, to have a footnote appended limiting the crimes by the "clear and present danger" doctrine. Sensing an impasse, he persuaded the committee to postpone action while members tried to negotiate a compromise.[22]

Maktos's initial optimism that the Ad Hoc Committee would approve a limited list of offenses partially vanished once the body adopted a Chinese proposal instead of Fite's template. It criminalized not only mass murder but also attempting to commit, conspiracy to commit, and public and private incitement. The Chinese delegate then moved to add a ban on preparatory acts. Maktos tried a new argument against the latter provision, claiming that the amendment overlapped with conspiracy and attempts to commit genocide and thus was redundant. The committee nonetheless passed the addition by a margin of one and approved the overall list of five crimes with Maktos casting the lone negative vote. One day later, with the Venezuelan delegate shifting his vote after further caucusing with Maktos, the committee replaced "preparatory acts" with the familiar Anglo-Saxon legal phrase of "complicity" in any of the acts mentioned in the treaty. The delegates understood that, in the words of legal commentator Nehemiah Robinson, the term referred to "accessorship before and after the act, and to aiding and abetting in the commission of any of the crimes included in the Convention." The United States won another major vote when the committee rejected a Soviet amendment to forbid the issuance of propaganda aimed at "provoking the commission of acts of genocide." Despite the victories, which prevented a possible collision with the Constitution's First Amendment, Maktos cast the lone abstention when the Ad Hoc Committee approved the entire article due to its unqualified inclusion of incitement, which the Supreme Court had rendered illegal only when directly contributing to a crime.[23]

Maktos had more success in persuading his colleagues to reject universal jurisdiction in favor of creating an international criminal tribunal. He found a nemesis in Soviet delegate Platon Morozov, who would serve in the Security Council and sit on the World Court for 15 years until retiring in 1985. He steadfastly reiterated the Soviet position of not giving up any measure of national sovereignty to an international body. Maktos replied that Moscow's position was "useless" as national courts would not always want or be able to try alleged perpetrators, particularly when a sitting government condoned or participated in genocide. Agreeing with Morozov that an international court, lacking a police force, could never enforce any of its verdicts, he nonetheless declared that the mere pronouncement of guilt might deter future genocides. As a compromise designed to isolate Morozov and insulate the United States from any potential oversight, Maktos proposed that an international tribunal would only prosecute when a national court either refused to act or did so inadequately. The committee followed his lead: it unanimously declared that courts of the nation where genocide occurred could first try the alleged perpetrators, added over Soviet and Polish objections that an international court could act only in cases where a "denial of justice" occurred, and rejected the concept of universal jurisdiction. The debate was a bit pedantic, though, as the treaty included no details at all about the creation, structure, or procedures of a transnational court. For the United States, then, supporting it in principle was a cost-free way of endorsing some extranational enforcement without compromising its own sovereignty in any practical or foreseeable way.[24]

Moscow and Washington also battled on one more treaty enforcement question: whether to require the legislatures of signatories to pass implementing legislation. Morozov argued that all treaty parties had an obligation to pass laws to at least specify appropriate punishments and to criminalize acts of genocide not covered by existing statutes. Maktos objected, arguing that legislatures did not always agree with a national leader's decision to sign a treaty. If Congress refused to pass implementing legislation, Maktos opined, the United Nations might find Washington in violation of the convention. He must have also worried that senators would look askew at a treaty that forced them to pass implementing legislation under the watchful eyes of the United Nations. In order to bury the Soviet draft while also providing an alternative, Maktos introduced an anemic clause that asked signatories "to undertake to enact the necessary legislation in accordance with their constitutional procedures." After explaining awkwardly that his feeble wording was necessary though it "in no way affected the obligation to be assumed by Governments," Maktos persuaded his committee allies to back the addition.[25]

With qualified American support, the Ad Hoc Committee and ECOSOC approved the Genocide Convention in late April and August respectively. The convention declared genocide to be a violation of international law punishable by national and international courts. Its terms extended to acts directed against national, racial, religious, and political groups committed with the intent to destroy the group because of its defining characteristic(s). After delineating physical and cultural genocide, the convention listed the five crimes of genocide: genocide itself, conspiracy to commit genocide, direct incitement to genocide, attempt to commit genocide, and complicity. Finally, signatories promised to pass implementing legislation according to their constitutional requirements and to extradite those charged with any of the crimes listed if they were unwilling or unable to try them.[26] Willard Thorp, the American delegate to the ECOSOC, outlined two American major reservations regarding the proposed convention. He objected to including cultural genocide and the crime of direct incitement, but he wished that none of his remarks "be interpreted as modifying his delegation's strong and wholehearted support of the essential parts of the draft Convention." ECOSOC, though, refused to reopen debate and sent the convention to the General Assembly unchanged.[27]

As the draft convention awaited discussion by the assembly, American religious organizations that had participated in wartime human rights lobbying led a charge for quick approval. The ecumenical Federal Council of the Churches of Christ in America, the largest coalition of Protestant denominations in the country, called for the treaty's passage at the General Assembly's next session. "We do this in the belief that genocide is a direct assault upon the Christian conception of the dignity and worth of men as children of the Heavenly Father," the statement asserted. Therefore, the U.S. delegates in ECOSOC should "do everything within their power" to facilitate the completion and approval of a treaty. The Catholic Association for International Peace asked the State Department to accept an international tribunal. What was most important was that "a start must be made, as great a start as possible but without compromising upon matters of principle, an effective start, limited though it may be." According to James Hendrick and James Simsarian, so many telegrams supporting the Genocide Convention flowed in from Jewish groups that they "dare not guess their number."[28]

To lobby on behalf of an effective treaty at the United Nations and consequently in the U.S. Senate, these religious supporters of the convention formed a broad-based coalition with secular organizations. In the spring of 1948, a group of men largely drawn from the National Conference of Christians and Jews (NCCJ) met in the New York City home of James Rosenberg. The NCCJ dated from 1927 as an ecumenical group of Jews, Protestants, and Catholics dedicated to fostering mutual understanding, combating religious bigotry, and fighting for progressive causes. Rosenberg, a bankruptcy lawyer, painter, and passionate art collector, knew many pillars of the Eastern establishment and the leaders of every major faith community in the country. In Rosenberg's house gathered Raphael Lemkin; Willard Johnson, the NCCJ's program director; Dr. Samuel Mc-Crea Cavert, the general secretary of the Federal Council of Churches; and Dr. Henry Noble McCracken, who served as co-chair of the International Council of Christians and Jews. Rosenberg and Lemkin had first connected in the fall of 1947, when Lemkin pleaded for Rosenberg's assistance after the United Nations had deadlocked about what to do on the subject of genocide. The group decided to form a grassroots-based lobbying force whose name became the United States Committee for a United Nations Genocide Convention. Rosenberg agreed to chair the organization, and Johnson became its general secretary. Within three months, its board of directors included leaders of the American Association for the United Nations, the Congress of Industrial Organizations, the Business and Professional Women's Clubs, and the Catholic Association for International Peace.[29]

Rosenberg and Lemkin, who also sat on the committee's board, wasted no time in lobbying for U.N. passage of the treaty by the end of the year. Lemkin was already well known to most, if not all, delegates at the United Nations who had discussed the treaty. He had become, in the words of his biographer John Cooper, "an accomplished lobbyist in the corridors of the United Nations at Lake Success . . . no mean feat for a solo player with only a few allies." In early June, Rosenberg publicized his group's request for quick approval of the Genocide Convention by the General Assembly. Cognizant of previous American policy, Rosenberg labeled as "committeecide" any State Department attempts to send the treaty to other bodies, such as the UNCHR or the International Law Commission. He gave Undersecretary of State Robert Lovett, ECOSOC President Charles Malik, and General Assembly delegates a list of groups around the world with over 20 million members who supported "prompt adoption of a genocide convention." While Lemkin and Rosenberg worked the United Nations and State Department, others in their group expanded the membership. On June 17, 1948, almost 50 organizations, including the National Association for the Advancement of Colored People, American Jewish Congress, United World Federalists, and the Young Men's Christian Association, gathered in a New York City "town meeting" under the U.S. committee's aegis to sign a petition in favor of a genocide convention. Upon receiving the document, Sandifer stated the department's belief that the General Assembly should pass the convention at its fall session, though he obliquely referred to "necessary changes" that should precede such approval.[30]

It was unclear whether the General Assembly, convening in Paris, would follow this timetable, as Great Britain and the Soviet Union stood poised to block passage. The British had long opposed the convention on pragmatic grounds, arguing that in a world of sovereign states, it would have symbolic value only. Eric Beckett, the Foreign Office's main legal advisor, characterized Resolution 96(I) as "a useless resolution, and I think our attitude on it generally must be that we should not mind if it got lost somewhere and died a natural death, and at the most we do not want much time and expense being wasted in drawing up a perfectly useless convention." Privately, the British worried that the inclusion of cultural genocide might bring scurrilous charges against them for actions taken in their chaotic mandate of Palestine. They also objected to the inclusion of political groups. To prevent U.N. approval, they proposed reviving the American position of referring the convention to the International Law Commission that was finally due to convene in early 1949. The Soviets sided with the British on deleting political groups from the treaty, and they also fervently wanted to omit any mention of international enforcement. Lemkin tried to short-circuit their opposition by calling upon his growing friendship with General Assembly President Herbert Evatt. When Evatt asked him who might lead discussions in the assembly's Legal Committee, Lemkin recommended treaty supporter Dr. Ricardo Alfaro, a former leader of Panama. Evatt agreed, increasing the odds that the Legal Committee could pass a revised draft to the assembly before it adjourned in mid-December.[31]

Once the General Assembly referred the convention to its Legal Committee for final editing, the State Department prioritized the elimination of cultural genocide and direct incitement. The Americans had mixed success. Latin American and European nations, troubled by a definition of cultural genocide so vague that it might prohibit even the voluntary assimilation of their indigenous minorities, joined with Maktos to delete it from the treaty. Maktos fought unsuccessfully, though, to strike the crime of "direct incitement in public and private to commit genocide." He claimed the clause did not adequately distinguish between "the right of freedom of the Press and an alleged violation of the convention. Protection against genocide should stop where freedom of speech began." Newspaper editors and reporters who printed stories critical of a racial, national, religious, ethnic, or political group might be charged with "incitement," and such charges would have a chilling effect on speech. He lost due to opposition from the Soviet bloc, some Latin American countries, and even Western allies such as France, Denmark, and Norway that had suffered under Nazi propaganda firsthand as occupied nations.[32] Another stinging defeat came when the Soviet bloc and most sovereignty-conscious nations in Europe and Latin America deleted all generic references to an international court. The inclusion of political groups in the convention made a majority fearful that their leaders might face trial abroad for suppressing insurrection at home or in its colonies. Without this admittedly sparse provision, the State Department worried that the treaty was toothless, as government officials who undertook a campaign of genocide would likely have immunity from prosecution in their own courts.[33]

The convention's definition of genocide underwent substantial revision by the Sixth Committee, though the changes proved more controversial in American ratification debates than at the United Nations. One puzzle was how to clarify the definition of genocide as acts committed "with the intent to destroy" a group. Did they have to be committed with the intent to destroy all or just a presumably large part of a group? The Sixth Committee sidestepped the issue by adopting a Norwegian amendment delimiting genocide as actions "committed with intent to destroy, *in whole or in part*," a protected group. This soon raised an interpretational problem that marred future attempts to enforce the treaty. Certainly genocide encompassed the intent to destroy an entire group, but intent is often difficult to prove, as those who commit genocide rarely admit to doing so. Moreover, even if suspects deliberately committed genocide against only part of a group, how large of a portion would need to be targeted before domestic and foreign forces had to intervene? The entire drafting history of this clause in the Sixth Amendment is short and vague, so that the connection between intent and "in whole or in part" remains a hindrance to prosecution to this day.[34]

Tragic events of the recent past caused the Legal Committee to further expand the list of prohibited acts. By a relatively narrow vote, the body approved a Greek proposal to criminalize the forced transfer of children from one group to another. The impetus was the kidnapping of thousands of Greek children by Communist forces in the closing days of World War II and their relocation to families in Communist areas of the Balkans. Lemkin argued strongly for the addition, citing Jewish children in pre-Communist Russia and kids in "racially pure" nations occupied by the Nazis who were raised by German families. He also started an international movement to return the Greek children home, a cause that may have found favor with John Maktos, who himself was born in Greece. The delegates also restored, from the Secretariat's draft, the ban on causing serious "mental harm" to members of a protected group. Ti-Sun Li, the Chinese representative, reminded representatives that the Japanese had manufactured hundreds of tons of opium in his country during World War II to create a nation of passive addicts. Those two words soon caused a firestorm in the Senate, some of whose members worried that the provision could invalidate segregation on the grounds that the latter allegedly harmed the self-esteem of African Americans. As passed by the Sixth Committee, the treaty outlawed five crimes: killing, causing "serious bodily or mental harm," lowering the living standards of a group "to bring about its physical destruction," preventing reproduction, and forcibly transferring children.[35]

As the Legal Committee wrapped up its work in late November, the United States and Latin American and Asian nations struck a crucial compromise that smoothed the way for the treaty's passage. Maktos knew that many delegates had voted against an international court due to the body's competence extending to charges of genocide against political groups. In particular, Brazil, Uruguay, and Iran were most concerned that political leaders would be able to be tried by an international tribunal for carrying out necessary measures against subversive political groups. These nations had almost succeeded in deleting political groups from the convention. Maktos still disagreed with this stance, but "in a conciliatory spirit and in order to avoid the possibility that the application of the convention to political groups might prevent certain countries from acceding to it," he was willing to reverse course. In return for American acquiescence in dropping political groups, Maktos wanted to restore the reference to an international tribunal. Latin American and Asian states supported the American amendment by a combined vote of 19 to 3. The revised convention posited that if national courts did not or could not try those charged with genocide, the alleged perpetrators would be tried by "such international penal tribunal as may have jurisdiction with respect to such Contracting Parties as shall have accepted the jurisdiction of such tribunal." By making the deal, Maktos explained, he had retained the principle of international enforcement, made its application unlikely in the United States, and obtained additional signatories to the treaty. He may have also acted in response to a furious lobbying effort by Lemkin and his committee, who perceived the inclusion of political groups as a death warrant for the whole convention.[36]

On December 1, the Sixth Committee unanimously recommended that the General Assembly approve the Convention on the Prevention and Punishment of the Crime of Genocide, which it did eight days later. Ernest Gross, summarizing the thoughts of many delegates, declared that the vote "reflected the determination of the peoples of the United Nations

... to assure that the barbarism which had so recently shocked the conscience of mankind would never take place again." Dr. Herbert V. Evatt, the Australian president of the General Assembly, termed the adoption "an epoch-making event. Our approval of the Convention marks an important advance in the development of international criminal law." He urged all members to sign and ratify the document "with the least possible delay." Raphael Lemkin triumphantly suggested that "it would be an inspiration to the world if the United States Senate showed the way and ratified it first." Though he knew that some American lawyers were skeptical about the United Nations' human rights work, he surmised that "those doubters and hair-splitters appear to be greatly outnumbered by those who are more horrified by genocide and want to stop it." President Truman must have agreed with this political calculation. After signing the treaty just four days later, he reported it to the Senate, remarking that its ratification would show the world that the United States "is prepared to take action on its part to contribute to the establishment of principles of law and justice."[37]

Lemkin counted on strong support from the Truman administration and advocacy groups such as the United States Committee for a United Nations Genocide Convention and the American Bar Association's Section of International and Comparative Law. Arrayed against this formidable coalition was the leadership of the American Bar Association, patriotic groups including the Daughters of the American Revolution, and conservative Senators Tom Connally (D-TX) and Walter George (D-GA). Such voices sought to bury the treaty in the Foreign Relations Committee through constitutional, political, and racist predictions. First, they argued persuasively, though with dubious legal accuracy, that the convention would overturn parts of the U.S. Constitution, upsetting the delicate federal-state balance of power and infringing on individual liberties guaranteed by the Bill of Rights. Second, they reoriented the debate away from the treaty's actual provisions to a polemical discussion of whether the document would bring about a nascent world government under the United Nations. The international tribunal created by the treaty, opponents argued, could seize and try American citizens on false charges of genocide before foreign judges and with no recourse to criminal protections contained in the Bill of Rights. Finally, convention foes exploited issues of race to generate fear and concern among Southern senators that the convention might grant civil rights to African Americans or hold members of lynch mobs legally liable, as well as public officials who "merely" enforced the system of segregation.[38]

Elements of the American Bar Association, particularly its Commit-tee on Peace and Law through United Nations, began to agitate against the Genocide Convention once Truman had affixed his signature. Having already developed a critical stance on the Universal Declaration of Hu-man Rights and the covenant, the committee began to sketch the domestic damage the treaty would allegedly cause. Its early work paid dividends when the House of Delegates, the ABA's policymaking body, met in Chi-cago in early February 1949. The gathering unanimously asked for a year-long delay in ratifying the Genocide Convention "until there has been accorded the time and opportunity for adequate discussion and under-standing." President Frank Holman informed the State Department that the resolution "was the considered judgment of the House of Delegates, representing over 40,000 lawyers," so that there could be a careful study of the treaty's impact on domestic law. To initiate this discussion, the ABA received a $15,000 grant from the Carnegie Endowment for International Peace to sponsor 16 regional conferences over a span of three months to "educate" lawyers on the United Nations' human rights work.[39]

The State Department attempted in good faith to engage the leadership of the bar, many of whom its lawyers knew personally. Warren Austin, the head delegate to the United Nations, received a list of questions from the chair of the ABA's Peace and Law Committee, Judge William Ransom. The eight queries, Ransom argued, encapsulated the House of Delegates' reser-vations about the Genocide Convention, including whether the treaty was self-executing and if an international tribunal could try U.S. citizens. Two weeks later, Carl Rix, the new president of the Committee on Peace and Law, and George Finch, who had written the foreword to Lemkin's foun-dational work on genocide, invited representatives of the State and Justice departments to attend the regional conferences. Simsarian agreed, but af-ter three of the gatherings, he was appalled at what he heard. The modera-tors, who included Holman, Rix, and Finch, "were in general prejudiced against both the Covenant on Human Rights and the Genocide Conven-tion and sought repeatedly to raise as many irrelevant theoretical issues as possible in an effort to rouse the meetings against these documents," he wrote. This overt lobbying by the ABA's leadership later led the Carnegie Endowment to charge that the ABA was using non-partisan grant money to advance a political agenda and not an educational purpose.[40]

Seven months later, emboldened by negative feedback solicited at the regional conferences, the Peace and Law Committee issued a lengthy re-port to the House of Delegates. The group raised four major constitutional objections to senatorial ratification of the Genocide Convention. By federalizing crimes previously punished by state statutes, the treaty would revise the Tenth Amendment and concentrate power in the nation's capital. Second, Americans tried by international judges abroad would lose their Sixth Amendment right to a trial by jury in the place where the crimes were committed. Third, the penalization of incitement could provide a pretext for governmental regulation of speech and press in violation of the First Amendment. Finally, both houses of Congress under Article I, Section 8, had the power to define offenses against the law of nations, but only the Senate had ratification authority. In making this last charge, Rix's committee assumed that the treaty, rather than the Constitution, was at fault because the former was self-executing, meaning it could enter into force after ratification without the need for any accompanying legislation passed by both houses of Congress. The report recommended that the Senate not ratify the convention as written. This report anticipated both the strident tone and doomsday arguments that the Peace and Law Committee's members would employ in upcoming Senate testimony.[41]

The treaty opponents did not speak for all in the American Bar Association, and this schism created a showdown in the House of Delegates. The Committee on International Law of the New York City Bar Association, a progressively minded group with extensive international legal experience, approved a resolution in favor of ratification. The ABA's own Section of International and Comparative Law, consisting of one thousand transnational lawyers, also had its roots in New York City and the larger East Coast. Its members submitted an alternative report to the House of Delegates. They favored ratification accompanied by clarifying statements they thought would meet the key objections of their disagreeable brethren. By proposing simple assertions that the treaty was non-self-executing and that individuals charged with genocide would face trial in federal court rather than abroad, the section hoped to defuse any opposition to ratification. The report's preface praised "some of the ablest lawyers in the world" who formulated the treaty, noting that given its international nature, it was not surprising that parts did not square with the details of each country's existing legal system. The answer to such inconsistencies, the section pointedly noted, was not to reject this important document but to harmonize it with American law. Noting the historical basis for the convention, the international lawyers concluded that "The killing of [huge groups of people] merely for the sake of killing is the most abominable of all crimes" and necessitates moral and legal condemnation.[42]

The twin reports came before the House of Delegates in early September in St. Louis, but the expected battle was more of a rout. President

Frank Holman and the Committee on Peace and Law had used Carnegie Endowment money to hold meetings, publish brochures, and write articles attacking the Genocide Convention, though many of their arguments were transparently spurious. Holman told an Omaha lunch meeting that "an American [could] be extradited to a foreign country for trial even though his only offense had been telling a joke on a member of another race" due to the prohibition on causing mental harm. In Boston, he warned that "if one had an auto accident and seriously injured someone of another race," they would face a foreign tribunal. After prolonged and heated debate, the House of Delegates approved a resolution condemning genocide but noting that "the convention raises important fundamental [constitutional] questions but does not resolve them in a manner consistent with our form of Government." The statement opposed ratification of the treaty "as written," thus allowing for the possibility of later passage with amendments by signatory nations or with reservations approved by the Senate. The former raised procedural obstacles as the treaty had already received U.N. approval; the latter might cause diplomatic trouble if other nations viewed the United States as shirking its legal responsibilities. Though Charles Tillett, the chair of the Section of International and Comparative Law, later told the Senate that the finding amounted to a compromise, ABA opponents of the convention now argued that no group within the nation's largest and most prestigious association of lawyers found the convention acceptable in its present form.[43]

It was supporters of the convention, though, who dominated the first Senate proceedings. Hearings began on January 23, 1950, before a five-member subcommittee of the Foreign Relations Committee chaired by Brien McMahon (D-CT), a firm convention supporter. McMahon had extensive experience in criminal law, serving as a special assistant to the U.S. attorney general following graduation from Yale Law School. He oversaw the Justice Department's Criminal Division under President Roosevelt before leaving to resume private practice and run for the Senate in 1944. In four days of testimony, only 5 of 45 witnesses opposed the convention, 3 of whom belonged to the ABA's Committee on Peace and Law. Those testifying in favor included Nuremberg prosecutor Thomas Dodd, former Secretary of State George Marshall, and ex-Secretary of War Robert Patterson from the U.S. Committee for a U.N. Genocide Convention, a coalition whose combined membership surpassed 100 million people. Raphael Lemkin had assembled a remarkable list of religious leaders who submitted favorable testimony from the Jewish, Catholic, Lutheran, Greek Orthodox, Methodist, Unitarian, Seventh-Day Adventist, Presbyterian, Episcopal, and Quaker faith communities.

Spearheading the movement for ratification was the United States Committee for a U.N. Genocide Convention, though internal schisms hampered its hearing preparations. One dispute pitted Raphael Lemkin, the organization's hyperactive, aggressive, and well-connected activist, with co-chairman James Rosenberg over the timing of Senate hearings. Lemkin, who was in constant contact with Senator McMahon, expressed optimism that "support for the convention is considerable throughout the country." Rosenberg was more skeptical given the ABA's opposition, and he wanted hearings only after his group had accomplished an extensive public education campaign. Rosenberg also had drafted testimony without clearing it with the organization, which infuriated Lemkin. The New York lawyer had repeatedly argued in public that the convention would advance minority rights, and Lemkin knew that such words would alarm Southern senators. The two men also disagreed on procedure; Lemkin favored a lengthy hearing to provide many supporters with the chance to testify, while Rosenberg wanted a briefer and more limited schedule. With an eye toward Genocide Convention opponents and possible unreliable allies, Lemkin predicted that "we face, I am afraid, an uphill fight," even if the treaty had popular support.[44]

Once the hearings began, treaty advocates made other strategic decisions that hurt their cause. One problem was the constant behind-the-scenes lobbying by the impatient and tenacious Lemkin. Senator H. Alexander Smith (R-NJ) was put off by "a man who comes from a foreign country who . . . speaks broken English," and he stated that other senators "have been irritated to no end by this fellow running around." Even McMahon called Lemkin the "least plus quantity" in weighing the advantages of ratification adherents. Whether such comments betray a combination of anti-Semitism or xenophobia, a refusal to understand the personal nature of Lemkin's crusade, or reasonable political differences is hard to determine. A second and far more important error was in not aggressively reacting to testimony given by the Peace and Law Committee, which thereby gave the impression that Carl Rix and George Finch spoke for the nation's lawyers. While a few did testify in favor, such as Charles Tillett, their measured tone and acceptance of reservations made their contrasting position, arguments, and opinions not often clear. Moreover, it was difficult to combat the unreasonable and at times plain silly arguments made by respected treaty opponents: the sound and temperate language of Genocide Convention defenders lacked the force, passion, simplistic reasoning, and memorable qualities of the opponents' testimony. While convention supporters unquestionably had the stronger legal arguments, opponents exploited political and emotional advantages for their side. Finally, supporters rarely mentioned the moral and diplomatic reasons for passing the treaty. The Holocaust and Japanese atrocities in the Pacific showed that genocidal dictators presented grave dangers to international peace and security; early international intervention against their barbarity could have saved the world from catastrophic war. They may have believed that the hardening of the Cold War made such claims sound naïve and utopian.[45]

Opponents also had larger political trends operating in their favor, as a postwar political backlash against big government, Communism at home and abroad, and civil rights climaxed in the early 1950s, just as the Senate took up the Genocide Convention. The increasing belligerency of the Cold War, capped off by the start of the Korean War, made Americans oppose on principle further expansion of federal power, equating such growth with Communism or socialism. As Senator Robert Taft (R-OH) argued, "The New Dealers really attacked the basic philosophy of American government, its belief in individual and local freedom, in competition and reward for incentive. They echoed the arguments of Moscow against it, and wanted to move our system toward that of Russia." The Second Red Scare, or McCarthyism, provided a simple explanation for Cold War setbacks in China and Korea, while civil rights agitation and increased federal economic regulation was allegedly caused by Communists or "fellow travelers" in high positions of government. These growing attacks threw Truman on the defensive, and he responded by distancing himself from the progressive faction of his own party, thereby alienating the strongest supporters of human rights treaty ratification. The Republicans, using red-baiting tactics and capitalizing on Korean War discontent, picked up 5 Senate and 28 House seats in the 1950 elections. In an increasingly polarized, fearful, and crisis-oriented political atmosphere, a United Nations treaty to outlaw genocide had little chance if opponents successfully characterized it as a socialist dagger aimed at the U.S. Constitution.[46]

Three members of the ABA's Committee on Peace and Law who testified, Chairman Alfred Schweppe, former chair Rix, and George Finch, made that assertion paramount by depicting the Genocide Convention as a dangerous new type of treaty that contradicted the U.S. Constitution. They argued that it could squelch freedoms of speech and press, diminish the Tenth Amendment by giving the federal government prosecutorial power over a large list of crimes that states had wielded previously, and deprive Americans of a trial in their nation's courts.[47] These dangers existed, the lawyers informed the increasingly uneasy senators, because the U.S. Supreme Court had never declared a treaty unconstitutional. The lawyers cited Article VI, which stated, "This Constitution, and the Laws of the United States which shall be made in Pursuance thereof; and all Treaties made, or which shall be made, under the Authority of the United States, shall be the supreme Law of the Land." The verbiage implied in their minds a legal equivalency between the Constitution and treaties, and while they did not fear that treaties could literally rewrite portions of the Constitution, they worried that judges would suddenly after 150 years allow treaties to compromise the Constitution's protections.[48]

The concern of Rix, Schweppe, and Finch with individual freedoms did not extend to discrimination against African Americans, and their critique of the Genocide Convention began with an analysis of how it could be used to invalidate Jim Crow laws. With President Harry Truman's civil rights initiatives to ban the poll tax, create a permanent Fair Employment Practices Committee, and pass an anti-lynching law stalled in Congress, they believed that the treaty could be a Trojan horse for invalidating segregation. Finch identified the "mental harm" provision as the most likely culprit for use toward this end. He asked, "Can it be successfully denied that segregation laws are susceptible of being denounced as causing mental harm to all members of the group against which such laws discriminate?" Tying the intent to exterminate a group "in part" with lynching, Alfred Schweppe, who stated that he took "a back seat to no one in being opposed to genocide," presented a scenario involving all five African Americans in the town of Rendon, Washington. "We'll say," he narrated, "that sometimes some crime of violence occurs, and as a result of it, some ill-meaning citizens of that community—I wouldn't call them well-meaning—decide that they want to get rid of these people." Could they face trial for genocide for wanting to kill or cause mental harm to five members of that racial group? If so, could such prosecutions be the death knell of Jim Crow laws and the start of forced integration in the South? These concerns had earlier persuaded the ABA's Section on International Law, which supported the convention, to define "mental harm" as limited to "permanent physical injury to mental faculties, such as that caused by the excessive use or administration of narcotics." McMahon's subcommittee, in an attempt to defuse the claims of Finch and Schweppe that had won over Senator Elbert Thomas (D-UT), recommended passing along the clarifying definition of "mental harm" to the full Foreign Relations Committee.[49]

Holman and other convention opponents tied the maintenance of individual freedoms to white supremacy and states' rights, and they warned that an enlargement of federal criminal jurisdiction came at the expense of existing constitutional liberties. By creating a new class of federal crimes under the rubric of genocide, the Tenth Amendment would erode, thereby upsetting the delicate balance of power between state and national authority. They frequently cited the 1920 Supreme Court case of *Missouri v. Holland*, which had allowed a treaty to override less restrictive state hunting regulations. On the one hand, this was hardly a surprising ruling, as the Constitution's Article VI plainly states that treaties are "the supreme Law of the Land; and the Judges in every State shall be bound thereby, any Thing in the Constitution or Laws of any State to the Contrary notwithstanding." The Peace and Law Committee's objection was political, therefore, and not constitutional in nature. As the power to prosecute crimes defined by the Genocide Convention traditionally fell under the purview of states, some ABA members worried that the convention would set a precedent toward federalizing the entire criminal code. Carl Rix asked the critical question: "If there is to be a succession of treaties from the United Nations dealing with domestic questions, are we ready to surrender the power of the States over such matters to the Federal Government?"[50]

The Genocide Convention would not only centralize government at the national level, according to convention opponents, but it would also grant foreign institutions unprecedented authority over Americans. The treaty declared genocide to be a breach of international law whose violators could be tried by international courts. Even though the treaty allowed foreign courts to intervene only if a nation had accepted the tribunal's jurisdiction *and* had refused to prosecute, the Peace and Law Committee assumed without any evidence that Americans would be extradited for trial. This scenario, the Peace and Law Committee argued, was a violation of Article III of the Constitution, which guaranteed Americans a trial in the place where the crime occurred. It also brought back memories of the American Revolution to George Finch, as the Declaration of Independence had condemned King George III "for transporting us beyond seas to be tried for pretended offenses." Once cast before a tribunal of foreign judges, Americans would be shorn of protections recognized by the Bill of Rights. The charges made an impression on New Jersey Senator H. Alexander Smith, who in executive session announced that they were the main reason for his opposition to ratification. "I do not want any American citizen to be tried by a tribunal, for example, such as the Russians may have," he declared. Senator Alexander Wiley (R-WI) agreed, stating that "I don't think the peoples of the earth are in any position where they can tell this great people on morals, politics, and religion, how they should live." These statements showed the level of xenophobia and Cold War fears that infused Genocide Convention debates in private.[51]

Genocide Convention supporters from the State Department and private organizations tried to rebut these challenges by laying out the moral and constitutional reasons for American accession. The first testimony came from Dean Rusk, the Deputy Undersecretary of State, and Solicitor General Philip Perlman. After noting that seven nations had already ratified the convention, Rusk asserted that

> the United States took a leading part in the United Nations in the international effort to outlaw this shocking crime of genocide. I can only express, on behalf of the State Department, our earnest hope that the Senate of the United States, by giving its advice and consent to the ratification of this convention, will demonstrate to the rest of the world that the United States is determined to maintain its moral leadership in international affairs, and to participate in the development of international law on the basis of human justice.[52]

Perlman focused on the constitutionality of entering into the convention. He asserted that the Holocaust and other wartime atrocities made genocide an appropriate subject for treaty-making. Any assertions that the treaty would diminish the authority of the Constitution were false, Perlman concluded, because the Supreme Court had consistently ruled in dicta that treaties could not invalidate parts of the U.S. Constitution. The clearest statement came in the 1890 case of *Geofroy v. Riggs*. Justice Stephen Johnson Fields, speaking for a unanimous court, declared that "it would not be contended that it [the treaty-making power] extends so far as to authorize what the Constitution forbids, or a change in the character of the government." Moreover, Genocide Convention supporters pointed out that their adversaries never offered any examples of unconstitutional treaties that the Supreme Court had nevertheless been forced to uphold.[53]

Though they believed that treaties could not override the Constitution, past and present Truman administration officials nonetheless strove to prove the constitutionality of the Genocide Convention. Perlman, State Department Legal Advisor Adrian Fisher, and former Nuremberg prosecutor (and dissenting ABA Committee on Peace and Law member) Thomas Dodd pointed out that a simple examination of the drafting history would demonstrate that the concepts of "mental harm" and "incitement to commit genocide" fit very well into existing American constitutional law. The former included only, in Fisher's words, the causing of "permanent impairment of mental faculty," and "not just embarrassment or hurt feelings, or even the sense of outrage that comes from such action as racial discrimination or segregation." This interpretation was clearly stated by the treaty's authors and reaffirmed by the State Department, which defined "mental harm" as the "disintegration of the mind by the imposition of stupefying drugs." Turning to the incitement clause, the Solicitor General argued that the Supreme Court had already denied First Amendment immunity to those charged with solicitation or incitement to commit a crime. Perlman quoted Justice Oliver Wendell Holmes, who wrote in *Frohwerk v. United States*, a case involving the publishing of antiwar editorials during World War I, "We venture to believe that neither Hamilton nor Madison, nor any other competent person then or later, ever supposed that to make criminal the counseling of a murder within the jurisdiction of Congress would be an unconstitutional interference with free speech."[54]

Lawyers supporting the Genocide Convention agreed with Holman, Schweppe, and Finch that its provisions were superior to local, state, and existing federal laws as stated quite plainly by Article VI of the Constitution. To them, then, *Missouri v. Holland* was just a restatement of the obvious: treaties are not restricted, in the words of Justice Oliver Wendell Holmes from that case, "by some invisible radiation from the general terms of the Tenth Amendment." The United States had, from its earliest post-Constitutional days until now, entered into treaties that nullified inconsistent state and local laws.[55] The Genocide Convention was also far from the first treaty that federalized crimes that had historically fallen under the jurisdiction of states. Multilateral conventions that criminalized drug trafficking, the sale of obscene publications, and prostitution provided only some examples of this power. Under these treaties, it is important to note, state and federal courts had *concurrent* criminal jurisdiction to prosecute alleged offenders; an individual could face trial in both state and federal courts without double jeopardy attaching. If the Genocide Convention became the law of the land, state courts could still prosecute individuals under state law if they incorporated the crime of genocide into their legal codes.[56]

In responding to the charge that an international tribunal would trample the rights of alleged American offenders, Robert Patterson of the United States Committee for a United Nations Genocide Convention provided a sensible two-part answer. The court could not exist until a U.N. body had drafted its statute, during which time Washington could negotiate its contents, after which the Senate would vote on ratification. Only if the Senate approved the statute, to which it could attach whatever reservations it felt necessary to safeguard the Bill of Rights and American sovereignty, could the court even potentially try an American citizen. Even by ratifying the court's statute, Patterson continued, the Senate did not relinquish the right of Americans to face trial before their own courts. The principle of territorial jurisdiction, whereby a country had primary jurisdiction to prosecute all crimes committed within its borders, was a cornerstone of international law that the convention itself affirmed. The State and Justice departments added a joint statement concluding that senatorial ratification "is in no way—legally or morally—committing the United States to send American citizens abroad for trial for acts committed in the United States." Perlman become so exasperated with the ABA's erroneous conclusions on this topic that he met personally with ABA leaders and "begged" them to stop repeating such falsehoods when speaking to regional bar associations.[57]

Having testified that the Genocide Convention would cause no constitutional problems, treaty supporters did not have to respond to charges that the agreement was self-executing. If the treaty already fit within the existing constitutional framework, then it mattered not whether the federal courts could enforce the treaty without congressional implementing legislation. Yet officials from the State and Justice departments and specialists in international law wanted to provide as much reassurance as possible to senators, and so they firmly denied that the convention was self-executing. They repeatedly pointed to the treaty's own clear words, under which signatories "undertake to enact, in accordance with their respective Constitutions, the necessary legislation to give effect to the provisions of the present Convention." This clause made it crystal clear to them that the treaty required national legislatures to pass implementation laws before the document obtained any internal legal standing. The convention could hardly be enforced on its own accord anyway since it contained no criminal penalties, which Congress would have to attach before any court could prosecute. Adrian Fisher, the State Department legal advisor, quoted no less an authority than the first Supreme Court Chief Justice, John Marshall, who observed that when the terms of a treaty "import a contract, when either of the parties engage to perform a particular act, the treaty addresses itself to the political, not the judicial, department, and the legislature must execute the contract before it can become a rule of the court."[58]

Genocide Convention backers also emphasized, though belatedly, the diplomatic advantages that would accrue to the United States as a treaty party. The State Department explained how ratification would redound to America's advantage in the Cold War. If, as Undersecretary of State Dean Rusk asserted, the United States "was engaged in a very fundamental struggle in our foreign relations" with the Soviet Union, passage of the convention would be proof of American leadership in the global fight to protect human rights. "We all know too well that millions of human beings are still subjected to the domination of ruthless totalitarian regimes, and that the specter of genocide still haunts mankind. It should be made clear to such governments that the United States and other civilized countries do not condone such conduct now any more than in the past." Senator McMahon, attempting to reach out to his skeptical anti-Communist, conservative colleagues, pointed out that, as a state party, the United States could charge the Soviet Union with genocide against Latvians, Ukrainians, and other ethnic minorities under the convention. Solicitor General Perlman agreed, asserting that such a move would inspire those living behind the Iron Curtain to believe "that the civilized nations of the world have not forgotten them and will join in a condemnation of a nation who attempts to wipe them out."[59]

Rusk, Perlman, and Lemkin found common ground with Peace and Law Committee members who argued that the convention would not protect African Americans from extralegal murders in the South. In Rusk's interpretation of the treaty, genocide occurred only when the intent existed to destroy an entire group, and those who committed lynchings lacked this requisite motivation. Lawyer and civil rights activist Eunice Carter had the unusual task of stating that she supported something that would not promote her larger cause in the least. In brief testimony on behalf of the National Council of Negro Women, she explained, "the situation of the Negro people in this country is in no way involved" in these deliberations. Lemkin agreed, offering that "the basic policy of the South is not to destroy the Negro but to preserve that race on a different level of existence." This narrow interpretation of intent did not rest on hard evidence, though, for the issue of whether genocide encompassed acts committed with the intent to eliminate part of a group was uncertain. Even in this case, though, Rusk and Perlman pointed out that a glance at the convention's drafting history showed that the enumerated genocidal acts had to affect a large portion of the targeted group. This was one human rights treaty that had no power to invalidate white supremacy in the United States, they asserted without apparent irony.[60]

After four days of contentious hearings, Senator McMahon's subcommittee unanimously recommended ratification subject to the inclusion of several understandings that showed the influence of the Peace and Law Committee. Concerned that the Convention might invalidate segregation laws and prosecute vigilantism, the senators declared that a "substantial portion" of a group must be actually affected for genocide to occur, and it defined "mental harm" as "permanent physical injury to mental faculties."

Lynch mobs, in contrast, did not aim to destroy "the Negro race as a whole or in part, but to frighten local Negroes from doing certain things or to visit mob justice and punishment outside of the regular courts upon those believed guilty of having committed certain acts." By defining "complicity to commit genocide" as "participation before and after the fact and aiding and abetting in the commission of the crime of genocide," the body hoped to square it with existing federal law. To allay the objections of states' rightists, a legally ambiguous addendum pronounced that ratification in no way abridged "the traditional jurisdiction of the several states of the Union with regard to crime." As months dragged on without a full committee vote scheduled, McMahon proposed a fifth reservation to ensure that the federal government did not intrude, as a result of the treaty, into *any* area of policymaking reserved to states under the Tenth Amendment. Treaty advocates were in no position to object to these neutering statements that could inspire other nations to make similarly qualified commitments to prevent genocide. As the U.S. Committee for a U.N. Genocide Convention ran a deficit and its members talked of dissolution, Foreign Relations Committee Chair Tom Connally and ranking Democrat Walter George favored indefinite postponement of full committee discussion. Lemkin reported gloomily, "I found out that the ABA did quite a devastating job on the senators."[61]

The sudden start of the Korean War provided an unexpected catalyst for renewed lobbying on behalf of the convention. On June 25, 1950, North Korean forces overran the five-year-old line of demarcation on a mission to unite the peninsula under Communist rule. Advancing southward, they took Seoul in three days and began hunting and killing South Korean civil servants, Christians, and other sympathizers of the American-backed dictator Syngman Rhee. On July 31, the South Korean ambassador to the United States, John Myun Chang, sent an urgent letter to Warren Austin, the American ambassador to the United Nations, claiming that North Korea was bent on exterminating the "national, cultural, and religious leadership" of his country. He asked for American ratification of the convention to further enshrine the principle against genocide in international law and call attention to the North's brutality. A week earlier, representatives of 32 religious and labor organizations had sent a telegram to Secretary of State Acheson urging him to lobby for convention ratification, which would help protect "religious and national groups from destruction" in South Korea. President Truman made the same point, sending a note to Foreign Relations Committee Chair Connally along with Chang's telegram, and concluding that "speedy" ratification was "essential to the effective maintenance of our leadership of the free and civilized nations of the world in the present struggle against the forces of aggression and barbarism." Having the United States as a party might deter rulers from committing mass murder, including against South Korean Christians, he added for emphasis. The administration released the letter to the *New York Times* and other major newspapers.[62]

Senators Connally and Alexander Wiley (R-WI) nonetheless maintained a hostile attitude during executive sessions in May, August, and September 1950. They were convinced that the convention would sacrifice American sovereignty to the United Nations and other nations, constitutional rights to an international tribunal, and segregation statutes to an irresponsible use of the treaty power. Wiley railed against U.N. human rights treaties that would "crack the Constitution" and overturn state and federal laws. "I don't want to sell America short in the sense that we are going to put ourselves in a position where [other nations] can take us for a ride . . . they are [sic] different breed from us. We are an American breed, a mixture of all of them, and we have created different ideals, different concepts." Lemkin, with his broken English and passionate lobbying, had turned off at least three senators on the committee. "If you see him," convention supporter Senator Henry Cabot Lodge told Fisher, "you ought to tell him he has done his own cause a great deal of harm." Given these negatives, Wiley and Connally did not see the need to ratify what they saw as a problematic treaty, given that in their opinion genocide was exceedingly unlikely to occur in the United States. When State Department Legal Advisor Adrian Fisher discussed the possibility of filing charges against the Soviet Union for genocide against ethnic minorities, Connally cut him off. He deplored State Department officials for "coming up here and lecturing to Congress about the morals or morality of the United States." After reading aloud the 1949 ABA House of Delegates Resolution opposing ratification, he refused to take a committee vote, believing that a "bitter controversy" would erupt on the Senate floor if it passed out of his committee.[63]

Complicating the ratification debate in the Senate was the uncertain legality of any reservations the United States and others might propose to the Genocide Convention. The treaty itself contained no allowance for such exceptions, though the Soviet Union, Poland, Bulgaria, Romania, and the Philippines had attached several, to which some other parties to the treaty objected. Past practice yielded conflicting guidance on what constituted a legal reservation. The Pan American Union, the predecessor of the Organization of American States, allowed nations to reject the reservations of others, and it was up to each nation to decide for itself if it considered the reserving nation to still be a party to the treaty. If no state objected, the reserving state, with its reservation included, became a party to the treaty. This created a complex web of partial and total state parties to a treaty, and it also made it hard to enforce such contracts if countries widely differed in their terms of acceptance. In contrast, the League of Nations simply recognized that a valid reservation had to have the unanimous consent of all signatories to the treaty. ABA leaders and several senators worried that if the United Nations adopted the League of Nations system, any signatory nation could exercise veto power over what American legislators saw as constitutionally necessary modifications. Pending General Assembly guidance, Secretary-General Trygve Lie settled ad interim on a modified League of Nations practice. He allowed only ratifying countries, and not just those that had signed the convention, to accept or object to reservations. Under these terms, the necessary 20 nations adopted the convention, and the United Nations' first human rights treaty became law on January 12, 1951. The General Assembly asked the International Court of Justice to render a definitive judgment on the reservation conundrum.[64]

Controversy over Lie's interim actions on reservations further marred the convention's chances of ratification in the Senate. Because the assembly had included no instructions for Lie to follow while the ICJ deliberated, he was unclear on whether to continue his interim policy. The State Department feared that any change would allow the Soviet Union, as a signatory, to veto any reservations attached by the Senate, and the *New York Times* carried a page-two story under the provocative headline "U.S. Senate Faces Soviet Veto in U.N." In addition, Senator Hubert Humphrey (D-MN), a prominent convention supporter, told President Truman that sending the issue to the ICJ would force the secretary-general to decline all reservations under the legal doctrine of pendente lite, or "while the litigation is pending." Such uncertainty and delays, expected to last a year before the ICJ issued its decision, could freeze Senate consideration of the convention at a time when momentum to ratify was rising from the Korean War. Although the State Department soon denied the likelihood of such a change in policy by the secretary-general, it immediately proposed an amendment instructing him to accept all reservations without prejudice until the ICJ had decided otherwise. The amendment passed the General Assembly by a wide margin. Truman had bought additional time for the Senate Foreign Relations Committee to report out the convention with reservations. Yet such legal machinations could hardly have impressed domestic treaty opponents, who had continuously railed against the United Nations and its member nations for exercising influence over foreign policymaking.[65]

The United States pushed hard for ICJ acceptance of the Pan American system, which would allow American ratification of the convention with controversial reservations intact. In a brief filed with the ICJ, the State Department's lawyers asked the court to balance the need for the document's maximum acceptance among nations with "avoid[ing] either a general undermining of the standards accepted by many without reservation, or imposing any new obligations without the necessary consent on all upon whom they fall." The brief dismissed the unanimity required by the League of Nations system as almost impossible given the more diverse geographical, legal, and cultural membership of the United Nations. The net effect of affirming that procedure would be a reduction in the number of signatories to any convention. The Pan American system, in contrast, allowed signatory and ratifying nations to decide for themselves which reservations were legally permissible. This power to bilaterally nullify another state's reservations, the State Department argued, would persuade nations to limit the number of reservations offered, would act as a check on frivolous reservations, and would result in a maximum number of states signing and ratifying the Genocide Convention. Left unspoken was the expectation that the Senate would ratify with treaty with controversial reservations that even American allies might find objectionable, let alone the Soviet Union—but they would lack the power to invalidate them.[66]

The World Court, in a fractured opinion delivered on May 28, 1951, agreed with most of the American position. Seven of the twelve justices ruled

> that a State which has made and maintained a reservation which has been objected to by one or more of the parties to the Convention but not by others, can be regarded as being a party to the Convention if the reservation is compatible with the object and purpose of the Convention; otherwise, that State cannot be regarded as being a party to the Convention.[67]

It would be up to the ICJ to decide whether specific reservations met the "object and purpose" standard in specific cases. The court upheld the right only of ratified nations to object to a reservation, and it ruled that the objecting country could consider at its discretion the reserving state not to be a party to the treaty. A reserving nation would be a party to an international convention, therefore, to the extent that other nations did not reject its reservations. With the decision, the pace of ratifications sped up; between the court's decision and the end of 1955, 22 nations ratified the treaty, all but one without any reservations. The decision opened the door for qualified U.S. ratification, as the reservations proposed by McMahon's subcommittee would be legally valid unless every other ratifying nation objected to them.[68]

Any excitement generated by the World Court's decision was tempered by the growing realization that the Senate would not ratify the Genocide Convention even in a qualified manner. In early November 1950, Solicitor General Philip Perlman sent all Foreign Relations Committee members a pointed response to the ABA's Peace and Law Committee testimony. He attached a statement by Nuremberg prosecutor and committee member Thomas Dodd, whose dissent from the body's opposition to the Genocide Convention made him persona non grata in ABA committee meetings. Perlman also noted that the ABA's Section on International and Comparative Law and the International Bar Association had also supported ratification. He concluded that "there is not a single good argument why ratification should be withheld, especially in light of the clarifying reservations recommended by your subcommittee." In mid-September 1951, McMahon tried one more time to have the Foreign Relations Committee report the treaty to the Senate. Chairman Connally again dissented, declaring its consideration would "cause a hell of a row" and that he opposed "making treaties that bind us to do things in our own domestic jurisdiction." Senator Walter George agreed and added that the convention was "filled with subtle and obscure and doublemeaning things that really aim to attack the constitutional setup we have under our dual [federal-state] system." Despite McMahon's begging Connally for a future roll call vote, the meeting adjourned without a quorum, and the Foreign Relations Committee would not discuss the treaty again until 20 years had passed.[69]

The Genocide Convention met with a slow death in the Senate, in a way that its domestic and foreign supporters could not have expected back in 1948. In the wake of horrific suffering from the Holocaust and other World War II atrocities, survivors and their governments pushed for a global ban on genocide. Their efforts, spearheaded by a Polish Jew who lost dozens of family members to the Nazis, resulted in the world's first ban on the mass killing of civilians whether in wartime or peace. The unanimous vote in the United Nations reflected the shame and guilt that many felt toward recent events and the determination to avoid a repetition. Although the treaty did not include everything that American negotiators wanted, President Harry Truman submitted it to the Senate and endorsed its ratification. Hearings promptly began, and a grassroots effort to lobby members of the Foreign Relations Committee started in earnest. At this point the momentum stalled. Conservative senators, reacting against New Deal liberalism, United Nations idealism, and civil rights activism, viewed the convention with skepticism. Fearing it would harm Americans over-seas and the constitutional status quo at home, they, along with a segment of the American Bar Association, increasingly doubted the wisdom of ac-ceding to a treaty that the State Department had played such an important and influential role in drafting. Not even a series of understandings and reservations offered by their colleagues could assuage their concerns. As a result, the Senate refused to ratify the Genocide Convention until 1986, and then only accompanied by a similar list of exceptions. By that time Lemkin was dead of heart failure, having perished alone and penniless in a New York City apartment. His tombstone reads, "Dr. Raphael Lemkin (1900–1959), the Father of the Genocide Convention."[70]

By not ratifying the Genocide Convention, the Senate effectively con-ceded American leadership in the worldwide movement against genocide at the United Nations. Supporters tried again to leverage the Cold War as a reason for passage of the treaty, noting that it could be used to spotlight repression behind the Iron Curtain. On January 11, 1952, over a hundred Republican congressmen signed a letter to Secretary of State Dean Ache-son asking him to start "a campaign [at the United Nations] to expose So-viet genocide" committed against Poles, Lithuanians, Czechs, Ukrainians, and other ethnic groups. They claimed to represent 12 million Americans born in those "captive" nations or regions. The administration had a deli-cate problem, as a close presidential race was unfolding, and voters with Eastern European roots had traditionally supported Democratic candi-dates. Assistant Secretary of State Jack McFall responded by acidly not-ing that "our failure to ratify the convention keeps this Government from exerting its full moral influence to deter and prevent this deplorable crime. We cannot very well insist," he continued, "that other nations abide by the principles to which we have not given our own endorsement."[71]

The policy reversal also caused the United States actual embarrassment at the United Nations. On August 3, 1953, the Economic and Social Coun-cil approved a resolution entreating states to hasten approval of the conven-tion. The Eisenhower administration, placed in a difficult position due to its own opposition to ratification, wanted to abstain in the vote. When the resolution came before the General Assembly's Legal Committee, though, U.S. delegate Archibald Carey insisted, due to his personal beliefs, on vot-ing affirmatively. Even a meeting with American ambassador to the United Nations Henry Cabot Lodge could not sway him. Lodge tried to schedule a meeting between Carey and Secretary of State John Foster Dulles, but Dulles told him to solve the problem on his own. Despite Lodge's extraor-dinary efforts to delay a vote by trying to cancel the Legal Committee's meeting, the body including Carey unanimously approved the resolution on October 8. After the General Assembly passed the resolution a month later, again with American support, Lodge had to issue an awkward press release explaining that the vote was "not a commitment as to the timing of action by the United States on the Genocide Convention, either on behalf of the Executive or Legislative Branch." He added in a pointed warning to the secretary-general that "the United States does not interpret the resolution as authorizing propaganda in the United States in relation to a matter pending before the United States Senate." That statement generated a rebuke from Senator Herbert Lehman (D-NY), who decried Lodge's attempts to dictate what the secretary-general could do in carrying out a General Assembly directive. "We cannot expect to be the leader of free nations within the United Nations if we insist on treating the United Nations as if it was an organ of the United States Government," he added. Lodge wrote an extremely apologetic letter to Dulles for his handling of the Carey matter, signing it "with regret"; Dulles did not reply. He had his hands full trying to stop the American Bar Association and a group of conservative senators who, inspired by the Genocide convention's defeat, set about passing a constitutional amendment to negate the domestic impact of all future human rights treaties.[72]

CHAPTER 6

The End of a Crusade, 1951–1953

THE RISING DOMESTIC AND international backlash against the Genocide Convention and the human rights covenant soon forced Presidents Harry S. Truman and Dwight D. Eisenhower to change policy at the United Nations. The victorious struggle against the convention waged by conservative senators and leaders of the American Bar Association had generated the publicity, legal arguments, and political connections that they now used to attack the human rights covenant. By asserting that the covenant and other United Nations agreements could invalidate parts of the U.S. Constitution, abolish federalism by creating a centralized national government, and transport socialism to American shores, this coalition, led by Senator John Bricker (R-OH), battled for a constitutional amendment to limit the internal power of all treaties. State Department officials, growing increasingly anxious, tried to blunt such criticism by advancing proposals in the United Nations Commission on Human Rights (UNCHR) to protect states' rights and strike all references to economic and social guarantees. UNCHR members, though, not only rejected the American proposals, but also added an expansive article on self-determination, attached a long list of economic guarantees, and omitted a federal-state article. Truman and Eleanor Roosevelt left office with U.S. human rights policy in shambles, a UNCHR polarized along East-West and North-South lines, and a hostile Senate on the verge of approving a constitutional amendment to repudiate their human rights proposals. It was an inglorious and bitter end for both policymakers, one who had championed American membership in the United Nations, and the other who had served for five years as the inaugural chair of the first ever global human rights commission.

To thwart passage of a constitutional amendment that he believed would cripple the president's powers in foreign affairs, incoming President Dwight D. Eisenhower radically altered American human rights policy. He and Secretary of State John Foster Dulles proposed to replace the treaty-based program of their predecessors with an "Action Program," which would restrict the UNCHR's work to educating and advising governments on human rights issues. To deflect foreign criticism of this proposal and diminish support for Bricker's amendment, Eisenhower, Dulles, and U.N. Ambassador Henry Cabot Lodge launched a propaganda offensive at the United Nations to highlight the woeful human rights records of Communist nations. Eisenhower's substitute recommendations, though, met with disdain in the UNCHR. American withdrawal from the treaty-drafting process helped to create deadlock in the commission; the body would debate the covenants aimlessly for 13 more years. Another consequence would be the reluctance of future presidents to submit human rights treaties, including the Genocide Convention, for Senate consideration. Without having ratified the basic legal instruments that defined international human rights law, Washington's Cold War–tinged human rights rhetoric often sounded hypocritical, hollow, and opportunistic.

John Foster Dulles himself had traveled the trajectory from Wilsonian idealist to nationalistic Cold Warrior, and his evolution provides a window into a changing domestic political climate. His Presbyterian-infused worldview led him to fight during World War II for causes related to universal justice, a recognition of human rights, and a United Nations that had the power to enforce peace between countries. Lobbying for such principles on behalf of the Federal Council of Churches raised Dulles's stature enough to secure an invitation as a delegate to the San Francisco Conference. It was in dealing with the practical application of theological principles that his more narrow, nationalistic views emerged. He fought for a strong domestic jurisdiction clause and a weak full employment requirement in the U.N. Charter, for example. When a friend questioned Dulles about the gap between his theological exhortations and his positions in San Francisco, he replied, "one who has official responsibility must conduct himself somewhat differently than one who, as a private citizen, stands on the side-lines giving advice."[1]

The developing Cold War only sharpened his situational distinction between "proper" U.N. activities such as peacemaking and intrusive acts that were contrary to state sovereignty, such as going beyond promoting human rights (as in the Universal Declaration) and into their enforcement (as with the U.N. covenants). Once the covenants contained controversial articles on self-determination and economic and social rights that the U.S. Constitution did not recognize, Dulles became an outspoken opponent of Senate ratification. In his mind, such requirements smacked of Communism, statism, and United Nations intervention; the first attacked Christianity itself, the second undermined individual free will, and the third compromised the notion of American exceptionalism that had made the United States the defender of the free world against Soviet aggression and answerable to no one.[2]

By early 1951, with the Genocide Convention stalled in the Senate and a backlash growing against the latest version of the human rights covenant, even the strongest domestic backers of the U.N. human rights program searched for an alternative way to promote human rights at home. They disagreed, though, on the content and focus of a new policy, and three different paths emerged. Union leader A. Philip Randolph, Walter White of the NAACP, and the National Council of Negro Women's Mary McLeod Bethune, joined by a dozen other African American labor and civil rights leaders, asked Truman to adopt a domestic focus by "not only talking democracy and fighting for it across the earth, but . . . demonstrating it in practice here at home." The abolition of segregation in the nation's capital, the hiring of African Americans into federal positions including the diplomatic corps, and the issuance of an executive order banning job discrimination in the defense industry, they believed, would comprise necessary and effective responses to "forces which weaken our democracy in the eyes of the world and which all too frequently give our enemies a justifiable reason to spread dangerous propaganda against us." They delivered these demands to an ambivalent President Truman in late February 1951. Portrayed as weak on Communism at home by McCarthyites and abroad due to a Korean War stalemate, the Democrats lost 5 Senate and 28 House seats in the November 1950 elections, barely retaining a majority in both chambers. With Southerners in control of key congressional committees, it was unlikely that the executive or legislative branches would summon the necessary political will to make civil rights progress.[3]

Other groups were not willing to give up on the covenant, though they disagreed on its proper content. The American Jewish Committee embraced this view, noting that the "United States, as the leader of those nations carrying out the United Nations' decisions on aggression in Asia, should also assume the leadership in the movement for human rights and freedoms in the world organization." The American Civil Liberties Union agreed, endorsing the State Department's position that economic and social rights belonged in a separate treaty. The National Federation of Business and Professional Women's Clubs endorsed a covenant that allowed for NGO petitions and the right to participate in government, both of which the State Department opposed. At a conference in Chicago sponsored by the American Association for the United Nations, almost one hundred NGOs approved a statement calling for American ratification of the covenant and for a global educational campaign on the principles enshrined in the Universal Declaration of Human Rights. Inserting their proposals into a Cold War context, the signers argued that "these efforts strike at the tyrannies of the police state, whether Communist or Fascist, and also at the causes of manifold grievances and injustices which arouse strife and endanger peace. As such, they constitute one of the greatest hopes of human progress through the United Nations."[4]

A third position emphasized staying engaged in the UNCHR but radically altering its agenda. Disillusioned by the actions of the 1951 General Assembly, these groups advocated giving low priority to covenant completion and instead attacking Communist nations for violating human rights. The Jewish Labor Committee alerted the State Department to practices of "cultural and spiritual genocide" against Soviet Jews and demanded an on-site investigation by the United Nations. A late January meeting of State Department officials and a dozen NGOs wrestled with a core dilemma: as the United States continued to lose on controversial issues in the UNCHR, it was becoming less likely that the Senate would ratify any resulting covenant. Attendees, who included longtime human rights experts Ben Cohen, Frederick Nolde, Clark Eichelberger, and James Shotwell, split over whether to lobby for a covenant or propose a different method of promoting human rights. Proposals for the latter might require governments to file periodic reports on their human rights practices or convene regional commissions to study human rights issues. The consensus, though, pointed away from human rights treaties. As these individuals had been passionate supporters of the Universal Declaration of Human Rights and early work on the covenant, their latest recommendations showed how quickly the political landscape in Washington had changed.[5]

Amid these schisms born of despair, Eleanor Roosevelt, James Simsarian, Jack Tate, and other covenant supporters in the State Department were pleasantly surprised by the unexpected vote of the U.N. Economic and Social Council (ECOSOC) in late August to place political and economic rights in separate covenants. After the Human Rights Commission had drafted a list of such guarantees for inclusion in one covenant, Roosevelt and her advisors had deemed any future lobbying for two covenants "unproductive and unwise." They feared the ill will from non-aligned, poorer nations that such a likely unsuccessful campaign would generate. The State Department therefore accepted one covenant with the understanding that economic and social "rights" were "to be treated [only] as objectives" by U.N. members and did not require an internal or global redistribution of wealth. Yet, due to a unified Western presence in ECOSOC, the body voted to reconsider the call for a single covenant. It was a narrow vote, with influential India, Iran, Peru, and Uruguay agreeing with the West that the immediate enforcement of civil rights, as compared with the gradual realization of economic guarantees, necessitated placing each group in a separate convention. The body also affirmed the need for a federal-state article. Though these were two clear American wins, Durward Sandifer was cautious, for persuading the more diverse General Assembly to approve these decisions would be difficult. Senator John Bricker was similarly unimpressed. "A few more 'victories,'" he glumly stated soon after the vote, "and the Constitution will be lost."[6]

Bricker found a high-profile opportunity to demonstrate his critique during the trial of Associated Press Reporter William Oatis in Czechoslovakia. On July 4, 1951, the Czech government convicted Oatis of espionage for what the prosecution ironically termed "his discretion and insistence on obtaining only accurate, correct, verified information." He faced ten years in prison. The State Department quickly condemned the detention and sponsored a successful ECOSOC resolution that called on governments generically to "do all within their power to safeguard the right of correspondents freely and faithfully to gather and transmit news." Bricker saw the episode as another opportunity to criticize the human rights covenants. Citing the draft article that allowed governments to limit freedom of the press in order to protect "public order, safety, health, or morals," the Ohio senator declared that the covenant would condone similar harassment of reporters. "How can the State Department complain about the imprisonment of William Oatis," Bricker inquired, when the covenant "would legitimize such action?" Three weeks later, Bricker introduced his first constitutional amendment to bar the signing of any treaty "respecting the rights and freedoms of citizens of the United States recognized in this Constitution." Written by Bricker and an aide, the amendment was poorly worded and received little attention in the Senate, but it marked the beginning of his crusade to "defend" the Constitution from U.N. human rights pronouncements.[7]

As covenant opponents upped the constitutional ante, their antagonists in the State Department faced desertion by domestic allies and non-aligned nations due to Cold War politics. At home, the Second Red Scare's condemnation of civil rights activism tore liberal coalitions apart, weakening a key segment of covenant supporters. The NAACP under Walter White made the controversial decision to abandon U.N. petitions, conduct an anti-Communist internal purge, and align the group politically with the Truman administration. He hoped the strategy would defuse accusations that the prestigious group was a Communist front, especially as he now collaborated with Eleanor Roosevelt and Truman to criticize Soviet denunciations of American civil rights violations. These moves caused the Civil Rights Congress (CRC) to charge the NAACP with minimizing Jim Crow at home and apologizing for it abroad. The CRC, formed in the mid-1940s, consisted of remnants of the National Negro Congress (which had petitioned the United Nations in 1946) and elements of the American Communist Party. Copying the NNC's strategy, on November 12, CRC President William Patterson published *We Charge Genocide* to a national and international audience. Using data compiled ironically from the NAACP and the U.S. government, the heavily researched document argued that the U.S. government had violated the Genocide Convention by supporting segregation. The document made clear that

> Words and statistics are but poor things to convey the long agony of the Negro people. We have proved "killing members of a group"—but the case after case after case cited does nothing to assuage the helplessness of the innocent Negro trapped at this instant by police in a cell which will be the scene of his death. We have shown "mental and bodily harm" in violation of Article 2 of the Genocide Convention but this proof can barely indicate the life-long terror of thousands on thousands of Negroes forced to live under the menace of official violence, mob law and the Ku Klux Klan. We have tried to reveal something of the deliberate infliction "on the group of conditions which bring about its physical destruction in whole or in part"—but this cannot convey the hopeless despair of those forced by law to live in conditions of disease and poverty because of race, of birth, of color. We have shown incitements to commit genocide, shown that a conspiracy exists to commit it, and now we can only add that an entire people, not only unprotected by their government but the object of government-inspired violence, reach forth their hands to the General Assembly in appeal.[8]

The State Department immediately focused on damage control, summoning White and other NAACP leaders to refute the allegations before the General Assembly. This mission, though, tore apart the group's own leadership, as not only had the CRC utilized NAACP research, but, as Roy Wilkins stated, the "State Department cannot expect that we will . . . assume the role of 'blaster' of this petition" given the civil rights commitment of the association. Washington also turned the screws on any delegation that might place the petition on the General Assembly's agenda, and Patterson found that delegations from Egypt, Liberia, Haiti, and the Dominican Republic greatly valued continued U.S. aid. The Soviet bloc also demurred, arguing predictably that the United Nations had no mandate to intervene in the internal affairs of states. When Eleanor Roosevelt cautioned that the document had emboldened non-aligned nations of color to resist American policy on weakening the covenant, the Truman administration hatched a plot to silence Patterson, who had traveled to Paris to lobby assembly delegates personally. He was charged with contempt of Congress for not releasing the names of CRC contributors, put on a plane to New York, and strip-searched upon arrival. With his passport subsequently confiscated, he could do no more trouble overseas.[9]

Such forceful tactics were out of place in the halls of the General Assembly, of course, where Roosevelt, Simsarian, and Acheson had a Gordian knot to cut. Triangulating a covenant policy that offered concessions to non-aligned nations, satisfied increasingly skeptical senators, and mobilized domestic activist groups required finesse and obfuscation. After reassuring Senate Foreign Relations Committee Chair Tom Connally that the draft covenant was "unsatisfactory" and needed alterations "so that it will conform to American constitutional principles and practices," State Department lawyers formulated policy for the 1951 General Assembly. One strategy involved discrediting the human rights record of the Soviet Union, which had often sided with the Third World on issues of decolonization. This would involve preparing a "fully documented exposure of Soviet bloc [human rights] practices for use as necessary" to persuade neutralist countries to desert their Communist friends. One major policy change involved a concession to Asian, Latin American, and Middle Eastern nations that saw economic and social rights as "a symbol of the[ir] needs and aspirations." Acheson permitted the United States to vote for one *or* two covenants, depending on the majority's wishes in the assembly. To assuage Bricker's charges of socialism, though, the delegation made it clear that economic provisions were only "objectives which States adhering to the Covenant will within their resources undertake to achieve progressively by private as well as public action." Foggy Bottom also demanded the inclusion of a federal-state clause to silence states' rightists and the omission or the placement in separate protocols of machinery for receiving NGO and individual petitions in order to satisfy sovereignty-conscious senators.[10]

Betraying Acheson's seemingly flexible approach, the State Department privately spent the rest of 1951 in discussions with foreign allies on pressing for two covenants. A month before the General Assembly convened, Acheson and Warren Austin lobbied the British, French, Canadian, and Australian delegations to embrace dual covenants. Roosevelt aide James Frederick Green, decrying the "general emotionalism" of underdeveloped countries, and Roosevelt, who explained the 1950 decision to draft one covenant as based on "emotion rather than reason," described what was at stake to her aides. If the United Nations voted for one covenant, she predicted, the Senate would likely reject the document they had now labored over for four years to complete. The adoption of two covenants, though, would permit the Senate to ratify only the treaty of familiar civil and political guarantees. On December 5, in her first speech of the new General Assembly's session, though, Roosevelt disingenuously claimed that having two covenants would not result in privileging civil and political rights. "I consider each group of rights of equal importance," she concluded, and her proposal for two treaties "would maintain this equality of importance." Determined American lobbying paid off, as one month later, a sharply divided General Assembly approved the dual-covenant plan. While Washington had won, the image of an overbearing superpower transparently defending its own narrow interests now replaced the collaborative human rights crusader of World War II. In hindsight, this was the last hurrah for American covenant policy at the United Nations.[11]

The endorsement of white supremacy at home, in colonial empires, and in South Africa provided the immediate pretext for a full-fledged revolt by less developed nations of color. The first stinging defeat for Washington came over the right of self-determination, which America's colonial allies and conservative senators strongly opposed. Neither the UNCHR nor ECOSOC had yet discussed the topic as requested by the General Assembly. Frustrated by the delay, 13 Asian and Middle Eastern nations moved that "all peoples shall have the right to self-determination," and the Soviet Union attached an amendment to force colonial nations to promote this right in their dependent areas. Although the U.N. Charter already included such verbiage, these nations argued that its importance as a prerequisite for the enjoyment of other rights and the need to provide inspiration and legal cover for those struggling against colonialism mandated its inclusion. Acheson and Roosevelt sought to bury it in a UNCHR subcommittee or address it in a non-binding resolution; above all, they wanted the UNCHR, where the United States had more influence, to forge the exact text. Any of these options would avoid "adding another rivet to this super-heated steamboiler" of problematic amendments and promote needless factionalization in the world body. The Senate would surely find a clause unacceptable, especially if it required Washington to schedule independence or statehood referendums in its own colonies of Alaska and Hawaii.[12]

The American delegation's desire to stifle discussion could not prevent a Soviet–Third World coalition from passing a strong self-determination article. The topic, which merged the struggle of Asian, African, and Middle Eastern peoples to gain political and economic independence from the West with Moscow's drive to cultivate global influence by charging the imperialist United States with "trying to enslave the world," provoked bitter debate. France and Britain vociferously argued against American betrayal in the full assembly, warning that any resolution would legalize the expropriation of Western businesses and military bases. "They tried to frighten us in every possible way," Roosevelt informed Acheson, but such threats were unnecessary. On February 5, the General Assembly, with only the United States and Western Europe dissenting, voted that both covenants would state that "all peoples shall have the right to self-determination" and asked all colonial countries to "promote the realization of that right in relation to the peoples" in their dependent territories. John Allison, the assistant secretary of state for Far Eastern Affairs, asserted that "the U.S. thus appeared in opposition to a resolution relating to a particularly American concept, while the overwhelming majority of the UN—with the Soviet bloc of course included—registered support for it. For the Far East, and Asia as a whole, the propaganda consequences of this vote are obvious and unfortunate."[13]

Providing further evidence of American insincerity to people of color, Washington became complicit in South Africa's rejection of U.N. mediation over discrimination against Indian nationals. Pretoria, under Nationalist Party Prime Minister Daniel Malan, had dismissed the 1950 U.N. overture that proposed a three-member mediation commission and a repeal of the Group Areas Act, which mandated residential segregation by race. Malan, a die-hard Afrikaner nationalist and architect of apartheid, viewed any U.N. action as illegal intervention in Pretoria's internal affairs. Aware of Malan's intransigence, Acting Secretary of State James Webb strongly preferred that Great Britain handle the problem as a Commonwealth affair, fearing any U.N. involvement would set a precedent for intervention and "open [the] way for propaganda counter-charges by unfriendly states re racial situation in U.S." Eleanor Roosevelt and advisor Channing Tobias (who sat on the NAACP's board of directors) advocated confronting South Africa over apartheid, the latter encouraging the delegation to "take the same attitude with the South Africans as with the Soviets in cases of such extreme violations of human rights." Durward Sandifer and Ben Gerig, though, favored working privately to promote reconciliation between the parties concerned, as Pretoria had become a loyal anti-Communist ally while India retained substantial U.N. influence. Acheson sided with the latter group, repeating a year-old rumor that Pretoria might withdraw from the United Nations if the organization criticized apartheid. The State Department used the Christmas break to search for an acceptable compromise that would "not unduly emphasiz[e] HR [human rights] issue."[14]

The resulting attempt to yet again push the issue to the secretary-general revealed to the non-aligned bloc that Washington was not serious about confronting a blatant case of racial discrimination. Delegates Roosevelt and Anna Lord Strauss, a former president of the League of Women Voters, had the job of articulating Secretary of State Acheson's contradictory policy goals. The State Department desired to stay out of a conflict between two allies while demonstrating American opposition to racism to the Third World in a way that would not precipitate a South African withdrawal from the world body. Employing shuttle diplomacy, the delegation proposed that the secretary-general, in consultation with India, Pakistan, and South Africa, appoint an impartial mediator to start negotiations if South Africa refused to talk directly with the other two states. The gambit worked, and the General Assembly approved the plan unanimously in mid-January. Pretoria again refused to negotiate, though, and the General Assembly subsequently voted to discuss the matter again in 1953. By then, most non-aligned nations had grown tired of compromise, and the United States soon found itself alone again with its colonial allies. American support for a state founded upon white supremacy, due to its need for a Cold War ally in southern Africa and to access uranium ore for nuclear weapons, negatively affected America's standing in the developing world for decades.[15]

The maintenance of racial discrimination at home fueled yet another defeat at the United Nations, this time rendering the United States unable to complain about the illegal treatment of one of its own citizens overseas. When ECOSOC's report on William Oatis came before the Third (Social, Humanitarian, and Cultural Affairs) Committee, Roosevelt told Acheson that the United States should only make a speech, rather than sponsor a resolution, that condemned Czechoslovakia for keeping him behind bars. Due to the United States' loss of credibility to speak on human rights matters, the

State Department worried that even U.S. allies would vote against censure on the grounds that Oatis just might be the American spy that Prague charged and the reporter confessed (under extreme duress) to being. Roosevelt also worried that pressing for a written rebuke would allow the Soviets and Arabs to "exploit such an opportunity . . . [to make] many speeches on other human rights matters, such as Negroes in US," using raw material from the Civil Rights Congress's *We Charge Genocide*. Acheson concurred, and in late January, delegate Channing Tobias denounced the arrest and trial of Oatis as "constitut[ing] a direct attack on freedom of information." Czechoslovakia responded that the United Nations had no jurisdiction in its internal affairs, a point Washington had cited often too. That was the end of the issue at the United Nations. Due to the loss of human rights leadership, past positions on domestic jurisdiction, and the desire to avoid *tu quoque* charges, American delegates found themselves unable to create a majority sympathetic to an innocent imprisoned reporter. Oatis served 18 months in jail until Stalin's death ushered in a period of liberalization that led to his release.[16]

As the State Department defended or weakly protested human rights violations at home and abroad, it was Bricker and ABA leaders who adopted the mantle of freedom's true defenders by battling against what Bricker called the "Covenant on Human Slavery." The Ohio senator condemned the latest draft for allowing governments to ban press coverage of criminal trials to protect national security, thereby running roughshod over the public trial requirement of the Sixth Amendment. "It is time for the Senate," Bricker concluded, "to say whether the rights of the American people are to be determined under international law or the Constitution." Two months later, Bricker criticized the covenant's restrictions on free speech in the interest of "national security, public order, safety, health or morals, or of the rights, freedoms or reputations of others." Noting that "it is impossible to summarize decades of judicial decisions in a few lines," he worried that such language gave governments a virtual blank check to censor media outlets. He concluded that "the only reason for defining these rights in a U.N. treaty is to advance world government . . . a fantastic king-size edition of Brook Farm." The Constitution itself must forever ban the Senate, he declared, from approving any treaty that limited the Bill of Rights. By the fall of 1951, Bricker was scheduling regular conversations with Frank Holman, Alfred Schweppe, and Eberhard Deutsch, the latter two of the Committee on Peace and Law through United Nations. He also proposed a new version of his constitutional amendment when the 82nd Congress convened in January 1952.[17]

These meetings soon turned ugly, though, as the ABA and Bricker quarreled over whose ideas best protected the Constitution from overreaching United Nations treaties. Although Deutsch congratulated Bricker for his "brilliant and courageous defense of human rights," Peace and Law Committee members under Chairman Schweppe spent four months crafting an alternative amendment. They parted with Bricker by proposing to make *all* treaties non-self-executing, thereby forcing both houses of Congress to pass enforcement legislation before *each* agreement became law. They also included what became known as the notorious "which" clause to safeguard states' rights: "A treaty shall become affective as internal law in the United States only through legislation by Congress which it could enact under its delegated powers in the absence of such treaty." This would reverse the *Missouri v. Holland* doctrine that had made the federal government responsible for enforcing all treaty contents, even if those matters were ordinarily beyond Congress's reach given the Tenth Amendment. Bricker thought both positions unrealistic and dangerous. He knew that most treaties were not controversial, and he did not want Congress to waste time crafting enforcement legislation for each one. In 1951 alone, the Senate considered 21 treaties, and since 1945, the number had fluctuated between 15 and 22 annually. Deutsch shot back that any additional burden on Congress "would be a far lesser evil than the danger of finding our liberties threatened or lost under an international covenant Utopian on its face." Arguing against the "which" clause, Bricker asserted that reciprocal treaties that gave aliens property rights and business privileges in return for identical guarantees for Americans overseas were desirable and necessary even though they overrode state probate and business laws. Despite these substantial differences, Deutsch told Bricker that a compromise must be possible if they could discover language succinctly delineating the proper subjects for treaty-making.[18]

By early 1952, the political winds in Washington were blowing with gale force against the dwindling supporters of a human rights treaty. With American troops bogged down in the two-year-old Korean War, the economy in a slump, and Senator William Fulbright (D-AR) investigating corruption within the executive branch, President Harry Truman received his lowest public approval rating ever of 22 percent. Attacks on the United Nations as a nascent world government and Communist front by Senator Joseph McCarthy and his allies decreased Americans' confidence in the world body. As the 1952 presidential campaign began, Robert Taft (R-OH) emerged as the front-runner. He articulated an isolationist foreign policy vision that derided the United Nations' inability to prevent or mediate conflict due to deadlock among the five Security Council permanent members. On February 8, just days after the General Assembly voted for two covenants and a self-determination article, 58 senators joined John Bricker in sponsoring his constitutional amendment to limit the internal effects of treaties. Taft was a co-signer, telling Bricker that it was "most important that the subject be examined." The Truman administration's use of the United Nations to craft an international code of human rights conduct was now under full-fledged assault by General Assembly members who thought Truman's policies too timid and by domestic groups who thought them too radical.[19]

Bricker and the American Bar Association, seeking to harness this favorable political climate, each seized the offensive for their divergent constitutional amendments. Bricker employed provocative language to describe the dire social and political consequences that the covenant would wreak on an unsuspecting nation. He warned that allowing individuals to "seek, receive, and impart information" could force Notre Dame University to admit atheist students, hire non-believing professors, and invite Communists like Paul Robeson to speak. In a form letter to an expanding list of backers, Bricker called for a "thorough educational campaign at the grass-roots level" to protect the integrity of the Constitution and U.S. sovereignty from the "heavily financed one-world propaganda of public and private agencies." The climax of his efforts was another constitutional amendment. Senate Joint Resolution 130 was similar to his 1951 offering, except for an attempt to meet one of the ABA's objections by defining all treaties as non-self-executing if their content could overturn state law. It also prohibited treaties from transferring any judicial, legislative, or executive power to an international organization. "I do not want any of the international groups, and especially the group headed by Mrs. Eleanor Roosevelt, which has drafted the Covenant of Human Rights, to betray the fundamental, inalienable, and God-given rights of American citizens enjoyed under the Constitution," he told his colleagues. "That is what I am driving at."[20]

The American Bar Association, viewing Bricker's text as still offering too little protection to the Tenth Amendment, passed its own version in late February. The Peace and Law Committee effort contained the "which clause," making all treaties affecting domestic statutes non-self-executing and subservient to those state laws. When the full House of Delegates discussed the draft, lawyers from the ABA's Section on International and Comparative Law fought a rearguard action, claiming that the amendment would prevent Congress from ratifying treaties that gave aliens in the United States and Americans abroad crucial property guarantees and would severely restrict the president's foreign policy powers. By allowing state laws to determine foreign policy, the nation would repeat the failed decentralized foreign policy experiment that had occurred under the Articles of Confederation. Former section chair Charles Tillett castigated to no avail the "almost complete and total ignorance of the average run-of-mine members of the House of Delegates [who required] words of one syllable . . . and illustrations easily within their mental grasp" to understand the issues at stake. On February 24, the House of Delegates voted to cease compromise talks with Bricker and send the Peace and Law Committee's draft to Congress. Holman, though, soon regretted the existence of two versions that only created confusion and division in the Senate.[21]

Roosevelt and her advisors, dismissing Bricker and ABA criticism as uninformed and unrepresentative of public opinion, responded slowly to anti-covenant tirades in two ways. The first strategy was to defend the covenant as a Cold War document that would buttress America's moral leadership position in the world. Walter Kotschnig made the point in a reply to Marvin Mohl, a leader of the Washington State Bar Association, the home state of Frank Holman and Alfred Schweppe. American support of the United Nations' human rights undertakings, he wrote, "has been and must continue to be one of the bases for our role of leadership in the Western civilization's opposition to the Soviet Union's repression of fundamental liberties." Assistant Secretary of State Jack McFall asserted that the failure of the country to support the covenants "would furnish a propaganda weapon to the Kremlin which would question our sincere interest in the rights of the individual." Roosevelt wrote in her *My Day* column that "if we are unwilling to enter into a treaty on human rights, we are putting ourselves in the same position as is the U.S.S.R." What was lacking, though, was a strong defense of human rights treaties on grounds cited during and immediately after World War II: that they might assist in the creation of a more peaceful, stable, and humane world. Confrontation with the Soviet Union and waging the Korean War had made such idealism seem unacceptably naïve. The weak substitute defense instead centered on upholding American credibility by avoiding international embarrassment at the hands of Moscow. The covenant was a means to this political end, not a means to help directly individuals who faced wrongful imprisonment, extrajudicial execution, or cruel torture.[22]

The second strategy was to respond to the near apocalyptic criticisms of covenant opponents. In a December 1951 editorial, John Cates of the State Department tore into the objections of Bricker and the American Bar Association. Quoting a covenant article that forbade governments from using the covenant to limit existing rights, he asserted that nations could not enact new curbs on the press or create secret tribunals without violating their general treaty responsibilities. Moreover, he observed that the federal-state clause and an article making treaties non-self-executing would provide enough protection for the Tenth Amendment. Five days after Bricker introduced Joint Resolution 130, Assistant Secretary of State John Hickerson, belatedly observing that anti-covenant arguments "could no longer be dismissed as isolated misrepresentation," told Legal Advisor Adrian Fisher that some kind of sharp public reply was necessary. Roosevelt agreed with the prescription. Her mail, which was "quite frightening," had tripled in volume, and she worried to Acheson that the "old forces fighting for isolationism and fascism in this country" were on the march. To meet the challenge, she advocated a public relations campaign to demonstrate similarities between the covenant and the U.S. Constitution. This effort never got off the ground due to divisions within the Truman administration on whether such an effort should mention the covenant or ignore it and focus solely on defending the constitutional status quo against any Bricker or ABA-sponsored alterations. Doing the former might provide even more momentum to anti-treaty forces while the latter risked signaling abandonment and betrayal to covenant supporters at home and in the United Nations.[23]

Roosevelt and Simsarian believed that the only way to support continued American participation in drafting the covenant would be to have the UNCHR, at its spring 1952 session, strike its most controversial components. Priorities included reaffirming only the general principle of self-determination, allowing for the submission of individual and NGO petitions but only in separate protocols, and revising the economic and social rights to emphasize their gradual fulfillment by private and public actors. The Bricker-ABA axis also made it even more critical to include, in both covenants, federal-state and non-self-executing articles and a clear statement that governments could not use the covenant to limit the human rights of their citizens. "Every effort has been made to have the proposals prepared for the United States Delegation consistent with American law and tradition," Roosevelt's briefing papers began. With the Democratic Party on the defensive, the current UNCHR session might be the State Department's last chance to complete the covenants before the November elections perhaps resulted in a Republican taking the presidential oath of office. If the commission accepted two covenants along the lines Roosevelt proposed, the campaign by Bricker and the ABA might become irrelevant, and the Democratic Party could trumpet a diplomatic victory as elections loomed in November.[24]

Hopes for sending at least one covenant to the Senate in late 1952 fell quickly when the UNCHR, in *its* first clear rejection of American direction, lapsed into a prolonged debate over the concept of self-determination. Meeting in New York City in mid-April, the 18 members placed the issue first on the commission's agenda and proceeded to spend three weeks in intense discussion. The General Assembly had already proposed the wording of an article to include in both covenants, but delegates from Communist and developing countries wanted a more explicit and immediate guarantee. The debate highlighted some of the uncertainties and controversies that the principle evoked. Was the right of self-determination an individual right, one which allowed for maximum individual control over one's destiny? Or was it a group right that promised some undefined measure of autonomy for populations living under foreign domination? Was it a political right in either case, or did it also confer sovereignty over proximate economic resources? A final dispute over the article's purpose divided delegates: Should the text recognize a simple principle, or should the commission draft a detailed provision in language specific enough to comprise a contractual obligation? With anti-colonial grievances and claims of economic exploitation fueling the determination of Communist and developing nations for a substantive provision, Roosevelt remarked in her *My Day* column, "The sins of the past are rising up to make life difficult for us today in many ways!"[25]

Those past wrongs provided a clear rejection of the middle ground that Roosevelt tried to cultivate. Her weak affirmation that all peoples had the "right freely to determine their political status" in subordination to "constitutional processes and with the proper regard for the rights of other States and peoples" came under fire from the Communist bloc. Her intermediate position between obstructionist colonial nations and pro-revolution Communist states allowed for only peaceful and legal means of seeking political independence. This moderate course partially succeeded at first, as the commission adopted identical articles for both covenants substantially based on her proposal.[26] Her satisfaction turned to displeasure, though, when the Chilean representative defined self-determination to include "permanent sovereignty over [a people's] wealth and resources." Worried the amendment might legalize the nationalization of American assets abroad, the State Department considered it objectionable "not only with regard to substance, but because its inclusion in the Human Rights Covenants would unquestionably have an adverse effect upon ratification of any such Covenants by the U.S. Senate." The plea did not work, and the United States joined the other five Western nations in the UNCHR in voting no. It passed by a wide margin, as even America's allies in Latin America joined the revolt against Western political and economic domination. The alliance of Communist nations and the developing world also forwarded resolutions to the General Assembly that mandated self-government for peoples who voted for it in United Nations-sponsored plebiscites and that asked colonial nations to report on efforts to promote indigenous rule. The State Department realized that large majorities would ensure their passage. Roosevelt diplomatically told the devoted readers of her daily column that "what amounts practically to confiscation of property of foreigners without compensation being legalized by a treaty is going to be extremely difficult for a great many nations to accept."[27]

After disposing of its most controversial agenda item, the UNCHR ironically devoted the next six weeks to revising both covenants along lines substantially recommended by the United States. Western delegates handily defeated all Communist attempts to mandate the ultimate enforcement of economic rights by governments. Roosevelt also succeeded in keeping the implementation article vague and flexible; the final version bound nations to take individual and collaborative steps "to the maximum of its available resources, with a view to achieving progressively the full realization" of the economic, social, and cultural rights contained in the covenant.[28] The lack of a federal-state article and the approval of problematic self-determination provisions were unsurprising, but the committee could revisit them in the future. Roosevelt expressed great relief that the treaties met many of the criticisms coming from Bricker and the ABA. "It has been accepted from the beginning," she awkwardly wrote in her column, "that we would try primarily as a delegation to have accepted what we felt our own Senate could accept but to make every effort at the same time to meet the views of others where they did not conflict with what we felt was possible for us to accept." To this end, the State Department had tried to ensure that both treaties contained non-self-executing articles and clauses that banned governments from using either agreement to limit existing freedoms. "Neither of the Covenants as now drafted contains any provisions which depart from the American way of life in the direction of communism, socialism, syndicalism, or statism," Roosevelt asserted in June after the UNCHR had adjourned. James Simsarian made similar arguments in the *Department of State Bulletin* that was distributed to libraries nationwide.[29]

Roosevelt and Simsarian aimed their words squarely at Bricker, who had criticized the covenant for supporting "some form of socialism, communism, fascism, or feudalism" during the first formal Senate hearings on his amendment in late May. The opportunity to testify provided a national platform for the arguments that Bricker, Holman, and the American Bar Association's Peace and Law Committee would champion over the next two years. While they presented constitutional arguments in favor of limiting the treaty power, isolationist-oriented free-enterprise and patriotic groups developed economic and political critiques of the covenants. The U.S. Chamber of Commerce, the American Flag Committee, and the Daughters of the American Revolution viewed the United Nations as a nascent world government whose handiwork would bring socialism to the United States and the rest of the free world. They also warned that human rights treaties by design could strip away national sovereignty, create a centralized government in Washington at the expense of states' rights, and destroy American constitutional freedoms. Although they organized a massive and impressive grassroots campaign around such apocalyptic arguments, Bricker and his ABA partners exerted more profound influence in the halls of the Senate through their legal arguments.[30]

Bricker and Holman trotted out two objections to senatorial ratification that they had formulated during hearings on the Genocide Convention: The covenants would limit the constitutional freedoms of Americans and erode states' rights. They darkly warned that due to awkward constitutional phrases and unclear past Supreme Court decisions, treaties could nullify parts of the Constitution, including the Bill of Rights. Although the U.S. Supreme Court had repeatedly declared the opposite in dicta, the justices had never actually ruled a treaty unconstitutional. The Peace and Law Committee explained this absence by remarking that the courts could not do so, as the Constitution's Article VI maintained the alleged distinction that "This Constitution, and the Laws of the United States which shall be *made in Pursuance thereof*; and all Treaties made, or which shall be made, *under the Authority of the United States*, shall be the supreme Law of the Land." The Peace and Law Committee read the clause to mean that laws had to follow constitutional principles whereas treaties did not given the different derivations cited. Bricker furthermore noted that the First Amendment placed prohibitions only on "Congress." By not including the treaty-making offices of the president and Senate, he saw another loophole that placed treaties above the Constitution. Therefore, the constitutional amendments offered by Senator Bricker and the American Bar Association were needed to prohibit treaties from invalidating any part of America's governing charter.[31]

If treaties could override the Constitution, Bricker and his allies argued, the human rights covenants could neuter the Bill of Rights. They zeroed in on broadly worded permissible restrictions to specific rights. *The Free-man*, a conservative publication of the Foundation for Economic Educa-tion, lambasted the covenant's freedom of religion article, which allowed for "such limitations as are necessary to protect public safety, order, health or morals, or the fundamental rights and freedoms of others." Bricker re-peatedly pointed out that the covenants allowed governments to impose restrictions on many of the rights contained therein by simply declaring a state of "public emergency." Moreover, the economic rights contained in the covenants would bring socialism to the United States, Bricker and the ABA argued, since the federal government would be obliged to grant all Americans rights to employment, health care, housing, and education. To Bricker and Holman, these consequences of treaty law were not acciden-tal: American "internationalist" delegates at the United Nations wanted to use treaties as "Trojan horses" to undermine the Constitution and bring the United States under a tyrannical and Communistic world government. President Dwight D. Eisenhower soon characterized the crusade for an amendment as founded upon "saving the United States from Eleanor Roo-sevelt."[32]

Mandating a broad definition of the Tenth Amendment by preventing treaties from invalidating state law also preoccupied supporters of a con-stitutional amendment. The Supreme Court, citing the clear language of the Constitution's Article VI, had ruled that treaties nullified any conflict-ing state laws. Given the wide scope of the covenants, Bricker and Hol-man worried that the federal government stood poised to supplant state jurisdiction in the fields of education, workplace regulation, and criminal procedure. The two men disagreed on how best to preempt this. Bricker's amendment specified that all treaties that might alter state laws be non-self-executing, or unenforceable without congressional enabling legisla-tion. Such supplemental laws, Bricker believed, would require the assent of a majority in both houses of Congress, which would jealously safeguard the Tenth Amendment. He did not want all treaties to be non-self-exe-cuting nor did he support making state laws automatically immune from alteration by treaty. Bricker's experience as a senator had convinced him that "there are some subjects within the retained jurisdiction of the States which may nevertheless be of legitimate international concern."[33]

Frank Holman and ABA members of the Peace and Law Committee continued to fear that Bricker's amendment did not go far enough to pro-tect states' rights. Holman, who summed up his commitment by announc-ing that "it would have been better for this country, better for the world, [and] better for civilization if the South had won the Civil War," feared that the covenants would provide President Truman and other liberal Democrats with the authority to enact expansive Fair Deal housing, health care, and civil rights legislation. His anxiety was rooted in the crucial 1920 Supreme Court case of *Missouri v. Holland*. Holman worried that the decision allowed Congress to pass any legislation implementing the human rights covenant, even though Congress ordinarily, without a treaty, lacked the authority under its delegated powers to do so. To reverse *Missouri*, prevent the expansion of federal power, and restore authority to the Tenth Amendment, the ABA demanded that any constitutional amendment include the "which clause." Whereas Bricker would tolerate some bleeding by treaties into state jurisdiction, the bar association wanted a bright red separation line.[34]

Representatives of the Truman administration and a dissenting group of lawyers testified that an impenetrable barrier between the covenants and the Constitution already existed due to provisions either already in the treaty or awaiting UNCHR approval. Undersecretary of State David Bruce testified that the proposed federal-state article would safeguard the integrity of the Tenth Amendment, and the non-self-executing clause gave Congress adequate power to mold implementation legislation to meet any other constitutional requirements. In response to concerns that courts might use covenant qualifications to restrict the broader First Amendment, he pointed out that the treaties already banned governments from using any provision to circumscribe existing freedoms. Not only was Bricker's amendment unneeded, Bruce asserted, but its passage would "so seriously interfere with the historic and fundamental functions of the Executive in the field of foreign affairs that it would jeopardize the influence of the United States in the world today." The proposal would, for example, invalidate treaties that allowed aliens to own and transfer property in the United States in exchange for extending those rights to Americans abroad. Forcing both houses of Congress to act before any treaty could take effect and preventing international agreements from ever altering state laws amounted to unconstitutional transfers of power to the legislative branch and to the states, Bruce claimed. Such limitations would also "furnish a propaganda weapon to the Kremlin which would question our sincere interest in the rights of the individual," he concluded. Such reasonable arguments, just as in testimony over the Genocide Convention, were not as influential or memorable for senators or the general public as the starkly foreboding claims made by Bricker and Holman.[35]

International lawyers provided invaluable support by showing that the entire profession did not share Holman's and the Peace and Law Committee's alarmist and troublesome views. Members of the ABA's Section on International and Comparative Law had unsuccessfully fought to postpone a House of Delegates vote on the ABA's amendment three months earlier, and former chair Charles Tillett testified at the May hearings. Also appearing were two members of the Association of the Bar of the City of New York, a group whose clients had many foreign interests. The bar group criticized Bricker's amendment for placing "unnecessary and ill-advised limitations on our chief executive in handling the delicate and urgent problems of diplomacy." The addition was unneeded, the members explained, because the Supreme Court (even in *Missouri v. Holland*) had often stated that treaties could not abridge constitutional rights; it was also ill-advised because the broad ban on treaties "respecting the rights" of Americans would have prevented Senate ratification of the U.N. Charter and treaties of friendship, commerce, and navigation. The report concluded by warning that it was "unwise to tinker with the existing safeguards lest the cure should prove worse than the disease." For example, allowing state laws to trump international agreements would require the State Department to negotiate with all 48 state legislatures and governors prior to signing a treaty. The barrier to enacting unconstitutional treaties already existed in the Constitution: the requirement that the president with two-thirds of senators concur. These reassurances fell on deaf ears, as the Senate subcommittee approved a modified Bricker Amendment, though the Senate took no action before adjourning for the summer.[36]

This auspicious result for treaty opponents placed the State Department so much on the defensive that its diplomats stopped publicly defending the human rights covenants. In a plea to Acheson, Roosevelt explained that the State Department did not have to say they were going to reject the covenant in order to deprive the opposition of a lightning-rod justification for their amendment. Acheson, believing that a victory by the Bricker forces would place the country "in grave danger of a retreat to the same kind of isolationist attitude that wrought such damage to our interests after the First World War," cast the covenants adrift. In a speech to the National Committee for United Nations Day, he blamed unnamed countries for "putting insincere provisions into these documents . . . which are so fanciful in many cases that people who really wanted to carry them out couldn't do it." He did not enunciate a replacement policy, as those discussions continued within the walls of the State Department. In the face of strident attacks by Bricker, the American Bar Association, and conservative patriotic groups, the covenants were left to twist in the election-year partisan wind.[37]

   Republican and Democratic leaders reacted cautiously to the growing criticism of the United Nations' human rights program, uncertain
how best to navigate the controversy while maintaining party unity. The
party of Lincoln came into its Chicago convention divided. Senator Robert Taft had the backing of isolationists in the South and Midwest, while
former General Dwight D. Eisenhower represented the more cosmopoli-
tan Northeast and West. John Foster Dulles, former U.N. delegate and the
GOP's top spokesperson on foreign policy, drafted a platform plank that
once again declared Republican opposition to any "treaty or agreement
with other countries [that] deprives our citizens of the rights guaranteed
them by the Federal Constitution." By omitting the means to accomplish
that goal, Dulles hoped to unite Bricker, Holman, and other isolationists
with internationalists like himself, Clark Eichelberger of the American Association for the United Nations, and Eisenhower. The vague wording also
reflected the uncertain path that Dulles himself had taken. He supported
the drafting of the Universal Declaration of Human Rights and called upon
the Senate to ratify the Genocide Convention. Yet at a regional meeting of
the American Bar Association, he cryptically warned that "human rights
should have their primary sanction in community will, and when Treaties ignore that, and try to substitute an alien will, the Treaties themselves
usually collapse through disrespect, dragging down the whole structure of
international law, order, and justice." He arrived at a politically convenient
agnostic conclusion on the Bricker Amendment, explaining that "there is
room for honest difference of opinion" on its passage.[38]
   The Democratic Convention, held in the same coliseum vacated by
the Republicans, showed division too. Tennessee Senator Estes Kefauver
had bested Truman in the New Hampshire primary, and he came into
the gathering as the favored nominee. He could not obtain the blessing
of party bosses, though, and those state delegations that were free to offer
a candidate from the floor nominated Illinois Governor Adlai Stevenson.
Stevenson was an avowed U.N. supporter, having served on the American
delegation in 1946 and 1947. Offered a major speaking role at the convention, Roosevelt took the opportunity to rebuke Bricker Amendment supporters. Asserting that the Senate would never ratify a treaty that abridged
the Constitution, she denounced as "shameful" the idea that her country
should not work with other nations "to bring about the recognition and
acceptance throughout the world of [human rights] standards and values.
For us to serve notice that we would not today accept our own Bill of Rights
if it were presented to us is a statement which should make everyone of us
blush." Though she received a standing ovation, party officials knew that a

Gallup poll showed that less than 25 percent of Americans had a positive view of the United Nations. Caution was the watchword, and the party platform only stated blandly that Democrats would "continue our efforts to strengthen the United Nations, improve its institutions as experience requires, and foster its growth and development." Due to the prudence exhibited by both parties, the human rights covenants and constitutional amendments played no role in the 1952 elections in which issues of Korea and McCarthyism predominated.[39]

While the politicians focused on other issues during the campaign, all-out war over whether to amend the Constitution broke out among the lawyers. Confident that the Democrats would lose control of the executive and legislative branches, Bricker and ABA leaders foresaw a brighter political landscape. The position articulated by the Republican Party platform offered some hope, even though Eisenhower made no reference to it on the campaign trail. Frank Holman took solace in Dulles's speech to a bar association gathering, which, in Holman's words, "vividly pictured the dangers of 'treaty law,'" and in similar addresses by prominent Eisenhower supporter Clarence Manion, the former dean of Notre Dame Law School. On the opposite side, noted Harvard Law Professor Zechariah Chafee published a dismissive piece in the *American Bar Association Journal* that concluded with the need "to trust our President and our Senators to act carefully and wisely, under the guidance of public opinion, in enabling our nation to play its part in this troubled world." Bricker derided such advice in another law review article, warning that "even a superficial knowledge of American history proves that the President and the Senate should not be trusted not to abridge the inalienable rights of American citizens." Holman himself published a fifty-page exposé of what he called a State Department "propaganda effort *at the taxpayers' expense*" (italics his) entitled *State Department Half-Truths and False Assurances Regarding the U.N. Charter, Genocide Convention, and Proposed Covenant on Human Rights.* The heated rhetoric was a sign that pro-amendment forces viewed 1953 as the climactic year of their half-decade struggle to protect the Constitution from the United Nations.[40]

Eisenhower's landslide victory brought an end to the Roosevelt era at the United Nations at a time when her efforts in the Human Rights Commission had come under domestic and foreign attack. Despite Durward Sandifer's urging that she press for a position in Eisenhower's State Department, Roosevelt hesitated for political and personal reasons. In a form letter to friends who shared Sandifer's views, she wrote that partisan differences and her lack of a personal relationship with the incoming president mitigated against her remaining as an effective U.N. delegate. Privately, she also did not respect incoming Secretary of State Dulles, with whom she had had frequent clashes when both were U.N. delegates. Yet she also yearned to complete her five-year term on the Human Rights Commission and finish up the covenant, a sentiment encouraged by Sandifer, James Simsarian, and John Hickerson. She submitted her resignation, hoping that the president-elect might refuse and reappoint the woman known as the "First Lady of the World." To her surprise and disappointment, Eisenhower accepted it with a short and sterile reply. Whether due to her stature as a prominent Democrat, as a staunch human rights advocate, or as a critic who faulted Eisenhower for failing to defend former Secretary of Defense George Marshall from Joseph McCarthy's charges of disloyalty, hers was one of the first resignations he sought.[41]

Republican control of the White House and both houses of Congress injected uncertainty into the debate over U.S. human rights policy and the Bricker Amendment. White House Chief of Staff Sherman Adams, Secretary of Agriculture Ezra Taft Benson, and Defense Secretary Charles E. Wilson all endorsed some sort of constitutional amendment, and Eisenhower's liaison to Congress, Gerald Parsons, told Bricker of the White House's desire for immediate consultations. Bricker appreciated the gesture, writing to Dulles that he was "most anxious to work out this problem in close co-operation with the new Administration so that there is no danger of hamstringing the President in the conduct of the Nation's foreign policy." Holman remained skeptical of the new secretary of state's sincerity. "Mr. Dulles for the past three years has been associated with the Acheson personnel and policies," he wrote to the Ohio senator in late December. Dulles's refusal to answer Holman's questions on the treaty-making power due to the secretary's "devoting all his time and energies to the reorganization and staffing of the Department" was hardly encouraging. Convinced that a renewed offensive was necessary, Holman mailed copies of his articles, Peace and Law Committee reports, and lists of supporters to every member of Congress. Bricker came around to Holman's suspicions. After initially postponing at Eisenhower's request his introduction of a slightly revised constitutional amendment, he reversed course in early January. Almost every Senate Republican and 18 Democrats, totaling the necessary two-thirds majority, cosponsored Senate Joint Resolution 1. Eisenhower's first foreign policy crisis erupted just down Pennsylvania Avenue.[42]

Dulles quickly conceived a two-track response that would remove the immediate justification for an amendment while allowing for a vigorous defense of the constitutional status quo. Both he and Eisenhower regarded the covenants doubtfully due to their conviction that only education, rather than legislation, could realistically improve human rights at home and abroad. To the perceptive listener, the president portended this shift in his inaugural address. "Honoring the identity and the special heritage of each nation in the world, we shall never again use our strength to try to impress upon another people our own cherished political and economic institutions," he promised. His gradualist approach meant that he might condemn some human rights violations, but he hoped that enlightenment and economic development would slowly erase injustice. His skepticism of U.N. treaties also derived from a twin defense of American sovereignty and an intrinsic sympathy for states' rights in opposition to an activist federal role. Dulles thought in broadly similar terms, praising the ideal standards of the Universal Declaration of Human Rights but opposing their metamorphosis into binding international and federal law. Their decision to reexamine the U.S. role in drafting the covenants not only dovetailed with their personal beliefs but might, they thought, also remove the catalyst for any constitutional amendment that would heavily restrict the president's foreign affairs powers.[43]

Their desire for alternatives to a covenant-based human rights policy at the United Nations generated some pushback from career foreign service officers. In early February, Assistant Secretary of State for U.N. Affairs John Hickerson suggested to Dulles some relatively minor policy changes to maintain U.S. leadership "in rallying and strengthening the free peoples of the world" and to contain domestic criticism of the covenants. He recommended continued engagement in the treaty-drafting process and in particular fighting for non-self-executing and federal-state clauses. Abandoning the covenants now, he asserted, "would greatly weaken the position of leadership of the United States in the UN as a whole, and would be exploited to the full by countries hostile to the United States, and particularly the U.S.S.R." Withdrawal would also likely lead to U.N. approval of final drafts even more unacceptable to the United States, which would become standards of international conduct even without American adherence. Responding to covenant critics, he also recommended having the UNCHR investigate non-legislative ways that nations could improve living standards and support the free dissemination of news and information in developing countries. Given that Hickerson's Bureau of U.N. Affairs contained personnel who had advised Eleanor Roosevelt for seven years, the embrace of continuity could not have surprised the new secretary of state.[44]

Dulles pushed back strongly, determined to chart a new policy direction that would not fuel moves to hamstring the president's foreign policy powers. Just one week after demanding that Hickerson present a more robust set of options, a five-page list of alternatives without recommendations arrived on the secretary's desk. The memo reflected the nagging doubts over the covenant that the State Department had wrestled with the previous year, and it in essence amounted to a surrender on continued human rights treaty work. Hickerson admitted that nations including the United States were simply not ready politically to accept meaningful enforcement provisions. Moreover, if Washington nevertheless signed the covenants, they "would be a source of propaganda attack on positions taken by the United States and on conditions within this country. The Covenants might contain provisions on economic self-determination and the right of nationalization which would be detrimental to United States interests in certain areas abroad." Even continued participation in the drafting process was hazardous, as the American Bar Association would have a catalyst around which to campaign for the Bricker Amendment. Dulles had forced up the white flag by State Department veterans who viewed the protection of human rights as best done through the prism of declarations and binding treaties.[45]

Hickerson and the Bureau of U.N. Affairs also developed new strategies in case Dulles and Eisenhower agreed to change policy. The first option involved urging the world body to stop work on the covenants and take up other measures to promote human rights. Such new programs might include the appointment of an independent rapporteur to file reports on specific nations, the submission of self-studies by countries on their own efforts to improve human rights, and the creation of a UNCHR advisory panel to offer technical expertise to willing governments. If Dulles thought this plan too sweeping, the memo proposed working on only the political and civil rights covenant, while holding to the position that economic, social, and cultural rights were inappropriate subjects for a treaty.[46]

Dulles and Eisenhower seized this early opportunity to recast American human rights policy. Within two days of receiving Hickerson's memo, the secretary of state and the president agreed that the United States would offer only technical assistance should the UNCHR continue work on the covenants. American delegates would no longer actively participate in deliberations. The administration would press the UNCHR to examine other means of promoting the standards set by the Universal Declaration of Human Rights. Acting just two days after a subcommittee of the Senate Judiciary Committee had begun another round of hearings on amendments proposed by Bricker and the ABA, Dulles viewed the new policy as a way to dampen the brewing firestorm. Though Dulles worried that the human rights rapporteur "might give the Soviets an opportunity for prying around in human rights conditions in the United States," he told the cabinet that the end of American advocacy for human rights treaties could be the key to preventing passage of any constitutional limitations on the treaty power. Dulles, State Department Legal Advisor Herman Phlegar, and Hickerson decided to inform Americans and foreign nations of the shift by publishing the briefing instructions to Mary Pillsbury Lord, Eleanor Roosevelt's replacement on the UNCHR, just before the body convened.[47]

The appointment of Lord, the granddaughter of the flour magnate and co-chair of the Citizens for Eisenhower-Nixon movement, touched a sensitive nerve in Holman and others. Worried that other U.N. delegates would capitalize upon her total inexperience in international law to make the covenants even more unacceptable, he again argued the need for the ABA's amendment. "One does not send novices into important conferences," he bitingly told Phlegar. "We have had enough of this casual attitude toward important posts during the recent Democratic administrations." Henry Cabot Lodge, the new head of the American delegation to the United Nations, also voiced doubts about Lord's ability to Eisenhower. Dulles replied to Sherman Adams that if Cabot's "doubts are well founded then we should not have offered her *anything*! I'm personally confident she can do the job *well*!" (Emphases in the original.) It was true that Lord had no legal or United Nations experience aside from chairing the U.S. Committee for the U.N. International Children's Emergency Fund. She did have an extensive background in volunteer civic, wartime mobilization, and anti-poverty efforts in New York State, and those activities brought her into Republican circles. A friendship with Eisenhower began in 1945, when she toured Europe as a member of the Women's Army Corps. It could hardly have mollified Holman that she noted, in an interview with *Time Magazine* following her appointment, "I have a lot of homework to do." A meeting between Holman and Phlegar hardly calmed the tension, nor did the latter's assurance that Lord would rely upon quality legal advisors. "You may be sure I will check up on him," Holman wrote after Phlegar disclosed the name of one of Lord's aides, to ascertain "whether he belongs to the Acheson school which compromised American rights and American conceptions of government in order to appease communist and socialist representatives and in effect destroyed the fundamental principles of our Bill of Rights and our form of government."[48]

Ignorant of the administration's still-secret policy change, Bricker and Holman also kept up their angry but discordant attacks on the human rights covenant. Despite sharing a common desire to limit the internal effects of treaties, the ABA and Bricker still could not agree on a common text. Holman and the Peace and Law Committee convinced Senator Arthur Watkins (R-UT) to introduce their version as Senate Joint Resolution 43. They included the "which" clause again to prevent Congress from gaining power via treaty implementation that it did not possess otherwise. Hearings by a subcommittee of the Senate Judiciary Committee, which lasted from mid-February to mid-April, presented additional opportunities for Bricker, Holman, and Peace and Law Committee Chair Alfred Schweppe to explain why their amendments were needed to prevent the human rights covenants from divesting Americans of Bill of Rights protections.[49]

In a decision that disappointed Bricker but left Holman unsurprised, the Eisenhower administration publicly affirmed its Democratic predecessors' opposition to both amendments, asserting they would render the executive branch essentially powerless and disrespected in foreign affairs. Dulles, Phlegar, and Attorney General Herbert Brownell, Jr., testified before the Senate that the Bricker and ABA proposals would upset the separation of powers between the president and Congress and between states and the federal government. Bricker's desire to make all treaties non-self-executing was unreasonable and constitutionally suspect, they argued, since it would give the House of Representatives veto power in the treaty ratification process by requiring its approval to pass any implementation legislation. Bricker's sweeping prohibition on treaties that transferred general powers to any international organization, moreover, might ban the president from signing multilateral narcotics trafficking agreements, nuclear arms control treaties, and the pending NATO Status of Forces Agreement. Attorney General Herbert Brownell concluded that the proposed amendments would "substitute a new inflexible standard which would seriously restrict the ability of the United States to conduct foreign relations effectively." Dulles argued that the ABA's "which" clause would allow states to nullify all treaty articles that dealt with matters traditionally within their authority. "We cannot bargain effectively if we speak with 49 tongues," he warned, as individual states would acquire veto power over foreign policy matters as had occurred under the ineffective Articles of Confederation. Eisenhower summed up his frustration with Bricker and Holman by telling his cabinet, "I am so sick of the Bricker Amendment I could scream. We talk about the French not being able to govern themselves—and we sit here wrestling with a *Bricker Amendment*."[50]

In dramatic fashion designed to undercut the raison d'être for any amendment, Dulles publicly revealed Eisenhower's new human rights policy in his Senate testimony. He told the subcommittee on April 6, only one day before the UNCHR convened in Geneva, that

> While we shall not withhold our counsel from those who seek to draft a treaty or covenant on Human Rights, we do not ourselves look upon a treaty as the means which we would now select as the proper and most effective way to spread throughout the world the goals of human liberty to which this nation has been dedicated since its inception. We therefore do not intend to become a party to any such covenant or present it as a treaty for consideration by the Senate.[51]

The next day, Eisenhower himself announced that the continued denial of human freedom demanded a "new approach to the development of a human rights conscience in all areas of the world" as Lord outlined the details of a new three-part "Action Plan" in the UNCHR. Although, she assured the delegates, her government "continues to support wholeheartedly the promotion of respect for and observance of human rights," the time had come for a "new and urgent approach to take account of changed conditions in the world." Any movement toward fulfilling the standards set by the Universal Declaration of Human Rights, she opined, required building a human rights consensus through education and not condemnation. Appointing a human rights rapporteur to make recommendations regarding specific guarantees (Lord proposed starting with the right to a fair trial and freedom of religion), asking nations to file annual reports of compliance with the UNCHR, and training consultants to advise governments on securing human rights protections were three steps that she argued could improve the global human rights climate immediately. If the UNCHR continued work on the covenants, she concluded, her nation would passively assist but could not ratify them. She maintained that it would be ineffective to work on codifying human rights into law until a "human rights conscience will be sufficiently developed throughout the world," which was the "Action Plan's key objective."[52]

The reaction by members of the Human Rights Commission, even staunch U.S. allies, was negative, driven by a lack of prior consultation and worries that Lord's plan allowed far more U.N. oversight in their countries and colonies than a hypothetical treaty. Lord advisor James Green told John Humphrey of the U.N. Secretariat that neither the rest of the American delegation nor the United States' NATO allies had viewed the specific proposals until en route to Geneva. UNCHR members also criticized Washington for not waiting until the end of the UNCHR's session to announce the package, as the commission was bound by General Assembly instructions to work on the covenant. Responding to the proposals' substance, British delegate Samuel Hoare was "violently adverse," in Lord's words, to allowing the Soviet bloc and non-aligned nations to discuss human rights conditions in his country's empire. His government was "unalterably opposed" to Lord's suggestions, and though he did not want a public "show down" on them, he would "fight them and fight them hard" if the United States put them to a formal commission vote. Other colonial allies opposed the appointment of a rapporteur, fearing that political pressures by ex-colonies would negatively shape the mandate, choice of topics (such as self-determination and racial discrimination), and recommendations made. The governments of France, Sweden, Belgium, Australia, and Great Britain so severely criticized the "Action Program" that the American U.N. mission pulled it from circulation pending further State Department advice.[53]

Stark criticism also came from the non-aligned and Communist nations that defended continued work on the covenants. India severely criticized Lord for not understanding the utility of the covenants in raising human rights standards throughout the world, especially in nations that lacked a human rights tradition. The Lebanese delegate worried that the "Action Plan" was "based upon a wholly American orientation," by which he meant that their content spoke more about domestic political pressures in the United States than about outlining effective plans to improve human rights standards worldwide. Uruguay, the Philippines, and Chile likewise strongly condemned the proposals, the latter, in Lord's words, "in a rather violent way" due to their transparent deficiencies. Each proposal depended upon voluntary compliance by countries, and the UNCHR lacked any means of holding nations accountable by exposing and remedying human rights abuses. The Soviet delegate's reaction was therefore tellingly muted, due to his nation's unwillingness to sacrifice any sovereignty, though he wondered how the United States could refuse to sign a still unfinished document. Only China and Egypt consistently supported the United States. Dulles's refusal to compromise or make concessions only worsened the backlash. After discussions in a dozen meetings, UNCHR members voted to transmit, without any recommendation, the American proposals to U.N. members for comment prior to the General Assembly's fall meeting. After only half a dozen nations even bothered to critique the initiative, the General Assembly punted it back to the UNCHR for discussion at its 1954 session.[54]

The abandonment of the covenants unsurprisingly raised domestic criticism by pro-covenant activists who denounced the "Action Plan" as mistitled. Roosevelt and human rights activists from the International League for the Rights of Man, the World Jewish Congress, and the World Federation of United Nations Associations were very disappointed and angry. Their major objection focused on the annual human rights reports that countries would make, after consulting with national "advisory committees." Such bodies in totalitarian countries would be "stooges" that would "whitewash" incomplete and inaccurate reports, thus providing legitimacy and protection for abuses to continue. Although she doubted the Senate would ever pass the economic covenant, Roosevelt told Sandifer that the political covenant, even with the controversial non-discrimination and self-determination clauses, would be of immense legal value in gradually leading all governments to respect human rights. She angrily denounced the "Action Plan" as "comic," remarking that "anything emptier than to go to Geneva with these positions, I cannot imagine." The veteran liberal activist who had presided over the Human Rights Commission for four years and sat as a U.N. delegate on various committees for six even uncharacteristically rebuked Lord directly for serving as its messenger, predicting that "it will be hard for you to get along with the other representatives and to do any worthwhile work, I am sure."[55]

More significantly for Eisenhower and Dulles, the announcement did nothing to slow Holman's and Bricker's crusade, as they finally agreed on the text for a common amendment. It included the "which" clause, would nullify treaties that conflicted with the Constitution, and defined all treaties with any domestic implications as non-self-executing. Bricker conceded the "which" clause after ABA leaders convinced him that the wording would not invalidate international agreements that gave Americans economic rights and protections abroad. He also perhaps realized that a united front was essential to victory. On June 4, the full Senate Judiciary Committee approved the revised Senate Joint Resolution 1 by a two-to-one margin, as five of the eight Republicans joined with three Southern Democrats. The majority report affirmed the amendment's necessity, given that evidence presented at the hearings "certainly establishes that there exists no express limitation on the treatymaking power, and the existence of an implied limitation is shrouded in doubt." The minority report, which quoted heavily from statements submitted by the State Department and Attorney General, responded to every point raised by the majority before arguing for the status quo. "There is no need to change the Constitution just because bad treaties may have been or may be submitted," the four dissenting senators asserted. "The obvious course is to vote the treaties down and leave the Constitution alone." The Senate now headed for a showdown with the Eisenhower administration.[56]

To deflect foreign criticism of the "Action Plan" by Western and non-aligned governments and realign domestic staunch anti-Communists with Eisenhower, several executive branch agencies launched an effort to expose the terrible human rights records of Communist nations. The Central Intelligence Agency (CIA), Psychological Strategy Board (PSB), and Henry Cabot Lodge, Jr., the U.S. ambassador to the United Nations, began to co-ordinate a bold new psychological warfare initiative. Marrying modern radio, film, and mass-produced print technology with psychological studies of knowledge acquisition and human behavior, psywar advocates recognized the importance of generating favorable public opinion at home and abroad for American diplomatic initiatives. Similar to businesses that used images and carefully crafted messages to appeal to consumers, the Eisenhower administration sought to market an American "brand" internationally. The Cold War's expansion into Asia and the Middle East made it even more imperative to discredit Soviet attempts to position itself as the supporter of decolonization and self-determination. As historian Kenneth Osgood noted, "The fragile political and economic state of the postwar world provided fertile ground for meddling abroad, and the superpowers found that they could influence international politics through economic warfare, covert intervention, and propaganda at less cost and less risk than through direct military action." The point was not to improve human rights conditions behind the Iron Curtain, though if that happened all the better. Success would depend on what happened diplomatically outside of the Soviet bloc to expose Eastern bloc human rights abuses.[57]

The "Lodge Human Rights Project," under which intelligence agencies would collect data on Soviet bloc human rights violations for dissemination at the United Nations, had specific domestic and foreign goals. In Africa, Asia, and the Middle East, the Eisenhower administration sought to win the allegiance of neutralist countries by illustrating the hypocrisy of Moscow's human rights record and its hollow criticisms of the "Action Plan." At home, the program might unite liberal civil rights activists and conservative U.N. critics through a post-covenant promotion of human rights principles. Lodge, a staunchly anti-Communist and former Republican senator from Massachusetts, initiated and co-ordinated progress on these fronts. He conversed with C. D. Jackson, Eisenhower's special assistant for psychological warfare, as early as April about leading an anti-Soviet propaganda offensive when the General Assembly met in August 1953. Jackson gave the assignment to the Psychological Strategy Board, an agency created by Truman in April 1951 to co-ordinate most psywar programs run by the State Department, the military, the CIA, and other agencies. Its work in dozens of countries followed the vision of Gordon Gray, the board's first director, who wanted his organization "not to act as planner or co-ordinator with respect to any one major effort, but to act as planner and co-ordinator with respect to all" psywar activities. This framework required the buy-in of all PSB constituents, but the State Department balked from the beginning. To career foreign policy officials, a new body with sweeping influence over potentially all aspects of diplomacy was either a nuisance or a competitor for jurisdiction over foreign relations policymaking.[58]

Intragovernmental tensions notwithstanding, the Psychological Strategy Board had provided valuable assistance to the American U.N. delegation in the last two years of Truman's presidency. The PSB had provided "backstopping" intelligence to prepare the U.S. delegation for the 1951 and 1952 General Assembly meetings on topics ranging from disarmament to atomic energy, but not on human rights. The agency also had trained public affairs staffers to brief the domestic and international press corps on American policy. PSB Director of Information Porter McKeever outlined the importance of having an active U.N. office, stating, "The General Assembly is the biggest single propaganda platform in the world. Failure to organize ourselves to wage an effective propaganda campaign at the General Assembly means depriving ourselves of the outstanding opportunity to present to governments and peoples throughout the world the objectives of our foreign policy." The presence in Paris of 500 delegates, 3,000 U.N. staffers from 60 governments, and 2,000 reporters made McKeever overjoyed at the prospect of launching an information offensive. "It is doubtful if there is any comparable situation in which so many opinion leaders, representatives of the foreign media, and mechanisms for dissemination of propaganda are brought together in relation to a foreign policy forum for a comparable period of time," he wrote to PSB leaders. Now given Joseph Stalin's death on March 5, 1953, PSB officials worried that the Soviet Union would launch a "peace offensive" under the more moderate leadership of Georgy Malenkov once the General Assembly convened.[59]

Henry Cabot Lodge saw in the assembly's session an opportunity to offer a heavy-handed rebuke to the Soviet bloc, but his vision was not without problems. The State Department's reluctance to work with the Psychological Strategy Board meant that Lodge had to bypass his colleagues in Washington if he wanted to create a new psywar program. This was a marriage of convenience: Lodge could draw upon the past expertise and growing personnel of the PSB, while PSB officials could expand the young agency's influence. Lodge instructed C. D. Jackson that he wanted both to illuminate Soviet bloc hypocrisy and respond aggressively to Soviet attacks on American human rights shortcomings. Charles Norberg of the PSB promptly formed a small working group to prepare a list of human rights-related topics likely to come before the United Nations in 1953 with an eye toward their respective propaganda values. By the end of April, the PSB had developed a list of 20 topics for exploitation ranging from the "destruction of religion," "police terror, purges, and political murders," "mass deportations," and "cultural genocide of national minorities" by Soviet leaders against their own citizens and those of neighboring countries. Lodge readily approved the list, and he asked PSB to develop items under each into "five-minute punch speeches . . . in order to make headlines." When a PSB staffer revealed the plan informally to personnel in State's Bureau of U.N. Affairs, the reply was surprise and consternation. The State Department was not in a position to assist Lodge in these matters, they explained, because the U.N. ambassador had not asked them to do so. The answer raised a red flag in a PSB worried about avoiding a turf war with the State Department. Jackson told Lodge personally that he and others in the PSB "would all be happier if the Department of State were informed officially" that Lodge was working with the board on psywar activities.[60]

Lodge's attempts to bypass the State Department and create a strident propaganda campaign doomed the effort from the start. Fearing that the State Department might sabotage the initiative, Lodge continued to communicate directly only with the PSB. In an unusual twist, PSB officials tried to mitigate any fallout by briefing officials from the Bureau of U.N. Affairs on the Lodge Project themselves, even revealing Jackson's advice to Lodge on keeping State informed. Such meetings hardly erased bad feelings about the initiative, and bureau officials refused to co-operate until clear lines of responsibility, which placed the State Department firmly in control, emerged. Lodge also alienated PSB head Edward Lilly by insisting that his project be stridently anti-Soviet, rather than pro-American, as it would expose "Soviet actions against ethnic, religious, and other groups in the free world" using material that "would make headlines [with] no limitations on subject matter." This was a bit of a shock to PSB officials. Lilly responded cautiously at first, suggesting to Lodge that "the U.N. could be used more effectively for presenting positive American views of human rights." By July, after Lodge had called for PSB to uncover sensationalistic items of which, according to Lodge aide Charles Allen, "factual certainty is desired but should not be a fetish," Lilly and PSB dug in their heels. Such an unscrupulous project might estrange the very neutral nations and non-Communist intellectuals whose support the United States desired, turn the United Nations into a "debating society," diminish U.S. credibility, and cause European allies to view the United States as "trigger-happy and hysterical." Lodge's insistence on using only lurid and scandalous "ammunition" also meant postponing the program, as PSB could initially uncover none within the fields that Lodge had requested.[61]

These delays and obstacles notwithstanding, PSB officials tried to piece together a psywar campaign acceptable to Lodge and skeptics in the State Department. The start of a possible Soviet peace offensive targeting non-aligned nations and fears that American allies might view détente with Moscow as a favorable alternative to war made the success of such a strategy urgent. By the end of May, PSB had generated a rough outline of the Lodge Project whose objective was to "promote the solidarity and firmness of the free world against the Soviet bloc, and to promote discord and indecision within the Soviet bloc," by developing a psywar initiative at the United Nations for the fall. In early June, PSB created a Human Rights Working Group with representatives from the PSB, State and Defense departments, and the CIA, which immediately began discussing what categories of information to pass on to Lodge. By serving as a screen of all relevant stakeholders, the body could potentially censor untruthful, extraneous, or uselessly shocking items while gaining buy-in from the recalcitrant State Department. Wallace Irwin of the PSB's Office of Evaluation and Review chaired the committee, which soon collected reports of Soviet concentration camps, restrictions on religious observances, and examples of forced labor. In mid-June, the group agreed to prioritize two issues: discrediting the Communist Chinese government so as to prevent it being seated at the United Nations and publicizing Soviet repression of religious minorities.[62]

The institutionalization of the Lodge Project generated a bitter debate over its proper audience, content, and tone. The battle pitted those who demanded a moderate, truth-based propaganda campaign on a few key issues and those who wanted to smear the Communist nations with whatever charges they could find so as to turn them into international pariahs. PSB officials placed themselves in the former camp. Edward Lilly, the PSB's director, repeated his previous warning to Lodge that as the audience would be U.N. delegates from neutralist nations who comprised an intellectual elite, propaganda would only make an impact "if the approach is reasoned and rational, if the ideas are logically consistent, and if the factual background is objective." Such delegates would not be persuaded by crude messages or by totally negative accusations that did not recognize the aspirations and contributions of developing nations. Irwin agreed,

proposing a long memo that stressed a bold propaganda initiative containing "a reasoned rather than 'hysterical' attitude on our part." A campaign
of bluster and polemics, Irwin warned, could make the developing world
believe that the United States was preparing for another war and ignoring
the real economic and political needs of their nations and peoples.[63]

U.N. Ambassador Henry Cabot Lodge, Jr., dismissed such concerns,
and through Charles Allen of the Bureau of U.N. Affairs, who sat on the
PSB Committee on the General Assembly (formerly the Human Rights
Working Group), demanded attention-getting information, graphic pic-
tures, and dramatic charts for circulation to U.N. delegations. He also opposed the twin priorities that the interdepartmental committee had set,
and instead wanted all the embarrassing intelligence on the Soviet Union
from which he could pick and choose what to employ. In a meeting with
the PSB Committee in late June, he also denigrated the positive tone that
PSB officials had pushed, remarking that neutral nations would see such
speech as consisting of mere platitudes. The target audience would only respond to "the shocking fact, evidence of brutality, of conspiratorial action,
ect [sic]" that could be put across in three to four press statements a week
and in damning U.N. resolutions. Lodge, whose first post-Harvard occupation was as a reporter in Boston, believed that a rapid but questionably
accurate reply to an accusation by a Soviet bloc delegate was superior to
issuing a late but fact-checked response. In the latter case, the media often
ignored the rebuttal simply because the issue was current no longer.[64]

These differences of opinion, when added to bureaucratic infighting and
the lack of PSB intelligence acceptable to Lodge, caused the propaganda effort to fail. By mid-July, Wallace Irwin had had enough of the stonewall-
ing and belittling by the Bureau of U.N. Affairs (UNA), which opposed the
PSB's existence, and the American mission to the United Nations, which
denigrated PSB personnel. He suggested telling the bureau that the "PSB is
not about to dry up and blow away, and in fact is still a dangerous animal
to kick around." "The Lodge Project is in jeopardy," he revealed to Jackson,
because UNA, "unreconciled to the 'invasion' of its backyard" by PSB, was
dismissing as unusable all PSB intelligence passed to it. Although Irwin admitted the lack of sensationalistic items that PSB possessed, he again cried
out for a more moderate program. Equating "smoking gun" information
to precious metals, he tried to convince Jackson that while "the millions of
customers around the world will probably be more impressed with nuggets
of gold . . . there are connoisseurs too—and they will be more impressed
with works of art. Are we to ignore this refined taste? If we do, half of the
effectiveness of the project will be lost." No resolution of these bureaucratic,

political, and philosophical disagreements occurred by late August, though, when the General Assembly convened. According to a former PSB staffer, the entire situation "resulted in a paralysis in the highest echelons. The USUN [American delegation to the United Nations] was only able to present weak and fragmentary attacks on the highly efficient, well organized Communist propaganda machine." Paul Nitze, who had served on the State Department's policy planning staff under Truman, identified PSB overreach as a contributing factor. He had earlier told Gordon Gray, "Look, you just forget about the policy, that's not your business; we'll make the policy and then you can put it on your damn radios." With few defenders, the Psychological Strategy Board soon dissolved, replaced by a new agency that functioned under the National Security Council, with the State Department occupying a seat on the latter body.[65]

The failure of the Lodge Project continued a string of defeats on human rights issues at the United Nations that dated back to the momentous decision by the 1950 General Assembly to incorporate economic, social, and cultural guarantees into a single covenant. This unexpected turn of events followed the adoption of the U.S.-supported Universal Declaration of Human Rights and the UNCHR's largely acceptable revisions to the two covenants on human rights. However, the refusal of the Senate to ratify the Genocide Convention, the addition of a self-determination clause, and the omission of a federal-state provision soon cast a pall over the State Department and domestic human rights NGOs that had supported the standard-setting work of the Human Rights Commission. While experienced human rights activists inside and outside of government who had worked together during the planning days of World War II disagreed on what strategies to pursue, Senator John Bricker and the American Bar Association began to mobilize in opposition to all human rights treaties. Their differing proposals for a constitutional amendment to limit the domestic legal effect of all treaties had the same basic goals: to prevent any multilateral human rights treaty from overriding state laws and centralizing political and economic power in Washington. It remained to be seen, though, whether they could organize conservative Republicans and Democrats in the Senate to their states' rights and isolationist standards.

Into this delicate political environment came the developing nations of the General Assembly. Led by India, Yugoslavia, Saudi Arabia, and Pakistan, they had felt, directly or indirectly, the economic and political consequences of colonialism. Their governments cast a skeptical eye toward growing multinational corporations with headquarters in the West and extractive mines and factories in the Third World. Some nurtured resentments against Western Europe for imposing foreign rule and for continuing to oppose movements for self-determination in Africa and Asia. This bloc of nations strove to be independent in world affairs, refusing to join the Communist or non-Communist alliances. Viewing economic, social, and cultural rights as important aspirational objectives, these nations initially refused to compartmentalize them into a separate covenant. This coalition also fought for recognizing the right of peoples to political and economic self-determination in the covenants and to ensure that the colonial powers applied all human rights guarantees to their dependent areas. Though the number of U.N. members from the developing world increased only slightly between 1945 and 1953, what was more important was their coalescence into a voting bloc that could, in alliance with the Communist world, comprise a majority.

The confluence of these domestic and foreign forces caused a reorientation of American human rights policy by the Republican administration of Dwight Eisenhower. The "Action Plan," though, received harsh criticism even from U.S. allies, while the "Lodge Project" foundered before it could even begin. Worse, neither policy slowed the growing momentum by Bricker and his ABA allies for a constitutional amendment that Eisenhower thought would "be notice to our friends as well as our enemies abroad that our country intends to withdraw from its leadership in world affairs." In private, the president also denigrated Bricker himself, writing in his diary that the campaign for an amendment was the senator's "one hope of achieving at least a faint immortality in American history." Eisenhower and Dulles decided that the price of declaring all-out war on Bricker was the repudiation of American wartime and postwar human rights commitments. With the covenants off the Senate's foreseeable calendar, Eisenhower and his cabinet would now challenge directly the forces seeking to change the Constitution's standards for permissible treaties. In his clearest public statement to date on July 22, 1953, Eisenhower declared that he was "unalterably opposed to any amendment which would change our traditional treaty-making power or which would hamper the President in his constitutional authority to conduct foreign affairs."[66]

Conclusion

The Impact of a Crusade, 1953–2011

What has been accomplished? This: we have kept a

vision alive; we have held to a great ideal, we have established a

continuity, and some day when unity and co-operation come, the

importance of all these early steps will be recognized.

—W.E.B. Du Bois[1]

BETWEEN 1941 AND 1953, the United States government, often prodded by non-governmental organizations and in response to perceived diplomatic and domestic political interests, led a worldwide crusade for the international protection of human rights. The campaign, launched by President Franklin Roosevelt in the dark days of World War II as the British and the Chinese directly faced the forces of Fascism alone, derived as much from current events as from an American ideology as old as the Puritans. Beginning with their seventeenth-century mission to found in Massachusetts Bay a "city on a hill," the religious dissenters bestowed upon what would become the United States a perceived twentieth-century God-given duty to spread the blessings of liberty and freedom across the seas. Historians have given several contextual names to this evangelical impulse, from "Manifest Destiny" in the mid-1800s, to "imperialism" and the "white man's burden" in the late nineteenth century, and "Wilsonian internationalism" during the World War I era. Two decades later, speaking before a joint session of Congress in a muted atmosphere of solemn anticipation, Roosevelt conjured up this exceptionalist history. In this time of Fascist advance, the president explained,

> This nation has placed its destiny in the hands and heads and hearts of its millions of free men and women; and its faith in freedom under the guidance of God. Freedom means the supremacy of human rights everywhere. Our support goes to those who struggle to gain those rights or keep them. Our strength is our unity of purpose.[2]

As historians Michael Hunt, John Dower, and Anders Stephanson have shown, ideologies are malleable, organic, and contain internal contradictions. Thus presidents from Thomas Jefferson to Andrew Jackson to Woodrow Wilson believed in spreading freedom and liberty even as they defended white supremacy, sexual inequality, and colonialism. Few politicians can afford to be true believers and not compromise on even essential principles, and ideologies provide broad road maps rather than arrows pointing to single courses of action. Wilson's embrace of self-determination did not encompass peoples in Asia and Africa who had begun to organize nationalist movements, and his desire to liberate ethnic and national minorities from dictatorial oppression applied only to Europe and not to African Americans in the southern region of his own nation. Likewise, in the period during and after World War II, Franklin D. Roosevelt, Harry S. Truman, and Dwight D. Eisenhower found it extremely difficult to advocate for global human rights while protecting or condoning domestic racial segregation, disenfranchisement, legal and economic inequality, and colonialism. These leaders at first attempted to keep the racial status quo at home intact by trying ironically to incorporate protections for Jim Crow within human rights treaties. When underdeveloped nations in Asia, Africa, and the Middle East rebelled by seeking to include enforceable political, economic, social, and cultural rights, Truman, Eleanor Roosevelt, and their legal advisors were unwilling to alter the essential underpinnings of U.S. policy.[3]

The Roosevelt administration employed the soaring rhetoric of human rights to unify and prepare a nation for war and plan for its aftermath. In the Four Freedoms speech, the Atlantic Charter, and the Declaration of the United Nations, Franklin Roosevelt outlined an expansive postwar vision in which all governments would acquire some responsibility to grant political, civil, and economic rights. He firmly believed that heads of state who treated their own citizens peacefully and humanely would behave similarly toward peoples in other nations. The previous 30 years had provided too much evidence of the converse, as the leaders of Germany, Italy, and Japan had launched waves of repression at home before embarking on overseas conquests. He asked the State Department to translate this abstract vision into pragmatic proposals that would avoid the same type of isolationist backlash that had slain the League of Nations.

Roosevelt's bold words inspired American religious and secular organizations to undertake parallel studies, though their efforts soon met with unexpected indifference by the State Department and Roosevelt himself. Led by Clark Eichelberger, W.E.B. Du Bois, Quincy Wright, and James Shotwell, this new generation of activists came of intellectual age during the tumultuous senatorial debate over the Treaty of Versailles. They watched with increasing horror as the League collapsed in the wake of Fascist aggression. Once a second international conflagration broke out in 1939, they joined the Commission to Study the Organization of Peace, the Federal Council of Churches, and the American Civil Liberties Union, among other lobbying groups. Their proposals contained a common thesis: no longer would national governments have exclusive jurisdiction over how they treated those living under their sovereign domain. By 1943, though, Roosevelt and the State Department had responded disinterestedly. Soviet leader Joseph Stalin and British Prime Minister Winston Churchill opposed sacrificing national sovereignty to an oversight body because they continued to define human rights issues as strictly internal matters. Moreover, they and Roosevelt believed that a community of nations controlled by the world's regional military powers was the best means of preventing another war. Stalin, Roosevelt, and Churchill approved such a blueprint at the 1944 Dumbarton Oaks Conference.

Domestic human rights activists responded quickly and angrily to the marginalization of human rights in the Dumbarton Oaks plan. With an enthusiasm and determination born of a desire to escape a war-torn past and achieve a world based on peace and transnational co-operation, the Commission to Study the Organization of Peace, the American Jewish Committee, the National Association for the Advancement of Colored People, and other groups called for the State Department to amend the proposal. They were joined by Latin American and Asian nations whose desire for economic justice, human dignity, and political self-determination derived from a shared colonial past. Their joint lobbying at the 1945 San Francisco Conference helped lead to changes in what became the United Nations Charter. The final document obligated U.N. members to "promote universal respect for, and observance of, human rights and fundamental freedoms for all." To formulate specific standards that governments were expected to follow, the charter created an Economic and Social Council (ECOSOC) and a Human Rights Commission (UNCHR). President Harry S. Truman, believing that a domestic jurisdiction clause prevented both bodies from compelling compliance by national governments, supported these amendments, as did leaders of Great Britain and the Soviet Union.

It fell to President Truman and his State Department legal advisors to balance demands by NGOs and foreign nations for a binding U.N. Bill of Rights on one hand, with domestic political interests and imperatives on the other hand. Concerned that human rights treaties might invalidate Jim Crow laws and thereby split the Democratic Party along a North-South axis, Truman and UNCHR Chair Eleanor Roosevelt suggested a conservative structure and agenda for the UNCHR. They proposed to staff the Human Rights Commission with governmental delegates instead of independent experts as advocated by American and foreign NGOs. To protect national sovereignty and prevent embarrassing attacks on their nation's human rights violations, Roosevelt also encouraged passage of a "self-denying rule" that prohibited the UNCHR from accepting human rights petitions from individuals and NGOs. Roosevelt then asked the commission to draft a non-binding list of political, civil, and economic rights. On December 10, 1948, U.N. members unanimously approved the symbolic Universal Declaration of Human Rights. The Human Rights Commission then started work on a more controversial agenda item: a contractual bill of rights that the United Nations would actually enforce against all signatories.

As the UNCHR and other U.N. bodies turned to drafting binding treaties, Truman and State Department lawyers adopted new strategies to safeguard segregation. Roosevelt and the State Department tirelessly pushed for language in a human rights covenant that encapsulated two hundred years of American jurisprudence and allowed for the maintenance of white supremacy. They also demanded the inclusion of federal-state and non-self-executing articles that mitigated against the domestic application of the treaty. The Genocide Convention, passed by the United Nations on December 9, 1948, demonstrated the skillful and persuasive lobbying of U.S. delegates John Maktos and Eleanor Roosevelt. The convention provided a narrow definition of the international crime of genocide, incorporated statutory elements already recognized in American law, and relied on national courts to undertake prosecutions. Confident that the Senate would ratify the Genocide Convention and that the covenant was in almost final form, Truman and Roosevelt could then claim credit for leading a conservative human rights revolution at the United Nations.

The concurrent emergence of a new balance of power within the United Nations and growing domestic opposition to assuming binding human rights responsibilities caught Truman and the State Department by surprise. In late 1950, a coalition of underdeveloped nations from Asia and the Middle East, sometimes allied with the Communist bloc, attached to the covenant a list of economic and social guarantees and the right of all peoples to self-determination. These states saw promises of individual access to food, medical care, education, and housing as aspirational objectives; their insertion in international agreements would demonstrate their importance to the majority of the world's people. Roosevelt tried unsuccessfully to defeat both proposals, which U.S. law did not recognize and which provoked hostility from America's colonial allies. These amendments also provided critical fuel for conservatives in the Senate and leaders of the American Bar Association, who castigated the Genocide Convention and the covenant for compromising American sovereignty. Senator John Bricker and ABA leaders Frank Holman, Alfred Schweppe, and George Finch also charged that the covenant could place limitations on the Bill of Rights, promote the creation of a world government, and bring socialism to the United States. They claimed that only a constitutional amendment that circumscribed both the president's foreign affairs powers and the internal impact of treaties could prevent these consequences.

Incoming President Dwight D. Eisenhower and Secretary of State John Foster Dulles tried to silence foreign and domestic criticism by reorienting human rights policy. By announcing that he would not sign the covenants, ask the Senate to ratify the Genocide Convention, or participate in future covenant discussions, Eisenhower hoped to defuse the Bricker Amendment controversy. He called for the UNCHR to replace its work on the controversial covenant with an "Action Program," under which the commission would educate and advise willing governments on how to implement human rights. Eisenhower also launched a psychological warfare campaign to spotlight abuses behind the Iron Curtain. The project fell apart before it could mature due to bureaucratic rivalries between the two principal agencies involved in the hasty planning for its execution. With this propaganda offensive, President Eisenhower had returned U.S. human rights policy to its World War II–era rhetoric that demonized America's enemies and celebrated the nation's political and civic ideals but eschewed any commitment to achieving specific standard-setting goals.

Unsatisfied with Eisenhower's policy concessions, Bricker and the leaders of the American Bar Association continued advancing a constitutional amendment to restrict the executive's foreign policy powers and limit the internal impact of human rights treaties. Efforts by Bricker to enlist Eisenhower's support fell apart over the legislator's insistence on including a provision that would restrict Congress's ability to implement treaties to those areas in which it could already legislate without a treaty. The Ohio senator reacted angrily to Eisenhower's opposition. Putting his cause above party unity, Bricker publicly criticized the president and asked traditionally Republican groups of lawyers, veterans, small businessmen, and isolationists for their endorsement. His opponents, led by the president, dissenting international lawyers, multinational corporations, and progressive political activists, mobilized as well. After Holman vetoed a "which-less" compromise that Bricker and Eisenhower finally hammered out in January 1954, the Senate responded to Eisenhower's renewed opposition by defeating, with a single vote to spare, a weak constitutional amendment. For the Ohio senator, losing on his signature issue was personally shattering, and his electoral defeat while seeking a third term in 1958 also ended his cause. Eisenhower was relieved but livid after the crucial 1954 vote. "If it's true that when you die the things that bothered you the most are engraved on your skull," he said, "I am sure I'll have there the mud and dirt of France during [the] invasion and the name of Senator Bricker." Holman was defiant. "The first round is over, but only the *first* round," he wrote in 1954. "It will be continued for as many 'rounds' as necessary to achieve victory."[4]

Thirty years later Frank Holman and Senator John Bricker could claim victory, for their legacy of opposition to ratifying human rights treaties remained intact. Although the Senate finally ratified the Genocide Convention a month before the senator's death in 1986, it did so only after attaching two reservations and five understandings. The former were so broad that even Western European allies objected that they ran counter to the "object and purpose" of the treaty itself. The Senate also appended five reservations, five understandings, and three declarations to its approval of the International Covenant on Civil and Political Rights (ICCPR) in 1992. Due partially to Bricker's ideological successor, Senate Foreign Relations Committee Chairman Jesse Helms (R-NC), the United States is one of only two nations yet to ratify the Convention on the Rights of the Child (CRC), and it is the only industrialized nation that has not approved the Convention on the Elimination of All Forms of Discrimination against Women (CEDAW). The International Covenant on Economic, Social, and Cultural Rights (ICESCR), signed by President Jimmy Carter in 1977, also remains unratified. In June 1998, the United States was one of only seven nations (out of 130 present) to vote against the statute for an International Criminal Court, which can try persons accused of war crimes, crimes against humanity, and genocide. Although President Bill Clinton in 2000 made the United States one of over 130 nations that signed the statute, he did not send it to the Senate for approval. Two years later, President George W. Bush "unsigned" the document, declaring that the country "has no legal obligations arising from its signature." State Department spokesperson Richard Boucher explained, "We cannot allow our peacekeepers to be subject to the extranational legal jurisdiction of the International Criminal Court, nor can we allow the International Criminal Court to second-guess our legal system." The ghosts of John Bricker and Frank Holman are today very much alive.[5]

The unmistakable irony that intrudes into this refusal to assume binding human rights responsibilities is that the main reason for justifying such a policy has completely changed. In the 1950s, Bricker and Holman worried primarily that the covenants and the Genocide Convention would lower existing constitutional standards. By the 1990s, though, international law had progressed to the point where, in some cases, it provided more guarantees than American practices. The imposition of torture, the utilization of indefinite detention without charge or trial, the denial of habeas corpus, the use of secret extraordinary rendition, and the creation of military commissions, all of which the administration of George W. Bush designed for use in the war against Islamic extremism, demonstrate a disregard for international human rights standards.[6] The judicial branch has recognized this divide, but in looking to international law for guidance, justices have fueled a Bricker-esque backlash from congressional conservatives. In opinions outlawing the death penalty for juveniles and the mentally retarded, invalidating sodomy laws, and permitting the use of affirmative action policies, Justices John Paul Stevens, Anthony Kennedy, Ruth Bader Ginsburg, and Stephen Breyer in particular have noted the practices of other nations and the decisions of foreign courts. In *Lawrence v. Texas*, for example, which struck down state sodomy laws, Justice Kennedy's majority opinion referred to the decriminalization of sodomy by the British Parliament in 1967, the European Convention on Human Rights, and a 1981 ruling by the European Court of Human Rights. Conservative members of the House of Representatives were outraged. A non-binding resolution introduced by Tom Feeney (R-FL) and Bob Goodlatte (R-VA), with 50 cosponsors, asserted that Supreme Court decisions should not be based on foreign law or practice. As Feeney expressed in words that could have come from the mouth of John Bricker, "This resolution advises the courts that it is improper for them to substitute foreign law for American law or the American Constitution."[7]

Despite the hostility by Eisenhower and his successors toward incorporating international human rights law, American allies in Europe and Latin America forged ahead to create revolutionary international and regional instruments. Ironically, the ICCPR and the ICESCR, both completed in 1966, contain weak and largely ineffective enforcement machinery similar to proposals made by the Truman administration. The ICCPR created a Human Rights Committee to receive periodic reports from ratifying countries and hear state-to-state complaints, and an optional protocol allows it to consider petitions from aggrieved individuals. State parties to the ICESCR must report every five years on how they have implemented the treaty's principles. Latin American and European nations have also adopted regional agreements, but those include robust supranational enforcement mechanisms. The European Court of Human Rights, founded in 1959 and reformed substantially in 1998, allows for nations, individuals, and NGOs to file complaints against states. The judges can order states to take remedial action and award compensation for wrongs committed. In the Western hemisphere, the Inter-American Commission on Human Rights, also created in 1959, interprets compliance with the American Declaration of the Rights and Duties of Man and the 1969 American Convention on Human Rights. The commission's duties include visiting nations and preparing progress reports, mediating interstate disputes, and making recommendations on petitions from states, individuals, and NGOs. The Inter-American Court on Human Rights can hear cases recommended to it by the commission and by state parties that have accepted its jurisdiction. The United States, unsurprisingly, has neither ratified the convention nor recognized the right of the court to hear lawsuits brought against it by other nations.[8]

Successive American leaders have refused to take on these binding commitments despite the increasingly important, though still equivocal, role that human rights issues have in influencing U.S. foreign policy. Most notably since the presidency of Jimmy Carter, Congress and the executive branch have struggled to balance traditional support for promoting human rights abroad with other, conflicting interests. Contemporary debates over selling arms and military equipment to brutal dictators in Asia, Africa, and the Middle East and approving policies on the interrogation of suspected terrorists all require balancing human rights standards with issues of national security. Discussions over including labor, environmental, and human rights standards in bilateral and multilateral trade agreements (such as the North American Free Trade Agreement [NAFTA]) pit advocates of the free exchange of goods against those who oppose the presence of sweatshops, rapacious corporations, and governing elites that view their own and their nation's economic interests as one and the same. Even conservatives in Congress, who have been historically more willing to place other interests ahead of human rights concerns, now advocate economic sanctions against nations that persecute Christians and the elimination of slavery in northern Africa. As descendants of NGOs in the 1940s and 1950s, non-partisan lobbying groups such as the American Civil Liberties Union, the National Council of Churches, and the United Nations Association of the United States of America lobby for Senate ratification of human rights treaties and their worldwide enforcement by the United Nations. They are joined by truly transnational agencies, such as Amnesty International, Human Rights Watch, and the Centre on Housing Rights and Evictions, which publicize, campaign against, and seek to prevent violations along a broad spectrum of human rights.

The global activism of citizens and non-governmental organizations has not stopped genocide, crimes against humanity, and war crimes from occurring, but it has nudged the United Nations to reform its human rights program. Two recent changes show that even sovereignty-conscious countries are willing to admit that the status quo is unable to prevent or stop atrocities from occurring. In 2006, the General Assembly replaced the Human Rights Commission with a forty-seven-member Human Rights Council. The election of notoriously repressive regimes to sit on the commission (and the precedent-setting failure of the United States to win a seat in 2001), the body's unwillingness to censor governments for obvious violations, and the commission's resulting loss of credibility mandated its elimination. It is by no means certain that the council will be any more effective, though candidates for membership are explicitly supposed to possess solid human rights credentials. The council is required to undertake a "universal periodic review" of all countries, including China, Russia, and the United States that in the past have escaped notice due to their diplomatic, economic, or military power. A second change is the approval by the Security Council of the Right to Protect (R2P) doctrine in the aftermath of atrocities in Rwanda, the Balkans, Chechnya, and the Congo. Under an April 2006 resolution, the Security Council affirmed the duty of all states to prevent genocide, war crimes, ethnic cleansing, and crimes against humanity from occurring within their borders. If they failed, though, the United Nations had an obligation to act:

The international community, through the United Nations, also has the responsibility to use appropriate diplomatic, humanitarian and other peaceful means, in accordance with Chapter VI and VIII of the Charter, to help protect populations from genocide, war crimes, ethnic cleansing and crimes against humanity. In this context, we are prepared to take collective action, in a timely and decisive manner, through the Security Council, in accordance with the UN Charter, including Chapter VII, on a case by case basis and in co-operation with relevant regional organizations as appropriate, should peaceful means be inadequate and national authorities manifestly failing to protect their populations from genocide, war crimes, ethnic cleansing and crimes against humanity. We stress the need for the General Assembly to continue consideration of the responsibility to protect populations from genocide, war crimes, ethnic cleansing, and crimes against humanity and its implications, bearing in mind the principles of the Charter of the United Nations and international law. We also intend to commit ourselves, as necessary and appropriate, to help states build capacity to protect their populations from genocide, war crimes, ethnic cleansing and crimes against humanity and to assist those which are under stress before crises and conflicts break out.[9]

Whether the R2P principles will provide a new jurisdictional basis for real international action in the face of systemic and serious human rights abuses is hard to predict, but the history of U.N. action in the human rights arena provides plenty of ground for skepticism.

The historical implications of this book for present and future U.S. human rights policy are several. First, it is important to note that the United States has never regained the position it had when Eleanor Roosevelt worked as a leading defender of human rights at the United Nations. In 1945, the country had just helped to win a global war and played a major role in founding the United Nations, and it comprised the world's only economic and military superpower. Despite its substantial domestic shortcomings, the Truman administration demonstrated real though cautious initiative in helping to craft the Universal Declaration of Human Rights, the Genocide Convention, and early work on the covenants. Since the early 1950s, though, the country has been largely on the defensive, with Presidents Ronald Reagan and George H. W. Bush acting with disdain and arrogant disregard for U.N. mandates. Special mention must be made of President G.W. Bush's appointment of U.N. Ambassador John Bolton, who declared, "There is no such thing as the United Nations. There is an international community that occasionally can be led by the only real power left in the world, and that's the United States, when it suits our interest and when we can get others to go along." Although Washington still exerts some influence on the United Nations' human rights agenda, it flows from the nation's military and economic power and its veto on the Security Council more than its moral authority. The defeat in the 2004 General Assembly of U.S.-sponsored resolutions condemning human rights violations in Belarus, Zimbabwe, and the Sudan demonstrate how little respect and influence Washington possesses. To regain credibility on human rights issues, the nation must accept greater international treaty responsibilities while also eliminating domestic human rights abuses, such as the use of capital punishment, the existence of racial disparities in the judicial system, the occurrence of discrimination against gay, lesbian, and transgendered individuals, and the unsavory practices adopted to detain and torture suspected terrorists. George Washington University Law Professor Jonathan Turley describes the deplorable, illegal, and inhumane methods used against suspected terrorists in a provocative but accurate *Washington Post* editorial headlined "10 Reasons the U.S. Is No Longer the Land of the Free."[10]

Second, any change in U.S. policy will probably not occur without strong lobbying by domestic and international NGOs. Wanting maximum freedom of action and dedicated historically to opposing the transnational oversight of human rights issues (unless Washington could find a way to escape such scrutiny), the United States has consistently sought to postpone or defeat human rights reforms proposed at the United Nations. Moreover, presidents from Eisenhower to Bush have rarely discussed human rights concerns with other governments unless NGOs and the media have publicized them and public opinion has reacted strongly. To be successful lobbyists, NGOs must show how massive human rights violations promote political instability, cause economic underdevelopment, and fuel civil wars and military intervention by other nations. In other words, activists must go beyond giving idealistic and moralistic reasons as to why the promotion of human rights should be a top priority for the State Department. Such justifications might include the arguments that the Bush administration's anti-terrorism policies have harmed the United States' image overseas, provided propaganda for armed extremist groups to use in recruiting members, and undermined the rule of law at home.

Finally, as the world's only remaining superpower, the United States must use its own laws, multilateral diplomacy, and unilateral military and economic leverage more forcefully and prudently to stop genocide and other massive human rights abuses. The killing fields of Rwanda and the

Balkans show how dictators who assume impunity and non-intervention by the world community can lead their peoples to war by advocating genocide. The ad hoc criminal tribunals created by the Security Council to try the perpetrators of unspeakable horrors in both regions provide a useful starting point for discussions of ending impunity through multilateral legal co-operation. Washington provided logistical support, technical aid, and funding for both efforts. The United States should also be at the forefront of holding accountable in its own courts those who have committed grave crimes overseas. The 1789 Alien Tort Statute and the 1991 Torture Victim Protection Act provide for civil suits against perpetrators living in the United States. In the first verdict of its kind, in October 2008 a Miami jury convicted Chucky Taylor, the son of former Liberian President Charles Taylor, of criminal charges of torture. The conviction rested on the Extraterritorial Torture Statute that Congress passed in 1994 that allows for federal charges against anyone living in the United States who committed torture anywhere abroad. To build upon these actions, the nation should ratify the statute of the International Criminal Court, embrace the Right to Protect, and support efforts to punish those responsible for terrorist attacks in domestic or international courts.

Though these changes to American human rights policy will be difficult to achieve given the history recounted in this work, they are small steps when compared to the accomplishments of other countries and by a majority in the United Nations. These possible reforms also pale in scope when seen against the revolutionary development of international human rights law over the past 50 years. From the vague promises of the Atlantic Charter to the founding of an International Criminal Court, from the collapse of the League of Nations to a United Nations with evolving human rights responsibilities, from the existence of a handful of NGOs concerned with human rights issues to the formation of a global, Internet-linked network of lawyers, activists, and academics, the internationalized institutionalization of human rights is a recent phenomenon. But the revolution is not done; one hopes that Louis Henkin's appellation, the "Age of Rights," will also apply to future decades. If so, we will understand the truth spoken above by W.E.B. Du Bois: though the Roosevelt and Truman administrations launched a most uncertain crusade to protect human rights, their first steps help to make contemporary and future human rights history possible.

Notes

Introduction

1. James Simsarian, "United Nations Action on Human Rights," 28 December 1948, box 2, Papers of James P. Hendrick, Harry S. Truman Presidential Library.

2. Dulles to Eisenhower, 31 March 1953, Papers of John Foster Dulles, subject series, box 2, Dwight D. Eisenhower Presidential Library [DDEL].

3. Article 55, United Nations Charter.

4. Warren Zimmerman, *First Great Triumph: How Five Americans Made Their Country a World Power* (New York: Farrar, Straus, and Giroux, 2002), 348.

5. See Gordon S. Wood, *The Radicalism of the American Revolution* (New York: Alfred A. Knopf, 1992); Stephen Wrage, "Human Rights and the American National Myth" (PhD diss., Johns Hopkins University, 1987); Frederick Merk, *Manifest Destiny and Mission in American History: A Reinterpretation* (New York: Vintage Books, 1963); Thomas Hietala, *Manifest Design: Anxious Aggrandizement in Late Jacksonian America* (Ithaca: Cornell University Press, 1985); Stephen Kinzer, *Overthrow: America's Century of Regime Change from Hawaii to Iraq* (New York: Times Books, 2006); and Anders Stephanson, *Manifest Destiny: American Expansion and the Empire of Right* (New York: Hill and Wang, 1995).

6. Thomas J. Knock, *To End All Wars: Woodrow Wilson and the Quest for a New World Order* (Princeton: Princeton University Press, 1992); and N. Gordon Levin, Jr., *Woodrow Wilson and World Politics: America's Response to War and Revolution* (London: Oxford University Press, 1968).

7. Peter Balakian, *The Burning Tigris: The Armenian Genocide and America's Response* (New York: Perennial, 2003); Paul G. Lauren, *The Evolution of International Human Rights: Visions Seen* (Philadelphia: University of Pennsylvania Press, 1998), 38–71; James Frederick Green, *The United Nations and Human Rights* (Washington, DC: Brookings Institution, 1956), 3–7; Robert Beisner, *Twelve Against Empire: The Anti-Imperialists, 1898–1900* (New York: McGraw-Hill, 1968); James B. Stewart, *Holy Warriors: The Abolitionists and American Slavery* (New York: Hill and Wang, 1996); Melvin Small, *Democracy and Diplomacy: The Impact of Domestic Politics on U.S. Foreign Policy, 1789–1994* (Baltimore: Johns Hopkins University Press, 1996), 26–52; and Bill Seary, "The Early History: From the Congress of Vienna to the San Francisco Conference," in *The Conscience of the World: The Influence of Non-Governmental Organisations in the U.N. System*, ed. Peter Willetts (Washington, DC: Brookings Institution, 1996), 15–19.

8. Adam Hochschild, *King Leopold's Ghost: A Story of Greed, Terror, and Heroism in Colonial Africa* (London: Pan Books, 2002); Robert C. Tucker, ed., *The Marx-Engels Reader* (New York: W. W. Norton, 1978); Micheline R. Ishay, *The Human Rights Reader: Major*

Political Writings, Essays, Speeches, and Documents from the Bible to the Present (New York: Routledge, 1997), 175–232; Lauren, *Evolution of International Human Rights*, 52–57; and Antony Alcock, *A History of the International Labor Organization* (New York: Octagon Books, 1971).

9. Lauren, *Evolution of International Human Rights*, 72–82; Sheila M. Rothman, *Woman's Proper Place: A History of Changing Ideals and Practices, 1870 to the Present* (New York: Basic Books, 1978); Seary, "The Early History," 19–22; and Leila J. Rupp, *Worlds of Women: The Making of an International Women's Movement* (Princeton: Princeton University Press, 1997).

10. Green, *The United Nations*, 7–8; Howard Tolley, *The U.N. Commission on Human Rights* (Boulder, CO: Westview Press, 1987), 1–2, 16; Lauren, *Evolution of International Human Rights*, 92–99; and Arno J. Mayer, *Politics and Diplomacy of Peacemaking: Containment and Counterrevolution at Versailles, 1918–1919* (New York: Vintage Books, 1967).

11. W.E.B. Du Bois, *The Souls of Black Folk*, in *Three Negro Classics* (New York: Avon Books, 1965), 221. See also Paul Gordon Lauren, "Human Rights in History: Diplomacy and Racial Equality at the Paris Peace Conference," *Journal of Diplomatic History* 2 (June 1978): 257–78; Knock, *To End All Wars*, 210–51; Mayer, *Politics and Diplomacy*; and Akira Iriye, *Across the Pacific: An Inner History of American–East Asian Relations* (New York: Harcourt Brace & World, 1967), 135–43.

12. Lauren, *Evolution of International Human Rights*, 106–30; Gary B. Ostrower, *The League of Nations, 1919 to 1929* (Garden City Park, NY: Avery Publishing, 1996); Robert Divine, *Second Chance: The Triumph of Internationalism in America during World War II* (New York: Atheneum, 1967), 6–28; Seary, "The Early History," 22–24; and Elmer Bendiner, *A Time for Angels: The Tragicomic History of the League of Nations* (New York: Knopf, 1975).

13. Philip Dray, *At the Hands of Persons Unknown: The Lynching of Black America* (New York: Modern Library, 2002), 303–62; John Egerton, *Speak Now Against the Day: The Generation Before the Civil Rights Movement in the South* (New York: Knopf, 1994), 1–197; Robert S. McElvaine, *The Great Depression: America, 1929–1941* (New York: Times Books, 1993), 187–95, 287–305; and Michael Hiltzik, *The New Deal: A Modern History* (New York: Free Press, 2011), 308–25.

14. Kofi Annan, "In Larger Freedom: Report of the Secretary-General," A/59/2005, 21 March 2005.

1: Defining a Crusade

1. "President Roosevelt's Message to Congress on the State of the Union," *New York Times*, 7 January 1941, 4. In June 1940, Roosevelt announced cautiously that his administration was dedicated to the elimination of "four fears," which he changed to the "four freedoms" in a press conference one month later and repeated in his 1941 State of the Union address. See Jonathan Daniels, ed., *Complete Presidential Press Conferences of Franklin D. Roosevelt* (New York: Da Capo Press, 1972), 15:497–99, 16:18–21.

2. Harley Notter, *Postwar Foreign Policy Preparation, 1939–1945* (Washington, DC: U.S. Government Printing Office, 1950), 18; Stephen C. Schlesinger, *Act of Creation: The Founding of the United Nations* (Boulder, CO: Westview Press, 2003), 35, see also 20–31; Cordell Hull, *The Memoirs of Cordell Hull* (New York: Macmillan, 1948), 2:1626–30, 1640; Daniels, *Complete Presidential Press Conferences*, 15:497–99, 16:18–21; and Graham Stuart, *The Department of State: A History of Its Organization, Procedure, and Personnel* (New York: Macmillan Company, 1949), 340–51.

3. For the history of the council, see Robert Schulzinger, *The Wise Men of Foreign Affairs: The History of the Council on Foreign Relations* (New York: Columbia University Press, 1984); and Laurence H. Shoup and William Minter, *Imperial Brain Trust: The Council on Foreign Relations and United States Foreign Policy* (New York: Monthly Review Press, 1977).

4. Walter Sharp, "Basic American Interests," in *Studies of American Interests in the War and the Peace: Political Series* (New York: Council on Foreign Relations, 1941), 3. See also Robert A. Divine, *Second Chance: The Triumph of Internationalism in America during World War II* (New York: Atheneum, 1967), 20–23; Notter, *Postwar Foreign Policy Preparation,* 19, 56; Hull, *Memoirs,* 2:1625; and Assistant Chief of Division of Special Research Harley A. Notter to Chief of Division of Special Research Leo Pasvolsky, 14 September 1942, Harley A. Notter Papers, Record Group 59, box 8, National Archives and Records Administration [hereafter NARA].

5. Commission to Study the Organization of Peace, *Preliminary Report* (New York: Commission to Study the Organization of Peace, 1940), 12; and Notter, *Postwar Foreign Policy Preparation,* 19. See also Divine, *Second Chance,* 30–32; Clark Eichelberger, executive director of the Commission to Study the Organization of Peace to Franklin Roosevelt, 6 April 1941, box 4351, Office Files, Franklin D. Roosevelt Library [hereafter FDRL]; and Clark Eichelberger, *Organizing for Peace: A Personal History of the Founding of the United Nations* (New York: Harper & Row, 1977), 111–18.

6. Quoted in Robert Dallek, *Franklin D. Roosevelt and American Foreign Policy, 1932–1945* (New York: Oxford University Press, 1979), 254, 256–57.

7. Sumner Welles, *Where Are We Heading?* (New York: Harper & Brothers, 1946), 6.

8. Theodore Wilson, *The First Summit: Roosevelt and Churchill at Placentia Bay, 1941* (Lawrence: University Press of Kansas, 1991), 163, 164, see also 149–64; Winston Churchill, *The Second World War,* vol. 3, *The Grand Alliance* (Boston: Houghton Mifflin, 1950), 427–37; Undersecretary of State Sumner Welles to John G. Winant (U.S. ambassador to Britain), 14 July 1941, in *Foreign Relations of the United States, 1941* (Washington, DC: U.S. Government Printing Office, 1958), 1:342 [hereafter referred to as *FRUS 1941*]; Welles memo of conversation, 9 August 1941, *FRUS 1941,* 1:351–52. Most historians agree that the charter was of British origin. Sumner Welles states in *The Time for Decision* that he authored a preliminary draft of a joint declaration and gave a copy to British Foreign Minister Sir Alexander Cadogan. No copy survives, however, and *FRUS* makes no mention of it. Welles also does not repeat the assertion in his longer account of the conference in *Where Are We Heading?* See Welles, *The Time for Decision* (New York: Harper & Brothers, 1944), 175–76; and idem, *Where Are We Heading?,* 6–7.

9. Welles memo of conversation, 10 August 1941, *FRUS 1941,* 1:355. See also Welles memo of conversation, *FRUS 1941,* 1:354–56; Wilson, *The First Summit,* 164–89; Welles, *Where Are We Heading?,* 7–17; Ruth B. Russell, *A History of the United Nations Charter: The Role of the United States, 1940–1945* (Washington, DC: Brookings Institution, 1958), 34–39; Robert E. Sherwood, *Roosevelt and Hopkins: An Intimate History* (New York: Harper and Brothers, 1948), 359–61; Dallek, *Franklin D. Roosevelt,* 281–85; Georg Schild, *Bretton Woods and Dumbarton Oaks: American Economic and Political Postwar Planning in the Summer of 1944* (New York: St. Martin's Press, 1995), 33–37; and David Reynolds, "The Atlantic 'Flop': British Foreign Policy and the Churchill-Roosevelt Meeting of August 1941," in *The Atlantic Charter,* ed. Douglas Brinkley and David R. Facey-Crowther (New York: St. Martin's Press, 1994), 129–50.

10. H. V. Morton, *Atlantic Meeting* (New York: Dodd, Mead and Company, 1943), 149–50; Reynolds, "The Atlantic 'Flop,'" 144; and Robert Rhodes James, ed., *Winston S. Churchill: His Complete Speeches, 1897–1963* (New York: Chelsea House, 1974), 6:6481. See also Wilson, *The First Summit*, 223–26; and Joint Statement by Roosevelt and Churchill, 14 August 1941, *FRUS 1941*, 1:367–69.

11. Wilson, *The First Summit*, 200; and Daniels, *Complete Presidential Press Conferences*, 17:79; "Message of the President to the Congress Regarding Conference at Sea with British Prime Minister," *U.S. Department of State Bulletin* 133 (23 August 1941): 147; and Theodore A. Wilson, "The First Summit: FDR and the Riddle of Personal Diplomacy," in Brinkley and Facey-Crowther, *The Atlantic Charter*, 20. See also Welles memos of conversation, 11 August 1941, *FRUS 1941*, 1:360–63, 364–67; Wilson, *The First Summit*, 168–78; Russell, *History of the United Nations Charter*, 39–42; Dallek, *Franklin D. Roosevelt*, 285.

12. James, *Winston S. Churchill*, 6:6481; Wilson, *The First Summit*, 226–27. See also "Inter-Allied Council," *U.S. Department of State Bulletin* 5 (27 September 1941): 233–35; *FRUS 1941*, 1:378; William R. Lindley, "The Atlantic Charter: Press Release or Historic Document?" *Journalism Quarterly* 41 (Summer 1964): 375–79, 394; Wilson, *The First Summit*, 191–94, 199–204, 227; Morton, *Atlantic Meeting*, 148–51; and Dallek, *Franklin D. Roosevelt*, 358. For a particularly stark denial that the charter should be applied literally, see the Minutes of the Subcommittee on Political Problems, 24 October 1942, Notter Papers, RG 59, box 55, NARA.

13. Notter, *Postwar Foreign Policy Preparation*, 517–18, see also 41–42; Division of Special Research, "Comment on the Atlantic Joint Declaration of President Roosevelt and Prime Minister Churchill," 11 September 1941, Notter Papers, RG 59, box 13, NARA; and Notter to Leo Pasvolsky, chief of the Division of Special Research, 20 August 1941, Notter Papers, RG 59, box 8, NARA.

14. Hull, *Memoirs*, 2:1114–15; and Department of State, *Foreign Relations of the United States 1942* [hereafter *FRUS 1942*] (Washington, DC: U.S. Government Printing Office, 1960), 1:25, see also 1–26; Hull, *Memoirs*, 2:1114–26; Halifax to Churchill, 25 December 1941, *Foreign Relations of the United States: Conferences at Washington, 1941–1942, and Casablanca, 1943* (Washington, DC: U.S. Government Printing Office, 1968), 366–67; Memo by Harry Hopkins to Roosevelt, 27 December, ibid., 368; Sherwood, *Roosevelt and Hopkins*, 446–53; and Dallek, *Franklin D. Roosevelt*, 319.

15. Hull, *Memoirs*, 2:1125; and Russell D. Buhite, ed., *Calls to Arms: Presidential Speeches, Messages, and Declarations of War* (Wilmington, DE: Scholarly Resources, 2003), 183, 189. See also Hull memo of conversation, 29 December 1941, in *FRUS 1942*, 1:18–20; Welles memo of conversation, 29 December 1942, ibid., 21–22; Memos by Savage, 30 December 1941 and 2 January 1942, ibid., 22–23, 28–29; "Declaration by United Nations," 1 January 1942, ibid., 25–26; and "The President's Message," *New York Times*, 7 January 1942, 1. For names and dates of signatories of the U.N. Declaration, see *U.S. Department of State Bulletin* 6 (3 January 1942): 3–4.

16. Notter, *Postwar Foreign Policy Preparation*, 63, 65, 69. See also Pasvolsky to Welles and Assistant Secretary of State Gardiner H. Shaw, 7 February 1942, Notter Papers, RG 59, box 8, NARA; Divine, *Second Chance*, 50; Elmer Plischke, *U.S. Department of State: A Reference History* (Westport, CT: Greenwood Press, 1999), 298–300; Notter, *Postwar Foreign Policy Preparation*, 78–84, 97, 101–7; and Hull, *Memoirs*, 2:1634–37. For a summary of the responsibilities of the committee and its subcommittees, see Notter, "Work of the Committees Dealing with Post-War Political Foreign Policy," 10 June 1943, Notter Papers, RG 59, box 8, NARA.

17. "The Federal Council of the Churches in Christ in America . . . What It iI and What It Does," Official File 213, box 1, FDRL; Divine, *Second Chance*, 45; and John Foster Dulles, *Long Range Peace Objectives* (New York: Commission to Study the Bases of a Just and Durable Peace, 1941), 8. See also Divine, *Second Chance*, 36–37.

18. Commission to Study the Bases of a Just and Durable Peace, "Statement of Guiding Principles," 5 March 1942, in *A Righteous Faith for a Just and Durable Peace*, ed. John Foster Dulles (New York: Commission to Study the Bases of a Just and Durable Peace, 1942), 103.

19. Ibid., 101–4; and Commission to Study the Bases of a Just and Durable Peace, *A Message from the National Study Conference on Churches and a Just and Durable Peace* (New York: Commission to Study the Bases of a Just and Durable Peace, 1942).

20. Council on Foreign Relations, "Problems of Postwar International Organization: A Tentative Outline," in *Studies of American Interests in the War and the Peace: Political Series* (New York: Council on Foreign Relations, 1942), 3; Eichelberger, *Organizing for Peace*, 193; Eichelberger to Col. McIntyre, 21 May 1942, Official File 4351, box 1, FDRL. See also Divine, *Second Chance*, 53–55; and Eichelberger, *Organizing for Peace*, 192–94.

21. Henry Wallace, "The Price of Free World Victory," in *Democracy Reborn* (New York: Reynal & Hitchcock, 1944), 192; and Maxwell Hamilton, head of the Division of Far Eastern Affairs, to Hull, 18 June 1942, RG 59, box 3241, decimal file (1940–1944), 3. See also Divine, *Second Chance*, 35–36, 64–67.

22. Franklin D. Roosevelt, "Flag Day Address by the President," *U.S. Department of State Bulletin* 6 (20 June 1942): 545–46.

23. Quoted in Divine, *Second Chance*, 67; and Cordell Hull, "The War and Human Freedom," 22 July 1942, Records of the Office of United Nations Affairs, box 1, NARA. See also Hull, *Memoirs*, 2:1177–79; Notter, *Postwar Foreign Policy Preparation*, 93–95; and Divine, *Second Chance*, 67–68.

24. Notter, *Postwar Foreign Policy Preparation*, 82, see also 98, 114.

25. Durward Sandifer, interview by Richard D. McKinzie, 15 March 1973, Harry S. Truman Library, Independence, Missouri, <http://www.trumanlibrary.org/oralhist/sandifer.htm>, accessed 8 June 2007; and Sandifer, "Bill of Rights: Preliminary Draft," 31 July 1942, Records of the Advisory Commission on Post-War Foreign Policy, Notter Papers, RG 59, box 72, NARA. See also Sandifer, "Bill of Rights: Explanatory Comments," 31 July 1942, Records of the Advisory Commission on Post-War Foreign Policy, Notter Papers, RG 59, box 72, NARA. For the documents used by Sandifer to prepare his bill of rights, see "Guarantees of Personal Rights and Liberties in the Constitutions of the Countries of Occupied Europe," "American Bill of Rights: Articles I to VIII of Amendments to the Constitution of the United States," "English Bill of Rights of 1689," "French Declaration of the Rights of Man and of the Citizen of 1789," "Declaration of the International Rights of Man," and "Polish Minorities Treaty," all of 31 July 1942, Records of the Advisory Commission on Post-War Foreign Policy, Notter Papers, RG 59, box 72, NARA.

26. "Tentative Views of the Subcommittee on Political Problems," 12 August 1942, Records of the Advisory Committee on Post-War Foreign Policy, Notter Papers, RG 59, box 54, NARA. See also Minutes of Division of Special Research Staff Meeting, 10 August 1942, Notter Papers, RG 59, box 11, NARA; Notter, *Postwar Foreign Policy Preparation*, 114–16; Notter to Pasvolsky, 14 September 1942, Notter Papers, RG 59, box 8, NARA; and Minutes of the first meeting of the Subcommittee on Legal Problems, 21 August 1942, Records of the Advisory Commission on Post-War Foreign Policy, Notter Papers, RG 59, box 72, NARA.

27. Minutes of the Legal Subcommittee, 1 October 1942, Notter Papers, RG 59, box 72, NARA.

28. Minutes of the Legal Subcommittee, 1 October 1942, Notter Papers, RG 59, box 72, NARA.

29. Ibid.; and Minutes of the Legal Subcommittee, 22 October 1942, Notter Papers, RG 59, box 72, NARA. See also Sandifer, "Bill of Rights—Revised Draft of Articles 1–12," 6 October 1942, Notter Papers, RG 59, box 72, NARA.

30. Minutes of the second meeting of the Legal Subcommittee, 1 October 1942; Minutes of the third meeting of the Legal Subcommittee, 22 October 1942; Sandifer, "Bill of Rights—Revised Draft," and Sandifer, "Commentary on Revised Draft," 26 October 1942, Notter Papers, RG 59, box 72, NARA.

31. Minutes of the fourth meeting of the Legal Subcommittee, 29 October 1942, Notter Papers, RG 59, box 72, NARA.

32. Minutes of the fifth meeting of the Legal Subcommittee, 5 November 1942, Notter Papers, RG 59, box 72, NARA; and *Plessy v. Ferguson*, 163 U.S. 537.

33. Sandifer, "Bill of Rights—Second Revised Draft," 11 November 1942, Notter Papers, RG 59, box 72, NARA. See also Minutes of the fifth meeting of the Legal Subcommittee, 5 November 1942.

34. Sandifer, "Report of the Session of the American Law Institute for Discussion of International Bill of Rights Project," 10 November 1942, Notter Papers, RG 59, box 72, NARA. See also American Law Institute, *Annual Report of William Draper Lewis, Director* (New York: American Law Institute, 1942); William Draper Lewis, "An International Bill of Rights: Tentative Draft of Agenda," 9 November 1942, Notter Papers, RG 59, box 72, NARA; and Sandifer, "Bill of Rights—Second Revised Draft," 11 November 1942, Notter Papers, RG 59, box 72, NARA.

35. Minutes of the seventh meeting of the Legal Committee, 19 November 1942, Notter Papers, RG 59, box 72, NARA; Sandifer, "Bill of Rights—Fourth Draft," 28 November 1942, ibid.; Minutes of the eighth meeting of the Legal Subcommittee, 3 December 1942, ibid.; Sandifer, "Bill of Rights—Final Draft," 3 December 1942, ibid.; Minutes of the ninth meeting of the Legal Subcommittee, 10 December 1942, ibid.

36. Minutes of the sixtieth meeting of the Subcommittee on Political Problems, 19 June 1943, Notter Papers, RG 59, box 55, NARA.

37. Notter, *Postwar Foreign Policy Preparation*, 108–10; and Divine, *Second Chance*, 51–52.

38. James Shotwell, "Provisional Outline of International Organization," 28 October 1942, Notter Papers, RG 59, box 87, NARA. See also Minutes of the Special Subcommittee on International Organization, 30 October 1942, Notter Papers, RG 59, box 85, NARA; Notter, "A Note," 19 June 1943, Notter Papers, RG 59, box 8, NARA; Notter, *Postwar Foreign Policy Preparation*, 110–14; Townsend Hoopes and Douglas Brinkley, *FDR and the Creation of the U.N.* (New Haven: Yale University Press, 1997), 68–69; Eichelberger, *Organizing for Peace*, 198–208; Russell, *History of the United Nations Charter*, 110, 229–40, 278–84, 306–11, 323–24, 331–34; Welles, *Where Are We Heading?*, 23; Russell, *History of the United Nations Charter*, 219, 227–40. For the text of the Draft Constitution, see Notter, *Postwar Foreign Policy Preparation*, 472–83.

39. Arthur Krock, "The Situation in the State Department," *New York Times*, 6 August 1943, 14; Notter, *Postwar Foreign Policy Preparation*, 175–76; Hoopes and Brinkley, *FDR*, 76–82; Russell, *History of the United Nations Charter*, 219–20, 240–44, 284–90, 311–

12, 334–43, 354–58; O. Benjamin Gerig, chief of the Division of Political Studies to Notter, 14 August 1943, Notter Papers, RG 59, box 171, NARA; Hull, *Memoirs*, 2:1647; and Irwin F. Gellman, *Secret Affairs: Franklin Roosevelt, Cordell Hull, and Sumner Welles* (Baltimore: Johns Hopkins University Press, 1995), 302–17. For the text of the Staff Charter, see Notter, *Postwar Foreign Policy Preparation*, 526–32.

40. Notter, *Postwar Foreign Policy Preparation*, 530; and Staff Charter Group, "Draft Commentary—First Revision," 3 September 1943, Notter Papers, RG 59, box 171, NARA. For the full text of the Staff Charter, see Notter, *Postwar Foreign Policy Preparation*, 526–32.

41. Staff Charter Group, "Draft Commentary—First Revision," 3 September 1943, Notter Papers, RG 59, box 171, NARA. See also draft of article nine, 13 August 1943, and Staff Charter Group, "Commentary on the Tentative Draft Text of the Charter of the United Nations," September 1943, Notter Papers, RG 59, box 107, NARA.

The Subcommittee on Political Problems would come to the same conclusion on enforcing a bill of rights in a brief discussion on 15 May 1943. See Minutes of Subcommittee on Political Problems, 15 May 1943, Notter Papers, RG 59, box 55, NARA; and Subcommittee on Political Problems, "Views and Arguments Developed in the Political Subcommittee," 15 May 1943, Notter Papers, RG 59, box 54, NARA.

42. Russell, *History of the United Nations Charter*, 120. See also Hull, *Memoirs*, 2:1292–1307, 1640–47; Hoopes and Brinkley, *FDR*, 83–85; Russell, *History of the United Nations Charter*, 115–24; Notter, *Postwar Foreign Policy Preparation*, 187–89, 553; and Dallek, *Franklin D. Roosevelt*, 389–90, 419–20.

43. Department of State, "Radio Bulletin No. 1," 1 January 1943, Records of the Office of U.N. Affairs, RG 59, box 2, NARA; Cordell Hull, "Our Foreign Policy in the Framework of Our National Interests," 12 September 1943, Records of the Office of U.N. Affairs, RG 59, box 20, NARA. See also Franklin Roosevelt, "Radio Bulletin No. 38," 13 February 1943, Records of the Office of U.N. Affairs, RG 59, box 20, NARA; and Divine, *Second Chance*, 133–35.

44. Division of Political Studies, "International Bill of Rights: Problem of Protecting Individual Rights," 2 June 1943, and idem, "International Bill of Rights: Uses of Bill of Rights," 9 June 1943, and idem, "International Bill of Rights: Content of Bill of Rights," 14 September 1943, and idem, "International Bill of Rights: Implementation," 14 September 1944, Notter Papers, RG 59, box 175, NARA; Division of Political Studies, "Basic Objectives of Permanent Organization," 15 July 1943, Notter Papers, RG 59, box 90, NARA; Division of Political Studies, "Permanent International Organization—Functions, Powers, Machinery, and Procedure: Promotion of Observance of Basic Human Rights," 21 August 1943, Notter Papers, RG 59, box 89, NARA; Cordell Hull, Departmental Order 1124, 14 January 1943, Notter Papers, RG 59, box 8, NARA; Notter, *Postwar Foreign Policy Preparation*, 157–59, 173–76; "The Divisions of Political Studies and of Economic Studies," *U.S. Department of State Bulletin* 8 (16 January 1943): 63–64; Hull, *Memoirs*, 2:1638; and Stuart, *The Department of State*, 378–81. For members of each division, see Notter, *Postwar Foreign Policy Preparation*, 522–26.

45. Divine, *Second Chance*, 129–54; Hoopes and Brinkley, *FDR*, 86–93; Hull, *Memoirs*, 2:1258–63, 1292–1307, 1646–48; "Passage of the Fulbright Resolution by the House of Representatives," *U.S. Department of State Bulletin* 9 (25 September 1943): 207–8.

46. Russell, *History of the United Nations Charter*, 125–37; Notter, *Postwar Foreign Policy Preparation*, 194–99; "The Tripartite Conference in Moscow: Anglo-Soviet-American Communique," *U.S. Department of State Bulletin* 9 (6 November 1943): 307–9; ibid. (20

November 1943), 341–45. For the drafting history of the Moscow Declaration, see Notter to Pasvolsky and Hull, 14 December 1943, Notter Papers, RG 59, box 8, NARA.

47. Commission to Study the Organization of Peace, *Fundamentals of the International Organization: General Statement*, in *Building Peace: Reports of the Commission to Study the Organization of Peace* (Metuchen, NJ: Scarecrow Press, 1973), 89–90. See also Eichelberger, *Organizing for Peace*, 217; Divine, *Second Chance*, 101–2, 164–65; and Commission to Study the Organization of Peace, *Winning the War on the Spiritual Front* (New York: Commission to Study the Organization of Peace, 1943).

48. Commission to Study the Bases, *A Righteous Faith*, 11; John Foster Dulles to Franklin Roosevelt, 30 March 1943, Official File 213, box 1, FDRL. See also "'Six Pillars of Peace' Program of Federal Council of Churches," *New York Times*, 6 June 1943, 32; Divine, *Second Chance*, 161–63; and Frederick Roblee, Chairman of the Commission on Public Affairs of the Bay City Council of Churches to Franklin Roosevelt, 1 April 1943, Roosevelt Papers, Official File, box 4351, FDRL.

49. Percy Bordwell to Franklin Roosevelt, 18 January 1943, Official File 4351, box 2, FDRL; and Roosevelt to State University of Iowa Law Professor Percy Bordwell, 9 March 1943, Official File 4351, box 2, FDRL. See also Clarence Streit, *Union Now: A Proposal for a Federal Union of the Democracies of the North Atlantic* (New York: Harper & Brothers, 1939).

50. Quincy Wright, "Human Rights and the World Order," *International Conciliation* 389 (April 1943): 250.

51. Durward Sandifer, "Report of Session of Annual Meeting of the American Law Institute on Its International Bill of Rights Project," 13 May 1943, Notter Papers, RG 59, box 72, NARA; and American Law Institute International Bill of Rights Project, "Reports (Preliminary) of Subcommittees of the Committee of Advisors, February 1943," 13 May 1943, Notter Papers, RG 59, box 72, NARA.

52. Notter, *Postwar Foreign Policy Preparation*, 160–64; Hoopes and Brinkley, *FDR*, 78–82; Leo Pasvolsky, "Survey of Organization of Preparations on Post-War Foreign Policy," 10 June 1943, Notter Papers, RG 59, box 8, NARA; and Notter to Pasvolsky, Chief of Division of Departmental Personnel John Ross, and Assistant Secretary of State G. Howland Shaw, 9 October 1943, Notter Papers, RG 59, box 8, NARA.

53. Notter, *Postwar Foreign Policy Preparation*, 96–97, 160–76.

2: Implementing a Vision

1. Quoted in Thomas G. Paterson and J. Garry Clifford, *America Ascendant: U.S. Foreign Relations Since 1939* (Lexington, MA: D. C. Heath and Company, 1995), 23.

2. "Conference of President Roosevelt, Prime Minister Churchill and Premier Stalin at Tehran," *U.S. Department of State Bulletin* 9 (11 December 1943): 409. See also Hoopes and Brinkley, *FDR*, 100–102, 106–8; Schild, *Bretton Woods*, 42–45; Notter, *Postwar Foreign Policy Preparation*, 199–201; Sherwood, *Roosevelt and Hopkins*, 785–87; Russell, *History of the United Nations Charter*, 154–65; and William L. Neumann, *Making the Peace, 1941–1945: The Diplomacy of the Wartime Conferences* (Washington, DC: Foundation for Foreign Affairs, 1950), 65–71.

3. *New York Times*, 12 January 1944, 12.

4. Hull to Roosevelt, 29 December 1943, in *Foreign Relations of the United States, 1944* [hereafter *FRUS 1944*] (Washington, DC: U.S. Government Printing Office, 1966), 1:616 and 615. See also Hull, *Memoirs*, 2:1649; Russell, *History of the United Nations Char-*

ter, 166–67, 244–51, 315–17, 328; Notter, *Postwar Foreign Policy Preparation*, 169–73, 247–51; Hoopes and Brinkley, *FDR*, 111; and Schild, *Bretton Woods*, 61–62. For text of Outline Plan, see *FRUS 1944*, 1:614–20.

5. Wright, "Memorandum on the Charter," undated, and Norman Padelford to Sandifer, Notter, and Gerig, 30 December 1943, Notter Papers, RG 59, box 90, NARA; Robert Hilderbrand, *Dumbarton Oaks: The Origins of the United Nations and the Search for Postwar Security* (Chapel Hill: University of North Carolina Press, 1990), 34–37; Minutes of the Informal Political Agenda Group, 16 December 1943, Notter Papers, RG 59, box 170, NARA; Cordell Hull to Franklin Roosevelt, 29 December 1944, in *FRUS 1944*, 1:615; Notter, *Postwar Foreign Policy Preparation*, 256; and Notes on Hull-Roosevelt meeting, 3 February 1944, in *FRUS 1944*, 1:620–22. At Hull's suggestion, the Agenda Group drafted an attached "Principal Obligations of a Member State" that included the duties to refrain from using force, to settle all disputes through negotiation, and to participate in arms control agreements. The list did not include any human rights responsibilities. See *FRUS 1944*, 620.

6. Informal Political Agenda Group, "The General Assembly," 13 March 1944, Notter Papers, RG 59, box 141, NARA; and Minutes of the Informal Political Agenda Group, 23 February 1944, Notter Papers, RG 59, box 170, NARA. See also Russell, *History of the United Nations Charter*, 329; Informal Political Agenda Group, "The General Assembly," 10 February 1944, Notter Papers, RG 59, box 171, NARA; idem, "General Character and Functions of an International Organization," 23 February 1944; idem, "The General Assembly," 23 February 1944; idem, "The General Assembly," 24 February 1944, Notter Papers, RG 59, box 171, NARA; idem, "General Character and Functions of an International Organization," 13 March 1944, Notter Papers, RG 59, box 141, NARA; and Minutes of the Informal Political Agenda Group, 18 February 1944, Notter Papers, box 170, NARA.

7. Cordell Hull, "Bases of Foreign Policy of the United States," *U.S. Department of State Bulletin* 10 (25 March 1944): 275–76; Hull, "Foreign Policy of the United States of America," ibid. (15 April 1944): 335–42; Divine, *Second Chance*, 194; Notter, *Postwar Foreign Policy Preparation*, 258; and Hull, *Memoirs*, 2:1321–23.

8. Quoted in Divine, *Second Chance*, 197; and Hoopes and Brinkley, *FDR*, 125. See also Notter, *Postwar Foreign Policy Preparation*, 258–69, 582–91; Hull, *Memoirs*, 2:1658–69; Russell, *History of the United Nations Charter*, 193–97; and Divine, *Second Chance*, 195–203.

9. U.S. ambassador to Britain John G. Winant, "Tentative Proposals by the United Kingdom for a General International Organization," 22 July 1944, in *FRUS 1944*, 1:671. See also Acting Secretary of State Stettinius to U.S. ambassador to the Soviet Union W. Averell Harriman and U.S. ambassador to Britain John G. Winant, 10 February 1944, "Tentative Proposals by the United Kingdom for a General International Organization," 22 July 1944, in *FRUS 1944*, 1:622–23, 670–93; Undersecretary of State Stettinius to Pasvolsky, 26 May 1944, Notter Papers, RG 59, box 12, NARA; Hilderbrand, *Dumbarton Oaks*, 37–55; Notter, *Postwar Foreign Policy Preparation*, 257–582, 266, 283; Schild, *Bretton Woods*, 66–70; and Hull, *Memoirs*, 2:1675–77.

10. "Memorandum on an International Security Organization, by the Soviet Union," 12 August 1944, in *FRUS 1944*, 1:707. See also Schild, *Bretton Woods*, 70–72; Hilderbrand, *Dumbarton Oaks*, 44–47; Telegram from British embassy in Soviet Union to Foreign Office, 5 April 1944, in *FRUS 1944*, 1:635; Harriman to Hull, 29 June 1944, ibid., 1:643; Hull to Harriman, 7 July 1944, ibid., 1:644; Soviet embassy to State Department, 9 July 1944, ibid., 1:645; Harriman to Hull, 24 July 1944, ibid., 1:694–96; and "Memorandum on an International

Security Organization, by the Soviet Union," 12 August 1944, ibid., 706–11; Hoopes and Brinkley, *FDR*, 121; and Hull, *Memoirs*, 2:1672–77.

11. Manley Hudson to Roosevelt advisor Harry Hopkins, 20 July 1944, Papers of Harry Hopkins, box 329, FDRL. See also American Law Institute, "Report to the Council and Statement of Essential Human Rights by a Committee of Advisors, Representing the Principal Cultures of the World," 24 February 1944, files of Alger Hiss, 1940–1946, subject files of the Office of Special Political Affairs, box 2, NARA; and Divine, *Second Chance*, 214.

12. Commission to Study the Organization of Peace, *International Safeguard of Human Rights* (New York: Commission to Study the Organization of Peace, 1944), 6, 15. See also Heber R. Harper of the Division of Cultural Co-operation to Office of Public Information Director John Dickey, Acting Chief of the Division of Science, Education, and Art, and Assistant Chief of the Division of Science, Education, and Art Ralph Turner, 18 August 1944, decimal file 500.CC/8-1844 (1940–1944), RG 59, box 1460, NARA.

13. "United States Tentative Proposals for a General International Organization," 18 July 1944, in *FRUS 1944*, 1:655. See also Post War Programs Committee, "Summary of the Papers Relating to the Establishment of International Organization," 15 March 1944, Notter Papers, RG 59, box 141, NARA; Division of International Organization and Security, "General Assembly," 7 April 1944, Notter Papers, RG 59, box 171, NARA; Minutes of the Informal Political Agenda Group, 11 April 1944, and Minutes of the International Organization Group, 14 and 30 June 1944, Notter Papers, RG 59, box 170, NARA.

14. Roosevelt press conference, 30 May 1944, in Daniels, *Complete Presidential Press Conferences*, 23:192–93.

15. Ibid. See also press statement by Roosevelt, 15 June 1944, in *FRUS 1944*, 1:642–43; Hull to Roosevelt, 11 July 1944, in *FRUS 1944*, 1:647–50; and Roosevelt to Hull, 15 July 1944, in *FRUS 1944*, 652. Roosevelt press conferences, 30 May and 2 June 1944, in Daniels, *Complete Presidential Press Conferences*, 26:191–97, 211–12, 215; Notter, *Postwar Foreign Policy Preparation*, 278–85, 294–300; Divine, *Second Chance*, 204–8; Hoopes and Brinkley, *FDR*, 121–22; Hilderbrand, *Dumbarton Oaks*, 64–66; and Russell, *History of the United Nations Charter*, 392–94.

For an angry response to Roosevelt's lack of attention to human rights matters, see Doris Washington, secretary to National Association for the Advancement of Colored People leader Walter White, to Harold Young, Administrative Assistant to Vice President Henry Wallace, 3 August 1944, Wallace Papers, box 75, FDRL.

16. Soviet embassy in the United States to the Department of State, 9 July 1944, in *FRUS 1944*, 1:645.

17. Hull speech at Opening of Dumbarton Oaks Conversations, 21 August 1944, Records of the Office of U.N. Affairs, RG 59, box 31, NARA. See also Group 1, A and B, "Background Books," undated, Notter Papers, RG 59, box 175, NARA; "Staff Charter: Introductory Comment," and "Preamble," undated, Notter Papers, RG 59, box 171, NARA; "Progress Report on Postwar Programs," book 2, Notter Papers, RG 59, box 145, NARA; Group 1, working book A, "General Character and Establishment," Notter Papers, RG 59, box 176, NARA. For histories of the conference that present a distorted summary of human rights issues, see Hilderbrand, *Dumbarton Oaks*, 86–93; and Hoopes and Brinkley, *FDR*, 142–43. Schild does not even mention debates over the Economic and Social Council in his chapter on Dumbarton Oaks.

18. Hilderbrand, *Dumbarton Oaks*, 86–87; Informal record of meeting of American delegation, 25 August 1944, Notter Papers, RG 59, box 174, NARA; and Informal minutes

of the Joint Steering Committee, 25 August 1944, *FRUS 1944*, 1:735–36. See also Hilderbrand, *Dumbarton Oaks*, 87–90; Personal diary of Edward R. Stettinius, Jr., 24 and 29 August 1944, in *FRUS 1944*, 1:732 and 749–50; Hull memo of conversation with Gromyko, 31 August 1944, in *FRUS 1944*, 1:760; Hoopes and Brinkley, *FDR*, 142–43. Informal minutes of the Joint Steering Committee, 25 August 1944, in *FRUS 1944*, 1:734–36; Stettinius to Hull, 29 August 1944, ibid., 1:746–47; Stettinius to Hull, 6 September 1944, ibid., 1:771–72; Stettinius to Hull, 7 September 1944, ibid., 1:776–78; and Stettinius to Hull, 8 September 1944, ibid., 1:783–84. Hull to American embassies in London and Moscow, 30 August 1944, Records of the Office of U.N. Affairs, Notter Papers, RG 59, box 30, NARA.

19. Stettinius diary entry, 28 August 1944, in *FRUS 1944*, 1:744. See also diary of Stettinius, 29 August and 6 and 8 September 1944, in *FRUS 1944*, 1:748–50, 772–76, and 784–88; Minutes of the Joint Steering Committee, 13 September 1944, in *FRUS 1944*, 1:798–804; Hoopes and Brinkley, *FDR*, 147–56; and Schild, *Bretton Woods*, 156–66.

20. Stettinius to Roosevelt, 8 September 1944, President's Secretary's Files, box 131, FDRL; Informal record of meeting of U.S. delegation, 9 September 1944, Notter Papers, RG 59, box 174, NARA; Informal minutes of the Joint Steering Committee, 9 September 1944, Notter Papers, RG 59, box 178, NARA; and Stettinius to Hull, 9 September 1944, in *FRUS 1944*, 1:789. See also Stettinius diary, 9 September 1944, Notter Papers, RG 59, box 190, NARA; Notes on meeting of the American delegation, 9 September 1944, and Minutes of meeting of U.S. delegation, 12 September 1944, Notter Papers, RG 59, box 174, NARA; Informal minutes of the Joint Steering Committee, 17 September 1944, Notter Papers, RG 59, box 178, NARA; Hilderbrand, *Dumbarton Oaks*, 91–92; Russell, *History of the United Nations Charter*, 423–24; Stettinius to Hull, 9 September 1944, and Stettinius to Hull, 19 September 1944, in *FRUS 1944*, 1:789–91, 824–26.

21. Stettinius to Hull, 20 September 1944, Notter Papers, RG 59, box 182, NARA; Stettinius diary, 20 September 1944, Notter Papers, RG 59, box 190, NARA; Informal minutes of Joint Steering Committee, 20 September 1944, Notter Papers, RG 59, box 178, NARA; Hilderbrand, *Dumbarton Oaks*, 92–93; and Informal record of meeting of U.S. delegation, 20 September 1944, Notter Papers, RG 59, box 174, NARA.

22. Diary of Stettinius, 21 September 1944, in *FRUS 1944*, 1:834; and Informal minutes of Joint Steering Committee, 27 September 1944, Notter Papers, RG 59, box 178, NARA. See also Stettinius to Roosevelt, 20 September 1944, President's Secretary's Files, box 131, FDRL; Hull to U.S. embassies in London and Moscow, 21 September 1944, Records of the Office of U.N. Affairs, RG 59, box 30, NARA; Stettinius diary, 21 September 1944, in *FRUS 1941*, 1:831–34; Stettinius to Roosevelt, 21 September 1944, and Informal record of meeting of U.S. delegation, 27 September 1944, Notter Papers, RG 59, box 174, NARA; Stettinius diary, 23 and 27 September 1944, Notter Papers, RG 59, box 190, NARA; Alger Hiss, special assistant to the head of the Office of Special Political Affairs, to Stettinius, 23 September 1944, and Stettinius to Hiss, 25 September 1944, Notter Papers, RG 59, box 181, NARA; and Russell, *History of the United Nations Charter*, 424.

23. Stettinius to Roosevelt, 27 September 1944, in *FRUS 1944*, 1:838–41. See also "Proposals for the Establishment of a General International Organization," 9 October 1944, in *FRUS 1944*, 1:890–900. For a concise history of human rights considerations at the Dumbarton Oaks Conversations, see Alice McDiarmid, "Promotion of Respect for Basic Human Rights and Fundamental Freedoms," 26 September 1944, Notter Papers, RG 59, box 162, NARA.

24. Dorothy B. Robins, *Experiment in Democracy: The Story of U.S. Citizen Organizations in Forging the Charter of the United Nations* (New York: Parkside Press, 1971),

38; see also 35–39; Divine, *Second Chance*, 245–46, and Notter, *Postwar Foreign Policy Preparation*, 378–80.

25. Hull, "Statement by the Secretary of State," 9 October 1944, *U.S. Department of State Bulletin* 11 (8 October 1944): 366; Stettinius speech to New York University, 23 October 1944, Records of the Office of U.N. Affairs, RG 59, box 31, NARA; Hilderbrand, *Dumbarton Oaks*, 26–27; Divine, *Second Chance*, 244–47; Robins, *Experiment in Democracy*, 40–45, 178–81; and Edward Stettinius, *Charter of the United Nations: Report to the President on the Results of the San Francisco Conference* (Washington, DC: U.S. Government Printing Office, 1945), 26–27.

Stettinius stated that Americans sent over twenty thousand letters a week to the State Department by April 1945. *Charter*, 27. For a list of the organizations present at the 16 October meeting, see Robins, *Experiment in Democracy*, 182–88.

26. William Allan Neilson, chair of the executive committee of the Commission to Study the Organization of Peace to Hull, 15 September 1944, decimal file 500.CC/9-1344 (1940–1944), RG 59, box 1461, NARA; Hull to Neilson, 28 September 1944, decimal file 500.CC/9-1544 (1940–1944), RG 59, box 1461, NARA; Neilson to Edwin Wilson, 7 October 1944, decimal file 500.CC/10-744 (1940–1944), RG 59, box 1462, NARA; Edwin Wilson, memo of conversation with Neilson and others, 17 October 1944, decimal file 500. CC/10-1744, RG 59, box 1463, NARA; Commission to Study the Organization of Peace, *Toward Greater Freedom: Problems of War and Peace*, 3rd ed. (New York: Commission to Study the Organization of Peace, 1944); Divine, *Second Chance*, 247–49; and Robins, *Experiment in Democracy*, 35–44.

27. Hudson to Stettinius, 19 December 1944, decimal file, 500.CC/12-1944 (1940–1944), RG 59, box 1468, NARA. See also Roosevelt advisor Benjamin V. Cohen to Hopkins, undated, Hopkins Papers, box 329, FDRL; Lewis to Sandifer, 27 December 1944, Sandifer to Hiss, John Dickey, director of the Office of Public Information, and Pasvolsky, 9 December 1944, Hiss to Sandifer, 13 December 1944, Sandifer to Hiss, Dickey, and Pasvolsky, 4 January 1945, and Sandifer to Lewis, 13 January 1945, decimal file 501-BD-Human Rights/12-2744 (1940–1944), RG 59, box 1468, NARA; and Divine, *Second Chance*, 167, 249–50.

28. Joseph M. Proskauer, president of the American Jewish Committee to Roosevelt, 23 October 1944, Official Files, box 1581, FDRL; and Edward A. Conway, S.J., National Catholic Welfare Conference, 30 November 1944, decimal file 500.CC/11-3044 (1940–1944), RG 59, box 1465, NARA. See also Proskauer to Stettinius, 28 November 1944, decimal file 500.CC/11-2844 (1940–1944), RG 59, box 1465, NARA; David S. Wyman, *Abandonment of the Jews: America and the Holocaust, 1941–1945* (New York: Pantheon Books, 1984), 67, 329; Proskauer to William A. Fowler, chief of the Division of Commercial Policy, 23 October 1944, decimal file 500.CC/10-2344 (1940–1944), RG 59, box 1463, NARA; Robins, *Experiment in Democracy*, 56; Wilson memo of conversation with O. Frederick Nolde of the Federal Churches of Christ in America, 31 October 1944, Records of the Office of U.N. Affairs, RG 59, box 30, NARA; Emory Ross, executive secretary of the Foreign Missions Conference of North America to Roosevelt, 12 January 1945, Official Files, box 5557, FDRL; Commission for a Just and Durable Peace, "A Message to the Churches," Notter Papers, RG 59, box 95, NARA; and Divine, *Second Chance*, 251–52.

29. Inter-American Juridical Committee, *The Dumbarton Oaks Proposals: Preliminary Comments and Recommendations* (Washington, DC: Pan American Union, 1944), 5. See also Notter memo of conversation, 17 October 1944, and Carlton Hayes, U.S. ambassador to Spain to Stettinius, 24 October 1944, Records of the Office of U.N. Affairs, RG 59,

box 30, NARA; and Notter, *Postwar Foreign Policy Preparation*, 436; Charles W. Sawyer, U.S. ambassador to Belgium to Stettinius, 25 November 1944, *FRUS 1944*, 1:940.

30. Alice McDiarmid, "Commitments of the United States Relating to the Promotion of the Observance of Basic Human Rights," 27 October 1944, Notter Papers, RG 59, box 74, NARA. See also Walter Kotschnig, "Additional Commissions to Be Appointed by Economic and Social Council," 7 November 1944, and Division of International Security and Organization, "International Co-operation in the Political Field," 20 November 1944, Notter Papers, RG 59, box 163, NARA.

31. Notter to Wilson, Pasvolsky, and Stettinius, 21 December 1944, Notter Papers, RG 59, box 9, NARA; Sandifer to Gerig, Lawrence Preuss, assistant chief of section on judicial organization and legal problems of the Division of International Security and Organization, Charles Rothwell, executive secretary of the Committee on Post-War Problems, and the director of the Division of African Affairs Henry Villard, 28 November 1944, Notter Papers, RG 59, box 208, NARA; State Department, "Organization of the Department of State," 20 December 1944, press release, *U.S. Department of State Bulletin* 11 (17 December 1944), Supplement, 777–813; and Notter, *Postwar Foreign Policy Preparation*, 348–52.

"Mr. Pasvolsky's Committee" consisted of Pasvolsky, Notter, Wilson, Hiss, Sandifer, Gerig, acting chief of the Division of International Security Affairs Joseph E. Johnson, and Pasvolsky's assistant, Robert Hartley. See Notter, *Postwar Foreign Policy Preparation*, 386.

32. "'People Fooled' About Charter, View in Capital," and "Offspring in Search of a Parent," *Chicago Tribune*, 21 December 1944, 4; "Atlantic Charter Unsigned but Still Intact, Roosevelt Says," *New York Times*, 21 December 1944, 1; and quoted in Divine, *Second Chance*, 259. See also Daniels, *Complete Presidential Press Conferences*, 24:266–71, 275–78, and Russell, *History of the United Nations Charter*, 484.

33. For an excellent recent overview of the conference, see S. M. Plokhy, *Yalta: The Price of Peace* (New York: Viking, 2010).

34. "Resolution 30 of the Inter-American Conference on Problems of War and Peace," *U.S. Department of State Bulletin* 12 (18 March 1945): 449–50. See also Committee 2, "An Account of the Essential Comments Made by the Delegates to the Inter-American Conference on Problems of War and Peace Concerning the Bases of Dumbarton Oaks," Records of the Office of U.N. Affairs, RG 59, box 30, NARA; "Proposal of the Delegation of Cuba for the Declaration of the International Duties and Rights of the Individual," Notter Papers, RG 59, box 23, NARA; and Department of State, *Report of the Delegation of the United States of America to the Inter-American Conference on Problems of War and Peace* (Washington, DC: U.S. Government Printing Office, 1946), 82, 102–4, 108–9, 141–44, 156–60, 258–59, 344, and 355–56.

For general background and information about the conference, see Russell, *History of the United Nations Charter*, 553–69; and Notter, *Postwar Foreign Policy Preparation*, 398–407. For documentation about the human rights aspects of the conference and the U.S. preparation, see memo by William Sanders, technical officer to U.S. delegation, 29 January 1945, in *Foreign Relations of the United States, 1945* (Washington, DC: U.S. Government Printing Office, 1969), 9:74; Memo by Sanders, 2 February 1945, ibid., 9:82; and Memo by Sanders, 7 February 1945, ibid., 9:92.

35. Telegram from U.S. embassy in Norway to State Department, 2 March 1945, Notter Papers, RG 59, box 185, NARA; Division of International Organization Affairs, "Comments and Suggestions by Other Governments, *Chapter 2: Principles*," undated, Notter Papers, RG 59, box 164, NARA; and U.S. Department of State, *The United Nations*

Conference on International Organization: Selected Documents (Washington, DC: U.S. Government Printing Office, 1946), 92–110. See also Division of International Organization Affairs, "Comments and Suggestions on the Dumbarton Oaks Proposals," 28 March 1944, Notter Papers, RG 59, box 214, NARA; and Elbridge Durbrow, chief, Division of European Affairs to Sandifer, 5 February 1945, in *Foreign Relations of the United States, 1945* [hereafter *FRUS 1945*] by the U.S. Department of State (Washington, DC: U.S. Government Printing Office, 1969), 1:58–60.

36. Quincy Wright, "The Dumbarton Oaks Proposals," 20 January 1945, Notter Papers, RG 59, box 94, NARA; Jacob Robinson, "The Dumbarton Oaks Proposals and the Problem of Human Rights and Fundamental Freedoms," 27 February 1945, Notter Papers, RG 59, box 168, NARA; Eichelberger, *Organizing for Peace*, 253; Robins, *Experiment in Democracy*, 63–64; Ulric Bell, executive vice president of Americans United for World Organization to Eleanor Roosevelt, 9 March 1945, Notter Papers, RG 59, box 197, NARA; Lewis to Stephen Early, Roosevelt's secretary, 2 April 1945, and Early to Lewis, 7 April 1945, Official Files, box 4351, FDRL; and Herbert Hoover, "Summary of the Hoover Amendments," 25 March 1945, in *Dumbarton Oaks*, ed. Robert E. Summers (New York: H. W. Wilson, 1945), 138–39.

See also the very detailed U.N. Constitution submitted by the Free World Association, a member of Americans United, that began with a bill of rights. Free World Research Bureau, "The Constitution of the United Nations," April 1945, Papers of Henry Reiff, box 5, Harry S. Truman Library [hereafter cited as HSTL].

Churches also participated in this final push. See National Catholic Welfare Conference, "Summary of the Statement Issued by the Archbishop and Bishops of the Administrative Board," 17 April 1945; and E. Hilton Jackson, Chairman of the Joint Conference Committee on Public Relations of the Northern, Southern, and National Baptist conventions to the U.S. delegation to the San Francisco Conference, 14 April, Notter Papers, RG 59, box 191, NARA.

For a text of Davis's statement, see "Davis Sees Dark Future if Present Efforts Fail," *Changing World* 17 (January 1945): 5.

37. Division of International Organization Affairs, "Comments and Suggestions on the Dumbarton Oaks Proposals," 28 March 1944, Notter Papers, RG 59, box 214, NARA; and Robins, *Experiment in Democracy*, 84–86, 196–99.

38. Henry S. Villard, "The Positive Approach to an Enduring Peace," 22 January 1945, Notter Papers, RG 59, box 177, NARA. See also "International Bill of Human Rights to Be Offered at World Peace Parley," *New York Times*, 21 March 1945, 13; Memo by Charles E. Bohlen, assistant to the Secretary of State, 29 March 1945, in *FRUS 1945*, 1:166–68; and Department of State, "International Bill of Rights," *Foreign Affairs Outlines* 4 (Spring 1945): 3–4; Robins, *Experiment in Democracy*, 93–96.

39. Division of International Organization Affairs, "Promotion of Respect for Human Rights and Fundamental Freedoms," 7 April 1945, Notter Papers, RG 59, box 208, NARA. See also Division of International Organization Affairs, "Proposals and Suggestions for Consideration," 9 April 1945, Notter Papers, RG 59, box 213, NARA.

40. Robins, *Experiment in Democracy*, 86–90, 199–205; Minutes of the second meeting of the American delegation to the San Francisco Conference, 23 March 1945, in *FRUS 1945*, 1:148–50; Acting Secretary of State Joseph Grew to John Winant, American ambassador to Great Britain, 23 March 1945, in *FRUS 1945*, 1:153; Memo by Charles Bohlen, assistant to the secretary of state for White House Liaison, 29 March 1945, in *FRUS 1945*,

1:166–68; Minutes of the third and fourth meetings of the American delegation to the San Francisco Conference, 30 March and 3 April, in *FRUS 1945*, 168–73 and 183–89; Schlesinger, *Act of Creation*, 122–23; and Notter, *Postwar Foreign Policy Preparation*, 414–23.

For a list of consultants invited to the conference, see Robins, *Experiment in Democracy*, 200–202, and Stettinius press release, 10 April 1945, Records of the Office of U.N. Affairs, RG 59, box 31, NARA. The groups included the American Jewish Committee, Federal Council of Churches, Catholic Association for International Peace, National Catholic Welfare Conference, Church Peace Union, Commission to Study the Organization of Peace, Americans United for World Organization, and the Council on Foreign Relations, all of whom had made previous human rights recommendations.

41. Minutes of the seventh meeting of the U.S. delegation, 11 April 1945, in *FRUS 1945*, 1:252 and 253; and Minutes of the eighth meeting of the U.S. delegation, 11 April 1945, in *FRUS 1945*, 1:263. See also Minutes of fifth meeting of the U.S. delegation, 9 April 1945, in *FRUS 1945*, 1:223; Minutes of sixth meeting of the U.S. delegation, 10 April 1945, ibid., 1:231; Minutes of the seventh meeting of the U.S. delegation, 11 April 1945, ibid., 250–53; Minutes of the eighth meeting of the U.S. delegation, 11 April 1945, ibid., 259–68; Minutes of the twelfth meeting of the U.S. delegation, 18 April 1945, ibid., 338–44 and 347; and Stettinius to President Harry S. Truman, 19 April 1945, ibid., 353–55.

42. Schlesinger, *Act of Creation*, 65–92; and Hoopes and Brinkley, *FDR*, 179–85.

43. Schlesinger, *Act of Creation*, 111–22.

44. Stettinius, "Speech to the First Plenary Session of the San Francisco Conference, 26 April 1945," *U.S. Department of State Bulletin* 12 (29 April 1945): 793; and Department of State, *The United Nations Conference*, 482–83.

45. Quoted in Robins, *Experiment in Democracy*, 104. See also Eichelberger, *Organizing for Peace*, 269–72; Robins, *Experiment in Democracy*, 106–8, 130; Divine, *Second Chance*, 291; Schlesinger, *Act of Creation*, 122–23.

46. Quoted in Robins, *Experiment in Democracy*, 219. The full text of the letter is in Robins, 218–21. See also 130–31; Divine, *Second Chance*, 292; Schlesinger, *Act of Creation*, 123–24.

47. Minutes of the Meeting of Consultants to the American delegation, 2 May 1945, Notter Papers, RG 59, box 195, NARA. See also Divine, *Second Chance*, 291–92; Robins, *Experiment in Democracy*, 112, 130–31; Diary of Stettinius, 2 May 1945, Notter Papers, RG 59, box 30, NARA; National Catholic Welfare Conference press release on a bill of rights, 15 April 1945, Reiff Papers, box 5, HSTL; National Association of Manufacturers, "International Economic Peace," 1 May 1945, Reiff Papers, box 5, HSTL; World Jewish Conference, American Jewish Conference, and Board of Deputies of British Jews, "Memorandum," Reiff Papers, box 5, HSTL; Proskauer and Blaustein to Hiss, 4 May 1945, Notter Papers, RG 59, box 201, NARA; and American Veterans Committee statement, 1 May 1945, Notter Papers, RG 59, box 197, NARA.

48. Minutes of the Meeting of the U.S. delegation, 2 May 1945, *FRUS 1945*, 1:532–48. See also Department of State, *The United Nations Conference*, 97–99 and 103–5.

49. Minutes of the first Four-Power Consultative Meeting on Charter Proposals, 2 May 1945, in *FRUS 1945*, 1:551. See also "Amendments to the Dumbarton Oaks Proposals as Suggested by the United States, the United Kingdom, the Soviet Union, and China," 3 May 1945, Notter Papers, RG 59, box 255, NARA. See also Notter, *Postwar Foreign Policy Preparation*, 442–43; Diary of Stettinius, 3 May 1945, Notter Papers, RG 59, box 30, NARA; Stettinius to Truman, 4 May 1945, President's Secretary's Files, box 139, HSTL;

and Minutes of the First Four-Power Consultative Meeting on Charter Proposals, 2 May 1945, in *FRUS 1945*, 1:548–62. For the text of all U.S. amendments to the charter, see Notter, *Postwar Foreign Policy Preparation*, 679–81.

50. Minutes of the U.S. delegation, 3 May 1945, in *FRUS 1945*, 1:581; "Consultation of the United States, United Kingdom, Soviet Union, and China on Their Amendments to the Dumbarton Oaks Proposals: Status of Consultation," 4 May 1945, Notter Papers, RG 59, box 197, NARA; Minutes of the Meeting of Consultants, 5 May 1945, Notter Papers, RG 59, box 195, NARA; and "Amendments Proposed by the Governments of the United States, the United Kingdom, the Soviet Union, and China," 5 May 1945, Notter Papers, RG 59, box 227, NARA. See also Minutes of the Second Four-Power Consultative Meeting on Charter Proposals, 3 May 1945, in *FRUS 1945*, 1:570; Minutes of the U.S. delegation, 3 May 1945, in *FRUS 1945*, 1:581; and Minutes of the Third Four-Power Consultative Meeting on Charter Proposals, 3 May 1945, in *FRUS 1945*, 1:584; Minutes of the Meeting of Consultants, 22 May 1945, Notter Papers, RG 59, box 196, NARA; Robins, *Experiment in Democracy*, 132; Stettinius press statement, 5 May 1945, Notter Papers, RG 59, box 197, NARA; Stettinius, "Report to the President on the Results of the San Francisco Conference," in *Hearings Before the Senate Foreign Relations Committee on the United Nations Charter*, 79th Cong., 1st sess. (Washington, DC: U.S. Government Printing Office, 1945), 47–49, 105; Stettinius to Truman, 5 May 1945, President's Secretary's Files, box 139, HSTL; and Minutes of Meeting of Commission 2, 11 June 1945, Notter Papers, RG 59, box 202, NARA. For a list of the Big Four amendments, see Notter, *Postwar Foreign Policy Preparation*, 681–85; "United Nations Conference on International Organization: Amendments Offered to Dumbarton Oaks Proposals," *U.S. Department of State Bulletin* 12 (6 May 1945): 851–54; and Stettinius to Truman, 4 May 1945, President's Secretary's Files, box 139, General File, HSTL.

51. Stettinius press statement, 5 May 1945, Notter Papers, RG 59, box 197, NARA; Divine, *Second Chance*, 292; and Minutes of the Meeting of Consultants, 5 May 1945, Notter Papers, RG 59, box 195, NARA.

52. U.S. Delegation, "Recommendation on Major Issues, Committee 2/3," 25 May 1945, Notter Papers, RG 59, box 198, NARA. See also "Seven Proposals on the Dumbarton Oaks Proposals Submitted by the Delegation of Cuba," 2 May 1945, "Additional Amendments Offered by the Delegation of the Republic of Panama Concerning the Proposals for the Maintenance of Peace and Security Agreed Upon at the Conference of Dumbarton Oaks," 5 May 1945, and "Additional Amendments and Proposals by the Delegation of Chile," 6 May 1945, Notter Papers, RG 59, box 227, NARA; Department of State, *The United Nations Conference*, 96, 130; Minutes of the meeting of the U.S. delegation, 7 May 1945, Notter Papers, RG 59, box 193, NARA; Stettinius diary, 7 May 1945, Notter Papers, RG 59, box 30, NARA; and U.S. Delegation, "Amendments to the Dumbarton Oaks Proposals Which Require Consideration by the Delegation," 8 May 1945, Notter Papers, RG 59, box 197, NARA; Summary record of fifth meeting of Committee 1/1, 14 May 1945, and Minutes of sixth meeting of Committee 1/1, 15 May 1945, Notter Papers, RG 59, box 202, NARA; U.S. Delegation, "Progress Report of Work in Commissions and Committees, Committee 1/1/A," 24 May 1945, Notter Papers, RG 59, box 198, NARA; Minutes of the meeting of the U.S. delegation, 3 May 1945, in *FRUS 1945*, 580; Minutes of the Fourth Four-Power Consultative Meeting on Charter Proposals, 4 May 1945, in *FRUS 1945*, 1:599; Schlesinger, *Act of Creation*, 237–39; Carol Anderson, *Eyes off the Prize: The United Nations and the African American Struggle for Human Rights, 1944–1955* (Cambridge: Cambridge University Press, 2003), 48–50.

53. "Dumbarton Oaks Amendments Suggested by Big Four and by Separate Powers," *New York Times*, 6 May 1945, 29; Stettinius diary, 15 May 1945, Notter Papers, RG 59, box 30, NARA; and Stettinius, "Provisions on Human Rights," 15 May 1945, *U.S. Department of State Bulletin* 12 (20 May 1945): 928–29. See also Minutes of the meeting of the U.S. delegation, 14 May 1945, Notter Papers, RG 59, box 192, NARA; and U.S. Delegation, "Daily Summary of Opinion Development," 16 and 17 May 1945, Notter Papers, RG 59, box 205, NARA.

54. U.S. Delegation, "Progress Report of Work in Commissions and Committees," 13 May 1945, and "Recommendations to United States Delegation on Various Issues," 16 May 1945, Notter Papers, RG 59, box 198, NARA; Minutes of fifth meeting of Committee 2/3, 14 May 1945, Notter Papers, RG 59, box 203, NARA; Minutes of the meeting of the U.S. delegation, 16 May 1945, in *FRUS 1945*, 1:749–52; and Minutes of the meeting of the U.S. delegation (Executive Session), 17 May 1945, in *FRUS 1945*, 1:777–78.

For the Big Four human rights amendment to the U.N.'s list of purposes (that would merge with the section on purposes), see Summary record of the meeting of Subcommittee A of Committee 1/1, 16 May 1945, and Summary reports of meetings of Committee 1/1, 1 and 2 June 1945, Notter Papers, RG 59, box 202, NARA. See also "Text as Passed by the Co-ordination Committee," 5 June 1945, "Technical Committee Text Submitted to the Co-ordination Committee without Change," 7 June 1945, "Revision of Technical Committee Text Suggested by the Secretariat as Submitted to the Co-ordination Committee," 14 June 1945, and Summary reports of meeting of the Co-ordination Committee, 15 and 16 June 1945, Notter Papers, RG 59, box 226, NARA; and Verbatim minutes of Commission 1, 15 June 1945, Notter Papers, RG 59, box 237, NARA.

For the General Assembly's human rights responsibilities, see Summary report of the third meeting of Committee 2/2, 9 May 1945, Notter Papers, RG 59, box 229, NARA; "Texts Passed by the Technical Committee," 18 May 1945, Notter Papers, RG 59, box 225, NARA; and Summary report of the meeting of Committee 2/3, 25 May 1945, Notter Papers, RG 59, box 231, NARA.

For the amendments to ECOSOC's list of objectives (including a revision of the Dumbarton Oaks text), see Committee 2/3, "First Report of Drafting Subcommittee," 16 May 1945, Notter Papers, RG 59, box 230, NARA; Summary record of meeting of Committee 2/3, 16 May 1945, Summary record of the meeting of Committee 2/3, 22 May 1945, and Summary record of meeting of Committee 2/3, 24 May 1945, Notter Papers, RG 59, box 203, NARA; Minutes of meeting of U.S. delegation, 22 and 23 May 1945, in *FRUS 1945*, 1:837–39, 850–57; "Texts Passed by the Technical Committee," 26 May 1945, Notter Papers, RG 59, box 25, NARA; Summary report of the meeting of Committee 2/3, 24 May 1945, Notter Papers, RG 59, box 231, NARA; and "Texts as Considered by the Co-ordination Committee," 28 and 29 May 1945, "Text Adopted by Committee 2/3," 6 June 1945, and Summary record of the meeting of the Co-ordination Committee, 14 June 1945, Notter Papers, RG 59, box 226, NARA.

For the debate over a human rights commission, see Summary record of Subcommittee A of Committee 2/3, 29 May 1945, Notter Papers, RG 59, box 203, NARA; Summary report of Committee 2/3, 31 May and 6 June 1945, Notter Papers, RG 59, box 232, NARA; "Text as Passed by the Technical Committee," 2 June 1945, and "Revision of Technical Committee Text Suggested by the Secretariat as Submitted to the Co-ordination Committee," 13 June 1945, Notter Papers, RG 59, box 225, NARA; and Summary report of the meeting of the Co-ordination Committee, 15 June 1945, Notter Papers, RG 59, box 226, NARA.

55. Stettinius, "Report on the San Francisco Conference," speech of 28 May 1945, Notter Papers, RG 59, box 21, NARA. See also U.S. Delegation, "Progress Report of Work in Commissions and Committees," 24 May 1945, and U.S. Delegation, "Recommendations on Basic Issues," 25 May 1945, Notter Papers, RG 59, box 198, NARA; Minutes of a meeting of the U.S. delegation, 16 May 1945, in *FRUS 1945*, 1:751; Summary report of the eleventh meeting of Committee 2/3, 25 May 1945, Notter Papers, RG 59, box 232, NARA; Report of rapporteur of Committee 2/3, 8 June 1945, Notter Papers, RG 59, box 233, NARA; and Stettinius, "Report on the San Francisco Conference," 28 May 1945, *U.S. Department of State Bulletin* 12 (3 June 1945): 1007–13.

The domestic jurisdiction clause was not new, though, for the Big Four had submitted a version with their other joint amendments on 4 May. For the official U.S. government interpretation of the human rights clauses in the U.N. Charter, see Stettinius, *Charter*, 53, 56–57, 101–8.

56. Harry S. Truman, "Address by the President of the United States of America Closing Plenary Session of the United Nations Conference on International Organization," 26 June 1945, President's Secretary's Files, box 189, HSTL; and quoted in Anderson, *Eyes off the Prize*, 70.

57. Congress, Senate, Committee on Foreign Relations, *Hearings Before the Senate Committee on Foreign Relations on the United Nations Charter*, 79th Cong., 1st sess., 307 and 320. See also 309–12, 319–21, 454, 512, 576–77, and 641–43. For written comments in support of the charter's human rights clauses, see statements by the American Jewish Committee, the Federal Council of Churches, and the Catholic Association for International Peace to the Senate Foreign Relations Committee, ibid., 665–66, 698, and 703–4. See also Hull, "Senate Approval of Charter of the United Nations," *U.S. Department of State Bulletin* 13 (29 July 1945): 138.

58. Brenda Gayle Plummer, *Rising Wind: Black Americans and U.S. Foreign Affairs, 1935–1960* (Chapel Hill: University of North Carolina Press, 1996), 140–46.

3: A Conservative Revolution Begins

1. P. Bernard Young, editor of the *Norfolk Journal and Guide*, to Truman, 28 August 1945, White House Central Files, Truman Papers, box 10, HSTL.

2. Clark Eichelberger to President Harry S. Truman, 30 July 1945, Official Files, 85, Truman Papers, box 528, HSTL. See also United Nations Preparatory Commission, *Report of the Preparatory Commission to the United Nations* (New York: United Nations, 1946).

3. McDiarmid, "Status, Scope, and Functions of the Commission for the Promotion of Human Rights," 5 September 1945, Eleanor Roosevelt Papers, box 4575, FDRL. See also Notter to John Ross and Hiss, 8 and 17 August 1945, Notter Papers, RG 59, box 9, NARA; and U.S. Delegation to the United Nations Preparatory Commission, "Tentative and Partial List of Topics for Discussion with Reference to the Economic and Social Council," 4 September 1945, Notter Papers, RG 59, box 273, NARA.

4. Notter, "Comments on Memoranda to Be Submitted to Mr. Stettinius on the General Assembly, and on the Commission for the Promotion of Human Rights," 18 September 1945, Notter Papers, RG 59, box 9, NARA; and U.S. State Department, "United Nations Preparatory Commission: Background Information," 21 November 1945, RG 59, box 283, Notter Papers, NARA. See also United Nations Preparatory Commission, "Revised Draft Recommendations with Regard to the Economic and Social Council," 17 October 1945, PC/EX/95/Rev.1.

5. *Report by the Executive Committee to the Preparatory Commission of the United Nations* (New York: Preparatory Commission of the United Nations, 1945), 36, 39. See also United Nations Preparatory Commission, *Report of the Preparatory Commission of the United Nations* (London: United Nations, 1945), 28–39; Walter Kotschnig, "Structure of the System," in *The United Nations and Promotion of the General Welfare*, by Robert E. Asher, et al. (Washington, DC: Brookings Institution, 1957), 46–47; and Durward Sandifer, "Progress in Establishment of the United Nations Organization," *U.S. Department of State Bulletin* 13 (23 December 1945): 1010–14.

6. For biographies that cover Eleanor Roosevelt's life after her husband's death (though few examine her U.N. activities in adequate detail, with the exception of Mower), see Jason Berger, *A New Deal for the World: Eleanor Roosevelt and American Foreign Policy* (New York: Social Science Monographs, 1981); Allida Black, *Casting Her Own Shadow: Eleanor Roosevelt and the Shaping of Postwar Liberalism* (New York: Columbia University Press, 1996); Joseph P. Lash, *Eleanor: The Years Alone* (New York: W. W. Norton, 1972); Eleanor Roosevelt, *On My Own* (New York: Harper & Brothers, 1958); and A. Glenn Mower, Jr., *The United States, the United Nations, and Human Rights: The Eleanor Roosevelt and Jimmy Carter Eras* (Westport, CT: Greenwood Press, 1979), 11–52. For two excellent interviews of people who knew her well, see oral histories of Durward Sandifer and Porter McKeever by Emily Williams, FDRL; and Arthur Vandenberg, Jr., *The Private Papers of Senator Vandenberg* (Boston: Houghton Mifflin, 1952), 240–41. For an intimate account of Roosevelt's human rights work by her legal advisor, see Marjorie M. Whiteman, "Mrs. Franklin D. Roosevelt and the Human Rights Commission," *American Journal of International Law* 62 (1968): 918–21. Two examples of private dissent in addition to those examined here were later letters to Truman and Secretary of State George Marshall decrying the loyalty program, and the American abandonment of the U.N. partition plan for Palestine, respectively. She offered her resignation after the latter, but Marshall refused to accept it.

7. Eleanor Roosevelt, *The Autobiography of Eleanor Roosevelt* (New York: Harper & Brothers, 1958), 299. See also Mary Ann Glendon, *A World Made New: Eleanor Roosevelt and the Universal Declaration of Human Rights* (New York: Random House, 2001), 21–28; Roosevelt, *Autobiography*, 299–303; and M. Glen Johnson and Janusz Symonides, *The Universal Declaration of Human Rights: A History of Its Creation and Implementation, 1948–1998* (Paris: UNESCO, 1998), 20–22.

8. Nolde, "Memorandum Suggesting a Program of Action for the Commission on Human Rights of the United Nations Organization," 14 November 1945. See also Henry Atkinson, General Secretary of the Church Peace Union, to Roosevelt, 27 December 1945, Eichelberger to Roosevelt, 28 December 1945, and Walter White to Roosevelt, 28 December 1945, Eleanor Roosevelt Papers, box 4561, FDRL; Truman to Roosevelt, 21 December 1945, Eleanor Roosevelt Papers, box 4560, FDRL; and Anderson, *Eyes off the Prize*, 93. See also Constance Sporborg, Chair of the Department of International Relations of the General Federation of Women's Clubs to Eleanor Roosevelt, 28 December 1945, Eleanor Roosevelt Papers, box 4561, FDRL; Eichelberger to Truman, 23 December 1946, Official File 421, box 1270, HSTL; and G. Bromley Oxnam, President of the Federal Council of the Churches of Christ in America to Truman, 15 March 1946, Official File 213, Truman Papers, box 803, HSTL. Nolde expanded upon the points in "Possible Functions of the Commission on Human Rights," *Annals of the American Academy of Political and Social Science* 243 (January 1946): 144–49. In 1945, the Commission on the Organization of Peace became the research arm of the American Association for the United Nations.

9. Notter to Hiss, 29 November 1945, Notter Papers, RG 59, box 9, NARA. See also Notter to Hiss, 14 and 27 November 1945, Notter Papers, RG 59, box 9, NARA; United Nations, *United Nations Action in the Field of Human Rights* (New York: United Nations, 1983), 8; *Report of the Preparatory Commission*, 28–29; Harry S. Truman, *Report by the President to the Congress for the Year 1946*, United States and United Nations Report Series 7 (Washington, DC: U.S. Government Printing Office, 1947), 55–56, 89–90 [hereafter referred to as *1946 Report*]; "General Assembly of U.N.O.," *U.S. Department of State Bulletin* 14 (20 January 1946): 62–65, 83; Felipe Pazoa, member of Cuban delegation to the United Nations to Sir Ramaswami Mudaliar, president of ECOSOC, 12 February 1946, E/HR/1; Resolution 5(I) of the ECOSOC, 16 February 1946; United States Delegation to the General Assembly of the United Nations, *Report of the United States Delegation to the First Part of the First Session of the General Assembly of the United Nations* (Washington, DC: U.S. Government Printing Office, 1946), 8–10; Glendon, *A World Made New*, 28–30; and Roosevelt, *Autobiography*, 305–8.

10. Sandifer memo of conversation, 19 March 1946, and Proskauer to Stettinius, 19 April 1946, decimal file, 501.BD/3-1946 (1945–1949), RG 59, box 2186, NARA; Sandifer to Hiss and Leroy Stinebower, 28 March 1946, and Sandifer and Kotschnig to Hiss, Stinebower, and William Benton, 22 April 1946, subject files of Sandifer, lot file 55D 429, box 8, NARA; William Ransom to Roosevelt, 4 May 1946, Roosevelt Papers, box 4587, FDRL; and Durward V. Sandifer, interview by Emily Williams, 27 April 1979, FDRL.

11. Hendrick, "Commission on Human Rights," 19 April 1946, and Ross to Hiss, "Commission on Human Rights," subject files of Sandifer, lot file 55D 429, box 8, NARA. See also Hiss to Acheson, 23 April 1946, decimal file 501.BD/4-2346 (1945–1949), box 2186, NARA; Sandifer to Roosevelt, 22 April 1946, Roosevelt Papers, box 4593, FDRL; Summary record of the third meeting of the UNCHR, 30 April 1946, and "Report of the Commission on Human Rights to the Second Session of the Economic and Social Council," 21 May 1946, E/38 Rev.1; Sandifer to Hiss and Stinebower, 2 May 1946, subject files of Sandifer, lot file 55D 429, box 8, NARA; U.S. Delegation to the United Nations, "Composition of the Commissions of the Economic and Social Council," E/Commissions/3, 6 May 1946, Roosevelt Papers, box 4589, FDRL; Summary record of the second meeting of the UNCHR, 30 April 1946, Summary record of the third meeting of the UNCHR, 30 April 1946, Summary record of the fourth meeting of the UNCHR, 2 May 1946, Summary record of the fifth meeting of the UNCHR, 2 May 1946, and Summary record of the seventh meeting of the UNCHR, 8 May 1946, Roosevelt Papers, box 4589, FDRL; and ECOSOC resolution 9(II), 1 July 1946, E/56/Rev.2. During its first 30 years, ECOSOC never rejected a recommendation for the UNCHR. See John Humphrey, *Human Rights and the United Nations: A Great Adventure* (Dobbs Ferry, NY: Transnational Publishers, 1984), 17–18; and Philip Alston, ed., *The United Nations and Human Rights: A Critical Appraisal* (Oxford: Clarendon Press, 1992), 193–94.

12. Summary record of the first meeting of the UNCHR, 29 April 1946, E/HR/6.

13. Report of the Commission on Human Rights, 21 May 1946, E/38/Rev.1. See also Kotschnig and Sandifer to Benton, Hiss, and Stinebower, 22 April 1946, subject files of Sandifer, lot file 55D 429, box 8, NARA; John G. Winant, U.S. representative to ECOSOC, "The Economic and Social Council: Report to the Secretary of State," 15 July 1946, Official File 85, box 532, HSTL; United Nations, *Yearbook of the United Nations, 1946–1947* (New York: Department of Public Information, United Nations, 1947), 523–24; and Mower, *The United States*, 54. For Roosevelt's participation in the nuclear commission's work, see Lash, *Eleanor*, 56–58; and Roosevelt, *On My Own*, 72–75.

14. Anderson, *Eyes off the Prize*, 19–80.

15. "Summary Record of the Presentation of a Petition by Dr. Max Yergin, President, National Negro Congress," 6 June 1946, and "The Oppression of the Negro: The Facts," Roosevelt Papers, box 4587, FDRL. See also Anderson, *Eyes off the Prize*, 79–81.

16. Max Yergin, president of the National Negro Congress to Truman, 15 May 1946, Official File 93, White House Central Files, box 543, HSTL; "Summary Record of the Presentation of a Petition by Dr. Max Yergin, President, National Negro Congress," 6 June 1946, and "The Oppression of the Negro: The Facts," Roosevelt Papers, box 4587, FDRL; Carol Anderson, "From Hope to Disillusion: African Americans, the United Nations, and the Struggle for Human Rights, 1944–1947," *Diplomatic History* 20 (Fall 1996): 544–53; and Anderson, *Eyes off the Prize*, 81–85, 90–92, 245–46, 261–62.

17. Channing Tobias, member of the NAACP Board of Directors, et al., to Truman, 19 September 1946, President's Secretary's files, White House Central Files, box 131, HSTL; and Dr. Metz Lochard, editor of the *Chicago Defender*, to Roosevelt, 25 October 1946, Roosevelt Papers, box 4587, NARA. See also Walter White to Roosevelt, 18 September 1946, Eleanor Roosevelt Papers, box 3337, FDRL; and Anderson, *Eyes off the Prize*, 84–85, 92–95.

18. Michael L. Krenn, *Black Diplomacy: African Americans and the State Department, 1945–1969* (Armonk, NY: M. E. Sharpe, 1999), 163, also 58–65.

19. UNCHR, "Report to the Economic and Social Council on the First Session of the Commission," E/259; and Humphrey, *Human Rights*, 28. See also UNCHR, "Working Paper on Consideration of Communications Received," 13 January 1947, E/CN.4/W.3; Hendrick memo of conversation, 18 September 1946, and Minutes of the first meeting of the Human Rights Working Group, 1 October 1946, subject files of Sandifer, lot files 55D 429, box 8, NARA; Provisional agenda for the first session of the Commission on Human Rights, E/CN.4/1, 18 December 1946; "Mrs. Roosevelt Is Elected Chairman of U.N. Human Rights Commission," *New York Times*, 28 January 1947, 13; UNCHR, "Communications Concerning Human Rights," E/CN.4/19/Add.1; Nabiel Jamiel Fareed, "The United Nations Commission on Human Rights and Its Work for Human Rights and Fundamental Freedoms" (PhD diss., Washington State University, 1977), 83; UNCHR, "Report of the Subcommittee on the Handling of Communications," 6 February 1947, E/CN.4/14/Rev.2; UNCHR, "Communications Concerning Human Rights," 6 February 1947, E/CN.4/19/Add.1; Summary record of the 20th meeting of the UNCHR, 7 February 1947, E/CN.4/SR.20; and Committee on International Social Policy, "Suggested Position Paper: Report of Commission on Human Rights," ISP D-36/47, 19 February 1947, records of the Committee on International Social Policy (ISP), RG 353, box 99, NARA.

20. Thomas Borstelmann, *Apartheid's Reluctant Uncle: The United States and Southern Africa in the Early Cold War* (New York: Oxford University Press, 1993), 29–31.

21. Anderson, "From Hope to Disillusion," 549. See also David Emblidge, ed., *Eleanor Roosevelt's My Day: Her Acclaimed Columns, 1945–1952* (New York: Pharos Books, 1990), 2:89; General Assembly Resolution 44(I), 8 December 1946; Truman, *The United States and the United Nations: Report by the President to the Congress for the Year 1947* (Washington, DC: U.S. Government Printing Office, 1948), 12–13, 100–101; Anderson, "From Hope to Disillusion," 548–51; Borstelmann, *Apartheid's Reluctant Uncle*, 75–79; and James Frederick Green, "Efforts to Deal with Violations of Human Rights," in Asher, *The United Nations*, 779–83.

22. Quoted in Anderson, *Eyes off the Prize*, 115; Executive Order 9808, in *To Secure These Rights: The Report of the President's Committee on Civil Rights* (New York: Simon and

Schuster, 1947), viii. For an excellent history of Truman's civil rights initiatives, see William C. Berman, *The Politics of Civil Rights in the Truman Administration* (Columbus: Ohio State University Press, 1970).

23. Clair Wilcox, Director of the Office of International Trade Policy, memo of conversation, 23 August 1946, Robert Carr, advisor in the Division of Commercial Policy to Wilcox, 26 August 1946, Carr to Wilcox, 27 August 1946, J. Robert Schaetzel, Special Assistant to the Director of the Office of International Trade Policy, Memorandum of Conversation with Assistant Secretary of Labor David Morse, 27 August 1946, Truman to Byrnes, 25 November 1946, "Committee on International Social Policy," undated, William Clayton, Chair of ISP and David Morse, ISP Deputy Chair, "Establishment of Interdepartmental Committee on International Social Policy," ISP D-18/47, undated, Minutes of the ISP, 12 December 1946, Records of the ISP, RG 353, box 98, NARA; ISP, "Terms of Reference for the Committee on Human Rights and Status of Women," D-11/47, 31 January 1947, Records of the Subcommittee on Human Rights and Status of Women (HRW), RG 353, box 109, NARA; and a brief biographical sketch of Walter Maria Kotschnig found at <http://library.albany.edu/speccoll/findaids/ger053.htm#bio>.

24. Working Group on Human Rights, "United States Proposals Regarding an International Bill of Rights," 16 January 1947, Roosevelt Papers, box 4592, FDRL. See also Hendrick to Sandifer, agenda of working group meeting, 30 September 1946, Hendrick, minutes of working group meeting, SD/E/HR/3/M-1, 1 October 1946, subject files of Sandifer, lot file 55D 429, box 8, NARA; "Declaration of Fundamental Human Rights and Freedoms Proposed by the Government of Panama," SD/A/C.3/3, 7 September 1946, Roosevelt Papers, box 4575, NARA; First and Third Committees of the General Assembly, "Report on the Draft Declaration of Human Rights and Fundamental Freedoms," A/234, 10 December 1946; U.N. General Assembly Resolution 43(I), "Draft Declaration on Fundamental Human Rights and Freedoms," 11 December 1946; Working Group on Human Rights, "Commission on Human Rights: Preparation of an International Bill of Rights," SD/E/CS.4/1; idem, "Legal Form of an International Bill of Rights," SD/E/CS.4/2; and idem, "Implementation of Human Rights and Fundamental Freedoms," SD/E/CS.4/8, 6 December 1946, Roosevelt Papers, box 4592, FDRL; Sandifer and Kotschnig to Elwood Thompson, 20 January 1947, decimal file 501.BD/1-2047 (1945–1949), box 2186, NARA.

25. Humphrey, *Human Rights*, 23–25; Glendon, *A World Made New*, 35–41; and United Nations, *Yearbook, 1946–1947*, 524.

26. UNCHR, Summary record of the seventh meeting of the UNCHR, 31 January 1947, E/CN.4/SR.7; Summary record of the fifteenth meeting of the UNCHR, 2 February 1947, E/CN.4/SR.15; and Division of International Organization Affairs and Office of the Legal Advisor, "Working Paper on International Bill of Rights Prepared by the Secretariat," undated, decimal file 501.BD/1-3147 (1945–1949). See also Secretary of State George Marshall to Roosevelt, 30 January 1947, Roosevelt Papers, box 4592, FDRL.

27. Quoted in Lash, *Eleanor*, 62. See also "United States Proposals Regarding an International Bill of Rights," E/CN.4/4 and E/CN.4/17, 28 January and 6 February 1947; U.N. Secretariat, "Working Paper on an International Bill of Rights," E/CN.4/W.4; Summary record of the fifteenth meeting of the UNCHR, 2 February 1947, E/CN.4/SR.15; Marshall to Roosevelt, 29 January 1947, decimal file 501.BD/1-2947 (1945–1949), and Warren Austin, Chief of U.S. Mission to the United Nations to Marshall, 31 January 1947, decimal file 501.BD/1-3047 (1945–1949), box 2186, NARA; UNCHR, "Draft Report of the Commission on Human Rights to the Economic and Social Council," E/CN.4/19, 6 February 1947;

Lash, *Eleanor*, 61–62; ECOSOC, "Report to the Economic and Social Council on the First Session of the Commission," E/259, 1947; John Humphrey, "The Universal Declaration of Human Rights: Its History, Impact, and Juridical Character," in *Human Rights: Thirty Years After the Universal Declaration*, ed. B. G. Ramcharan (The Hague: Martinus Nijhoff, 1979), 22–23; Roosevelt, *On My Own*, 77; Humphrey, *Human Rights*, 23–28; Glendon, *A World Made New*, 45–49; and ISP, "Report of Commission on Human Rights," ISP D-36/47, 19 February 1947, Records of the ISP, RG 353, box 99, NARA.

28. U.S. Congress, House Committee on Foreign Affairs, House Concurrent Resolutions 32 and 33, 80th Cong., 1st sess., 1947; and Representative Charles Eaton, Chair of the House Foreign Affairs Committee to Marshall, 4 April 1947, decimal file 501.BD/4-447 (1945–1949), box 2186, NARA.

29. Notter to Dean Rusk and Thompson, 1 May 1947, decimal file 501.BD/4-447 (1945–1949), box 2187, NARA; and Marshall to Eaton, 11 June 1947, decimal file 501. BD/4-447 (1945–1949), box 2186, NARA. See also Hendrick to Kotschnig, 30 April 1947, decimal file 501.BD/4-3047 (1945–1949), Fahy memorandum, 28 April 1947, decimal file 501.BD/4-2847 (1945–1949), and Fahy memorandum, 12 May 1947, decimal file 501. BD/5-1247 (1945–1949), box 2187, NARA; and Stella Alexander, *The Triple Myth: A Life of Archbishop Alojzije Stepinac* (New York: Columbia University Press, 1987). For the benchmark ruling, see the International Court of Justice, "Advisory Opinion on Nationality Decrees Issued in Tunis and Morocco (1923)," in *World Court Reports* (Washington, DC: Carnegie Endowment for International Peace, 1934), 143–62.

30. Fahy to Carr, 17 June 1947, decimal file 501.BD/4-2447 (1945–1949), box 2187, NARA; Carr to Acheson, 24 April 1947, decimal file 501.BD/4-2447 (1945–1949), Carr to Marshall, 23 May 1947, decimal file 501.BD/5-2347 (1945–1949), Carr to Marshall, 5 June 1947, decimal file 501.BD/6-547 (1945–1949), box 2187, NARA; and Carr to Roosevelt, 19 February 1947, files of the President's Committee on Civil Rights, box 9, HSTL; and President's Committee, *To Secure These Rights*, 100, 110–11.

31. John Howard in the Office of the Legal Advisor to Fahy, 24 February 1947, and Whiteman to Howard, 26 February 1947, decimal file 501.BD/2-2647, box 2187, NARA. See also Glendon, *A World Made New*, 47–48; Lash, *Eleanor*, 63–64; and Johnson and Symonides, *The Universal Declaration*, 24–25.

32. Notter to Rusk and Thompson, 14 March 1947, Notter Papers, box 10, NARA; and Thompson to Notter, Rusk, Miner, Kotschnig, and Hendrick, 18 March 1947, decimal file 501.BD/3-1847 (1945–1949), box 2187, NARA.

33. Humphrey, *Human Rights*, 31–32; and U.N. Secretariat, "Draft Outline of an International Bill of Rights," undated, E/CN.4/21, Annex A.

34. Minutes of the HRW, 2 April 1947, records of the HRW, RG 353, box 112, NARA; Hendrick, memo of conference with legal advisors and officers of the Division of International Organization Affairs, 23 April 1947, decimal file 501.BD/4-2847 (1945–1949), box 2187, NARA; Humphrey, *Human Rights*, 31–33; U.N. Secretariat, "Draft Outline of an International Bill of Rights," undated, E/CN.4/21, Annex A; HRW, "Liberty and Respect of Private Life," S/HRW D-53/47, "No Torture, Cruelty or Ill-Treatment," S/HRW D-49/47, and "Protection Against Arbitrary Arrest," S/HRW D-52/47, 15 May 1947, files of HRW, RG 353, box 110, NARA; idem, "Freedom of Aliens from Arbitrary Expulsion," S/HRW D-55/47, and "Right to Resist Oppression," S/HRW/D-56/47, 16 May 1947, files of HRW, RG 353, box 110, NARA; idem, "Right to Property," S/HRW D-35/47, 5 May 1947, files of HRW, RG 353, box 110, NARA; idem, "Right of Asylum," S/HRW D-39/47, "Nationality,"

S/HRW D-40/47, and "Immigration," S/HRW D-41/47, 6 May 1947, files of HRW, RG 353, box 110, NARA; idem, "No Discrimination," S/HRW D-73/47, 23 May 1947, files of the HRW, RG 353, box 10, NARA; ISP, "Position Papers on Draft International Bill of Rights," ISP D-88/47, 29 May 1947, Roosevelt Papers, box 4576, FDRL; Minutes of the HRW, 9, 13, 23, and 27–28 May 1947, files of HRW, RG 353, box 112, NARA; and HRW, "Memorandum on Rights of American Indians and American Territorial Citizens to Participate in Governments," S/HRW D-126/47, 18 September 1947, files of the HRW, RG 353, box 110, NARA.

35. ISP, "Position Papers on Draft International Bill of Rights," ISP D-88/47, 29 May 1947, Roosevelt Papers, box 4576, FDRL; and HRW, "Right to Work," S/HRW D-71/47, 23 May 1947, files of HRW, RG 353, box 110, NARA. See also idem, "Right to Participate in Cultural, Scientific and Artistic Life," S/HRW D-61/47, 19 May 1947, "Right to Education," S/HRW D-63/47, "Right to Health," S/HRW D-66/47, "Right to Social Security," S/HRW D-67/47, and "Right to Rest and Leisure," S/HRW D-68/47, 20 May 1947, files of the HRW, RG 353, box 110, NARA; Minutes of the HRW, 29 May 1947, and "Section 2: Social Rights," ISP D-89/47, 3 June 1947, files of the HRW, RG 353, box 112, NARA; and ISP, "Draft International Bill of Rights," ISP D-95/47, 20 June 1947, files of HRW, RG 353, box 100, NARA.

36. HRW, "Articles Concerning Duty to Respect Rights and Their International Character," ISP D-87/47, 28 May 1947, files of the HRW, RG 353, box 110, NARA. See also HRW, "Duty of the State to Respect and Protect the Rights Enumerated," S/HRW D-43/47, and "Observance of These Rights Is a Matter of International Concern," S/HRW D-45/47, 13 May 1947, files of the HRW, RG 353, box 110, NARA; Minutes of the HRW, 20 and 23 May 1947, files of the HRW, RG 353, box 112, NARA; and Minutes of the State Department's Committee on International Social Policy, 5 June 1947, files of the Interdepartmental Committee on International Social Policy, RG 353, box 98, NARA.

37. ISP, "Position Papers on Draft International Bill of Rights," ISP D-88/47, 29 May 1947, Roosevelt Papers, box 4576, FDRL. See also Article 48 of U.N. Secretariat, "Draft Outline of an International Bill of Rights," undated, E/CN.4/21, Annex A; HRW, "Right of Petition," S/HRW D-32/47, and S/HRW 46/47, 5 and 15 May 1947, files of the HRW, RG 353, box 110, NARA; idem, "Draft International Bill of Rights," ISP D-95/47, 20 June 1947, files of HRW, RG 353, box 100, NARA; and Minutes of the HRW, 9 May 1947, files of the HRW, RG 353, box 112, NARA. For the official State Department position on Article 2(7), see Ernest Gross, "Impact of the United Nations Upon Domestic Jurisdiction," *U.S. Department of State Bulletin* 18 (29 February 1948): 259–67.

38. Humphrey, *Human Rights*, 39 and 41. See also Drafting Committee of the United Nations Commission on Human Rights, "Report of the Drafting Committee to the Commission on Human Rights," E/CN.4/21, 1 July 1947; Humphrey, *Human Rights*, 29–36; Glendon, *A World Made New*, 53–55; Humphrey, "The Universal Declaration," 24–25; and United Nations, *Yearbook, 1946–1947*, 525–26.

39. Austin to Marshall, 26 June 1947, decimal file 501.BD 6-2547 (1945–1949), box 2187, NARA; and Marshall to Roosevelt, 8 July 1947, Notter Papers, box 10, NARA. See also Drafting Committee on an International Bill of Rights, "Suggestions of the Drafting Committee for Articles of an International Declaration on Human Rights," in "Report of the Drafting Committee to the Commission on Human Rights," 1 July 1947, E/CN.4/21, Annex F; UNCHR, "General Observations Made by Various Members of the Commission on Human Rights Concerning the Form and Content of the International Bill of Rights," 9 June 1947, E/CN.4/AC.1/7; and Hendrick to Fahy, Rusk, and John Halderman, 22 and 23 June 1947, Papers of James Hendrick, box 2, NARA.

40. Minutes of the ISP, 27 June 1947, files of the ISP, RG 353, box 98, NARA; Green, "Efforts to Deal with Violations," 762; and Hersch Lauterpacht, "Report to the Human Rights Committee of the International Law Association," Roosevelt Papers, box 4581, FDRL. See also Marshall to Roosevelt, 18 July 1947, decimal file 501.BD/7-1847 (1945–1949), box 2187, NARA; ISP, "Consideration of Communications Received by the Commission on Human Rights and the Commission on Status of Women," ISP D-110/47, 23 July 1947, files of the HRW, RG 353, box 110, NARA; idem, "Examination of Communications on Human Rights," ISP D-180/47, 10 November 1947, files of the HRW, RG 353, box 111, NARA; United Nations, *1947–1948 Yearbook of the United Nations* (New York: United Nations, 1949), 578–79; UNCHR, "Report of the Ad Hoc Committee Instructed to Consider Communications Received," 24 May 1948, E/CN.4/96; Economic and Social Council Resolution 75(V), 5 August 1947; and Alston, *The United Nations*, 139–40.

41. Marshall to Elinor Falvey, chair of the International Relations Committee of the National Council of Catholic Women, 8 August 1947, decimal file 501.BD/7-247 (1945–1949), box 2187, NARA; Representative Robert Ross to Marshall, 7 October 1947, decimal file 501.BD/10-747 (1945–1949), box 2188, NARA; and Rusk to State Department Legal Advisor Gross, 10 October 1947, decimal file 501.BD/10-747, box 2188, NARA. See also Falvey to Marshall, 20 July 1947, decimal file 501.BD/7-247 (1945–1949), box 2187, NARA; "K. of C. Requests U.S. to Bar Yugoslav Aid," *New York Times*, 25 May 1947, 33; and Robert Lovett to Ross, 23 October 1947, decimal file 501.BD/10-747 (1945–1949), box 2188, NARA.

42. Dean Rusk, Office of Special Political Affairs to Marshall, 15 July 1947, decimal file 501.BD/7-1547, box 2187, NARA; Marshall to Charles Wilson, 25 July 1947, and Rusk to Carr, 29 July 1947, decimal file 501.BD/6-547 (1945–1949), box 2187, NARA.

43. L. K. White of the Central Intelligence Group to Milton B. Stewart, Director of Research for the President's Committee on Civil Rights, 5 August 1947, papers of the President's Committee on Civil Rights, box 6, HSTL; Rusk to Carr, 29 July 1947, decimal file 501.BD/6-547 (1945–1949), box 2187, NARA; Carr to Rusk, 11 August 1947, decimal file 811.BD/8-1147 (1945–1949), NARA; and *Brief for the United States of America as Amicus Curiae, Shelley v. Kramer*, 334 U.S. 1, 19–20. See also White to Harry Krould of the State Department's Program Planning and Evaluation Board, 18 June 1947, and Krould to John Ottemiller, head of the State Department's Reference Division, 19 June 1947, papers of the President's Committee on Civil Rights, box 6, HSTL; President's Committee on Civil Rights memo to its subcommittee, 1 and 5 March 1947, papers of Philleo Nash, box 202, HSTL; and Will Maslow, director of the Commission on Law and Social Action of the American Jewish Congress to the President's Committee on Civil Rights, 1 May 1947, papers of the President's Committee on Civil Rights, box 9, HSTL.

44. Michael R. Gardner, *Harry Truman and Civil Rights: Moral Courage and Political Risks* (Carbondale: Southern Illinois University Press, 2002), 50; President's Committee, *To Secure These Rights*, 100; U.S. Constitution, Article VI, section 2; U.N. Charter, Article 55. See also President's Committee, *To Secure These Rights*, 100–101, 110–11; Virginia Pratt, *The Influence of Domestic Controversy on American Participation in the United Nations Commission on Human Rights, 1946–1953* (New York: Garland Publishing, 1986), 98–100; Berman, *The Politics of Civil Rights*, 67–73; "Public Interest in the President's Civil Rights Program," undated, David Niles Papers, box 27, HSTL; and Justice Department to President's Committee on Civil Rights, "Federal Criminal Jurisdiction over Violations of Civil Rights," 15 January 1947, Niles Papers, box 26, HSTL.

45. W.E.B. Du Bois, ed., *An Appeal to the World: A Statement on the Denial of Human Rights to Minorities in the Case of Citizens of Negro Descent in the United States of America and an Appeal to the United Nations for Redress* (New York: National Association for the Advancement of Colored People, 1947), 22–23, 148. See also Anderson, "From Hope to Disillusion," 553–58; and White to Roosevelt, 20 October 1947, Roosevelt Papers, box 3337, FDRL.

46. Quoted in Anderson, "From Hope to Disillusion," 558; "U.N. Gets Charges of Wide Bias in U.S.," *New York Times,* 24 October 1947, 9; and White to Roosevelt, 25 October 1947, Roosevelt Papers, box 3337, FDRL. See also White to Roosevelt, 20 and 21 October 1947, and Roosevelt to White, 22 October 1947, Roosevelt Papers, box 3337, FDRL; Roosevelt to White, 20 January 1948, Roosevelt Papers, box 3389, FDRL; Anderson, "From Hope to Disillusion," 557–62; Black, *Casting Her Own Shadow,* 99–102; Berman, *The Politics of Civil Rights,* 65–66; Lash, *Eleanor,* 66–67; Minutes of the HRW, 23 October 1947, RG 353, box 112, NARA; and Mary L. Dudziak, "Desegregation as Cold War Imperative," *Stanford Law Review* 41 (November 1988): 80–93.

47. A. L. Wirin, Charles Horsky, and Ernest W. Jennes, *Brief for Petitioners on Writ of Certiorari to the Supreme Court of California, Fred Oyama and Kajiro Oyama, Petitioners, in the Supreme Court of the United States,* 1947, 53. See also Bert Lockwood, "The United Nations Charter and United States Civil Rights Litigation: 1946–1955," *Iowa Law Review* 69 (May 1984): 917–23; Jo L. Southard, "Human Rights Provisions of the U.N. Charter: The History in U.S. Courts," *International Law Students Association Journal of International and Comparative Law* 1 (Spring 1995): 47–49; American Civil Liberties Union, *Brief of American Civil Liberties Union as Amicus Curiae on Petition for a Writ of Certiorari to the Supreme Court of the State of California, Fred Y. Oyama and Kajiro Oyama, Petitioners, in the Supreme Court of the United States,* 1946, 6–9; American Civil Liberties Union, *Brief of American Civil Liberties Union as Amicus Curiae on Writ of Certiorari to the Supreme Court of the State of California, Fred Y. Oyama and Kajiro Oyama, Petitioners, in the Supreme Court of the United States,* 1947, 13–14; Wirin, Horsky, and Jennes, *Brief for Petitioners,* 1947, 52–53; David K. Niles, administrative assistant to the president, to the president's legal counsel Clark Clifford, 8 April 1947, and George Elsey, Clifford's assistant to Clifford, 19 May 1947, Clark Clifford Papers, box 1, HSTL; and *Oyama v. California,* 332 U.S. 633.

48. Hendrick to Kotschnig, 28 August 1947, subject files of the Bureau of United Nations Affairs, lot file 55D 323, box 15, NARA. See also Minutes of the HRW, 15, 19, 22, and 29 August 1947, files of the HRW, RG 353, box 112, NARA; HRW, "Limitation on Exercise of Rights," "Equality Before the Law," "Life, Liberty, Security," "Freedom from Wrongful Arrest," "Fair Trial," "Right of Petition," "Right to Work," "Right to Education," "Right to Health," and "Right to Social Security," 12 September 1947, "Right to Privacy," "Freedom of Movement," "Right to Asylum," "Right to Property," "Right to Nationality," "Rights of Aliens," "Freedom of Opinion; Freedom of Information," and "Right to Resist Oppression," 11 September 1947, and "Right to Contract Marriage," 19 September 1947, S/HRW 122/47, Roosevelt Papers, box 4578, FDRL; and idem, "Right to Work," 12 November 1947, files of HRW, RG 353, box 111, NARA.

49. Robert McClintock, special assistant in the office of Special Political Affairs to Acting Secretary of State Robert Lovett, 25 November 1947, decimal file 501.BD/11-2547 (1945–1949), box 2189, NARA; and ISP, "Discussion of Changes Made by Under Secretary of State in U.S. Draft Declaration of Human Rights Subsequent to Approval by ISP," 4 December 1947, files of the HRW, RG 353, box 101, NARA. See also Lovett to Roosevelt and

Hendrick, 5 December 1947, decimal file 501.BD/11-2447 (1945–1949), box 2188, NARA; Lovett to Hendrick, 24 November 1947, decimal file 501.BD/11-2447 (1945–1949), box 2188, NARA; Hendrick to Kotschnig, 17 September 1947, subject files of the Bureau of United Nations Affairs, lot file 55D 323, box 15, NARA; Minutes of the HRW, 19 September, 3 October, and 12 November 1947, files of the HRW, RG 353, box 112, NARA; Truman, *The United States*, 122–23; Lash, *Eleanor*, 68–70; Rusk to Lovett, 18 November 1947, decimal file 501.BD/11-1847 (1945–1949), decimal file 501.BD/11-2047 (1945–1949), box 2189, NARA; Rusk to Lovett, 12 December 1947, Rusk to Kotschnig, 15 December 1947, and Rusk to Morse, 23 December 1947, decimal file 501.BD/12-1247 (1945–1949), box 2187, NARA; ISP, "Changes Made by Under Secretary of State in U.S. Draft Declaration of Human Rights (ISP D-178/47) and in U.S. Draft Convention on Human Rights (ISP D-179/47) Subsequent to Approval by ISP," ISP D-182/47, 11 November 1947, files of the HRW, RG 353, box 111, NARA; idem, "Declaration on Human Rights," ISP D-178/47 Rev.1, 21 November 1947, and Statement Submitted by the Department of Labor to the ISP, ISP D-187/47, 9 December 1947, files of the HRW, RG 353, box 101, NARA; Hendrick memo of conversation, 20 November 1947, Hendrick Papers, box 2, HSTL; U.N. Commission on Human Rights, "Proposal for a Declaration of Human Rights Submitted by the Representative of the United States on the Commission on Human Rights," 26 November 1947, E/CN.4/36; idem, "Explanatory Note on Derivation of Declaration on Human Rights Proposed by Representative of the United States on the Commission on Human Rights," 27 November 1947, E/CN.4/36/Add.1; idem, "Parallel Passages in Human Rights Drafting Committee Text and United States Proposal," 5 December 1947, E/CN.4/36/Add.2; State Department, "Proposal for a Declaration of Human Rights," *U.S. Department of State Bulletin* 17 (7 December 1947): 1075–76; "U.S. Submits Draft of Rights Treaty," *New York Times*, 2 December 1947, 16; and Minutes of the ISP, 11 December 1947, files of the HRW, RG 353, box 107, NARA.

50. Humphrey, *Human Rights*, 48; United Nations, *Yearbook of the United Nations, 1947–1948* (New York: U.N. Department of Public Information, 1949), 572; and Summary record of the Commission on Human Rights, 2 December 1947, E/CN.4/SR.25.

51. Article 2 of Commission on Human Rights, "Report of the Working Group on the Declaration on Human Rights," 10 December 1947, E/CN.4/57; ISP, "Report on Second Session, Commission on Human Rights," 7 January 1948, files of the HRW, RG 353, box 101, NARA; and Lash, *Eleanor*, 71. See also United Nations, *Yearbook of the United Nations, 1947–1948* (New York: United Nations, 1949), 572–73; Lash, *Eleanor*, 68–72; "18 Nations Hammer Out Bill of Rights" and "UN Agency Acts to Draft Human Rights Declaration," *Christian Science Monitor*, 4 and 10 December 1947, C11 and C4; United Nations, *Yearbook of the United Nations, 1948–1949* (New York: U.N. Department of Public Information, 1950), 572–73; Summary record of the Commission on Human Rights, 2, 4, and 5 December 1947, E/CN.4/SR.25, E/CN.4/SR.29, E/CN.4/SR.30; Hendrick to Kotschnig, 3 December 1947, decimal file 501.BD/12-347 (1945–1949), Consul in Geneva Harry L. Troutman to Rusk and Gross, 7 December 1947, decimal file 501.BD/12-747 (1945–1949), and Troutman to Marshall, 10 December 1947, decimal file 501.BD/12-1047 (1945–1949), box 2188, NARA; and Commission on Human Rights, "Report of the Working Group on the Declaration on Human Rights," 10 December 1947, E/CN.4/57.

52. Article 38 of Commission on Human Rights, "Report of the Working Group on the Declaration on Human Rights," 10 December 1947, E/CN.4/57; Commission on Human Rights, "Report to the Economic and Social Council on the Second Session of the

Commission," 17 December 1947, E/600; and Truman telegraph to Roosevelt, 23 December 1947, Official Files, box 533, HSTL. See also ISP, "Report on Second Session, Commission on Human Rights," ISP D-1/48, 7 January 1948, files of the HRW, RG 353, box 101, NARA; Hendrick to Gross, Rusk, and Kotschnig, 26 December 1947, decimal file 501. BD/12-2647 (1945–1949), box 2188, NARA; Emblidge, *My Day*, 118–19; Lash, *Eleanor*, 70–74; Commission on Human Rights, "Proposed Resolution by the Commission on Human Rights Submitted by the United States Delegation," 15 December 1947, E/CN.4/72; Summary record of the Commission on Human Rights, 16 December 1947, E/CN.4/SR.41; and James P. Hendrick, "An International Bill of Human Rights," *U.S. Department of State Bulletin* 18 (15 February 1948): 199–203, 207.

53. *Oyama v. California*, 332 U.S. 633 at 673. See also *Oyama v. California*, 332 U.S. 633 at 649–50 and 673–74; Lockwood, "The United Nations Charter," 919–21; Sidney Fine, *Frank Murphy: The Washington Years* (Ann Arbor: University of Michigan Press, 1984), 559–62; Joseph P. Lash, ed., *From the Diaries of Felix Frankfurter* (New York: W. W. Norton, 1975), 340–41; and J. Woodford Howard, Jr., *Mr. Justice Murphy: A Political Biography* (Princeton: Princeton University Press, 1968), 352–54.

54. Attorney General Tom C. Clark and Solicitor General Philip B. Perlman, *Brief for the United States as Amicus Curiae in Shelley v. Kramer, et al.*, December 1947, 334; Hendrick, memo of conversation, 2 January 1948, decimal file 501.BD/1-247, box 2189, NARA; and Lockwood, "The United Nations Charter," 935. See also National Association of Real Estate Boards, *Brief Amicus Curiae on Behalf of the National Association of Real Estate Boards in Shelley v. Kramer, et al.*, 546; American Association for the United Nations, *Motion for Leave to File Brief and Brief for the American Association for the United Nations as Amicus Curiae in Shelley v. Kramer et al.*; American Civil Liberties Union, *Brief of American Civil Liberties Union, Amicus Curiae in Shelley v. Kramer*; *Shelley v. Kramer*, 334 U.S. 1 (1948); Lockwood, "The United Nations Charter," 932–37; Halderman, "Interpretation of Articles 55 and 56 of United Nations Charter," 2 October 1947, and Hendrick, "Comment with Respect to Brief of the American Association for the United Nations," 31 December 1947, decimal file 501.BD/1-247, box 2189, NARA; Green, "Efforts to Deal with Violations," 658–61; Berman, *The Politics of Civil Rights*, 73–76; Jack Greenberg, *Crusaders in the Courts: How a Dedicated Band of Lawyers Fought for the Civil Rights Revolution* (New York: Basic Books, 1994), 110–12; and Kermit Hall, ed., *The Oxford Companion to the Supreme Court of the United States* (New York: Oxford University Press, 1992), 781–82.

For cases in which the petitioner or amicus briefs argued that racial discrimination violated the U.N. Charter, but the Supreme Court disagreed, see *Takahashi v. Fish & Game Commission*, 334 U.S. 410 (1948), *Sweatt v. Painter*, 339 U.S. 629 (1950); *Henderson v. U.S.*, 339 U.S. 816 (1950); *United States ex rel. Jaegelar v. Carusi*, 342 U.S. 347 (1952); *Zorach v. Clauson*, 343 U.S. 306 (1952); *Joseph Burstyn, Inc. v. Wilson*, 343 U.S. 495 (1952); *Bolling v. Sharpe*, 347 U.S. 497 (1954); and *Rice v. Sioux City Memorial Cemetery, Inc.*, 349 U.S. 70 (1955).

Lesser U.S. courts have cited the Universal Declaration to overturn obnoxious state laws. See *Namba v. McCourt*, 204 P.2nd 569 (Oregon, 1949), *Perez v. Lippold*, 198 P.2nd 17 (California, 1948), and *Wilson v. Hacker*, 200 Misc. 124 (New York Supreme Court, 1950). For later cases, see William R. Pabst and Ray Dickens, *The United Nations Charter and U.N. General Assembly Resolutions as Basis for Jurisdiction in Federal Court* ([Houston]: Center for the Independence of Judges and Lawyers of the United States, 1983), 20–21.

55. Hendrick to Kotschnig, 8 January 1948, subject files of Bureau of United Nations Affairs, lot file 55D 323, box 15, NARA; and ISP, "Observations, Suggestions, and

Proposals of the United States Relating to the Draft International Declaration on Human Rights, and the Draft International Covenant on Human Rights," ISP D-41/48 Rev.1, 15 April 1948, decimal file 501.BD/4-1548 (1945–1949), and Lovett to Roosevelt, 1 May 1948, decimal file 501.BD/5-148 (1945–1949), box 2188, NARA. See also Minutes of the ISP, 13 January 1948, files of the ISP, RG 353, box 107, NARA; Whiteman, Minutes of 13 January ISP meeting, 14 January 1948, decimal file 501.BD/1-1448 (1945–1949), box 2188, NARA; ISP, "Statement of Problems to Be Considered in Connection with Third Session of Commission on Human Rights," S/HRW D-8/48, 22 January 1948; idem, "Working Paper on Position to Be Taken in Connection with Third Session of Commission on Human Rights," S/HRW D-12/48 Rev.1, 16 February 1948, and "Human Rights Commission—Third Session—Declaration of Human Rights," S/HRW D-21/49, 4 March 1948, files of the HRW, RG 353, box 111, NARA; and idem, "Summary of Position Proposed in Attached Draft Letter of Comments of the United States on the Declaration, Covenant, and Implementation Report of the United Nations Commission on Human Rights," ISP D-41/48, 26 March 1948, files of the ISP, RG 353, box 101, NARA; Minutes of the HRW, 28 January and 24 March 1948, files of the HRW, RG 353, box 112, NARA; Commission on Human Rights, "Comments from Governments on the Draft International Declaration on Human Rights, Draft International Covenant on Human Rights and the Question of Implementation," 16 April 1948, E/CN.4/82; and ISP, "Instructions to the United States Representative to the Third Session of the Commission on Human Rights," ISP D-60/48 Rev.2, 29 April 1948, files of ISP, RG 353, box 12, NARA.

56. Minutes of the ISP, 8, 28, and 30 April 1948, files of ISP, RG 353, box 107, NARA. See also ISP, "Working Paper on Position to Be Taken in Connection with Third Session of Commission on Human Rights," S/HRW D-12/48 Rev.1, 16 February 1948, files of the HRW, RG 353, box 111, NARA; idem, "Position Paper on Draft Negotiating Declaration and Covenant of Human Rights, supplementary to U.S. Letter of Comments," 6 April 1948, files of ISP, RG 353, box 101, NARA; and idem, "Recommendations with Respect to Specific Articles Formulated by the United Nations Commission on Human Rights at Its Second Session in Geneva in December 1947," ISP D-58/48, 23 April 1948, Roosevelt Papers, box 4579, FDRL; and Minutes of the HRW, 1 April 1948, files of HRW, RG 353, box 112, NARA.

57. Quoted in Pratt, *Influence of Domestic Controversy*, 117. See also *New York Times*, 3 and 26 February and 11 May 1948; Berman, *The Politics of Civil Rights*, 82–96; Pratt, *Influence of Domestic Controversy*, 100–118; *Shelley v. Kramer*, 334 U.S. 1 (1948); NAACP, "Declaration of Negro Voters," 27 March 1948, Official File 413, box 1235, HSTL; and Statement by 21 black organizations to the Platform Committee of the Democratic Party, 8 July 1948, Niles Papers, box 27, HSTL.

58. "Speech by Mr. A. N. Pavlov, Representative of the Union of Soviet Socialist Republics in the Drafting Committee of the Commission on Human Rights," 11 May 1948, E/CN.4/AC.1/29; "Report of the Drafting Committee to the Commission on Human Rights," 21 May 1948, E/CN.4/95; Glendon, *A World Made New*, 107–11; and Lash, *Eleanor*, 74–75.

59. U.N. Commission on Human Rights, "United States of America: Proposed Alternative for the Preamble of the Draft International Declaration on Human Rights," 10 June 1948, E/CN.4/119. See also U.N. Commission on Human Rights, "Report to the Economic and Social Council on the Third Session of the Commission," undated, E/800.

60. Minutes of the meetings of the Commission on Human Rights, 26 May and 7, 8, 11, and 15 June 1948, E.CN.4/SR.48, E/CN.4/SR.61; E/CN.4/SR.64; E/CN.4/SR.69; and E/CN.4/SR.74; U.N. Commission on Human Rights, "India and the United Kingdom:

290 Notes to Pages 123–27

Proposed Amendments to the Draft Declaration on Human Rights," 24 May 1948, E/ CN.4/99; idem, "Report to the Economic and Social Council on the Third Session of the Commission," undated, E/800; ISP, "Right to Work," S/HRW D-52/48, 24 May 1948, files of HRW, RG 353, box 112, NARA.

61. Roosevelt press release, 18 June 1948, Roosevelt Papers, box 4580, FDRL. See also Marshall to U.S. delegation to the United Nations, 8 June 1948, decimal file 501. BD/6-848 (1945–1949), and Hendrick to Gross, Sandifer, and Kotschnig, 16 June 1948, decimal file 501.BD/6-1648 (1945–1949), box 2189, NARA; Hendrick to Gross, Sandifer, and Kotschnig, 15 June 1948, Hendrick Papers, box 2, HSTL; United Nations, *1947–1948 Yearbook*, 574–76; "Human Rights," *U.S. Department of State Bulletin* 18 (6 June 1948): 732; Hendrick, "Progress Report on Human Rights," *U.S. Department of State Bulletin* 19 (8 August 1948): 159–61, 167–72, 186; and Mallory Browne, "Charter of Rights Is Adopted in U.N.," *New York Times*, 19 June 1948, 1.

62. Du Bois to White, 1 July 1948, Roosevelt Papers, box 3337, FDRL; and quoted in Anderson, *Eyes off the Prize*, 149. See also Richard Winslow of U.S. delegation to United Nations to Hendrick, 25 May 1948, and Lovett to U.S. delegation to United Nations, 22 April 1948, Roosevelt Papers, box 4579, FDRL; and Anderson, *Eyes off the Prize*, 138–50.

63. ECOSOC, "U.S.S.R.: Amendment to the Chilean Amendment," 23 August 1948, E/1003. See also Green, "Efforts to Deal with Violations," 798–802; Marshall to U.S. embassy in Moscow, 1 and 6 July 1948, decimal file 501.BD/6-2448 (1945–1949), box 2189, NARA; Resolution 154D of the Commission on the Status of Women in "Report of the Human Rights Committee of the Commission on the Status of Women," 11 August 1948, E/950; ECOSOC, "Chile: Amendment to Resolution D of Document E/950," 19 August 1948, E/981/Corr.1; Summary record of ECOSOC plenary, 20 and 23 August 1948, E/SR.207 and E/SR.210; ECOSOC Resolution 154D(VII), 30 August 1948, E/1065; and Roger N. Baldwin, *Human Rights: World Declaration and American Practice* (New York: Public Affairs Committee of the ACLU, 1950), 15.

64. Notter to Rusk, 18 August 1948, and Notter to Rusk and Sandifer, 2 September 1948, Notter Papers, box 10, NARA; Sandifer to Roosevelt, 9 September 1948, Roosevelt Papers, box 4566, FDRL; and quoted in Glendon, *A World Made New*, 138–39. See also Lash, *Eleanor*, 77–78; Roosevelt, *On My Own*, 84–85; Marshall to U.S. embassy in Paris, 25 August 1948, decimal file 501.BD/8-2548 (1945–1949), and U.S. embassy in Paris to Marshall, 2 September 1948, decimal file 501.BD/9-148 (1945–1949), box 2189, NARA; M. Glen Johnson, "The Contributions of Eleanor and Franklin Roosevelt to the Development of International Protection for Human Rights," *Human Rights Quarterly* 9 (February 1987): 39–40; Emblidge, *My Day*, 149–50; Pete Stewart of the U.S. delegation to the United Nations to Roosevelt, 25 August 1948, Roosevelt Papers, box 4567, FDRL; and Rusk to Marshall, 23 August 1948, Notter Papers, box 10, NARA.

65. State Department press release of Roosevelt's speech, 27 September 1948, Roosevelt Papers, box 4588, FDRL; and U.S. embassy in Moscow to Marshall, 2 November 1948, decimal file 501.BD/11-248 (1945–1949), box 2189, NARA.

66. Marshall, "No Compromise on Essential Freedoms," 23 September 1948, *U.S. Department of State Bulletin* 19 (3 October 1948): 432.

67. Ibid.

68. American Bar Association, "Report and Recommendations to the House of Delegates by the Committee on Peace and Law through United Nations with Action Voted by the House of Delegates upon the Recommendations," 7 September 1948, Hendrick Papers, box 2, HSTL; and Gladwin Hill, "U.N. Rights Drafts Held Socialistic," *New York Times*, 18 September 1948, 4.

69. Frank Holman, "An 'International Bill of Rights': Proposals Have Dangerous Implications for U.S.," *American Bar Association Journal* 34 (November 1948): 984–86, 1078–81. See also Humphrey, *Human Rights*, 46, 60.

70. Hendrick to Ransom, 18 November 1948, Hendrick Papers, box 2, HSTL. See also Ransom to Hendrick, 13 October 1948, Hendrick Papers, box 2, HSTL; Duane Tananbaum, *The Bricker Amendment Controversy: A Test of Eisenhower's Political Leadership* (Ithaca: Cornell University Press, 1988), 7–11; Simsarian to Proskauer, 16 October 1948, decimal file 501.BD/10-1648 (1945–1949), Simsarian memo of conversation with Holman, 9 November 1948, decimal file 501.BD/11-948 (1945–1949), and Chairman of the Special Committee on Peace and Law through United Nations William Ransom to Acting Director of the Office of United Nations Affairs William Sanders, 29 November 1948, decimal file 501.BD/11-2948 (1945–1949), box 2189, NARA; Robert Marcus, "The U.N. Bill of Rights: Reply Made to Recent Statements Criticizing Present Drafts," *New York Times*, 20 October 1948, 28; Holman to Marshall, 2 November 1948, and Marshall to Holman, 12 November 1948, in Frank Holman, *The Dangers of Treaty Law: A Constitutional Amendment Is the Only Answer* (Yakima, WA: Veterans of Foreign Wars, 1952), 31–35; Holman, "'World Government' No Answer to America's Desire for Peace," *American Bar Association Journal* 32 (October 1946): 642–45, 718–21; and idem, *The Life and Career of a Western Lawyer, 1886–1961* (Baltimore: Port City Press, 1963), 361, 372–74; and William Ransom, "United Nations Will Proceed with Declaration and Covenant on Human Rights," *American Bar Association Journal* 34 (December 1948): 1091.

For an excellent reply to Holman's and Ransom's charges, see Moses Moskowitz, "Is the U.N.'s Bill of Human Rights Dangerous? A Reply to President Holman," *American Bar Association Journal* 35 (April 1949): 283–88, 358–59. Holman's rejoinder is on pages 288–90, 360–62.

71. Minutes of the HRW, 24 June 1948, and "Annotated Draft International Declaration on Human Rights," ISP D-124/48 (is also S/HRW D-1/48 Rev.1), 30 June 1948, and "Position Paper: Report of the Third Session of the Commission on Human Rights," ISP D-29/48, 2 July 1948, and "General Assembly—Third Session: Draft International Declaration of Human Rights," S/HRW D-70/48, 16 September 1948, files of HRW, RG 353, box 112, NARA; United Nations, *1948-1949 Yearbook*, 576–78; ECOSOC Resolution 151(VIII), 26 August 1948; Green, "Efforts to Deal with Violations," 668; Humphrey, *Human Rights*, 55–60; "Economic and Social Council," *U.S. Department of State Bulletin* 19 (22 August 1948): 238; State Department, "Draft International Declaration of Human Rights," SD/A/C.3/65, 20 August 1948, Roosevelt Papers, box 4579, FDRL; James Simsarian of the Office of United Nations Affairs memo of conversation, 24 August 1948, subject files of Durward Sandifer, lot file 55D 429, box 8, NARA; Hendrick to Simsarian, 27 July 1948, Hendrick Papers, box 2, HSTL; Sandifer to Roosevelt, enclosing State Department, "Draft International Declaration of Human Rights," SD/A/C.3/69 and SD/A/C.3/70, 26 August 1948, Roosevelt Papers, box 4595, FDRL; Minutes of the U.S. delegation to the U.N. General Assembly, 24 September 1948, in *Foreign Relations of the United States, 1948* (Washington, DC: U.S. Government Printing Office, 1975), 1:289–91 [hereafter cited as *FRUS 1948*]; and Minutes of the U.S. delegation to the U.N. General Assembly, 25 September 1948, in *FRUS 1948*, 291–95.

72. Black, *The Eleanor Roosevelt Papers*, 939. See also Glendon, *A World Made New*, 139–52; and Humphrey, *Human Rights*, 64–70.

73. "Searching Study of Human Rights Declaration," *United Nations Bulletin* 5 (1 November 1948): 858–61; Lash, *Eleanor*, 78–79; Humphrey, *Human Rights*, 63–71; "Progress on

Human Rights Declaration," *United Nations Bulletin* 5 (15 November 1948): 932–35; "Shaping the Declaration of Human Rights," *United Nations Bulletin* 5 (1 December 1948): 966–70; "Universal Declaration of Human Rights," *United Nations Bulletin* 5 (15 December 1948): 1003–8; Glendon, *A World Made New*, 159–63, and Third Committee of the General Assembly, "Draft International Declaration of Human Rights: Report of the Third Committee," 7 December 1948, A/777.

74. "Statement by Roosevelt to U.N. General Assembly Plenary," 9 December 1948, *U.S. Department of State Bulletin* 19 (19 December 1948): 751; Glendon, *A World Made New*, 170; and James Simsarian, "United Nations Action on Human Rights in 1948," *U.S. Department of State Bulletin* 20 (2 January 1949): 18. See also U.S. Delegation to the United Nations, "Position Paper on Draft International Declaration of Human Rights," 8 December 1948, in *FRUS 1948*, 302–4; Summary record of the General Assembly Plenary, 10 December 1948, A/PV183; Harry Truman, *United States Participation in the United Nations: Report by the President to the Congress for the Year 1948* (Washington, DC: U.S. Government Printing Office, 1949), 6; Pratt, *Influence of Domestic Controversy*, 65; Transcript of "Conference on the International Declaration of Human Rights," 31 October 1947, Roosevelt Papers, box 4578, FDRL; "The Human Rights Assembly," *United Nations News* 4 (January 1949): 1–4; and James Simsarian, "United Nations Action on Human Rights in 1948," *U.S. Department of State Bulletin* 20 (2 January 1949): 18–19.

4: Opposition at Home and at the United Nations

1. Summary minutes of the U.N. General Assembly Plenary, 10 December 1948, A/PV 183.

2. Hendrick memo of conversation, 3 July 1947, Eleanor Roosevelt Papers, box 4587, FDRL. See also J. Halderman to Fahy and Rusk, 9 July 1947, Hendrick Papers, box 2, HSTL; and Notter to Rusk, 11 July 1947, Notter Papers, RG 59, box 10, NARA.

3. HRW, "Position Paper on the Human Rights Convention," S/HRW D-113/47, 28 July 1947, files of HRW, RG 353, box 110, NARA.

4. Minutes of HRW, 5 and 13 August 1947, files of HRW, RG 353, box 112, NARA; Minutes of ISP, 11 August 1947, files of ISP, RG 353, box 98, NARA; ISP, "Proposal for a Human Rights Convention," 10 November 1947, Eleanor Roosevelt Papers, box 4589, FDRL; Whiteman, "The Treaty-Making Power and Federal and State Rights," S/HRW D-125/47, 12 September 1947, files of HRW, RG 353, box 110, NARA; and UNCHR, "Proposal for a Human Rights Convention Submitted by the Representative of the United States on the Commission on Human Rights," 26 November 1947, E/CN.4/37.

5. ISP, "Provisions of Human Rights Conventions Regarding Discrimination on Account of Race, Sex, Language, and Religion," 26 September 1947, files of ISP, RG 353, box 110, NARA. See also ISP, "Working Draft on the Subject of Implementation and Procedural Articles for Human Rights Convention," 9 October 1947, files of ISP, RG 353, box 110, NARA; ISP, "Proposal for a Human Rights Convention," 10 November 1947, Eleanor Roosevelt Papers, box 4589, FDRL; and UNCHR, "Proposal for a Human Rights Convention Submitted by the Representative of the United States on the Commission on Human Rights," 26 November 1947, E/CN.4/37.

6. HRW, "Working Draft on the Subject of Implementation and Procedural Articles for Human Rights Convention," S/HRW D-131/47, 9 October 1947, files of HRW, RG 353, box 110, NARA. See also State Department, "United States Proposals Regarding an Inter-

national Bill of Rights," SD/C.S. 4/3, 16 January 1947, Roosevelt Papers, box 4592, FDRL; UNCHR, "United States Proposals Regarding an International Bill of Rights," E/CN.4/4, 28 January 1947; Marshall to Roosevelt, 29 January 1947, decimal file 501.BD/1-2947 (1945–1949), box 2186, NARA; UNCHR, "Report of the Working Party on an International Convention on Human Rights," E/CN.4/56, 11 December 1947; UNCHR, "Report of the Drafting Committee to the Commission on Human Rights," E/CN.4/21, 1 July 1947; Minutes of HRW, 17 and 24 October 1947, files of HRW, RG 353, box 112, NARA; Robert McClintock of Office of Special Political Affairs (SPA) to Lovett, 20 November 1947, decimal file 501.BD/11-2047 (1945–1949), box 2189, NARA; ISP, "Changes Made by the Under Secretary of State in U.S. Draft Declaration of Human Rights and in U.S. Draft Convention on Human Rights Subsequent to Approval by ISP," ISP D-182/47, 21 November 1947, files of HRW, RG 353, box 111, NARA; Lovett to Hendrick, 24 November 1947, decimal file 501.BD/11-2447 (1945–1949), box 2188, NARA; and Department of Labor to ISP, 9 December 1947, ISP D-187/47, files of ISP, RG 353, box 101, NARA.

7. Lovett to Roosevelt, 26 November 1947, decimal file 501.BD/11-2547 (1945–1949), box 2188, NARA. See also McClintock to Lovett, 20 November 1947, decimal file 501.BD/11-2047, box 2189, NARA; ISP, "Changes Made by the Under Secretary of State in U.S. Draft Declaration of Human Rights (ISP D-178/47) and in U.S. Covenant on Human Rights (ISP D-179/47) Subsequent to Approval by ISP," 21 November 1947, ISP D-182/47, files of ISP, RG 353, box 111, NARA; Lovett to Hendrick, 24 November 1947, decimal file 501.BD/11-2447 (1945–1949), box 2188, NARA; Lovett to Roosevelt and Hendrick, 2 December 1947, decimal file 501.BD/11-2447 (1945–1949), box 2188, NARA; Kotschnig memo of conversation with Hendrick, 5 December 1947, decimal file 501.BD/12-547 (1945–1949), box 2188, NARA; Neal Sanford, "Broad World Bill of Rights Launched by U.S. in UN," *Christian Science Monitor*, 2 December 1947, C2; Minutes of the UNCHR, 2 December 1947, E/CN.4/SR.25; UNCHR, "Report to the Economic and Social Council on the Second Session of the Commission," 17 December 1947, E/600; Anderson, *Eyes off the Prize*, 132–33; and Lash, *Eleanor*, 69–74.

8. Minutes of ISP, 13 January 1948, files of ISP, RG 353, box 107, NARA. See also Minutes by Whiteman of meeting between Roosevelt, ISP, and other, 14 January 1948, decimal file 501.BD/1-1448 (1945–1949), box 2188, NARA; Lash, *Eleanor*, 72–74.

9. Lovett to Truman, 30 April 1948, and reply, 1 May 1948, Official File 85, box 533, HSTL. See also "U.N. Rights Court Opposed by Bar," *New York Times*, 26 February 1948, 4; ISP, "Report on Second Session, Commission on Human Rights," ISP D-1/48, 7 January 1948, files of ISP, RG 353, box 101, NARA; UNCHR, "Report to the Economic and Social Council on the Second Session of the Commission," E/600, Annex C, 17 December 1947; Hendrick memo of conversation with Ransom, 15 March 1948, decimal file 501.BD/3-1548 (1945–1949), box 2189, NARA; ISP, "Position Paper on Draft Negotiating Declaration and Covenant on Human Rights, Supplementary to U.S. Letter of Comments," ISP D-54/48, 6 April 1948, files of ISP, RG 353, box 101, NARA; ISP, "Statement of Problems to be Considered in Connection with Third Session of Commission on Human Rights," S/HRW D-8/48, 22 January 1948, RG 353, box 111, NARA; Minutes of HRW meeting, 28 January 1948, files of HRW, RG 353, box 112, NARA; Hendrick memo of conversation, 4 March 1948, Hendrick Papers, box 2, HSTL; Sandifer and Hendrick to Rusk, Gross, and Lovett, "Position of the United States for the Third Session of the Human Rights Commission," 2 April 1948, Roosevelt Papers, box 4579, FDRL; and HRW, "Recommendation with Respect to Provisions on Implementation Which Should Be Included in the Covenant on Human Rights,"

S/HRW D-34/48, 15 April 1948, Roosevelt Papers, box 4579, FDRL.

10. Minutes of ISP, 28 April 1948, files of ISP, RG 353, box 107, NARA; and Marshall to Roosevelt, 18 May 1948, decimal file 501.BD/5-18/48 (1945–1949), box 2188, NARA. See also Minutes of ISP, 30 April and 13 and 18 May 1948, files of ISP, RG 353, box 107, NARA; HRW, "Consistency of Proposed Covenant on Human Rights with Law in the United States," files of HRW, 12 April 1948, Roosevelt Papers, box 4581, FDRL; ISP, "Arguments Against Inclusion of the Right of Participation in Government in the Covenant," ISP D-61/48, and "Arguments in Favor of Inclusion of the Right of Participation in Government in the Covenant," ISP D-62/48, 28 April 1948, files of ISP, RG 353, box 112, NARA; ISP, "Recommendations with Respect to Specific Articles Formulated by the United Nations Commission on Human Rights at Its Second Session in Geneva in December, 1947," ISP D-57/48 Rev., 30 April 1948, decimal file 501.BD/4-3048 (1945–1949), box 2188, NARA; and ISP, "Covenant-Right of Participation in Government," ISP D-75/48, 20 May 1948, files of ISP, RG 353, box 102, NARA.

11. UNCHR, "Comments from Governments on the Draft International Declaration on Human Rights, Draft International Covenant on Human Rights, and the Question of Implementation," 16 April 1948, E/CN.4/82; and ISP, "Summary of Position Proposed in Attached Draft Letter of Comments of the United States on the Declaration, Covenant, and Implementation Report of the United Nations Commission on Human Rights," ISP D-41/48, 26 March 1948, RG 353, box 111, NARA. See also HRW, "Statement of Problems to Be Considered in Connection with Third Session of Commission on Human Rights," S/HRW D-8/48, 22 January 1948, and "Working Paper on Position to Be Taken in Connection with Third Session of Commission on Human Rights," S/HRW D-12/48 Rev.1, 16 February 1948, RG 353, box 111, NARA; Sandifer and Hendrick to Rusk, Gross, and Lovett, "Position of the United States for the Third Session of the Human Rights Commission," 2 April 1948, Roosevelt Papers, box 4579, FDRL; ISP, "Position Paper on Draft Negotiating Declaration and Covenant on Human Rights, Supplementary to U.S. Letter of Comments," ISP D-54/48, 6 April 1948, files of ISP, RG 353, box 101, NARA; HRW, "Consistency of Proposed Covenant on Human Rights with Law in the United States," S/HRW D-30/48, 12 April 1948, Roosevelt Papers, box 4581, FDRL; and UNCHR, "Comments from Governments on the Draft International Declaration on Human Rights, Draft International Covenant on Human Rights, and the Question of Implementation," 16 April 1948, E/CN.4/82, 7–12.

12. Justice Department, "Proposed Provision to Delay Operation of Covenant," ISP D-64/48, 28 April 1948, files of ISP, RG 353, box 102, NARA; and Minutes of ISP, 30 April 1948, files of ISP, RG 353, box 107, NARA. See also ISP, "Recommendations with Respect to Specific Articles Formulated by the United Nations Commission on Human Rights at Its Second Session in Geneva in December, 1947," ISP D-57/48 Rev., 30 April 1948, decimal file 501.BD/4-3048 (1945–1949), and Austin to Marshall, 14 May 1948, decimal file 501.BD/5-1448 (1945–1949), box 2188, NARA; HRW, "Covenant on Human Rights Not to Be Self-Execution," S/HRW D-87/48, 13 December 1948, files of HRW, RG 353, box 112, NARA; Tim Wu, "Treaties' Domains: When Do American Judges Enforce Treaties," <http://www.law.yale.edu/documents/pdf/Faculty/Tim_Wu_Treaties_Domains.pdf>, accessed 21 August 2008; and Legal Department of the Secretariat, "Opinion of the Legal Department on the Adaptation of Municipal Law to International Conventions," E/CN.4/116, 28 May 1948. For the origin of the non-self-executing treaty doctrine see *Foster & Elam v. Neilson*, 2 Pet. 253 (1829).

13. UNCHR Drafting Committee, "Report of the Drafting Committee to the Commission on Human Rights," E/CN.4/95, 21 May 1948. See also "Statement by Mrs. Franklin D. Roosevelt, United States Representative on the Commission on Human Rights," 18 June 1948, Roosevelt Papers, box 4580, FDRL; Summary records of the UNCHR Drafting Committee, 14 and 20 May 1948, E/CN.4.AC.1/SR.33 and 34; Austin to Marshall, 14 May 1948, decimal file 501.BD/5-14/48 (1945–1949), Hendrick to Sandifer and Gross, 3 and 5 May 1948, decimal file 501.BD/5-348 (1945–1949) and 501.BD/5-548 (1945–1949), box 2188, NARA; and UNCHR, "Report to the Economic and Social Council on the Third Session of the Commission on Human Rights," E/800, 18 June 1948.

14. Assistant Secretary of State Willard Thorp to Roosevelt, 25 May 1948, decimal file 501.BD/5-2548 (1945–1949), box 2188, NARA; Lovett to Roosevelt, 7 May 1948, decimal file 501.BD/5-748 (1945–1949), box 2188, NARA; and UNCHR, "China and the United States: Proposal on Implementation for the Covenant on Human Rights," E/CN.4/15, 16 June 1948. See also Australian Delegation to the United Nations, "Draft Proposals for an International Court of Human Rights," E/CN.4/AC.1/27; Hendrick to Gross and Sandifer, 18 May 1948, decimal file 501.BD/5-1848 (1945–1949), decimal file 501.BD/5-2548 (1945–1949), box 2188, NARA; U.N. Secretariat, "Suggested Regulations on the Subject of Petitions," E/CN.4/93, 19 May 1948; HRW, "Article on Implementation Proposed to Be Added to Covenant on Human Rights," S/HRW D-77/48, 30 September 1948, and "Article on Implementation Proposed to Be Added to Covenant on Human Rights: Alternative Draft," S/HRW D-84/48, 1 November 1948, and Minutes of HRW, 2 December 1948, files of HRW, RG 353, box 112, NARA.

15. Tananbaum, *The Bricker Amendment Controversy*, 8; "Bar Group Urges Fight on U.S. Reds, *New York Times*, 25 February 1948, 14; "Bar Group Revises Communist Purge," *New York Times*, 8 September 1948, 18; "Query on Race Dropped," *New York Times*, 30 May 1956, 14; "U.S. Bar Accused on Racial Query," *New York Times*, 24 February 1956, 10. See also Tananbaum, *The Bricker Amendment Controversy*, 7–8; Natalie Hevener Kaufman, *Human Rights Treaties and the Senate: A History of Opposition* (Chapel Hill: University of North Carolina Press, 1990), 19–35; and "Liberalized Admission for Negro Lawyers to Be Urged at U.S. Bar Group's Convention," *New York Times*, 5 September 1949, 15; "National Bar Bias Assailed in Jersey," *New York Times*, 11 December 1949, 78; "Bar Group Names First Negro," *New York Times*, 15 December 1950, 29; Anthony Lewis, "Lawyers on Civil Rights," *New York Times*, 18 August 1963, 154.

16. Holman, *Life and Career*, 357–59.

17. "The Declaration and the Covenant," *American Bar Association Journal* 35 (January 1949): 41–42. See also Simsarian to Proskauer, 16 October 1948, decimal file 501. BD/10-1648 (1945–1949), box 2189, NARA; American Bar Association, "Report and Recommendations to the House of Delegates by the Committee on Peace and Law Through United Nations: With Action Voted by the House of Delegates," 7 September 1948, Hendrick Papers, box 2, HSTL; Holman, *Life and Career*, 372–74; "U.N. Rights Court Opposed by Bar," *New York Times*, 26 February 1948, 4; Gladwin Hill, "U.N. Rights Drafts Held Socialistic," *New York Times*, 18 September 1948, 4; and Frank Holman, *The Story of the "Bricker" Amendment (The First Phase)* (New York: Committee for Constitutional Government, 1954), 8–9.

18. "Roosevelt speech to the U.N. General Assembly," 9 December 1948, *U.S. Department of State Bulletin* 19 (19 December 1948): 752.

19. "International Covenant: House Urges Study of Constitutional Questions,"

American Bar Association Journal 35 (March 1949): 196; and Dean Frederick K. Beutel of the University of Nebraska Law School to Jack Tate, 8 March 1949, decimal file 501. BD/3-849 (1945–1949), box 2189, NARA. See also "The Declaration and the Covenant," *American Bar Association Journal* 35 (January 1949): 40–42; George Eckel, "U.S. Delay Urged on U.N.'s Human Rights Plan," *New York Times*, 1 February 1949, 8; "International Covenant"; Simsarian to Joseph Proskauer, 16 October 1948, decimal file 501.BD/10-1648 (1945–1949), box 2189, NARA; Holman, "The President's Page," *American Bar Association Journal* 35 (March 1949): 202, and 195–97, 202–4; and Dulles to W. Jefferson Davis, 2 February 1949, Roosevelt Papers, box 3281, FDRL.

20. Minutes of ISP, 30 March 1949, files of ISP, RG 353, box 108, NARA. See also Simsarian to Sandifer, 28 March 1949, decimal file 501.BD/3-2849 (1945–1949), box 2189, NARA; and ISP, "Implementation Article," ISP D-36/49 Rev.1, 7 April 1949, files of HRW, RG 353, box 112, NARA.

21. Minutes of ISP, 30 March and 6 April 1949, files of ISP, RG 353, box 108, NARA. See also Simsarian to Sandifer, 28 March 1949, decimal file 501.BD/3-2849 (1945–1949), Tate to Sandifer, 9 May 1949, decimal file 501.BD/5-949 (1945–1949), Tate and Sandifer to Acheson, 10 May 1949, decimal file 501.BD/5-1049, Acheson to Roosevelt, 12 May 1949, decimal file 501.BD/5-1249, and Washington to Tate, 16 May 1949, decimal file 501.BD/5-1649, box 2189, NARA; Minutes of HRW, 18 March and 5 April 1949, and ISP, "Non-Self-Executing," D-19/49 Rev.1, 12 April 1949, and ISP, "International Covenant on Human Rights: U.S. Position," D-48/49 Rev.1, and ISP, "Implementation Article," ISP D-36/49 Rev.1, 7 April 1949, 18 April 1949, files of HRW and ISP, RG 353, box 112, NARA; Justice Department, "Proposed Amendments to Recommendations in the So-Called Non-Self-Executing Clauses to Paper ISP D-38/49," ISP D-44/49, 28 March 1949, and "Concerning Recommendation in ISP D-37/49 with Respect to Federal State Article for Covenant on Human Rights and Convention on Freedom of Information," 25 March 1949, files of ISP, RG 353, box 103, NARA; and UNCHR, "United States: Proposal for Article 25," 6 May 1949, E/CN.4/170.

22. "Statement by Roosevelt to U.N. General Assembly Plenary," 9 December 1948, *U.S. Department of State Bulletin* 19 (19 December 1948): 751. See also Nicholas Boer, *Cardinal Mindszenty and the Implacable War of Communism Against Religion and the Spirit* (London: B. U. E., 1949); Eduardo Anze Matienzo, Bolivian delegate to the United Nations to the U.N. Secretary-General, A/820, 16 March 1949; J. D. L. Hood of the Australian Mission to the United Nations to the U.N. Secretary-General, A/821, 19 March 1949; Senate Resolution 102, 81st Cong., 1st sess.; Frank J. Kendrick, "The United States and the International Protection of Human Rights" (Master's Thesis, University of Chicago, 1956), 57–66; and "National Conference of Christians and Jews Protest Denial of Religious Freedom in Hungary and Bulgaria," *U.S. Department of State Bulletin* 20 (10 April 1949): 454–55.

23. "U.S. Notes to Bulgaria, Hungary, and Rumania," *New York Times*, 3 April 1949, 4. See also "Bulgaria, Hungary, and Rumania Accused of Violating Human Rights and Fundamental Freedoms," *U.S. Department of State Bulletin* 20 (10 April 1949): 450–55; and Asher, *The United Nations*, 787–88.

24. Acheson to U.S. Mission to the United Nations, 5 April 1949, decimal file 501. BD/4-549 (1945–1949), box 2189, NARA. See also Asher, *The United Nations*, 787–89; and Minutes of the General Committee of the General Assembly, 6 April 1949, A/BUR/SR.58.

25. Minutes of the Ad Hoc Political Committee, 19 April 1949, A/AC.24/SR.35. See also Minutes of the Ad Hoc Political Committee, 19 and 22 April 1949, A/AC.24/SR.41; Ad Hoc Political Committee, "Report of the Ad Hoc Political Committee," 27 April 1949,

A/844; Minutes of the General Assembly, 29 and 30 April 1949, A/PV.201 and A/PV.203; U.N. General Assembly, Resolution 272(III), 30 April 1949; and Bertram D. Hulen, "U.S., Britain to Act Soon in Rights Case," *New York Times*, 5 May 1949, 1.

26. Minutes of the UNCHR, 11 May 1949, E/CN.4/SR.83; UNCHR, "Report to the Economic and Social Council on the Fifth Session of the Commission," 23 June 1949, E/1371; ISP, "Implementation Article," ISP D-36/49 Rev.1, 7 April 1949, files of ISP, RG 353, box 112, NARA; ISP, "Right of Petition," ISP D-71/49, 3 May 1949, files of ISP, RG 353, box 113, NARA; and Minutes of the UNCHR, 8 June 1948, E/CN.4/SR.118.

27. UNCHR, "United States of America: Amended Proposal, Article 4," 13 May 1949, E/CN.4/170/Add.1; Minutes of UNCHR, 18 May 1949, E/CN.4/SR.91; and Minutes of UNCHR, 13 June 1949, E/CN.4/SR.125. See also Minutes of UNCHR, 11, 17, 18 May 1949, E/CN.4/SR.83, E/CN.4/SR.88, E/CN.4/SR.90; Minutes of UNCHR, 13, 14, and 15 June 1949, E/CN.4/SR.125, E/CN.4/SR.126, E/CN.4/SR.127, and E/CN.4/SR.129; ISP, "U.S. Position on Article 4," ISP D-68/49, 12 May 1949, and idem, "Non-Self-Executing (Article 2)," 7 June 1949, ISP D-38/49 Rev.1, files of ISP, RG 353, box 112, NARA; UNCHR, "Report to the Economic and Social Council on the Fifth Session of the Commission," 23 June 1949, E/1371; UNCHR, "United States of America: Amendment to Article 2," 23 May 1949, E/CN.4/224; James Simsarian, "Human Rights: Draft Covenant Revised at Fifth Session of Commission on Human Rights," *U.S. Department of State Bulletin* 21 (11 July 1949): 3–12; and Arthur N. Holcombe, "The Covenant on Human Rights," *Law and Contemporary Problems* 14 (1949): 413–29.

28. HRW, "Statement in Answer to Possible Charge that the United States Discriminates Against Negroes in This Country," S/HRW D-40/49, 18 May 1949, files of HRW, RG 353, box 113, NARA. See also Hugh Smythe, review of the *1947 Negro Year Book*, ed. Jessie P. Guzman, *American Sociological Review* 13 (June 1948): 363–64.

29. Quoted in Pratt, *Influence of Domestic Controversy*, 109. See also Berman, *The Politics of Civil Rights*, 137–64; Pratt, *Influence of Domestic Controversy*, 102–9; J. Howard McGrath and Philip B. Perlman, *Brief of the United States as Amicus Curiae on a Writ of Certiorari to the Supreme Court of the United States, Elmer Henderson, Petitioner*, October 1949; and Philip B. Perlman and Philip Elman, *Brief of the United States as Amicus Curiae on a Writ of Certiorari to the Supreme Court of the United States, George W. McLaurin, Petitioner*, February 1950.

30. "U.S. Notes to Bulgaria, Hungary, and Rumania Invoke Peace Treaty Clauses to Settle Disputes on Violating Human Freedoms," *U.S. Department of State Bulletin* 20 (12 June 1949): 755–60; and "Statement by Acting Secretary Webb," *U.S. Department of State Bulletin* 20 (12 June 1949): 759. See also "U.S. Insists that Disputes Over Bulgarian, Hungarian, and Rumanian Rights Be Settled by Peace Treaties' Procedures," *U.S. Department of State Bulletin* 21 (11 July 1949): 29–30; James Webb, "The U.S.S.R. Refuses to Co-operate in Settling Disputes Under Bulgarian, Hungarian, and Rumanian Peace Treaties," 15 June 1949, *U.S. Department of State Bulletin* 20 (26 June 1949): 555; "U.S. Asks Bulgaria, Hungary, and Rumania to Refer Disputes to Peace Treaty Commissions," *U.S. Department of State Bulletin* 21 (15 August 1949): 238; and "Violation of Human Rights by Bulgaria and Hungary Placed on General Assembly Agenda," *U.S. Department of State Bulletin* 21 (26 September 1949): 456.

31. "Cohen to the Ad Hoc Political Committee, 4 October 1949," *U.S. Department of State Bulletin* 21 (24 October 1949): 618; "Cohen Speech to the Ad Hoc Political Committee, 12 October 1949," *U.S. Department of State Bulletin* 21 (31 October 1949): 659–61. See

also "Bulgaria, Hungary, and Rumania Accused of New Breach of Treaty Obligations," *U.S. Department of State Bulletin* 21 (3 October 1949): 514–15; "Austin to the U.N. Secretary-General, 20 September 1949," *U.S. Department of State Bulletin* 21 (10 October 1949): 541–42; "Cohen Speech to the General Assembly, 21 October 1949," *U.S. Department of State Bulletin* 21 (7 November 1949): 691–93; and U.N. General Assembly, "Resolution Adopted by the General Assembly at Its 235th Plenary Meeting on 22 October 1949," A/1043, 22 October 1949 (Resolution 294[IV]).

32. Roosevelt to Acheson, 24 June 1949, decimal file 501.BD/6-2149, box 2190, NARA; and Acheson to Roosevelt, 11 July 1949, decimal file 501.BD/6-2149, box 2190, NARA. See also UNCHR, "Report to the ECOSOC on UNCHR's Fifth Session," E/1371.

33. Kotschnig memo of conversation with John Boyd, first secretary of the British embassy in Washington, 19 December 1949, decimal file 501.BD/12-1949, box 2190, NARA; HRW, "Position of the United States with Respect to Proposals to Broaden the Covenant on Human Rights to Include Articles Relating to Social Security, Medical Care, and Education," S/HRW D-103/49, 8 November 1949, and "Proposal Re: Implementation," S/HRW D-102/49, 8 November 1949, files of HRW, RG 353, box 113, NARA; Minutes of HRW, 20 September and 10, 17, 18, and 29 November 1949, files of HRW, RG 353, box 112, NARA; and ISP, "Implementation: Second Position," 28 February 1950, Roosevelt Papers, box 4588, FDRL.

34. Article VI of the United States Constitution. See also Carl B. Rix, "Human Rights and International Law: Effect of the Covenant Under Our Constitution," *American Bar Association Journal* 35 (July 1949): 551–54, 618–21.

35. Rix, "Human Rights," 554. See also *Missouri v. Holland*, 252 U.S. 416 (1920).

36. Whiteman to Roosevelt, 26 August 1949, Roosevelt Papers, box 4588, FDRL; Tate to Gross, 20 February 1950, decimal file 340.1 AG/2-2050 (1950–1954), box 1326, NARA; and Gross to Wright, undated, decimal file 340.1 AG/2-1750 (1950–1954), box 1326, NARA. See also Wright to Austin, 17 January, and Simsarian to Green and Gross, 7 February 1950, decimal file 340.1 AG/2-1750 (1950–1954), box 1326, NARA; Tate to Whiteman, 17 February 1950, and Whiteman to Gross, 10 March 1950, decimal file 340.1 AG/2-1750 (1950–1954), box 1326, NARA.

37. State Department press release, "Statement of Mrs. Franklin D. Roosevelt," 3 January 1950, Roosevelt Papers, box 4588, FDRL; UNCHR, "Comments of Governments on the Draft International Covenant of Human Rights and Measures of Implementation: United States of America," 4 January 1950, E/CN.4/353/Add.1; and Assistant Secretary of State for United Nations Affairs John Hickerson to Acheson, 6 January 1950, decimal file 340.1 AG/1-650 (1950–1954).

38. Hickerson to Acheson, 6 January 1950, decimal file 340.1 AG/1-650 (1950–1954). For communications between the American and French governments, see Charles Bohlen, chargé d'affaires of the American embassy in Paris to State Department, 19 February 1950, and Acheson to U.S. embassy in Paris, 3 and 14 March 1950, decimal file 340.1 AG/2-1750 (1950–1954), box 1326, NARA; and U.S. ambassador to France David Bruce to Acheson, 16 March 1950, decimal file 340.1 AG/3-1650 (1950–1954), box 1326, NARA.

For communications between the American and British governments, see UNCHR, "Comments of Governments on the Draft International Covenant of Human Rights and Measures of Implementation: United Kingdom," 7 January 1950, E/CN.4/353/Add.2; U.S. Minister to Great Britain Julius Holmes to Acheson, 17 and 24 February and 14 March 1950, decimal file 340.1 AG/2-1720, 340.1 AG/2-2450, and 340.1 AG/3-1450 (1950–1954), Francis Willis, first secretary of the U.S. embassy in London to State Department, 23 February and 24 March 1950, decimal file 340.1 AG/2-2050 and 340.1 AG/3-2450 (1950–1954), box 1326, NARA; and Acheson to U.S. embassy in London, 3, 11, and 20 March 1950, decimal file 340.1 AG/2-1750, 340.1 AG/2-2450, and 340.1 AG/3-1450 (1950–1954), box 1326, NARA.

For communications between the United States and its allies, see Gross to U.S. Mission to the United Nations, and Acheson to U.S. embassy in Chile, 24 February 1950, decimal file 340.1 AG/2-2450 (1950–1954), box 1236, NARA; Sandifer to Minister of Lebanon Charles Malik, 13 March 1950, decimal file 340.1 AG/3-1350 (1950–1954), box 1326, NARA; Simsarian memos of conversation with diplomats from Lebanon and Uruguay, 7 March 1950, Roosevelt Papers, box 4588, FDRL; and Carlos Hall, first secretary to U.S. embassy in Chile to State Department, 31 March 1950, decimal file 340.1 AG/3-3150 (1950–1954), box 1326, NARA.

For comments by governments on the covenant and articles of implementation, see UNCHR, "Compilation of the Comments of Governments on the Draft International Covenant on Human Rights and the Proposed Additional Articles," 22 March 1950, E/CN.4/365; and UNCHR, "Compilation of Comments of Governments on Measures of Implementation," 22 March 1950, E/CN.4/366.

39. Thomas J. Hamilton, "Soviet Quits 2 U.N. Units; Rebuked by Mrs. Roosevelt," *New York Times*, 28 March 1950, 1; and Minutes of UNCHR, 27 March 1950, E/CN.4/SR.136.

For the debate on a general limitation clause, see Minutes of UNCHR, 30 March and 3, 5, 6, and 11 April 1950, E/CN.4/SR.139, 144, 146, 147, 148, 149, 152; "Human Rights Commission," *U.S. Department of State Bulletin* (1 May 1950): 703; UNCHR, "Observation by United States Concerning Proposal of the United Kingdom for Article 9," 3 April 1950, E/CN.4/401; and UNCHR, "Observation by United States Concerning Proposal of the United Kingdom for Article 5," 30 March 1950, E/CN.4/383.

For the debate over implementation, see U.N. Secretary-General, "The Right of Petition," 11 April 1950, E/CN.4/419; UNCHR, "United Kingdom and United States: Draft Proposal for Implementations of International Covenant on Human Rights," 22 April 1950, E/CN.4/444; Minutes of UNCHR, 25 April and 2 May 1950, E/CN.4/SR.168, 169, 176, and 177; "Right to Petition in U.N. Seen Weak," *New York Times*, 26 April 1950, 18; "U.N. Body Would Bar Individuals' Appeals," *New York Times*, 4 May 1950, 7; "Supervision Voted by U.N. Rights Unit," *New York Times*, 14 May 1950, 10; "Human Rights Commission," *U.S. Department of State Bulletin* 22 (1 May 1950): 703; "Human Rights Commission," *U.S. Department of State Bulletin* 22 (15 May 1950): 782; and "The United States in the United Nations," *U.S. Department of State Bulletin* 22 (19 June 1950): 1021–22; Austin to Acheson, 1 May 1950, and Acheson to U.S. delegation to United Nations, 2 May 1950, decimal file 340.1 AG/5-150 (1950–1954), box 1327, NARA; UNCHR, "France-India-United Kingdom-United States of America: Proposal Concerning Measures of Implementation/Establishment of a Human Rights Committee," 9 May 1950, E/CN.4/474; and UNCHR, "Report of the Commission on Human Rights (Sixth Session)," 25 May 1950, E/1681.

For the debate over including economic and social rights, see Minutes of UNCHR, 9–11 May, E/CN.4/SR.184–87; "U.N. Rights Treaty Will Go to Council," *New York Times*, 19 May 1950, 4; and UNCHR, "Report of UNCHR, Sixth Session," E/1681.

For a good summary of the session, see James Simsarian, "Proposed Human Rights Covenant: Revised at 1950 Session of Commission on Human Rights," *U.S. Department of State Bulletin* 22 (12 June 1950): 945–54.

40. Humphrey, *Human Rights*, 105; and Roosevelt, *My Day*, 20 May 1950, <http://www.gwu.edu/~erpapers/myday/displaydoc.cfm?_y=1950&_f=md001597> (accessed 5 September 2008). See also Humphrey, *Human Rights*, 105–7; and Glendon, *A World Made New*, 195–98.

41. Rabbi Irving Miller, president of the American Jewish Congress, to Webb, 5 May 1950, decimal file 340.1 AG/5-550 (1950–1954), box 1327, NARA; International League for the Rights of Man, "Proposals Relating to the Draft Covenant Submitted to the Council by the Commission on Human Rights," 27 June 1950, E/C.2/254; and World Jewish Congress, "Observations on the Draft First International Covenant on Human Rights," 4 July 1950, E/C.2/259. See also Rita Schaefer, secretary of the Ethics Committee of the Catholic Association for International Peace to Acheson, 21 March 1950, decimal file 340.1 AG/3-2150 (1950–1954), box 1326, NARA; Austin to Acheson, 29 April 1950, decimal file 340.1 AG/4-1550, John Cates of the Office of United Nations Affairs, memo of conversation with Sandifer, Hickerson, Tate, Kotschnig, and others, 10 May 1950, decimal file 340.1 AG/5-1050 (1950–1954), box 1327, NARA; Hickerson to Eichelberger, 11 May 1950, Roosevelt Papers, box 3372, FDRL; International League for the Rights of Man, "Proposals Relating to the Draft Covenant Submitted to the Council by the Commission on Human Rights," 27 June 1950, E/C.2/254; idem, "Statement Submitted by the International League for the Rights of Man, a Non-Governmental Organization Granted Consultative Status in Category B," 31 July 1950, E/C.2/276; ibid.; and World Jewish Congress, "Observations on the Draft First International Covenant on Human Rights," 4 July 1950, E/C.2/259.

42. *Sei Fujii v. State of California*, 24 April 1950, 217 P.2nd 488; U.S. Congress, House of Representatives, 81st Cong., 2nd sess., 24 April 1950, *Congressional Record*, 96:A3108; and Frank Holman, "Treaty Law-Making: A Blank Check for Writing a New Constitution," *American Bar Association Journal* 36 (September 1950): 788. See also Kendrick, "The United States," 87–88; Southard, "Human Rights Provisions," 49; Lockwood, "The United Nations Charter," 924–31; Pratt, *Influence of Domestic Controversy*, 128–31; *Kenji Namba v. McCourt*, 29 March 1949, 204 P.2d 569; Gladwin Hill, "U.N. Charter Voids a California Law," *New York Times*, 26 April 1950, 16; "Supreme Charter," *New York Times*, 30 April 1950, E2; "States' Laws Held Above U.N. Treaty," *New York Times*, 14 May 1950, 7; Arthur Krock, "In the Nation: The U.N. Charter and the Discrimination Issue," *New York Times*, 16 May 1950, 27; "Test for U.S. Laws Seen in U.N. Code," *New York Times*, 11 September 1950, 10; U.S Congress, Senate, 81st Cong., 2nd sess., 28 April and 19 May 1950, *Congressional Record*, 96:5993–6004, 7325–28; Holman, "Treaty Law-Making"; and Frank Ober, "The Treaty-Making and Amending Powers: Do They Protect Our Fundamental Rights?," *American Bar Association Journal* 36 (September 1950): 707–10, 787–90, and 715–19, 793–96.

43. Notter to Sandifer and Hickerson, 9 May 1950, decimal file 340.1 AG/4-2650 (1950–1954), box 1327, NARA. See also Reorganization Task Force #3 (Non-Military Interdepartmental Relationships), "The Interdepartmental Committee on International Social Policy," 16 June 1949, Executive Secretary for ISP Eleanor Dennison to Thorp, 22 November 1949, and deputy assistant secretary of state for Administration to head of the State Department's Secretariat Carlisle Humelsine, 22 November 1949, files of ISP, RG 353, box 98, NARA; ISP, "Proposed Dissolution of the ISP," ISP D-168/49, files of ISP, RG 353, box 105, NARA; and Minutes of ISP, 8 and 15 December 1949, files of ISP, RG 353, box 108, NARA.

For State Department strategy on the covenant, see Notter to Sandifer and Hickerson, 9 May 1950, Simsarian to Sandifer, 26 April 1950, and Sandifer to Simsarian, 11

May 1950, decimal file 340.1 AG/4-2650 (1950–1954), box 1327, NARA; Cates memo of conversation with Hickerson, Sandifer, Tate, Kotschnig, and legal advisor Marcia Maylott, 10 May 1950, decimal file 340.1 AG/5-1050 (1950–1954), decimal file 340.1 AG/6-2850 (1950–1954), box 1327, NARA.

44. James Simsarian, "Proposed Human Rights Covenant: Revised at 1950 Session of Commission on Human Rights," *U.S. Department of State Bulletin* 22 (12 June 1950): 945 and 949; and Tate to Solicitor General Philip Perlman, 28 June 1950, decimal file 340.1 AG/6-2850 (1950–1954), box 1327, NARA. The three civil rights cases were *Henderson v. United States*, 339 U.S. 816; *Sweatt v. Painter*, 339 U.S. 629; and *McLaurin v. Oklahoma State Regents*, 339 U.S. 637.

45. Simsarian to Otis Mulliken, 18 August 1950, decimal file 340.1 AG/8-1850 (1950–1954), box 1327, NARA. See also United Nations, *Yearbook of the United Nations, 1950* (New York: Columbia University Press, 1951), 521–24; Sandifer to Roosevelt, 28 July and 8 and 21 August 1950, decimal file 340.1 AG/7-2850, 340.1 AG/8-850, and 340.1 AG/8-2150 (1950–1954), box 1327, NARA; "Statement by Acting Secretary of State James Webb, 19 May 1950," *U.S. Department of State Bulletin* 22 (29 May 1950): 878–79; Sandifer to Roosevelt, 14 September 1950, decimal file 340.1 AG/9-1451, and Webb to U.S. embassy in Denmark, 4 October 1950, decimal file 340.1 AG/9-2750 (1950–1954), box 1328, NARA; Simsarian memo of conversation with Roosevelt and Sandifer, 10 August 1950, decimal file 340.1 AG/8-1050, box 1327, NARA; Minutes of ECOSOC, 4 and 5 July and 9 August 1950, E/SR.377–79 and E/SR.404; Minutes of ECOSOC's Social Committee, 17 to 31 July 1950, E/AC.7/146–55; Humphrey, *Human Rights*, 121–23; and ECOSOC Resolution 303 1 (XI).

46. State Department to fifty embassies, "Draft International Covenant on Human Rights and Draft Freedom of Information Convention in 1950 United Nations General Assembly," 19 August 1950, decimal file 340.1 AG/8-1850, and Acheson to embassies in London and Paris, "Draft International Covenant on Human Rights and Draft Freedom of Information Convention in 1950 United Nations General Assembly," 26 August 1950, decimal file 340.1 AG/8-2650, box 1327, NARA; Bernard Connally, first secretary in U.S. embassy in Pretoria to Acheson, 31 August 1950, decimal file 340.1 AG/8-3150, and Unsigned telegram from U.S. embassy in Haiti to Acheson, 8 September 1950, decimal file 340.1 AG/9-850, and Julius Holmes, U.S. minister to Great Britain to Acheson, 11 September 1950, decimal file 340.1 AG/9-1150, and Karl Rankin, counsel-general in Taipei to Acheson, 12 September 1950, decimal file 340.1 AG/9-1250, and Simsarian memo of conversation with J. M. Cote from the Canadian embassy to the United States, 13 September 1950, decimal file 340.1 AG/9-1350, and Eugenie Anderson, U.S. ambassador to Denmark to Acheson, 27 September 1950, decimal file 340.1 AG/9-2750, and Harold Schantz, counselor to U.S. embassy in Denmark to Acheson, 28 September 1950, decimal file 340.1 AG/9-2850 (1950–1954), box 1327, NARA; and Borstelmann, *Apartheid's Reluctant Uncle*, 83–133.

47. "Acheson Press Statement, 21 July 1950," *U.S. Department of State Bulletin* 23 (31 July 1950): 191. See also Holman, "Treaty Law-Making," 788; International Court of Justice (ICJ), "Interpretation of Peace Treaties with Bulgaria, Hungary, and Rumania (Second Phase)," 18 July 1950, in *International Court of Justice Reports 1950*, 221–61; idem, *International Court of Justice Yearbook, 1949–50*, 78–80; "State Department Press Release, 29 June 1950," *U.S. Department of State Bulletin* 23 (7 August 1950): 233–35; and Acheson to U.S. embassies, 29 July 1950, decimal file 340.1 AG/7-2950 (1950–1954), box 1327, NARA.

48. Benjamin Cohen, "Speech to the Ad Hoc Political Committee of the U.N. General Assembly on Human Rights in the Balkans, 2 October 1950," *U.S. Department of State Bulletin*

23 (23 October 1950): 670; and Green, "Efforts to Deal with Violations," 791. See also Acheson to U.S. embassies in Great Britain, Australia, Canada, and New Zealand, 28 August 1950, in *FRUS 1950*, 4:55; John Campbell, State Department's officer in charge of Balkan affairs, memo of conversation with Owen L. Davis, first secretary of Australian embassy in Washington, 9 August 1950, decimal file 340.1 AG/8-950, and Holmes to Acheson, 13 September 1950, decimal file 340.1 AG/9-1350 (1950–1954), box 1327, NARA; Webb to U.S. delegation to the United Nations, 22 September 1950, in *FRUS 1950*, 4:56–57; "General Assembly," *U.S. Department of State Bulletin* 23 (9 October 1950): 597; and "Reports of the Ad Hoc Political Committee," *U.S. Department of State Bulletin* 24 (22 January 1951): 143.

For the text of the resolution, see "Bulgaria, Hungary, and Rumania Condemned on Human Rights Issues," *U.S. Department of State Bulletin* 23 (27 November 1950): 872.

49. "Position Paper Prepared in the Department of State for the U.S. Delegation to the Fourth Regular Session of the General Assembly: The Treatment of Indians in South Africa," 2 September 1950, in *FRUS 1950*, 2:561. See also General Assembly Resolution 265(III), 14 May 1949; Borstelmann, *Apartheid's Reluctant Uncle*, 158–65; and B. N. Rau, permanent representative of India to the United Nations, to U.N. secretary-general, 20 July 1950, A/1289.

50. Minutes of a meeting of the U.S. delegation to the United Nations, 10 November 1950, in *FRUS 1950*, 2:565, 566. See also State Department, "Position Paper Prepared in the Department of State for the U.S. Delegation to the Fourth Regular Session of the General Assembly: The Treatment of Indians in South Africa," 2 September 1950, in *FRUS 1950*, 2:559–62.

51. Austin to Acheson, 7, 20, 22, 29, and 30 November 1950, in *FRUS 1950*, 2:562–63, 570–71, 572–73, 573–74, and 575; General Assembly Resolution 395(V); Green, "Efforts to Deal with Violations," 780–83; United Nations, *United Nations Action*, 60–61; Borstelmann, *Apartheid's Reluctant Uncle*, 142–43; and "Treatment of People of Indian Origin in South Africa," *U.S. Department of State Bulletin* 24 (22 January 1951): 145.

52. U.N. General Assembly, "Draft First International Covenant on Human Rights and Measures of Implementation: Report of the Third Committee," 29 November 1950, A/1559; Summary records of the Third Committee of the General Assembly, 8 November 1950, A/C.3/SR.308; and Roosevelt to Acheson, 14 December 1950, decimal file 340.1 AG/12-1450 (1950–1954), box 1327, NARA. See also Third Committee, "Yugoslavia: Amendment to the Joint Draft Resolution Submitted by Brazil, Turkey, and the United States of America A/C.3/L.76," 3 November 1950, A/C.3/L.92; Summary records of the Third Committee of the General Assembly, 14 November 1950, A.C.3/SR.313; State Department to the U.S. delegation to the Fifth Regular Session of the General Assembly, 5 September 1950, in *FRUS 1950*, 509–16; "Draft Resolution: Future Work of the Commission on Human Rights," 5 September 1950, in *FRUS 1950*, 519–20; "Working Paper on Human Rights: Report of the Third Committee," 29 November 1950, in *FRUS 1950*, 520–23; Minutes of the U.S. delegation to the General Assembly, 8 September 1950, in *FRUS 1950*, 516–18; Third Committee, "Union of Soviet Socialist Republics: Draft Resolution on the Draft First International Covenant on Human Rights and Measures of Implementation," 2 November 1950, A/C.3/L.77/Rev.1; Third Committee, "Brazil, Turkey, United States: Joint Draft Resolution on the Future Work of Commission on Human Rights," 1 November 1950, A/C.3/L.76; Third Committee, "Union of Soviet Socialist Republics: Amendments to Joint Draft Resolution Submitted by Brazil, Turkey, and United States," 6 November 1950, A/C.3/L.96; United Nations, *Yearbook, 1950*, 524–32; Green, "Efforts to Deal with Viola-

tions," 79–80; Tony Evans, *U.S. Hegemony and the Project of Universal Human Rights* (New York: St. Martin's Press, 1996), 129–30; General Assembly Resolution 421(V), 4 December 1950; and Paul Kennedy, *The Parliament of Man: The Past, Present, and Future of the United Nations* (New York: Random House, 2006), 122.

53. U.N. General Assembly, "Draft First International Covenant on Human Rights and Measures of Implementation: Report of the Third Committee," 29 November 1950, A/1559; and Roosevelt to Truman, 28 May 1950, Roosevelt Papers, box 4560, FDRL. See also Summary record of the Third Committee of the General Assembly, 9 November 1950, A/C.3/SR.309; Acheson to U.S. embassy in South Africa and U.S. Mission to the United Nations, 9 September 1950, decimal file 340.1 AG/8-3150, and Kotschnig to Gerig, 30 November 1950, decimal file 340.1 AG/1-3850 (1950–1954), box 1327, NARA; Third Committee, "Yugoslavia: Amendment to the Joint Draft Resolution," 3 November 1950, A/C.3/L.92; State Department to the U.S. Delegation, "The Draft First International Covenant on Human Rights," and "Working Paper: Report of the Third Committee," 29 November 1950, in *FRUS 1950*, 509–16, and 520–23; U.N. General Assembly, "Draft First International Covenant on Human Rights: Report of the Third Committee," 29 November 1950, A/1559; United Nations, *Yearbook, 1950*, 524–32; UNCHR, "Report of the Commission (Sixth Session)," 25 May 1950, E/1681; Third Committee, "Union of Soviet Socialist Republics: Draft Resolution on the Covenant," 2 November 1950, A/C.3/L.77/Rev.1; Minutes of the Third Committee, 8 November 1950, A/C.3/SR.308; Green, *The United Nations*, 55–57; General Assembly Resolution 421(V), 4 December 1950; General Assembly Resolution 422(V), 4 December 1950; and Secretary-General, "Federal and Colonial Clauses," 19 June 1950, E/1721.

54. General Assembly Resolution 421(V), 4 December 1950; and Truman speech to the National Council of Negro Women, 15 November 1949, Official File 93, box 544, HSTL. See also Summary record of the Third Committee of the General Assembly, 10 November 1950, A/C.3/SR.311; Third Committee, "Afghanistan and Saudi Arabia: Revised Amendment to the Joint Draft Resolution Submitted by Brazil, Turkey, and the United States of America," 7 November 1950, A/C.3/L.88/Rev.1; U.N. General Assembly, "Draft First International Covenant on Human Rights: Report of the Third Committee," 29 November 1950, A/1559; Third Committee, "U.S.S.R.: Amendments to the Joint Resolution," 6 November 1950, A/C.3/L.96; Third Committee, "U.S.S.R.: Draft Resolution on the Covenant," 2 November 1950, A/C.3/L.77/Rev.1; U.N. Secretary-General, "The Right of Peoples and Nations to Self-Determination," 2 March 1951, E/CN.4/516; idem, "The Right of Peoples to Self-Determination," 24 March 1952, E/CN.4/649; State Department, "Working Paper: Report of the Third Committee," 29 November 1950, in *FRUS 1950*, 2:520–23; Pratt, *Influence of Domestic Controversy*, 150–52; United Nations, *United Nations Action*, 16; and Minutes of the Third Committee, 10 November 1950, A/C.3/SR.310.

55. Green, "Post-Mortem on the Third Committee," 22 December 1950, Roosevelt Papers, box 4583, FDRL; and Roosevelt to Truman, 14 December 1950, Roosevelt Papers, box 4560, FDRL. See also Roosevelt to Acheson, 14 December 1950, decimal file 340.1 AG/12-1450 (1950–1954), box 1327, NARA.

56. Joseph E. Johnson, president of the Carnegie Endowment for International Peace to Tate, 30 March 1951, decimal file 340.1 AG/3-3051 (1950–1954), box 1327, NARA. See also Joseph E. Johnson to Whiteman, 22 January 1951, decimal file 340.1 AG/1-2251 (1950–1954), box 1327, NARA.

57. Unsigned, "Resolutions Adopted at the Chicago Conference," 25–27 February 1951, Official File 421, box 1270, HSTL. See also Eichelberger to the Board of Directors of

the American Association for the United Nations (AAUN), 20 February 1950, Roosevelt Papers, box 3249, FDRL; and Eichelberger to AAUN Board of Directors, 12 March 1951, Roosevelt Papers, box 3249, FDRL.

58. "Position Paper: Free Elections," undated, SD/E/CN.4/62, decimal file 340.1 AG/3-1951 (1950–1954), box 1327, NARA. See also Sandifer to Hickerson, 21 March 1951, decimal file 340.1 AG/3-1951 (1950–1954), box 1327, NARA; ECOSOC, "Observations of Governments of Member States on the Draft International Covenant on Human Rights and Measures of Implementation: United States," 20 February 1951, E/CN.4/515/Add.3; State Department, "Position Paper: Comments on Provisional Agenda," undated, SD/E/CN.4/61, State Department, "Position Paper: Present Text of the Draft Covenant," 7 March 1951, SD/E/CN.4/60, decimal file 340.1 AG/3-1951, box 1327, NARA.

59. State Department, "Position Paper: Economic, Social, and Cultural Rights," undated, SD/E/CN.4/56, decimal file 340.1 AG/3-1951, box 1327, NARA.

60. Ibid., "Position Paper: Petitions," undated, SD/E/CN.4/57, and "Position Paper: Right of Peoples and Nations to Self-Determination," undated, SD/E/CN.4/58, decimal file 340.1 AG/3-1951, box 1327, NARA.

61. UNCHR, "United States of America: Proposal on Economic, Social, and Cultural Rights," 16 April 1951, E/CN.4/539; Minutes of UNCHR, 16 April 1951, E/CN.4/SR.203; and "Mrs. Roosevelt Resigns as Head of U.N. Unit," *New York Times*, 17 April 1951, 20.

For general information on UNCHR's 1951 session, see Letitia A. Lewis, "International Negotiations Regarding the Human Rights Covenant: February 1951–February 1952," decimal file 340.1 AG/5-1452 (1950–1954), box 1328, NARA; UNCHR, "Report of the Seventh Session of UNCHR," 19 May 1951, E/1992; and James Simsarian, "Economic, Social, and Cultural Provisions in the Human Rights Covenant," *U.S. Department of State Bulletin* 24 (25 June 1951): 1003–14.

62. Summary record of the 217th meeting of the UNCHR, 28 April 1951, E/CN.4/SR.217. See also Summary record of the 221st meeting of the UNCHR, 1 May 1951, E/CN.4/SR.221; and UNCHR, "Report of the Seventh Session of UNCHR," 19 May 1951, E/1992.

63. U.N. Commission on Human Rights, "Observations of Governments on the Draft International Covenant on Human Rights," 26 July 1951, A/2059; Acheson to Roosevelt, 16 May 1951, decimal file 340.1 AG/5-1451 (1950–1954), box 1327, NARA; Article 19 of the covenant in UNCHR, "Report of the Seventh Session of UNCHR," 19 May 1951, E/1992; and Acheson to Roosevelt, 8 May 1951, decimal file 340.1 AG/5-551 (1950–1954), box 1327, NARA.

64. Hickerson to Rusk, 30 May 1951, office files of the assistant secretaries of state for U.N. Affairs, 1945–1954, lot file 58D 33, box 2, NARA; and Roosevelt, *My Day*, 30 April 1951, <http://www.gwu.edu/~erpapers/myday/displaydoc.cfm?_y=1950&_f=md001597> (accessed 11 September 2008). See also "Dangers Are Seen in U.S. Rights Code," *New York Times*, 24 April 1951, 6; Simsarian to Kotschnig, 29 April 1951, decimal file 340.1 AG/4-2951, Roosevelt to Acheson, 30 April 1951, decimal file 340.1 AG/4-3051, Roosevelt to Sandifer and Tate, 30 April 1951, decimal file 340.1 AG/4-3051, and Acheson to Roosevelt, 3 May 1951, decimal file 340.1 AG/5-151 and 340.1 AG/5-251 (1950–1954), box 1327, NARA; Roosevelt to Acheson, 3 May 1951, decimal file 340.1 AG/5-351, Roosevelt to Acheson, 10 May 1951, decimal file 340.1 AG/5-1051, Roosevelt to Sandifer and Tate, 11 May 1951, decimal file 340.1 AG/5-1151, and Acheson to Roosevelt, 12 May 1952, decimal file 340.1 AG/5-1251 (1950–1954), box 1327, NARA.

65. Roosevelt to Truman, 24 April 1951, quoted in Johnson, "Contributions of Eleanor and Franklin Roosevelt," 44; "Dangers Are Seen in U.N. Rights Code," *New York Times*, 24 April 1951, 6; Roosevelt, *My Day*, 11 May 1951, <http://www.gwu.edu/~erpapers/myday/displaydoc.cfm?_y=1950&_f=md001597> (accessed 11 September 2008); and Roosevelt, *My Day*, 27 August 1951, <http://www.gwu.edu/~erpapers/myday/displaydoc.cfm?_y=1950&_f=md001597> (accessed 11 September 2008). See also Sandifer to Kotschnig, 29 April 1951, decimal file 340.1 AG/4-2951 (1950–1954), box 1327, NARA.

66. Quoted in Tananbaum, *The Bricker Amendment Controversy*, 21, 24. For an excellent source on Bricker and his amendment, see Richard O. Davies, *Defender of the Old Guard* (Columbus: Ohio State University Press, 1993). For a hagiographic account of Bricker's early years, see Karl B. Pauly, *Bricker of Ohio: The Man and His Record* (New York: G. P. Putnam's Sons, 1944).

67. U.S. Congress, Senate, 82nd Cong., 1st sess., 17 July 1951, *Congressional Record*, 97:8255, Article 14(3) of the covenant, and Bricker to Holman, 23 July 1951, John Bricker Papers, box 160, Ohio Historical Society (hereafter referred to as Bricker Papers, OHS). See also Alfred Schweppe, chair of the ABA Committee on Peace and Law through United Nations, to Bricker, 20 July 1951, and Bricker to Schweppe, 24 July 1951, Bricker Papers, box 160, OHS; and Pratt, *Influence of Domestic Controversy*, 170–91.

5: United Nations Success Breeds Failure at Home

1. Raphael Lemkin, *Axis Rule in Occupied Europe: Laws of Occupation, Analysis of Government, Proposals for Redress* (Washington, DC: Carnegie Endowment for International Peace, 1944), viii.

2. Ibid., 79.

3. Ibid. See also editorial entitled "Genocide," in the *Washington Post*, 3 December 1944, B4. For information about his life, see Gertrude Samuels, "U.N. Portrait," *New York Times Magazine* (20 March 1949), 20–22. For an anti-Semitic polemic against Lemkin and his concept of genocide, see James J. Martin, *The Man Who Invented "Genocide": The Public Career and Consequences of Raphael Lemkin* (Torrance, CA: Institute for Historical Review, 1984). For Lemkin's thoughts on genocide, see Raphael Lemkin, "Genocide as a Crime Under International Law," *United Nations Bulletin* 4 (15 January 1948): 70–71; Lemkin, "Genocide as a Crime Under International Law," *The American Journal of International Law* 41 (January 1947): 145–51; Steven L. Jacobs, *Raphael Lemkin's Thoughts on Nazi Genocide: Not Guilty?* (Lewiston, NY: Edwin Mellen Press, 1992); and Lemkin, "Genocide," *American Scholar* 15 (April 1946): 227–30. For histories of genocide, see Jack Nusan Porter, ed., *Genocide and Human Rights: A Global Anthology* (Washington, DC: University Press of America, 1982); and Leo Kuper, *The Prevention of Genocide* (New Haven: Yale University Press, 1985).

4. Lemkin, "Genocide as a Crime," 148.

5. U.N. General Assembly's General Committee, "The Crime of Genocide," 2 November 1946, A/BUR/50; and "Genocide Before the U.N.," *New York Times*, 8 November 1946, 22.

6. U.N. General Assembly, Sixth Committee, "The Crime of Genocide: Draft Report and Proposed Resolution Adopted by Subcommittee 3," 6 December 1946, A/C.6/120; U.N. General Assembly, Sixth Committee, "The Crime of Genocide: Report of the Sixth Committee," 10 December 1946, A/231; Summary record of the Sixth Committee, 30 November 1946, A/C.6/91; Delegations to the United Nations from Chile, United States, Cuba,

France, India, Panama, Poland, Saudi Arabia, Great Britain, and the Soviet Union, "The Crime of Genocide," 2 December 1946, A/C.6/94 (1946); and "Law on Genocide Put to the Assembly," *New York Times*, 23 November 1946, 2; and James F. Bender, "Words in the News," *New York Times Sunday Magazine*, 1 December 1946, 21.

7. ECOSOC Resolution on genocide, 28 March 1947, E/325; Minutes of the HRW, 19 February 1947, RG 353, box 112, NARA; ISP, "Suggested Position Paper: Assembly Resolution on Crime of Genocide," ISP D-37/47, 19 February 1947, RG 353, box 99, NARA; Minutes of the ISP, 27 February 1947, RG 353, box 107, NARA; Summary record of ECOSOC, E/421, 15 March 1947; "Genocide Resolution Proposed by the United States," 17 March 1947, E/342; Memo of conversation by Carl Marcy, 25 February 1947, decimal file 501.BD/2-2547 (1945–1949), box 2186, NARA; and Summary record of ECOSOC, 20, 25, and 28 March 1947, E/AC.7/8, E/AC.7/15, and E/396/Rev.1.

8. "Historical Summary of the Genocide Convention from 2 November 1946 to 20 January 1948," 26 January 1948, E/621; and "Draft Convention Prepared by the Secretariat," 26 June 1947, E/447.

9. Telegram from Secretary of State George Marshall to Philip C. Jessup, 4 June 1947, decimal file 501.BD/6-447, Telegram from Jessup to Marshall, 5 June 1947, decimal file 501. BD/6-547 (1945–1949), box 2187, NARA; Summary record of the Twenty-Eighth Meeting of the Committee on the Progressive Development of International Law and Its Codification, 13 June 1947, A/AC.10/SR.128; Resolution submitted by England to the Committee on the Progressive Development of International Law and Its Codification, 6 June 1947, A/AC.10/44; Opinion of the Committee on the Progressive Development of International Law and Its Codification, 17 June 1947, E/447; and Lawrence J. LeBlanc, *The United States and the Genocide Convention* (Durham, NC: Duke University Press, 1991), 25–26.

10. HRW, "Genocide," S/HRW D-108/47, 30 June 1947, RG 353, box 110, NARA. Such a provision would violate a fundamental principle of international law, *pacta tertiis nec nocent nec prosunt*, which states that nations that are not parties to an international treaty cannot be bound by its provisions. It would also violate Anglo-Saxon law, which rests on the premise that law goes with the territory; thus even a non-party that wanted to prosecute under the Genocide Convention's terms would be legally unable to do so.

11. Minutes of the Subcommittee on Human Rights and Status of Women, 9 July 1947, RG 353, box 112, NARA; Memo from Notter to Rusk, 18 July 1947, decimal file 501.BD/7-1847 (1945–1949), box 2186, NARA; and "The Crime of Genocide," *New York Times*, 26 July 1947, 12; "U.N. Urged to Speed Its Ban on Genocide," *New York Times*, 1 August 1947, 4. See also HRW, "Genocide," S/HRW D-108/47, 30 June 1947, RG 353, box 110, NARA; Minutes of the ISP, 9 July 1947, RG 353, box 98, NARA; Minutes of the ISP, 14 July 1947, RG 353, box 107, NARA; "Economic and Social Council—5th Session, Comments on Item 11," HRW and ISP D-106/47, 24 July 1947, RG 353, box 100, NARA. For media pressure, see "Treaty on Genocide," *Washington Post*, 16 July 1947 as quoted in the *Congressional Record* 93, 80th Cong, 1st sess., 4020; and "Genocide Treaty Up For Action," *Christian Century* 64 (27 August 1947): 1013–14.

12. Summary record of the Social Committee of ECOSOC, 30 July 1947, E/AC.7/SR.15; and ECOSOC Resolution 77(V), 6 August 1947; and ISP, "General Assembly—2nd Session, Genocide," 2 September 1947, ISP D-144/47, RG 353, box 110, NARA. See also "Draft Resolution Submitted by the Delegation of the United States," 25 July 1947, E/AC.7/23; "Draft Resolution Presented to the Social Committee by the Delegations of Canada, Cuba, Norway, and United States," 1 August 1947, E/AC.7/31; Summary record

of the Social Committee of ECOSOC, 1 August 1947, E/AC.7/SR.17; and "The Crime of Genocide," *United Nations Bulletin* 3 (19 August 1947): 252–53.

13. "Commentary by the Government of the United States on the Genocide Convention," 30 September 1947, A/401/Add.2; and Memo to Lovett from Rusk and Gross, 10 September 1947, decimal file 501.BD/9-1047 (1945–1949), box 2186, NARA.

14. "Commentary by the Government of the United States on the Genocide Convention," 30 September 1947, A/401/Add.2.

15. Article I, Section 8 of the U.S. Constitution. See also Memo to Lovett from Rusk and Gross, 10 September 1947, decimal file 501.BD/9-1047 (1945–1949), box 2186, NARA.

16. Summary record of the General Assembly Plenary, 21 November 1947, A/PV.123. See also Summary record of the Sixth Committee of the General Assembly, 29 September, 6 October, and 20 November 1947, A/C.6/SR.39, A/C.6/SR.42, and A/C.6/SR.59; Subcommittee 2 of the Sixth Committee, "Report and Draft Resolution Adopted by Subcommittee 2 on Progressive Development of International Law and Its Codification," 11 November 1947, A/C.6/190/Rev.1; "Report and Draft Resolution Adopted by the Sixth Committee," 18 November 1947, A/510; and "Assembly Calls for Draft Convention on Genocide," *United Nations Bulletin* 3 (2 December 1947): 724.

17. ISP, "Genocide," ISP D-14/48, 23 January 1948, RG 353, box 101, NARA. See also Minutes of the ISP, 29 January 1948, RG 353, box 107, NARA.

18. John Maktos, interview by Richard D. McKinzie, May 28, 1973, transcript, Harry S. Truman Library and Museum, <http://www.trumanlibrary.org/oralhist/maktosj.htm> (accessed 23 September 2008). See also Summary record of ECOSOC, 12 February and 3 March 1948, E/SR.139 and E/SR.160; U.S. Delegation to the United Nations, "Proposal to ECOSOC," 12 February 1948, E/662; United States Delegation to the United Nations, "Draft Resolution," 13 February 1948, E/662/Add.1; "Drafting Convention on Genocide," *United Nations Bulletin* 4 (1 March 1948): 179; Minutes of the Social Committee, 21 February 1948, E/AC.7/SR.37; Draft Resolution by Venezuela to ECOSOC, 13 February 1948, E/663; and Hendrick, Sandifer, and Gross memo of conversation, 14 April 1948, subject files of Durward Sandifer, lot file 55-D-429, box 8, NARA.

19. Katherine Fite to Lovett, Gross, and Sandifer, "Position on Genocide Convention in ECOSOC Drafting Committee," 2 April 1948, subject files of Durward Sandifer, lot file 55-D-429, box 8, NARA; and Hendrick to American delegation to the United Nations, "Position on Genocide Convention in ECOSOC Drafting Committee," 8 April 1948, decimal file 501.BD/4-1048 (1945–1949), box 2186, NARA.

20. Soviet Delegation to the United Nations, "Basic Principles of a Convention on Genocide," 7 April 1948, E/AC.25/7. The Soviets thought that religion was a component of a larger national identity and so wished that the two characteristics be combined. See also Summary record of the Ad Hoc Committee on Genocide, 6, 19, and 20 April 1948, E/AC.25/SR.1, SR.12, and SR.13; Lovett to Maktos, 13 April 1948, decimal file 501.BD/4-1348, and Sandifer to Gross, 14 April 1948, decimal file 501.BD/4-1448 (1945–1949), box 2186, NARA. For domestic opposition to the provision on state complicity, see Letter from Mildred Burgess of the National Federation of Business and Professional Women's Clubs to Gross, 12 April 1948, decimal file 501.BD/4-1248 (1945–1949), box 2186, NARA. 21. Sandifer to Gross, 22 April 1948, decimal file 501.BD/4-224, box 2186, NARA; and Summary record of the Ad Hoc Committee, 8 April 1948, E/AC.25/SR.5. See also Summary record of the Ad Hoc Committee, 21 April 1948, E/AC.25/SR.14.

22. Summary record of the Ad Hoc Committee, 8, 9, 16, and 21 April 1948, E/

AC.25/SR.5, 6, 10, and 14; Sandifer to Gross, 14 April 1948, decimal file 501.BD/4-1448 (1945–1949), box 2186, NARA; Sandifer to Gross, 19 April 1948, D.F. 501.BD/4-1948 (1945–1949), NARA; *Schenck v. United States*, 249 U.S. 52 (1919); and *Abrams v. United States*, 250 U.S. 616 (1919).

23. Nehemiah Robinson, *The Genocide Convention: A Commentary* (New York: Institute of Jewish Affairs, 1960), 69. Ad Hoc Committee on Genocide, "Report to the Economic and Social Council on the Meetings of the Committee Held at Lake Success, New York from 5 April to 10 May 1948," undated, E/794. See also "Draft Articles for the Inclusion in the Convention on Genocide Proposed by the Delegation of China," 16 April 1948, E/AC.25/7; Summary record of the Ad Hoc Committee, 22, 23, and 28 April 1948, E/AC.25/SR.15, 16, 17, 18, 24; Hendrick memorandum of conversation with Gross and Sandifer, 14 April 1948, box 8, subject files of Sandifer, NARA; and Sandifer to Gross, 14 and 19 April 1948, decimal file 501.BD/4-1448 and 501.BD/4-1948 (1945–1949), box 2186, NARA.

24. Summary record of the Ad Hoc Committee, 12 April 1948, E/AC.25/SR.7. See also "Basic Principles of a Convention on Genocide," 7 April 1948, E/AC.25/SR.7; Summary record of the Ad Hoc Committee, 12, 13, and 26 April 1948, E/AC.25/SR.7, 8, and 20; Lovett to Maktos, 13 April 1948, decimal file 501.BD/4-1348 (1945–1949), box 2186, NARA; and Sandifer to Gross, 14 and 19 April 1948, decimal file 501.BD/4-1448 and 501. BD/4-1948 (1945–1949), box 218, NARA.

25. Article 6 of the Ad Hoc Committee's draft. See also Summary record of the Ad Hoc Committee, 23 and 27 April 1948, E/AC.25/SR.18 and 19; Lovett to Maktos, 13 April 1948, decimal file 501.BD/4-1348, Sandifer to Gross, 14 April 1948, decimal file 501.BD/4-1448, and Sandifer to Gross, 19 April 1948, decimal file 501.BD/4-1948 (1945–1949), box 2186, NARA.

Gross argued that implementation legislation was necessary before the United States could comply with the extradition requirements of the convention. See Gross to Maktos, 23 April 1948, box 8, subject files of Sandifer, lot file 55-D-429, box 8, NARA; and Tate to Gross, 9 November 1948, decimal file 501.BD/11-848 (1945–1949), box 2186, NARA.

26. Summary record of the Ad Hoc Committee, 30 April 1948, E/AC.25/SR.26; Ad Hoc Committee on Genocide, "Draft Convention on Prevention and Punishment of the Crime of Genocide," 19 May 1948, E/AC.25/12; and "Genocide Convention," *United Nations News* 3 (June 1948): 45–46.

27. Summary record of the ECOSOC Plenary, 26 August 1948, E/SR.219. See also Warren Austin to Gross and Sandifer, 28 April 1948, decimal file 501.BD/4-2848 (1945–1949), box 2186, NARA; Summary record of the ECOSOC Plenary, 26 August 1948, E/SR.218; and State Department, "Position on Genocide Convention Prepared by the Ad Hoc Committee on Genocide," undated, SD/E/148, records of the Bureau of International Organization Affairs, RG 59, box 28, NARA.

28. Walter W. Van Kirk to Thorp, 14 June 1948, decimal file 501.BD/6-1448 (1945–1949), box 2186, NARA; Rev. R. A. McGowan, executive secretary of the Catholic Association for International Peace to Secretary of State Marshall, 12 August 1948, decimal file 501.BD/8-1248 (1945–1949), box 2186, NARA; and Simsarian and Hendrick to Sandifer, Kotschnig, Mulliken, and Samuel DePalma, 27 July 1948, subject files of Sandifer, lot file 55-D-429, box 8, NARA.

29. John Cooper, *Raphael Lemkin and the Struggle for the Genocide Convention* (New York: Palgrave Macmillan, 2008), 104, 121–26.

30. Cooper, *Raphael Lemkin*, 109–10. See also Sandifer to James Rosenberg, undated, decimal file 501.BD/8-2648, Rosenberg to Lovett, 26 August 1948, decimal file 501.BD/8-2648, Johnson to Tate, 14 July 1948, decimal file 501.BD/7-1448, Rosenberg to Lovett, 17 August 1948, decimal file 501.BD/8-1748 (1945–1949), box 2186, NARA; and Cooper, *Raphael Lemkin*, 100–129.

31. Quoted in Cooper, *Raphael Lemkin*, 94. See also 102–8, 140–46.

32. Article 4(c) of the Ad Hoc Committee's Convention; and Summary record of the Sixth Committee, 27 October 1948, A/C.6/SR.85. See also Cooper, *Raphael Lemkin*, 158–59; and Summary record of the Sixth Committee, 26 October 1948, A/C.6/SR.84.

33. "Position on Genocide Convention Prepared by the Ad Hoc Committee on Genocide," 2 June 1948, subject files of Sandifer, lot file 55-D-429, box 8, NARA; and Union of Soviet Socialist Republics, amendments to the Ad Hoc Committee's draft, 9 October 1948, A/C.6/215/Rev.1. See also Summary record of the Sixth Committee, 25, 28, and 29 October and 4 and 10 November 1948, A/C.6/SR.83, 86, 87, 91, 98, and 99. For an analysis of votes in the Sixth Committee, see LeBlanc, *The United States*, 76–77 and 155–56.

34. "Norway: Amendment to Article 2 of the Draft Convention," 12 October 1948, A/C.6/288. See also Summary record of the Sixth Committee, 16 October 1948, A/C./SR.76 and 77; Robinson, *The Genocide Convention*, 62–63; and LeBlanc, *The United States*, 37–39.

35. Summary record of the Sixth Committee, 13–15 and 23 October 1948, A/C./SR.73–75, 82; Robinson, *The Genocide Convention*, 60–61; LeBlanc, *The United States*, 113–14; Cooper, *Raphael Lemkin*, 157–58; U.S. State Department, "Position on Genocide Convention Prepared by the Ad Hoc Committee on Genocide," 2 June 1948, subject files of Sandifer, lot file 55-D-429, box 8, NARA; and "Text Adopted by the Sixth Committee for Article 2 of the Draft Convention," 23 October 1948, A/C.6/245.

36. United Nations General Assembly, "Genocide: Draft Convention and Report of the Economic and Social Council, Report of the Sixth Committee," 3 December 1948, A/760; and Summary record of the Sixth Committee, 29 November 1948, A/C.6/SR.128. See also Summary record of the Sixth Committee, 10, 29, and 30 November 1948, A/C.6/SR.99, 128, 129, and 130; Sixth Committee, "United States of America: Amendment to Article 7 of the Draft Convention," 16 October 1948, A/C.6/235; Robinson, *The Genocide Convention*, 81–82; LeBlanc, *The United States*, 155–58; and Cooper, *Raphael Lemkin*, 167–70.

37. "Statement by Ernest A. Gross," *U.S. Department of State Bulletin* 19 (19 December 1949): 755; Summary record of the General Assembly Plenary, 9 December 1948, A/PV.179; Gertrude Samuels, "U.N. Portrait," *New York Times Magazine* (20 March 1949), 20–22; and U.S. Congress, Senate, Subcommittee of the Committee on Foreign Relations, *The Genocide Convention: Hearings on the International Convention on the Prevention and Punishment of the Crime of Genocide*, 81st Cong., 2nd sess., 1950, 2 (hereafter cited as Senate, *Genocide Convention Hearings*, 1950). See also "The United States in the United Nations," *U.S. Department of State Bulletin* 19 (12 December 1948): 729; "An Epoch-Making Event," *United Nations Bulletin* 5 (15 December 1948): 1009; Summary record of the Sixth Committee, 1 December 1948, A/C.6/SR.133; "Resolution of Approval of the Genocide Convention," December 1948, A/760; and "Draft Convention and Report of the Economic and Social Council: Report of the Sixth Committee," 3 December 1948, A/760.

38. LeBlanc, *The United States*, 39–56, 67–88, 96–108, 128–50, 164–74, 182–200; Kaufman, *Human Rights Treaties*, 37–63; and Cooper, *Raphael Lemkin*, 189–208.

39. Holman to Acheson, 8 February 1949, decimal file 501.BD/2-849 (1945–1949), box 2189, NARA. See also Sandifer to Rusk, 25 February 1949, decimal file 501.BD/2-849

(1945–1949), box 2189, NARA; and Holman, *Life and Career*, 389–90.

40. Ransom to Austin, 9 February 1949, decimal file 501.BD/2-1449, Maktos to Austin, 8 March 1949, decimal file 501.BD/2-1449 (1945–1949), box 2186, NARA; Memo of conversation between ABA leaders and State Department officials, 28 February 1949, decimal file 501.BD/2-2849, and Simsarian, "Three Regional Meetings of the American Bar Association on Human Rights: Summary Report," 22 March 1949, subject files of Sandifer, lot file 55-D-429, box 8, NARA.

41. Holman to Acheson, 9 March 1949, decimal file 501.BD/3-949 (1945–1949), box 2189, NARA; "Highlights of the Annual Meeting," *American Bar Association Journal* 35 (October 1949): 807; and Senate, *Genocide Convention Hearings*, 1950, 157–92.

42. Senate, *Genocide Convention Hearings*, 1950, 232–33. Minutes of the Committee on International Law, 2 February 1949, box 101, Adolf Berle Papers, FDRL; "Draft Report from the Committee on International Law to the Association of the Bar of the City of New York," box 90, Berle Papers, FDRL; Senate, *Genocide Convention Hearings*, 1950, 79; Association of the Bar of the City of New York, Committee on International Law, "Memorandum on the Genocide Convention," 14 February 1950, box 91, Berle Papers, FDRL; and Tananbaum, *The Bricker Amendment Controversy*, 13, 45, 58. For the report of the Section of International and Comparative Law, see Senate, *Genocide Convention Hearings*, 1950, 231–50.

43. Holman, *Life and Career*, 400, 416. See also Senate, *Genocide Convention Hearings*, 1950, 158; and "Highlights of the Annual Meeting," *American Bar Association Journal* 35 (October 1949): 806–7.

44. Quoted in Cooper, *Raphael Lemkin*, 190–91, 194. See also 189–96; and "Special Message to the Senate Transmitting Convention on the Preventing and Punishment of the Crime of Genocide, 16 June 1949," in *Public Papers of the Presidents of the United States: Harry S. Truman* (Washington, DC: U.S. Government Printing Office, 1964), 5:291–92.

45. Quoted in LeBlanc, *The United States*, 20.

46. Quoted in Mark Byrnes, *The Truman Years, 1945–1953* (Harlow, England: Longman, 2000), 70. See also Holman, *Dangers of Treaty Law*, 6, 53.

47. Holman, *Dangers of Treaty Law*, 43–46; Holman, *State Department Half Truths and False Assurances Regarding the U.N. Charter, Genocide Convention, and Proposed Covenant on Human Rights* (Seattle: Argus Press, 1952), 38–43; Holman, "The Greatest Threat to American Freedom," *Daughters of the American Revolution Magazine* 87 (August 1953): 982–83; and Kenneth S. Carlston, "The Genocide Convention: A Problem for the American Lawyer," *American Bar Association Journal* 36 (March 1950): 206–9.

48. See *The Cherokee Tobacco*, 11 Wall. 616, 620–21; *Geofroy v. Riggs*, 133 U.S. 258, 267; *Holden v. Joy*, 17 Wall. 211, 243, *New Orleans v. United States*, 10 Pet. 662 (1836), and *Dred Scott v. Sanford*, 19 Howard 393 (1857).

49. Senate, *Genocide Convention Hearings*, 1950, 204, 205, 217, and 232. See also 18–19, 169, 172, 199–205, 212, 217, 246–47, and 305–6; U.S. Congress, Senate, Committee on Foreign Relations, *Executive Sessions of the Senate Foreign Relations Committee* (Historical Series), 81st Cong., 1st and 2nd sess., 1949–1950, 2:367–73, 381–82 (hereafter cited as Senate, *Genocide Convention Executive Sessions*, 2, 1949–1950); and U.S. Congress, Senate, Committee on Foreign Relations, *Report on the International Convention on the Prevention and Punishment of the Crime of Genocide*, 81st Cong., 2nd sess., 1950, 794–95 (hereafter cited as Senate, *Report on the Genocide Convention*, 1950).

50. Senate, *Genocide Convention Hearings*, 1950, 208. See also 160–62, 207–10,

220, 306–7; Orie L. Phillips, "The Genocide Convention: Its Effect on Our Legal System," *American Bar Association Journal* 35 (August 1949): 623–25; Carlston, "The Genocide Convention," 206–9; Mary F. Barley, "Do Americans Want the Genocide Convention Ratified?" *Daughters of the American Revolution Magazine* 85 (April 1951): 289–90; Holman, *State Department Half Truths*, 15–19, 34–35, 38, 46–54; and *Missouri v. Holland*, 252 U.S. 416 (1920).

51. Senate, *Genocide Convention Hearings*, 1950, 216; and Senate, *Genocide Convention Executive Sessions*, 1949–1950, 2:384. See also Holman, *Dangers of Treaty Law*, 18; Senate, *Genocide Convention Hearings*, 1950, 168–69, 171–75, 198, 215–16; Senate, *Genocide Convention Executive Sessions*, 1949–1950, 2:379–80, 392–95; Phillips, "The Genocide Convention," 623–25; Carlston, "The Genocide Convention," 206–9; Barley, "Do Americans Want the Genocide Convention Ratified?," 289–90; Holman, *State Department Half Truths*, 15–19, 34–35, 38, 46–54; and Transcript of radio program on the Genocide Convention with Raphael Lemkin, George Finch, and Dr. Lev Dobriansky from the 1954 *Congressional Record*, 100:A9413–16.

52. Senate, *Genocide Convention Hearings*, 1950, 20.

53. Senate, *Genocide Convention Hearings*, 1950, 20; and *Geofroy v. Riggs*, 133 U.S. 258 (1890) at 267. See also Senate, *Genocide Convention Hearings*, 1950, 10–54; and Senate, *Genocide Convention Executive Sessions*, 1949–1950, 2:362–63; and Senate, *Report on the Genocide Convention*, 1950, 801, 803–4. For Supreme Court cases on the law of nations and treaty power, see *United States v. Arjona*, 120 U.S. 479; *Perkins v. Elg*, 307 U.S. 325 (1939); and *Ex Parte Quirin*, 317 U.S. 1 (1942).

54. Senate, *Genocide Convention Hearings*, 1950, 4, 49–50, and 263, and *Frohwerk v. United States*, 249 U.S. 206 (1919).

For testimony on the meaning of "mental harm," see Senate, *Genocide Convention Hearings*, 1950, 73–74, 246–47, 250, 255, 263–64, 498; Senate, *Genocide Convention Executive Sessions*, 1949–1950, 2:365, 371–73; Senate, *Report on the Genocide Convention*, 1950, 803; Robinson, *The Genocide Convention*, 63; and LeBlanc, *The United States*, 99, 101–7.

For testimony on the meaning of "incitement," see Senate, *Genocide Convention Hearings*, 1950, 49–51, 60, 72, 197–98, 264–65, 500; Senate, *Genocide Convention Executive Sessions*, 1949–1950, 2:364; Senate, *Report on the Genocide Convention*, 1950, 801; and Robinson, *The Genocide Convention*, 67–69.

For Supreme Court decisions denying a First Amendment application to those charged with incitement, see *Frohwerk v. United States*, 249 U.S. 204 (1919), *Giboney v. Empire Storage Co.*, 336 U.S. 490 (1949), and *Chaplinsky v. New Hampshire*, 315 U.S. 568.

55. *Missouri v. Holland*, 252 U.S. 433–34. For Supreme Court decisions on the supremacy of treaties, see *Ware v. Hylton* 3 Dallas 199 (1796), *Fairfax's Devisee v. Hunter's Lessee* 7 Cranch 603 (1813), *Hauenstein v. Lynham* 100 U.S. 483 (1879), *Asakura v. Seattle* 265 U.S. 332 (1924), and *Missouri v. Holland* 252 U.S. 416 (1920). For a long list of such Court decisions, see Oliver Schroeder, Jr., *International Crime and the U.S. Constitution* ([Cleveland]: Western Reserve University Press, 1950), 18–20; and Senate, *Genocide Convention Hearings*, 1950, 25–26, 45–47, 67–69.

56. Examples of treaties include: Convention to Suppress the Slave Trade and Slavery (1926), Convention and Final Protocol for the Suppression of the Abuse of Opium and Other Drugs (1912), Agreement for the Suppression of the Trade in White Women (1904), Convention for Protection of Submarine Cables (1884). See also Senate, *Genocide Convention Hearings*, 1950, 13–16, 33–36, 40–44, 70; State Department, "Memorandum on Constitutional Aspects of the Convention on the Prevention and Punishment of the Crime of Genocide," 30

December 1949, Berle Papers, box 90, FDRL, 6–7, 12–14; *United States v. Arjona* (120 U.S. 479), which involved counterfeiting, *United States v. Smith* (5 Wheat. 157 [1820]), which upheld Congressional penalties for pirates as called for by a treaty, and Wade J. Newhouse, "United Nations Convention on the Prevention and Punishment of Genocide: An Analysis of Its Legal Problems and Proposed Action for the United States" (Seminar Paper, University of Michigan Law School, 1950), 40–41, in decimal file 340.1 AJ/2-2554, box 1342, NARA.

57. Senate, *Genocide Convention Executive Sessions*, 1949–1950, 2:364 and 380. See also Senate, *Genocide Convention Hearings*, 1950, 4–5, 42–45, 72–73, 95, 257, 503–6; Senate, *Genocide Convention Executive Sessions*, 1949–50, 2:364–65, 368, 379–80, 392–93; U.S. Congress, Senate, Committee on Foreign Relations, *Executive Sessions on the Genocide Convention* (Historical Series), 82nd Cong., 1st sess., 1951, 3:381–82 (hereafter referred to as Senate, *Genocide Convention Executive Sessions*, 3, 1951); and Senate, *Report on the Genocide Convention*, 1950, 800.

58. Senate, *Genocide Convention Hearings*, 1950, 258 (the quotation is taken from *Foster v. Neilson*, 27 U.S. 253 at 314 [1819]). See also Senate, *Genocide Convention Hearings*, 1950, 4–5, 13, 24, 31–32, 58–59, 64, 257–59, 502–3; Senate, *Genocide Convention Executive Sessions*, 1949–50, 2:366, 383, 393–94, 643; and Senate, *Report on the Genocide Convention*, 1950, 799–800, 802.

59. Senate, *Genocide Convention Hearings*, 1950, 20–21 and 390–91. See also 19–20, 26, 54, 82–85, 89, 319–413, 416–68; Senate, *Genocide Convention Executive Sessions*, 1949–1950, 2:388–91, 396, 647; and Matthew Woll, chairman of American Federation of Labor's International Labor Relations Committee to Acheson, 27 June 1950, decimal file 340.1 AJ/6-2750 (1950–1954), box 1341, NARA.

60. Senate, *Genocide Convention Executive Sessions*, 1949–1950, 2:370. See also Senate, *Genocide Convention Hearings*, 1950, 4, 12, 48, 71–72, 131, 251, 263; Senate, *Genocide Convention Executive Sessions*, 1949–1950, 2:368–70, 381, 384, 391–92; and Senate, *Genocide Convention Report*, 1950, 802.

61. Lemkin to Adolf Berle, 5 June 1950, Berle Papers, box 90, FDRL. See also Senate, *Report on the Genocide Convention*, 1950, 799–804; "Approval of Pact on Genocide Urged," *New York Times*, 13 April 1950, 5; and Harold B. Hinton, "M'Mahon to Press for Genocide Pact," *New York Times*, 24 August 1950, 17.

62. "President Truman Urges Senate Approval of Genocide Convention in View of Korean Crisis," *U.S. Department of State Bulletin* 23 (4 September 1950): 379–80; Representatives from 32 groups to Acheson, 20 July 1950, decimal file 340.1 AJ/7-1950, and Truman to Connally, 25 August 1950, decimal file 340.1 AJ/8-2550 (1950–1954), box 1341, NARA. See also "President Urges Pact on Genocide," *New York Times*, 27 August 1950; and Cooper, *Raphael Lemkin*, 199.

63. Senate, *Genocide Convention Executive Sessions*, 1949–1950, 2:384, 391, see also 377–80, 384–86, 391–95, 643, 651–53; and "Genocide Action Put Off," *New York Times*, 2 September 1950, 7.

64. For the text of the reservations, see Jack K. McFall, assistant secretary of state, to McMahon, 28 March 1951, decimal file 340.1 AJ/3-2851; American delegation to the United Nations to State Department, 25 October 1950, decimal file 340.1 AJ/10-2550 (1950–1954), box 1341, NARA; "Reservations to Multilateral Conventions: Report of the Secretary-General," 20 September 1950, A/1372; Summary record of the General Assembly, 26 September 1950, A/SR.285; Summary record of the Sixth Committee, 6–20 October 1951, A/C.6/217-225; and United Nations, *Yearbook, 1950*, 873–78.

For descriptions of League of Nations and Pan American Union procedures with regard to reservations, see Newhouse, "United Nations Convention," 49–71; State Department, "Written Statement of the United States of America Regarding the Questions Submitted to the International Court of Justice by the United Nations General Assembly by Its Resolution Dated November 16, 1950 Relating to Reservations to the Genocide Convention," subject files of Sandifer, lot file 55-D-429, box 8, NARA; and "Genocide Convention Will Come into Force on January 12," *United Nations Bulletin* 9 (1 November 1950): 478.

65. Resolution 478(V) of 16 November 1950; "Court Consulted on Genocide Reservations," *United Nations Bulletin* 9 (1 December 1950): 651; United Nations, *Yearbook, 1950,* 878–79; "U.S. Senate Faces Soviet Veto in U.N.," *New York Times,* 28 October 1950; "U.S. Acts to Bar Veto on Genocide," *New York Times,* 4 November 1950, 2; Humphrey to Acheson, 20 October 1950, decimal file 340.1 AJ/10-1950, Humphrey to Truman, 24 October 1950, decimal file 340.1 AJ/10-2550 and Jack McFall, assistant secretary of state for congressional relations, to Humphrey, 27 October 1950, decimal file 340.1 AJ/10-2050 (1950–1954), box 1341, NARA.

Several organizations also wrote to the State Department expressing Humphrey's concern. See Mrs. Hiram Houghton, president of the General Federation of Women's Clubs to Truman, 20 October 1950, decimal file 340.1 AJ/10-2050, Roger Baldwin, chairman of the International League for the Rights of Man to Truman, 31 October 1950, decimal file 340.1 AJ/11-150, Samuel McCrea, Cavert Mahony, and James Baldwin of the U.S. Committee for a U.N. Genocide Convention to Truman, 31 October 1950, decimal file 340.1 AJ/11-150, and Walter Van Kirk, executive secretary of the Federal Council of Churches to Truman, 1 November 1950, decimal file 340.1 AJ/11-250 (1950–1954), box 1341, NARA.

66. State Department, "Written Statement of the United States of America Regarding the Questions Submitted to the International Court of Justice," page 9, subject files of Sandifer, lot file 55-D-429, box 8, NARA.

67. International Court of Justice, "Reservations to the Convention on the Prevention and Punishment of the Crime of Genocide," 28 May 1951, <http://icij.org/docket/files/12/4283.pdf> (accessed 6 October 2008).

68. Ibid. See also Jack Tate, State Department's deputy legal advisor to Senator Humphrey, 15 June 1951, decimal file 340.1 AJ/6-1551 (1950–1954), box 1341, NARA; Ivan S. Kerno, "Advisory Opinion on Reservations to Genocide Convention," *United Nations Bulletin* 10 (15 June 1951): 594–95; "Court Eases Rule for Genocide Pact," *New York Times,* 29 May 1951, 13; and LeBlanc, *The United States,* 214–19.

69. Perlman to Senate Foreign Relations Committee, 7 November 1950, decimal file 340.1 AG/1-1550 (1950–1954), box 1327, NARA. See also Senate, *Genocide Convention Executive Sessions,* 1951, 3:381–82.

70. Cooper, *Raphael Lemkin,* 271.

71. McFall to Representative Charles J. Kersten (R-WI), 19 February 1952, decimal file 340.1 AJ/1-1452 (1950–1954), box 1342, NARA. See also Kersten and 115 others to Acheson, 11 January 1952, decimal file 340.1 AJ/1-1152, William Sanders (planning advisor, Bureau of U.N. Affairs) to Acheson, 14 January 1952, decimal file 340.1 AJ/1-1452, Elizabeth Ann Brown of the Office of U.N. Political and Security Affairs, "Activities of Our United Nations Representatives in Paris on Genocide," 28 January 1952, decimal file 340.1 AJ/1-2852, Kersten to Acheson, 11 April 1952, decimal file 340.1 AJ/4-1152, McFall to Kersten, 19 May 1952, decimal file 340.1 AJ/4-1152, James J. Wadsworth, deputy representative to the United Nations, to Dulles, 19 July 1954, decimal file 340.1 AJ/7-1954, State Department to U.S. del-

egation to the United Nations, 30 July 1954, decimal file 340.1 AJ/7-1954 (1950–1954), box 1342, NARA; and *Congressional Record*, 83rd Cong., 1st sess., 1953, 99.2:1467–75.

72. Dulles to Lodge, 23 October 1953, box 5, Chronological Series, Dulles Papers, DDEL; "Lehman Criticizes Lodge on Genocide," *New York Times*, 5 November 1953, 9; and Lodge to Dulles, 9 October 1953, decimal file 340.1 AG/10-953, box 1357 (1950–1954), NARA. See also Sandifer to Robert Murphy, assistant secretary of state for U.N. affairs, 12 October 1953, decimal file 340.1 AJ/10-1253 (1950–1954), box 1342, NARA; Dulles memorandum of telephone conversation with Lodge, 21 October 1953, box 1, Telephone Call Series, Dulles Papers, DDEL; Lodge to Dulles, 28 October 1953, box 7, Subject Series, Dulles Papers, DDEL; Lodge to Dulles, 9 November 1953, box 5, Chronological Series, Dulles Papers, DDEL; United Nations, *Yearbook of the United Nations, 1953* (New York: Columbia University Press, 1954), 687–89; and "A Fortnightly Review," *United Nations Bulletin* 15 (15 November 1953): 445.

For press reaction to the vote, see Arthur Krock, "In the Nation," *New York Times*, 6 November 1953, 26; and "Lodge Defends Aim on News to Press," *New York Times*, 12 November 1953, 10.

6: The End of a Crusade

1. Ronald W. Pruessen, *John Foster Dulles: The Road to Power* (New York: Free Press, 1982), 257.

2. See Pruessen, *John Foster Dulles*, 404–31; Richard H. Immerman, *John Foster Dulles: Piety, Pragmatism, and Power in U.S. Foreign Policy* (Wilmington, DE: Scholarly Resources, 1999), 27–33; and Mark G. Toulouse, *The Transformation of John Foster Dulles: From Prophet of Realism to Priest of Nationalism* (Macon, GA: Mercer University Press, 1985), 253–54.

3. A. Philip Randolph to Truman, 28 February 1951, Official File 93, White House Central Files, box 544, HSTL. See also Randolph to Niles, 21 February 1951, Official File 93, White House Central Files, box 544, HSTL; and Berman, *The Politics of Civil Rights*, 186–87.

4. Jacob Blaustein to Acheson, 7 March 1951, decimal file 340.1 AG/3-751 (1950–1954), box 1327, NARA; and "Resolutions Adopted at Chicago Conference," 25–27 February 1951, Official Files, box 421, HSTL. See also Roger Baldwin, chairman of the National Committee of the ACLU to Acheson, 23 July 1951, decimal file 340.1 AG/8-1751 (1950–1954), box 1327, NARA; and Susanne P. Shallna, chairman of the International Relations Committee of the National Federation of Business and Professional Women's Clubs, to Acheson, 26 February 1951, decimal file 340.1 AG/2-2651 (1950–1954), box 1327, NARA.

5. Joseph Johnson of the Carnegie Endowment for International Peace to Tate, 30 March 1951, decimal file 340.1 AG/3-3051 (1950–1954), box 1327, NARA. See also Irving Salvert, director of public relations for the Jewish Labor Committee, to Cleon Swazey, labor advisor to the State Department, 27 March 1951, decimal file 340.1 AG/3-2751, Baldwin to Sandifer, 7 June 1951, decimal file 340.1 AG/6-751, and Baldwin, Dorothy Kenyon, and Robert MacIver of the ACLU to Acheson, 23 July 1951, decimal file 340.1 AG/8-1751, box 1327, NARA; Roosevelt to Sandifer, Roosevelt Papers, box 3362, FDRL; and Marian Neal of the Carnegie Endowment for International Peace, to Tate, 18 October 1951, decimal file 340.1 AG/10-1851 (1950–1954), box 1328, NARA.

6. Simsarian memo of conversation with Roosevelt, Hickerson, Sandifer, Tate, Sand-

ers, Green, et al., 29 May 1951, in *FRUS 1951*, 2:742; State Department, "Position Paper Prepared in the Department of State for the United States Delegation to the Thirteenth Session of the Economic and Social Council of the United Nations," 29 June 1951, in *FRUS 1951*, 2:745; ECOSOC Resolution 384(XIII), 29 August 1951; and Bricker speech in *Congressional Record*, 30 August 1951, 82nd Cong., 1st sess., 97:10795. See also UNCHR, "Observations of Governments on the Draft International Covenant on Human Rights: United Kingdom," 31 July 1951, E/2059/Add.2; UNCHR, "Observations of Governments on the Draft International Covenant on Human Rights: Yugoslavia," 27 July 1951, E/2059/Add.3; UNCHR, "Observations of Governments on the Draft International Covenant on Human Rights: Australia," 10 August 1951, E/2059/Add.4; UNCHR, "Observations of Governments on the Draft International Covenant on Human Rights: Norway," 11 August 1951, E/2059/Add.5; Roosevelt, "Report on the Covenant," *U.N. World* 5 (August 1951): 17–18; United Nations, *Yearbook, 1951*, 479–81; Evans, *U.S. Hegemony*, 130–31; "Draft International Convention on Human Rights," *U.S. Department of State Bulletin* 25 (3 September 1951): 396; U.N. Secretary-General, "Provisions Concerning Economic, Social and Cultural Rights," 10 March 1952, E/CN.4/650; and Sandifer to Roosevelt, 14 September 1952, in *FRUS 1951*, 2:752.

7. ECOSOC Resolution 387B(XIII); Article 14 of the Draft International Covenant on Human Rights; and Bricker speech in *Congressional Record*, 23 August 1951, 82nd Cong., 1st sess., 97:10537. See also "Trial of William N. Oatis," *U.S. Department of State Bulletin* 25 (20 August 1951): 283–89; "A. P. Correspondent's Trial Called Travesty of Justice," *U.S. Department of State Bulletin* 25 (16 July 1951): 92–93; Asher, *The United Nations and Promotion of the General Welfare*, 808–10; Bricker speech in *Congressional Record*, 16 August 1951, 82nd Cong., 1st sess., 97:10129; "Czechoslovakian Ambassador Presents Credentials to the President," *U.S. Department of State Bulletin* 25 (10 September 1951): 416–17; "The Story of the 'Secret' Telephone Line," *U.S. Department of State Bulletin* 25 (24 September 1951): 489–90; Tananbaum, *The Bricker Amendment Controversy*, 36–37, 221–22; and State Department, "Treatment in the General Assembly of the Case of William N. Oatis," undated, in *FRUS 1951*, 2:806–10.

8. Civil Rights Congress, *We Charge Genocide: The Historic Petition to the United Nations for Relief from a Crime of the United States Government Against the Negro People* (New York: International Publishers, 1970), 195. See also Anderson, *Eyes off the Prize*, 166–86.

9. Anderson, *Eyes off the Prize*, 187. See also 186–205; Carol Anderson, "Bleached Souls and Red Negroes: The NAACP and Black Communists in the Early Cold War, 1948–1952," in *Window on Freedom: Race, Civil Rights, and Foreign Affairs, 1945–1988*, ed. Brenda Gayle Plummer (Chapel Hill: University of North Carolina Press, 2003), 93–107; and Eleanor Roosevelt, "Reply to Attacks on U.S. Attitudes Toward Human Rights Covenant," *U.S. Department of State Bulletin* 26 (14 January 1952): 59–61.

10. Assistant Secretary of State Jack McFall to Connally, 23 August 1951, Roosevelt Papers, box 4584, FDRL; State Department, "United States Program in the General Assembly," 15 August 1951, Office Files of the Assistant Secretary of State for United Nations Affairs, 1945–1954, lot file 58-D-33, box 2, NARA; State Department, "Position Paper Prepared in the Department of State for the United States Delegation to the Sixth Regular Session of the General Assembly of the United Nations," in *FRUS 1951*, 2:756; and Acheson to Austin, 2 October 1951, decimal file 340.1 AG/10-251 (1950–1954), box 1328, NARA. See also Sandifer to Roosevelt, 6 August 1951, decimal file 340.1 AG/8-651 (1950–1954), box 1327, NARA; and State Department, "Position Paper Prepared in the Department of State

for the United States Delegation to the Sixth Regular Session of the General Assembly of the United Nations," in *FRUS 1951*, 2:753–60.

11. Minutes of the meeting of the U.S. delegation to the United Nations, 13 November 1951, in *FRUS 1951*, 2:766, 767; Minutes of the meeting of the U.S. delegation to the United Nations, 12 November 1951, in *FRUS 1951*, 2:764; and "Statement by Mrs. Franklin D. Roosevelt," in *U.S. Department of State Bulletin* 25 (31 December 1951): 1065–66. See also General Assembly Third Committee, "Belgium, India, Lebanon, and the United States of America: Amendment to the Draft Resolution Proposed by Chile, Egypt, Pakistan, and Yugoslavia," 20 December 1951, A/C.3/L.185/Rev.1; Minutes of the meeting of the U.S. delegation to the United Nations, 12 November 1951, in *FRUS 1951*, 2:753–55; Minutes of the meeting of the U.S. delegation to the United Nations, 13 November 1951, in *FRUS 1951*, 765–67; Acheson to Austin, 2 October 1951, decimal file 340.1 AG/10-251 (1950–1954), box 1328, NARA; Asher, *The United Nations*, 681–82; and Austin to Acheson, 7 December 1951, in *FRUS 1951*, 2:769.

12. Third Committee, "Resolution on Self-Determination Submitted by Afghanistan, Burma, Egypt, Indonesia, Iran, Iraq, Lebanon, Pakistan, Philippines, Saudi Arabia, Syria, and Yemen," 8 December 1951, A/C.3/L.186; and Minutes of the meeting of the U.S. delegation, 10 December 1951, in *FRUS 1951*, 2:777. See also State Department, "Department of State Instruction to the United States Delegation to the Seventh Session of the Commission on Human Rights," April 1951, in *FRUS 1951*, 2:772–74. See also Third Committee, "Report of the Third Committee," 3 February 1952, A/2112; General Assembly Third Committee, "United States of America: Amendment to the Joint Draft Resolution Submitted by Afghanistan, Burma, Egypt, India, Indonesia, Iran, Iraq, Lebanon, Pakistan, Philippines, Saudi Arabia, Syria, and Yemen," 5 January 1952, A/C.3/L.204; Emblidge, *My Day*, 2:248–49; Green, *The United Nations*, 48–50; Asher, *The United Nations*, 688; Evans, *U.S. Hegemony*, 132–37; Minutes of the meeting of the U.S. delegation, 10 December 1951, in *FRUS 1951*, 2:776–80; and Austin to Acheson, 8 December 1951, in *FRUS 1951*, 775–76.

13. Byelorussian delegate Kusov quoted in Pratt, *Influence of Domestic Controversy*, 152; Roosevelt to Acheson, 7 February 1952, in *FRUS 1951*, 2:787; Third Committee, "Report of the Third Committee," 3 February 1952, A/2112; Assistant Secretary of State for Far Eastern Affairs John Allison to Hickerson, 6 February 1952, in *FRUS 1951*, 2:784; and General Assembly Resolution 545(VI), 5 February 1952. See also Green, *The United Nations*, 48–50; Roosevelt to Acheson, 26 January 1952, in *FRUS 1951*, 780–81; Minutes of the meeting of the U.S. delegation to the United Nations, 31 January 1952, in *FRUS 1951*, 781–83; Third Committee, "Report of the Third Committee," 3 February 1952, A/2112; Summary record of the General Assembly Plenary, 4 February 1952, A/PV.374; Pratt, *Influence of Domestic Controversy*, 152–53; Green, "Efforts to Deal with Violations," 688–89; and United Nations, *Yearbook, 1951*, 485–87. For an excellent summary of the debate, see U.N. Secretary-General, "The Right of Peoples to Self-Determination," 24 March 1952, E/CN.4/649.

14. Webb to Austin, 5 December 1951, in *FRUS 1951*, 2:846; Minutes of the meeting of the U.S. delegation, 12 December 1951, ibid., 2:851; and Acheson to Austin, 13 December 1951, ibid., 2:853. See also "Department of State Instruction to the U.S. Delegation to the Sixth Regular Session of the General Assembly: Treatment of Indians in the Union of South Africa," 20 September 1951, in *FRUS 1951*, 2:842–45; Minutes of the meeting of the U.S. delegation, 12 December 1951, ibid., 2:847–52; Acheson to Austin, 13 December 1951, ibid., 2:852–53; Roosevelt to Acheson, 20 December 1951, ibid., 2:855–56; Acheson to Aus-

tin, 14 December 1951, ibid., 2:855; and U.N. Ad Hoc Political Committee, "Treatment of People of Indian Origin in the Union of South Africa," 8 January 1952, A/2046.

15. Austin to Acheson, 4 December 1951, in *FRUS 1951*, 2:846; Minutes of the meeting of the U.S. delegation to the United Nations, 21 December 1951, ibid., 856–59; Philip C. Jessup, U.S. Delegate to the U.N. General Assembly to Acheson, 23 December 1951, ibid., 860; Acheson to Austin, 28 December 1951, ibid., 860–61; Roosevelt to Acheson, 2 January 1952, ibid., 861; Minutes of the meeting of the U.S. delegation to the United Nations, 5 January 1952, ibid., 862–63; U.S. Delegation to the United Nations, "U.S. Delegation Position Paper: Treatment of People of Indian Origin in the Union of South Africa: Report of the Ad Hoc Political Committee," 10 January 1952, ibid., 863–65; U.N. Ad Hoc Political Committee, "Treatment of People of Indian Origin in the Union of South Africa," 8 January 1952, A/2046; and Green, "Efforts to Deal with Violations," 780–83.

16. Roosevelt to Acheson, 22 January 1952, in *FRUS 1951*, 2:817; and Summary record of the Third Committee, 30 January 1952, A/C.3/SR.413. See also U.S. delegation member Chester Williams to Adrian Fisher, 15 January 1952, decimal file 700.07/1-1552 (1950–1954), box 3050, NARA; Green, "Efforts to Deal with Violations," 808–10; Acheson to Austin, 23 January 1952, in *FRUS 1951*, 2:818; Minutes of the meeting of the U.S. delegation to the United Nations, 25 January 1951, ibid., 818–20; and Summary record of the Third Committee, 31 January 1952, A/C.3/SR.413.

17. Bricker, "Revival of the Star Chamber," speech to the U.S. Senate, 18 September 1951, Bricker Papers, box 40, OHS; and Bricker, "The Meaning of Freedom," speech to the Silurians, 12 November 1951, Bricker Papers, box 90, OHS. See also Tananbaum, *The Bricker Amendment Controversy*, 41–42.

18. Eberhard Deutsch, member of the ABA's Peace and Law Committee, to Bricker, 13 October 1951, Bricker Papers, box 160, OHS; Tananbaum, *The Bricker Amendment Controversy*, 41; and Deutsch to Bricker, 9 November 1951, Bricker Papers, box 160, OHS. See also Alfred Schweppe, chairman of the Peace and Law Committee, to committee members, 24 and 26 October 1951, Schweppe to Judge Orie Phillips, 6 November 1951, Bricker Papers, box 160, OHS; Tananbaum, *The Bricker Amendment Controversy*, 37–42, 47–48; and William Fleming, "Danger to America: The Draft Covenant on Human Rights," *American Bar Association Journal* 37 (October and November 1951): 739–42, 794–99, 816–20, 855–60.

19. "56 Senators Urge Curb on Treaties," *New York Times*, 8 February 1952, 12.

20. Article 14 of the Covenant on Human Rights; Bricker form letter, February 1952, Bricker Papers, box 90, OHS; Bricker speech, 7 February 1952, in *Congressional Record*, 82nd Cong., 2nd sess., 98:912. See also John Bricker, "U.N. Blueprint for Tyranny," *The Freeman* 2 (28 January 1952): 265–68; Bricker form letter, February 1952, and transcript of "Report from Washington," radio program broadcast on 4 March 1952, Bricker Papers, box 90, OHS; Bricker speech, 7 February 1952, in *Congressional Record*, 82nd Cong., 2nd sess., 98:907–14; Pratt, *Influence of Domestic Controversy*, 191–94; Tananbaum, *The Bricker Amendment Controversy*, 42–44; Davies, *Defender of the Old Guard*, 145–47; and Kaufman, *Human Rights Treaties*, 103–4.

21. Quoted in Tananbaum, *The Bricker Amendment Controversy*, 45. See also Schweppe to Bricker, 5 March 1952, Bricker Papers, box 160, OHS; Tananbaum, *The Bricker Amendment Controversy*, 39–41, 45–47, 222; Committee on Peace and Law through United Nations, "Report of the Standing Committee on Peace and Law through United Nations," 1 February 1952, Official File 116-H-4, box 583, White House Central Files, DDEL; and

Holman, *Life and Career*, 523–24.

22. Kotschnig to Marvin Mohl, 7 May 1952, decimal file 340.1 AG/4-1852 (1950–1954), box 1328, NARA; McFall to Senator Blair Moody, 29 April 1952, Jack B. Tate Papers, box 1, HSTL; and Roosevelt, *My Day*, 14 April 1952, <http://www.gwu.edu/~erpapers/myday/displaydoc.cfm?_y=1952&_f=md002195> (accessed 22 October 2008). See also Eleanor Roosevelt speech to the Third Committee, 5 December 1951, in *U.S. Department of State Bulletin* 25 (31 December 1951): 1059, 1064–66.

23. John Cates, Jr., "Expanding Concept of Individual Liberties," *U.S. Department of State Bulletin* 25 (31 December 1951): 1058–64; and Roosevelt to Acheson, 16 May 1952, decimal file 340.1 AG/5-1652, box 1328, NARA. See also Hickerson to Fisher, 12 February 1952, office files of the Assistant Secretaries of State for U.N. Affairs, 1945–1954, lot file 58D 33, box 3, NARA; and Memo of conversation between Roosevelt, Whiteman, Gross, Simsarian, and other U.N. delegation members by advisor James Hyde, 15 May 1952, in *Foreign Relations of the United States, 1952–1954* (hereafter *FRUS 1952–1954*) (Washington, DC: U.S. Government Printing Office, 1979), 3:1537–39.

24. Hickerson to Roosevelt, 16 April 1952, Roosevelt Papers, box 3306, FDRL. See also United Nations, *Yearbook, 1952*, 439; ECOSOC, "Provisional Agenda for UNCHR," 11 February 1952, E/CN.4/642; and U.N. Secretary-General, "Draft International Covenant on Human Rights and Measures of Implementation," 14 March 1952, E/CN.4/643.

25. Eleanor Roosevelt, *My Day*, 24 April 1952, <http://www.gwu.edu/~erpapers/myday/displaydoc.cfm?_y=1952&_f=md002204> (accessed 22 October 2008). See also UNCHR, "Report of the Eighth Session of the Commission on Human Rights," 16 June 1952, E/2256.

26. UNCHR, "Union of Soviet Socialist Republics: Draft Resolution," 15 April 1952, E/CN.4/L.21; U.N. Secretary-General, "The Right of Peoples to Self-Determination," 24 March 1952, E/CN.4/649; Minutes of UNCHR, 15, 17, and 21 April 1952, E/CN.4/SR.254, 256, 257, and 260; "Soviet Rights Plan Loses," *New York Times*, 19 April 1952, 3; UNCHR, "Report of the Eighth Session of the Commission on Human Rights," 16 June 1952, E/2256; and Third Committee, "Recommendations Concerning International Respect for the Self-Determination of Peoples," 13 December 1952, A/2309.

27. UNCHR, "Chile: Amendment to the Draft Resolution Submitted by the Union of Soviet Socialist Republics," 19 April 1952, E/CN.4/L.24; Edward Jamison to Charles Burrows, both in the Division of Inter-American Affairs, 21 April 1952, decimal file 340.1 AG/4-2152 (1950–1954), box 1328, NARA; and Roosevelt, *My Day*, 24 April 1952, <http://www.gwu.edu/~erpapers/myday/displaydoc.cfm?_y=1952&_f=md002204> (accessed on 22 October 2008). See also UNCHR, "Report of the Eighth Session of the Commission on Human Rights," 16 June 1952, E/2256; Gross to Acheson, 22 April 1952, decimal file 340.1 AG/4-2252 (1950–1954), Acheson to Roosevelt, 23 April 1952, decimal file 340.1 AG/4-2252 (1950–1954), and Acheson to Roosevelt, 24 April 1952, decimal file 340.1 AG/4-2352, box 1328, NARA; "Commission on Human Rights," *U.S. Department of State Bulletin* 26 (28 April 1952): 683; United Nations, *Yearbook, 1952*, 439–40; Green, "Efforts to Deal with Violations," 754–55; UNCHR, "United States: Revised Draft Resolution," 23 April 1952, E/CN.4/L.32/Rev.1; UNCHR, "Resolution Adopted by the Commission on Human Rights," 24 April 1952, E/CN.4/665; and Third Committee, "Recommendations Concerning International Respect for the Self-Determination of Peoples," 13 December 1952, A/2309.

28. Article 2 of the Draft Covenant on Economic, Social, and Cultural Rights. See also "Report of the Eighth Session of the Commission on Human Rights," 16 June 1952,

E/2256; Minutes of UNCHR, 25, 28, 29, and 30 April 1952, E/CN.4/SR.268, E/CN.4/
SR.269, and E/CN.4/SR.271–75; Minutes of UNCHR, 5, 7, 8, 9, and 13 May 1952, E/CN.4/
SR.278–79, E/CN.4/SR.282, E/CN.4/SR.286–87, and E/CN.4/SR.292; UNCHR, "Text of
Article 1 of the Draft Covenant on Economic, Social, and Cultural Rights as Adopted by
the Commission," 30 April 1952, E/CN.4/SR.666; UNCHR, "Article___of the Draft Cov-
enant on Economic, Social, and Cultural Rights as Adopted by the Commission," 5 and 6
May 1952, E/CN.4/SR.666/Add.1 and 2; and "Eleanor Roosevelt Press Statement, 13 June
1952," *U.S. Department of State Bulletin* 26 (30 June 1952): 1024–28.

 29. Roosevelt, *My Day*, 29 May 1952, <http://www.gwu.edu/~erpapers/myday/
displaydoc.cfm?_y=1952&_f=md002234> (accessed 22 October 2008); and Roosevelt,
"Progress Toward Completion of Human Rights Covenant, 13 June 1952," *U.S. Department of State Bulletin* 26 (30 June 1952): 1026. See also Roosevelt press release, 6 June 1952,
Roosevelt Papers, box 4588, FDRL; "Report of the Eighth Session of the Commission on
Human Rights," 16 June 1952, E/2256; Minutes of UNCHR, 23 and 26 May 1952, E/CN.4/
SR.307–10; Minutes of UNCHR, 9 and 10 June 1952, E/CN.4/SR.327–29; Pratt, *Influence
of Domestic Controversy*, 142–43; "Rights 'Umbrella' Voted by U.N. Unit, *New York Times*,
1 May 1952, 10; "Job Article Adopted for U.N. Rights Pact," *New York Times*, 6 May 1952,
4; "Conditions for Work Defined by U.N. Unit," *New York Times*, 7 May 1952, 10; "Soviets
Lose in U.N. on Science 'Misuse,'" *New York Times*, 15 May 1952, 5; "U.N. Group Approves
Basic Rights Text," *New York Times*, 16 May 1952, 5; "'Right to Life' Added to Planned U.N.
Pact," *New York Times*, 28 May 1952, 9; "'Federal State' Issue Is Clarified at U.N.," *New York
Times*, 9 June 1952, 11; UNCHR, "United States: Revised Amendment to Article 28," 9
May 1952, E/CN.4/L.80/Rev.2; UNCHR, "United States: Amendment to Article 30," 2 May
1952, E/CN.4/L.81; "Commission on Human Rights," *U.S. Department of State Bulletin* 26
(19 May 1952): 798, (2 June 1952): 877–78, and (9 June 1952): 918; UNCHR, "Australia, In-
dia, and United States of America: Draft of Proposed Federal State Article," 6 June 1952, E/
CN.4/L.199; James Simsarian, "Progress Toward Completion of Human Rights Covenant,"
U.S. Department of State Bulletin 27 (7 July 1952): 20–31; and U.N. Secretary-General,
"Draft International Covenant on Human Rights and Measures of Implementation: The
Federal Clause," 17 March 1952, E/CN.4/651.

 30. Statement of Senator Bricker before a subcommittee of the Senate Judiciary
Committee, 21 May 1952, Bricker Papers, box 90, OHS. See Tananbaum, *The Bricker
Amendment Controversy*, 53–55; U.S. Congress, Senate, Committee on the Judiciary, Sub-
committee of the Committee on the Judiciary, *Treaties and Executive Agreements: Hearings
on S. J. Res. 130—Proposing an Amendment to the Constitution of the United States Relative
to the Making of Treaties and Executive Agreements*, 82nd Cong., 2nd sess., 21, 22, 27, 28
May and 9 June 1952; and Holman, *Dangers of Treaty Law*, 40–71. For an example, see
Californians for the Bricker Amendment, "Attention Americans!," Box 3, General Files,
GF 3-A-5, White House Central Files, DDEL. For lists of pro-Bricker groups, see John M.
McElroy to Miss Mary McGrory, 20 January 1954, Bricker Papers, box 110, OHS.

 31. Article VI of U.S. Constitution. See also John Bricker, "A Proposal to Amend the
Constitution of the United States," 17 February 1952, Bricker Papers, box 90, OHS; Otto
Schoenrich, Speech to the New York State Association Annual Meeting, 30 January 1953,
Bricker Papers, box 92, OHS; and Alfred A. Schweppe, "Treaties and Executive Agree-
ments," 1 December 1953, box 583, Official Files, OF 116-H-4, DDEL; American Bar As-
sociation, "Report of Standing Committee on Peace and Law Through United Nations," 1
February 1952; American Bar Association, "Report of Standing Committee on Peace and

Law Through United Nations," 1 September 1952; Bricker to Frank Holman, 15 January 1953, and Bricker to Ray Murphy, 11 February 1953, Bricker Papers, box 91, OHS.

For cases in which the Supreme Court declared the Constitution above all treaties, see *New Orleans v. United States*, 10 Pet. 662, 736; *The Cherokee Tobacco*, 11 Wall. 616, 620–21; *Holden v. Joy*, 17 Wall. 211, 243, *Geofroy v. Riggs*, 133 U.S. 258, 267.

32. Articles 13 and 14 of the Draft Covenant on Civil and Political Rights; United Nations, Economic and Social Council, Commission on Human Rights, *Report of the Ninth Session of the Commission on Human Rights*, 1953, 42; and Supplementary notes, legislative leadership meeting, 11 January 1954, box 1, Legislative Series, Ann Whitman File, DDEL. See also Katharine G. Reynolds and Frances B. Lucas, "National Defense," *Daughters of the American Revolution Magazine* 86 (December 1952): 1300; Holman to Bricker, 20 July 1951, Bricker Papers, box 160, OHS; Bricker speech to U.S. Senate, "Revival of the Star Chamber," 18 September 1951, Bricker Papers, box 40, OHS; Bricker speech to the Silurians, "The Meaning of Freedom," 12 November 1951, Bricker Papers, box 90, OHS; Bricker, "U.N.: Blueprint for Tyranny," *The Freeman* 2 (28 January 1952): 265–68; Bricker, "Revival of the Star Chamber," 18 September 1951, Bricker Papers, box 40, OHS; Holman, "Constitutional Amendment Only Effective Protection Against 'Treaty Law,'" reprinted from *The Spotlight*, in Maurice Thatcher to Bricker, 30 December 1952, Bricker Papers, box 91, OHS; Holman to Bricker, 19 March 1952, Bricker Papers, box 160, OHS; and Joseph Ballew, "Assault on American Sovereignty," *The Freeman* 2 (24 March 1952): 397–400.

33. Bricker to Holman, 15 January 1953, Bricker Papers, box 91, OHS. See also U.S. Chamber of Commerce, "Legislative Outlook," 7 July 1952, Bricker Papers, box 91, OHS; Holman, "Memorandum RE New York Committee for 'Preserving the Treaty Power,'" 31 December 1953, Bricker Papers, box 95, OHS; Transcript of *See It Now* with Edward R. Murrow, 12 January 1954, Bricker Papers, box 110, OHS; *Oyama v. U.S.*, 332 U.S. 633 (1948); and *Sei Fujii v. California*, 217 Pac. (2nd), 481; 218 Pac. (2nd) 595 (1950).

For Supreme Court cases that declared treaties could override all state laws, see *Ware v. Hylton*, 3 Dallas 199 (1796), *Fairfax's Devisee v. Hunter's Lessee*, 7 Cranch 603 (1813), *Hauenstein v. Lynham*, 100 U.S. 483 (1879), *Asakura v. Seattle*, 265 U.S. 332 (1924), and *Missouri v. Holland*, 252 U.S. 416 (1920).

34. Holman, *Life and Career*, 348; and American Bar Association, Standing Committee on Peace and Law through United Nations, "Report of the Standing Committee on Peace and Law Through United Nations," 1 February 1952, box 583, Official Files, OF 116-H-4, White House Central Files, DDEL; and *Missouri v. Holland*, 252 U.S. 416 (1920). To place the *Missouri* decision in historical context, see Kurk Dorsey, "Scientists, Citizens, and Statesmen," *Diplomatic History* 19 (Summer 1995): 407–29.

35. Subcommittee of the Committee on the Judiciary, *Treaties and Executive Agreements*, 1952, 174; and Assistant Secretary of State Jack McFall to Senator Blair Moody (R-MI), 29 April 1952, Tate Papers, box 2, HSTL. See also Tananbaum, *The Bricker Amendment Controversy*, 56–58.

36. Association of the Bar of the City of New York, Committee on Federal Legislation and Committee on International Law, "Report on the 'Joint Resolution Proposing an Amendment to the Constitution of the United States Relative to the Making of Treaties and Executive Agreements,'" 13 May 1952, Tate Papers, box 1, HSTL. See also Tananbaum, *The Bricker Amendment Controversy*, 58–60; and Subcommittee of the Committee on the Judiciary, *Treaties and Executive Agreements*, 1952.

37. Roosevelt to Acheson, 16 May 1952, decimal file 340.1 AG/5-1652 (1950–1954),

box 1328, NARA; Acheson to Roosevelt, 20 June 1952, decimal file 340.1 AG/5-1652 (1950–1954), box 1328, NARA; and Acheson speech to the National Citizens' Committee for United Nations Day, 26 September 1952, Acheson Papers, box 58, HSTL. See also Acheson to Roosevelt, 18 June 1952, decimal file 340.1 AG/5-1652 (1950–1954), box 1328, NARA; Roosevelt to David Dubinsky, president of the International Ladies' Garment Workers Union, 19 May 1952, Roosevelt Papers, box 4572, FDRL; and Speech by former U.S. delegate to the United Nations Porter McKeever to the U.N. Correspondent's Association, 11 June 1952, Roosevelt Papers, box 4585, FDRL.

38. John Foster Dulles, "Treaty Making and National Unity," speech to a regional meeting of the American Bar Association in Louisville, Kentucky, 11 April 1952, Tate Papers, box 1, HSTL. See also Statement by Clark Eichelberger to the Republican Party's Committee on Resolutions, 30 June 1952, Roosevelt Papers, box 4584, FDRL; and Tananbaum, *The Bricker Amendment Controversy*, 60–64.

39. Roosevelt speech to the Democratic National Convention, 23 July 1952, Roosevelt Papers, box 3056, FDRL; and 1952 Democratic Party Platform, <http://www.presidency.ucsb.edu/ws/index.php?pid=29600> (accessed 27 October 1952). See also Lash, *Eleanor*, 209–11; Kendrick, "The United States," 115–17; and Tananbaum, *The Bricker Amendment Controversy*, 60–64.

40. Holman, *Story of the "Bricker" Amendment*, 32; Zechariah Chafee, Jr., "Stop Being Terrified of Treaties: Stop Being Scared of the Constitution," *American Bar Association Journal* 38 (September 1952): 734; and Bricker, "Safeguarding the Treaty Power," *Federal Bar Review* 13 (December 1952): 80. See also Eberhard P. Deutsch, "The Need for a Treaty Amendment: A Restatement and a Reply," *American Bar Association Journal* 38 (September 1952): 735–38, 793–96; American Bar Association, Committee on Peace and Law through United Nations, "Report of the Standing Committee on Peace and Law Through United Nations," 1 September 1952, Official File 116-H-5, box 583, White House Central Files, DDEL; Holman, *State Department Half Truths*; and Katherine G. Reynolds and Frances B. Lucas, "Threats to Americanism," *Daughters of the American Revolution Magazine* 86 (December 1952): 1299–1304.

41. Eisenhower to Roosevelt, 30 December 1952, Roosevelt Papers, box 3283, FDRL; Roosevelt to Ann Gilmen, 17 November 1952, Mary Pillsbury Lord Papers, box 1, DDEL; Oral history of Durward Sandifer by Emily Williams, 27 April 1979, FDRL; Johnson, "Contributions of Eleanor and Franklin Roosevelt," 45–46; Deputy Undersecretary of State Carlisle Humelsine to Roosevelt, 18 November 1952, Roosevelt to Sandifer, 10 December 1952, Roosevelt to Eisenhower, 15 December 1952, and Roosevelt to Eisenhower, 31 December 1952, Roosevelt Papers, box 3283, FDRL; Hickerson memo, 17 November 1952, office files of the Assistant Secretary of State for U.N. Affairs, box 3, NARA; Roosevelt to Sandifer, 22 December 1952, Roosevelt Papers, box 3362, FDRL; and Lash, *Eleanor*, 214–19.

42. Holman to Bricker, 17 December 1952, Bricker Papers, box 91, OHS. See also Davies, *Defender of the Old Guard*, 155–56; Tananbaum, *The Bricker Amendment Controversy*, 66–69; Bricker to Dulles, 7 January 1953, and Dulles to Bricker, 12 January 1953, Bricker Papers, box 91, OHS; Dulles to Sherman Adams, 2 January 1953, and Adams to Special Assistant for Congressional Affairs Gerald Parsons, 5 January 1953, Official Files 116-H-2-A, box 582, White House Central Files, DDEL; Bricker press release, 8 January 1953, Bricker Papers, box 91, OHS; John Stevenson, aide to Dulles, to Holman, 5 January 1953, Bricker Papers, box 161, OHS; and Holman, *Life and Career*, 548, 550.

43. Eisenhower inaugural address, 20 January 1953, Speech Series, Whitman File, box 3, DDEL. See also Dulles to Consul General at Geneva, 6 April 1953, in *FRUS*

1952–1954, 1568; and Assistant White House Staff Secretary L. Arthur Minnich, notes, 20 February 1953, files of the Office of the White House Staff Secretary, Minnich Series, box 1, DDEL.

44. Hickerson to Dulles, 9 February 1953, in *FRUS 1952–1954*, 1544. See also Hickerson to Dulles, 12 February 1953, files of the Assistant Secretary of State for U.N. Affairs, lot file 58D 33, box 3, NARA.

45. Hickerson, "United States Policy Regarding Draft International Covenants on Human Rights," 17 February 1953, subject files of Sandifer, lot file 55D 429, box 8, NARA.

46. Sandifer to Hickerson, 9 February 1953, subject files of Sandifer, lot file 55D 429, box 8, NARA; Hickerson to State Department Legal Advisor Adrian Fisher, 12 February 1953, in *FRUS 1952–1954*, 1548; and Legal Advisor Herman Phlegar and Hickerson to Dulles, 18 February 1953, ibid., 1549–54.

47. Sandifer to Kotschnig, 19 February 1953, subject files of Sandifer, lot file 55D 429, box 8, NARA. See also Dulles memo, 20 February 1953, in *FRUS 1952–1954*, 1555.

48. Holman to Phlegar, 17 March 1953, decimal file 340.1 AG/3-1753 (1950–1954), box 1329, NARA; *Time Magazine* 61 (26 January 1953), 23. <http://time.com/time/magazine/article/0,9171,817759,00.html> (accessed 30 October 2008); Dulles to Adams, 10 January 1953, Whitman File, box 1, DDEL.

49. Bricker to Holman, 15 January 1953, Bricker Papers, box 91, OHS; Holman to Bricker, 12 and 16 January 1953, and Bricker to Holman, 15 January 1953, Bricker Papers, box 91, OHS; ABA Committee on Peace and Law through United Nations, "Report of the Committee on Peace and Law Through United Nations," 1 February 1953, Official File 116-H-4, White House Central Files, box 583, DDEL; Dulles to U.S. Mission to the United Nations, 20 February 1953, decimal file 340.1 AG/2-2053 (1950–1954), box 1329, NARA; U.S. Congress, Senate, Committee on the Judiciary, *Treaties and Executive Agreements, Hearings on S. J. Res. 1 and S. J. Res 43—Proposing an Amendment to the Constitution of the United States Relative to the Making of Treaties and Executive Agreements*, 83rd. Cong, 1st sess., 18, 19, 25 February, 4, 10, 19, 27, 31 March, and 6, 7, 8, 9, 10, 11 April 1953, 2–19, 33–171 (hereafter referred to as *Hearings, 1953*); and Tananbaum, *The Bricker Amendment Controversy*, 82–87.

50. *Hearings, 1953*, 853; Statement by Dulles before the Senate Judiciary Committee, 6 April 1953, box 6, DDE Diary Series, Whitman File, DDEL; and Emmet John Hughes, *The Ordeal of Power: A Political Memoir of the Eisenhower Years* (New York: Atheneum, 1963), 144. The right of Congress to revise treaties was affirmed by the Supreme Court in *The Cherokee Tobacco*, 11 Wallace 616 (1870) and *The Head Money Cases*, 112 U.S. 584 (1884). See Dulles to Eisenhower, 2 March 1953, and "Outline of Presentation of Views by the Attorney General on S.J. Res. 1 and S.J. Res. 43," 12 March 1953, Official Files 116-H-2-A, White House Central Files, box 582, DDEL; Eisenhower to Edgar Eisenhower, 2 January 1954, box 5, DDE Diary Series, Whitman File, DDEL; and Dulles to President Eisenhower, 2 March 1953, box 582, Official Files OF-H-4, White House Central Files, DDEL; and Tananbaum, *The Bricker Amendment Controversy*, 87–90.

51. Dulles press release, 6 April 1953, Eisenhower Diary Series, Whitman File, box 6, DDEL.

52. Dulles press release, 6 April 1953, Eisenhower Diary Series, Whitman File, box 6, DDEL; Eisenhower press release, 7 April 1953, Dulles Papers, Subject Series, box 2, DDEL; and Lord statement to UNCHR, 8 April 1953, in *FRUS 1952–1954*, 1571, 1572. See also Phlegar and Hickerson to Dulles, 26 March 1953, decimal file 340.1 AG/3-2653

(1950–1954), and Dulles to Lord, 3 April 1953, decimal file 340.1 AG/4-353 (1950–1954), box 1329, NARA; Lord to Dulles, 30 March 1953, in *FRUS 1952–1954*, 1562–63; Hickerson to Phlegar, 26 March 1953, ibid., 1556–58; Phlegar and Hickerson to Dulles, 2 April 1953, ibid., 1563–64; Dulles to Lord, 3 April 1953, ibid., 1564–67; Dulles to Lord, 6 April 1953, ibid., 1568; Dulles to Eisenhower, 7 April 1953, ibid., 1569–71; and UNCHR summary record, 8 April 1953, E/CN.4/SR.340.

53. Lord to Dulles, 28 April 1953, decimal file 340.1 AG/4-2853 (1950–1954), box 1329, NARA; and Lord to Dulles, 30 April 1953, decimal file 340.1 AG/4-3053 (1950–1954), box 1329, NARA. See also Lord to Dulles, 30 March 1953, in *FRUS 1952–1954*, 1562–63; Dulles to American embassies in Britain, Belgium, Sweden, and France, 6 April 1953, in *FRUS 1952–1954*, 1567; Humphrey, *Human Rights*, 176.

54. Lord to Dulles, 28 April 1953, decimal file 340.1 AG/4-2853 (1950–1954), box 1329, NARA; and Lord to Dulles, 30 May 1953, in *FRUS 1952–1954*, 1579. See also Humphrey, *Human Rights*, 177; Lord to Dulles, 30 May 1953, in *FRUS 1952–1954*,1577–80; UNCHR summary record, 8 and 9 April 1953, E/CN.4/SR.340 and 41; Lord to State Department, 8 and 30 April and 9 May 1953, decimal file 340.1 AG/4-1153, 340.1 AG/4-3053, and 340.1 AG/5-953 (1950–1954), box 1329, NARA; UNCHR, "Report of the Ninth Session of the Commission on Human Rights," 2 June 1953, E/2256; U.S. Consul General in Geneva to Department of State, 8 April 1953, in *FRUS 1952–1954*, 1574; Lord to Department of State, 28 April 1953, in *FRUS 1952–1954*, 1575–77; and Dulles to Lord, 21 April 1953, decimal file 340.1 AG/4-2053 (1950–1954), box 1329, NARA.

55. Lord to Dulles, 28 April 1953, decimal file 340.1 AG/4-2853 (1950–1954), box 1329, NARA; Roosevelt to Sandifer, 20 March and 16 May 1953, Roosevelt Papers, box 3479, FDRL; and Roosevelt to Lord, 4 April 1953, Lord Papers, box 1, DDEL. See also Lord to Dulles, 11 April 1953, decimal file 340.1 AG/4-1153, and Roosevelt to Dulles, 20 March 1953, decimal file 340.1 AG/3-2053 (1950–1954), box 1329, NARA; Lord to Dulles, 30 April 1953, decimal file 340.1 AG/4-3053 (1950–1954), box 1329, NARA; Sandifer to Roosevelt, 18 March 1953, Roosevelt Papers, box 3479, FDRL; Lash, *Eleanor*, 221–22; and Oral history of Mary Pillsbury Lord by John T. Mason, Jr., 6 June 1967, DDEL.

56. U.S. Congress, Senate, Committee on the Judiciary, *Constitutional Amendment Relative to Treaties and Executive Agreements*, S. Report 412, 83rd Cong., 1st sess., 15 June 1953, 34 and 53. See also Tananbaum, *The Bricker Amendment Controversy*, 91–92; and Green, "Efforts to Deal with Violations," 713–16.

57. Kenneth Osgood, *Total Cold War: Eisenhower's Secret Propaganda Battle at Home and Abroad* (Lawrence: University Press of Kansas, 2006), 33. For a history of U.S. psychological warfare programs since World War II, see "Organizational Developments and Delineation of Psychological Warfare Responsibilities Since WWII," undated, Psychological Strategy Board (PSB) Files, box 22, HSTL; Undersecretary of State James Webb, "Report to the National Security Council on a Plan for Psychological Warfare," 10 July 1950, NSC-74, National Security Council Files, President's Secretary's Files, box 210, HSTL; Bureau of the Budget, "The Psychological Strategy Board: Selected Aspects of Its Concept, Organization, and Operations," 21 April 1952, Confidential Files, White House Central Files, box 31, HSTL; and Edward P. Lilly, "The Psychological Strategy Board and Its Predecessors, 1938–1953," in *Studies in Modern History*, ed. Gaetano L. Vincitorio (New York: St. John's University Press, 1968), 337–82.

58. Quoted in Osgood, *Total Cold War*, 41. See also Truman directive to establish the PSB, 4 April 1951, Confidential Files, White House Central Files, box 31, HSTL; and

Bureau of the Budget, "The Psychological Strategy Board: Selected Aspects of Its Concept, Organization, and Operations," 21 April 1952, Confidential Files, White House Central Files, box 31, HSTL.

59. Director of Information for the U.S. Mission to the United Nations Porter McKeever to PSB Director Gordon Gray, 3 August 1951, PSB Files, box 26, HSTL; and McKeever to PSB, 9 August 1951, PSB Files, box 26, HSTL. See also Acting Deputy Assistant Director of the PSB Office of Co-ordination Charles Norberg to McNair of the PSB Office of Evaluation and Review, 8 April 1953, White House Office, National Security Council (NSC) Staff: Papers, 1948–1961, PSB Central Files, box 23, DDEL.

60. PSB Assistant Director for Evaluation and Review Horace Craig to George Morgan of the PSB staff, 30 April 1953, White House Office, NSC Staff: Papers, 1948–1961, PSB Central Files, box 23, DDEL; and Craig memo of conversation with Lodge, Jackson, and others, 4 May 1953, White House Office, National Security Council (NSC) Staff: Papers, 1948–1961, PSB Central Files, box 23, DDEL. See also Minutes of PSB staff meetings, 1, 8, and 9 April 1953, Norberg to McNair, 8 April 1953, Norberg, "Program for Psychological Support for Ambassador Lodge during the 8th Session of the UN General Assembly," 10 April 1953, Morgan to Frank Wisner of the CIA, 3 June 1953, and Mallory Browne of the PSB to Horace Craig, 30 April 1953, White House Office, National Security Council (NSC) Staff: Papers, 1948–1961, PSB Central Files, box 23, DDEL; and Caroline Pruden, *Conditional Partners: Eisenhower, the United Nations, and the Search for a Permanent Peace* (Baton Rouge: Louisiana State University Press, 1998), 76–77. For information on Lodge's U.N. activities, see H. W. Brands, *Cold Warriors: Eisenhower's Generation and American Foreign Policy* (New York: Columbia University Press, 1988), 163–81. Brands also includes a chapter on C. D. Jackson. See 117–37.

61. Wallace Irwin, PSB Office of Evaluation and Review, memo of conversation with Lodge and Craig, 18 May 1953, Lilly to Craig and Irwin, 21 May 1953, Minutes of the PSB Committee on 8th General Assembly, 19 June 1953, and Arthur Cox of the PSB to Browne, 2 June 1953, White House Office, NSC Staff: Papers, 1948–1961, PSB Central Files, box 23, DDEL. See also Norberg to Acting Assistant Director for PSB's Office of Co-ordination Mallory Browne, 9 March 1953, Browne to Craig, 30 April 1953, Craig memo of conversation with Lodge, Jackson, and others, 4 May 1953, Albert Toner (PSB staff) summary of 31 July PSB meeting, 4 August 1953, and Lilly to Morgan, 31 July 1953, White House Office, NSC Staff: Papers, 1948–1961, PSB Central Files, box 23, DDEL; Arthur Cox of PSB staff to Browne, 2 and 3 June 1953, Jackson to Lodge, 21 April 1953, Memo of conversation between Herbert Fierst and Richard Sneider of the Bureau of U.N. Affairs and Wallace Irwin of the PSB, 14 May 1953, White House Office, NSC Staff: Papers, 1948–1961, PSB Central Files, box 23, DDEL; PSB, "Human Rights Project: Suggested Topics for Intelligence Development," 19 May 1953, Lilly to Craig and Irwin, 21 May 1953, Norberg to Irwin, 1 June 1953, and Irwin, "Human Rights: Consultation with Ambassador Lodge and USUN Staff," 22 May 1953, White House Office, NSC Staff: Papers, 1948–1961, PSB Central Files, box 23, DDEL; and Memo of conversation between Hickerson, Craig, and Irwin, 12 May 1953, C. D. Jackson Papers, box 4, DDEL.

62. PSB, "Exploitation of Soviet, Satellite, and Chinese Communist Psychological Vulnerabilities Before and During the Eighth U.N. General Assembly," 28 May 1953, White House Office, NSC Staff: Papers, 1948–1961, Operations Co-ordination Board (OCB) Secretariat Series, box 4, DDEL; Irwin to Morgan, 29 May 1953, Minutes of the PSB, 3 June 1953, and Toner to John Ross of the American Mission to the UN, 5 and 8 June 1953, White

House Office, NSC Staff: Papers, 1948–1961, PSB Central Files, box 23, DDEL; Minutes of the PSB Committee on the 8th General Assembly, 17 and 26 June 1953, and PSB, "List of Documents Sent to USUN, N.Y. from PSB," 23 June 1953, White House Office, NSC Staff: Papers, 1948–1961, PSB Central Files, box 23, DDEL; and Irwin, "Human Rights Working Group," 16 June 1953, White House Office, NSC Staff: Papers, 1948–1961, PSB Central Files, box 22, DDEL; Irwin to Charles Allen of the Bureau for U.N. Affairs, 16 and 17 July 1953, and Minutes of first meeting of the PSB Committee on 8th General Assembly, 17 June 1953, White House Office, NSC Staff: Papers, 1948–1961, PSB Central Files, box 23, DDEL; and Pruden, *Conditional Partners*, 75.

63. Lilly to Irwin, 14 July 1953, White House Office, NSC Staff: Papers, 1948–1961, box 4, DDEL; and Irwin to H. S. Craig of the PSB, 22 July 1953, White House Office, NSC Staff: Papers, 1948–1961, PSB Central Files, box 23, DDEL.

64. Minutes of the PSB Committee on 8th General Assembly, 26 June 1953, White House Office, NSC Staff: Papers, 1948–1961, box 23, DDEL. See also Pruden, *Conditional Partners*, 70–74.

65. Irwin to Craig and Jackson, 22 July 1953, White House Office, NSC Staff: Papers, 1948–1961, PSB Central Files, box 23, DDEL; and Osgood, *Total Cold War*, 45. See also Irwin to Craig, 19 August 1953, and Philip Corso to Craig, 21 October 1953, Jackson Papers, box 4, DDEL; Charles Taquey, PSB Office of Evaluation and Review, to Irwin, 14 July 1953, Irwin to Morgan and Jackson, 30 July 1953, and Minutes of the PSB Committee on the 8th General Assembly, 11 August 1953, White House Office, NSC Staff: Papers, 1948–1961, box 23, DDEL; Osgood, *Total Cold War*, 85–87; and Pruden, *Conditional Partners*, 80–82.

66. Eisenhower to Senator William Knowland, 25 January 1954, box 6, DDE Diary Series, Whitman File, DDEL; and Eisenhower diary entry, 24 July 1953, in *The Eisenhower Diaries*, ed. Robert Ferrell (New York: W. W. Norton, 1981), 248; and Eisenhower quoted in Tananbaum, *The Bricker Amendment Controversy*, 109.

Conclusion

1. Quoted in Lauren, *Evolution of International Human Rights*, vii.

2. Franklin and Eleanor Roosevelt Institute, "The Annual Message to Congress," 6 January 1941, <http://www.feri.org/common/news/details.cfm?QID=2089&clientid=11005> (accessed 8 November 2008); and "President Roosevelt's Message to Congress on the State of the Union," *New York Times*, 7 January 1941, 4.

3. Michael Hunt, *Ideology and U.S. Foreign Policy* (New Haven: Yale University Press, 1987); John Dower, *War Without Mercy: Race and Power in the Pacific War* (New York: Pantheon Books, 1986); and Stephanson, *Manifest Destiny*.

4. Quoted in Tananbaum, *The Bricker Amendment Controversy*, 151; and Holman, *Story of the "Bricker" Amendment*, 100–101. See also Tananbaum, *The Bricker Amendment Controversy*, 95–219; Davies, *Defender of the Old Guard*, 162–83; and Cathal J. Nolan, "The Last Hurrah of Conservative Isolationism: Eisenhower, Congress, and the Bricker Amendment," *Presidential Studies Quarterly* 22 (Spring 1992): 337–49.

5. Robert Bolton, American Ambassador to the United Nations, to U.N. Secretary General Kofi Annan, 6 May 2002, <http://www.state.gov/r/pa/prs/ps/2002/9968.htm> (accessed on 11 November 2008); and Statement by State Department spokesperson Richard Boucher on the International Criminal Court, 1 July 2002, <http://www.state.gov/r/pa/rmo/hglt/02/11603.htm> (accessed 11 November 2008). See also Natalie Hevener

Kaufman and David Whiteman, "Opposition to Human Rights Treaties in the United States Senate: The Legacy of the Bricker Amendment," *Human Rights Quarterly* 10 (1988): 309–37; and Louis Henkin, "U.S. Ratification of Human Rights Conventions: The Ghost of Senator Bricker," *American Journal of International Law* 89 (April 1995): 341–50.

6. William Schabas, *The Abolition of the Death Penalty in International Law* (Cambridge: Cambridge University Press, 1997), 81–90; and Amnesty International, *United States of America: Rights for All* (New York: Amnesty International, 1988).

7. Tom Curry, "A Flap Over Foreign Matter at the Supreme Court," *MSNBC News*, 11 March 2004, <http://www.msnbc.msn.com/id/4506232/> (accessed 12 November 2008).

8. Hurst Hannum and Dana D. Fischer, eds., *U.S. Ratification of the International Covenants on Human Rights* (Irvington-on-Hudson, NY: Transnational Publications, 1993); Mower, *The United States*; Scott Davidson, *The Inter-American Human Rights System* (Aldershot, England: Dartmouth, 1997); Evans, *U.S. Hegemony*; and United Nations, *United Nations Action*.

9. U.N. Security Council, Resolution 1674, 28 April 2006, <http://www.un.org/News/Press/docs/2006/sc8710.doc.html> (accessed 11 November 2008).

10. Ray Suarez, "Surprise U.N. Pick," *PBS Newshour*, 8 March 2005, <http://www.pbs.org/newshour/bb/fedagencies/jan-june05/bolton_3–8.html> (accessed 12 November 2008); and Jonathan Turley, "10 Reasons Why the U.S. Is No Longer the Land of the Free," *Washington Post*, 13 January 2012, <http://articles.washingtonpost.com/2012-01-13/opinions/35440628_1_individual-rights-indefinite-detention-citizens> (accessed 3 May 2013).

Bibliography

Primary Sources

Private Manuscript Collections

Dwight D. Eisenhower Library, Abilene, Kansas
    Sherman Adams Papers
    Herbert Brownell, Jr., Papers
    John Foster Dulles Papers
        Chronological Series
        Subject Series
        Telephone Call Series
    Dwight D. Eisenhower Papers
        Collection of Miscellaneous Manuscripts
        Personal Diary
        Presidential Papers (Ann Whitman File)
        Records of Daily Appointments
        White House Central Files
    James C. Hagerty Papers
    John W. Hanes, Jr., Papers
    C. D. Jackson Papers
    Henry C. Lodge Papers
    Mary Pillsbury Lord Papers
    Jack I. Martin Papers
    Records of the White House Cabinet Secretariat
    Records of the White House Office of the Staff Secretary
    Samuel C. Waugh Papers

Franklin D. Roosevelt Library, Hyde Park, New York
    Adolf Berle Papers
    Harry Hopkins Papers
    Eleanor Roosevelt Papers
    Franklin Roosevelt Papers
        Official Files
        President's Secretary's Files
    Henry Wallace Papers

Harry S. Truman Library, Independence, Missouri
  Dean Acheson Papers
  Tom C. Clark Papers
  Clark Clifford Papers
  James P. Hendrick Papers
  Robert A. Lovett Papers
  Philleo Nash Papers
  David K. Niles Papers
  President's Committee on Civil Rights Papers
  Psychological Strategy Board Files
  Henry Reiff Papers
  Samuel Rosenman Papers
  Edward R. Stettinius, Jr., Papers
  Jack B. Tate Papers
  Harry S. Truman Papers
    Confidential File
    Official File
    President's Secretary's Files
    White House Central Files
  James E. Webb Papers

Ohio Historical Society, Columbus, Ohio
  John W. Bricker Papers

Oral Histories

Donald C. Blaisdell, Truman Library
John W. Bricker, Eisenhower Library
Herbert Brownell, Eisenhower Library
Tom C. Clark, Truman Library
Dwight D. Eisenhower, Eisenhower Library
John D. Hickerson, Truman Library
Mary Pillsbury Lord, Eisenhower Library
Robert A. Lovett, Truman Library
John Maktos, Truman Library
Clarence Manion, Eisenhower Library
Porter McKeever, Roosevelt Library
Robert D. Murphy, Eisenhower Library
William Sanders, Truman Library
Durward Sandifer, Roosevelt Library
Durward V. Sandifer, Truman Library
James J. Wadsworth, Eisenhower Library
David W. Wainhouse, Eisenhower Library

Government Archives

National Archives of the United States, College Park, Maryland

Record Group 43, Records of International Conferences, Commissions, and Expositions
Record Group 59, General Records of the Department of State Decimal Files
    Harley A. Notter Papers
    Records of the Office of United Nations Affairs
    Subject Files of Durward Sandifer (lot file 55D 429)
    Subject Files of the Office of Special Political Affairs
Record Group 353, Records of Interdepartmental and Intradepartmental Committees
    Interdepartmental Committee on International Social Policy

United Nations and U.S. Government Documents

President's Committee on Civil Rights. *To Secure These Rights.* New York: Simon and Schuster, 1947.

United Nations. *Journal of the Economic and Social Council.*

———. *United Nations Action in the Field of Human Rights.* New York: United Nations, 1983.

———. *Who's Who: Delegates to the United Nations Conference on International Organization.* New York: U.N. Information Office, 1945.

———. *Yearbook of the United Nations.* 1947–1953.

United Nations, Economic and Social Council, Commission on Human Rights. *Report of the Ninth Session of the Commission on Human Rights,* 1953.

United Nations Preparatory Commission. *Report by the Executive Committee to the Preparatory Commission of the United Nations.* London: United Nations, 1945.

———. *Report of the Preparatory Commission to the United Nations.* New York: United Nations, 1946.

U.S. Congress. *Congressional Record,* 1944–1953.

U.S. Congress, Senate, Committee on Foreign Relations. *Confidential Committee Print No. 3. International Convention on the Prevention and Punishment of the Crime of Genocide, May 1950.* Executive Sessions. (Historical Series) 81st Cong., 1st and 2nd sess., 1949–1950. Made public July 1976.

———. *Executive Sessions of the Senate Foreign Relations Committee* (Historical Series) 2. 81st Cong., 1st and 2nd sess., 1949–1950. Made public August 1976.

———. *Executive Sessions of the Senate Foreign Relations Committee* (Historical Series) 3. 82nd Cong., 1st sess., 1951. Made public August 1976.

———. *Executive Sessions of the Senate Foreign Relations Committee* (Historical Series) 4. 82nd Cong., 2nd sess., 1952. Made public October 1976.

———. *Hearings Before the Senate Foreign Relations Committee on the United Nations Charter.* 79th Cong., 1st sess., 1945.

U.S. Congress, Senate, Subcommittee of the Committee on Foreign Relations. *The Genocide Convention: Hearings on the International Convention on the Prevention and Punishment of the Crime of Genocide.* 81st Cong., 2nd sess., 23, 24, 25 January and 9 February, 1950.

———. *Report on the International Convention on the Prevention and Punishment of the Crime of Genocide,* 81st Cong., 2nd sess., 1950.

U.S. Congress, Senate, Subcommittee of the Committee of the Judiciary. *Treaties and Executive Agreements: Hearings on S.J. Res. 1 and S.J. Res. 43—Proposing an Amendment to the Constitution of the United States Relative to the Making of Treaties and Executive*

Agreements. 83rd Cong., 1st sess., 18, 19, 25 February, 4, 10, 16, 27, 31 March, and 6, 7, 8, 9, 10, 11 April, 1953.

———. *Treaties and Executive Agreements: Hearings on S.J. Res. 130—Proposing an Amendment to the Constitution of the United States Relative to the Making of Treaties and Executive Agreements.* 82nd Cong., 2nd sess., 21, 22, 27, 28 May and 9 June, 1952.

United States. *Public Papers of the Presidents of the United States.* Vol. 5, *Harry S. Truman.* Washington, DC: U.S. Government Printing Office, 1964.

United States. Delegation to the General Assembly of the United Nations. *Report of the United States Delegation to the First Part of the First Session of the General Assembly of the United Nations.* Washington, DC: U.S. Government Printing Office, 1946.

U.S. Department of State. *Charter of the United Nations, Report to the President on the Results of the San Francisco Conference by the Chairman of the United States Delegation, the Secretary of State,* 26 June 1945. Conference Series 71, no. 2349.

———. *Foreign Relations of the United States, 1941.* Vol. 1. Washington, DC: U.S. Government Printing Office, 1958.

———. *Foreign Relations of the United States, 1942.* Vol. 1. Washington, DC: U.S. Government Printing Office, 1960.

———. *Foreign Relations of the United States, 1944.* Vol. 1. Washington, DC: U.S. Government Printing Office, 1966.

———. *Foreign Relations of the United States, 1945.* Vols. 1 and 9. Washington, DC: U.S. Government Printing Office, 1969.

———. *Foreign Relations of the United States, 1948.* Vol. 1. Washington, DC: U.S. Government Printing Office, 1975.

———. *Foreign Relations of the United States, 1949.* Vol. 5. Washington, DC: U.S. Government Printing Office, 1976.

———. *Foreign Relations of the United States, 1950.* Vol. 4. Washington, DC: U.S. Government Printing Office, 1980.

———. *Foreign Relations of the United States, 1951.* Vol. 2. Washington, DC: U.S. Government Printing Office, 1979.

———. *Foreign Relations of the United States, 1952–1954.* Vol. 3. Washington, DC: U.S. Government Printing Office, 1979.

———. *Foreign Relations of the United States: Conferences at Washington, 1941–1942, and Casablanca, 1943.* Washington, DC: U.S. Government Printing Office, 1968.

———. *Guide to the United States and the United Nations, United States–United Nations Information Series.* Washington, DC: U.S. Government Printing Office, 1947.

———. *Human Rights: Unfolding of the American Tradition.* Washington, DC: Office of Public Affairs, 1949.

———. "International Bill of Rights." *Foreign Affairs Outlines* 4 (Spring 1945): 3–4.

———. *Message from the President of the United States, Transmitting a Certified Copy of the Convention on the Prevention and Punishment of the Crime of Genocide.* 16 June 1949.

———. *Organizing the United Nations.* Washington, DC: U.S. Government Printing Office, 1946.

———. *Report of the Delegation of the United States of America to the Inter-American Conference on Problems of War and Peace.* Washington, DC: U.S. Government Printing Office, 1946.

———. *The United Nations Conference on International Organization: Selected Documents.* Washington, DC: U.S. Government Printing Office, 1946.

———. *The United States and the United Nations.* Washington, DC: U.S. Government Printing Office, 1946.

———. *The United States and the United Nations: Report by the President to the Congress.* Washington, DC: U.S. Government Printing Office, 1946–1948.

———. *The United States and the United Nations: Report of the United States Delegation to the First Part of the First Session of the General Assembly of the United Nations.* Washington, DC: U.S. Government Printing Office, 1946.

———. *United States Participation in the United Nations.* Washington, DC: U.S. Department of State, 1949.

U.S. Library of Congress. *Human Rights in the International Community and in U.S. Foreign Policy, 1945–1976.* Washington, DC: U.S. Government Printing Office, 1977.

U.S. President's Committee on Civil Rights. *To Secure These Rights.* Washington, DC: U.S. Government Printing Office, 1947.

U.S. Supreme Court and Lesser Court Documents

American Association for the United Nations. *Brief for the American Association for the United Nations as Amicus Curiae in Shelley v. Kramer, et al.*, 1947.

———. *Motion for Leave to File Brief for the United Nations as Amicus Curiae in Shelley v. Kramer, et al.*, 1947.

American Civil Liberties Union. *Brief of the American Civil Liberties Union, Amicus Curiae, in Shelley v. Kramer*, 1947.

———. *Brief of the American Civil Liberties Union as Amicus Curiae on Petition for a Writ of Certiorari to the Supreme Court of the State of California, Fred Y. Oyama and Kajiro Oyama, Petitioners, in the Supreme Court of the United States*, 1946.

———. *Brief of American Civil Liberties Union as Amicus Curiae on Writ of Certiorari to the Supreme Court of the State of California, Fred Y. Oyama and Kajiro Oyama, Petitioners, in the Supreme Court of the United States*, 1947.

Clark, Tom C., and Philip B. Perlman. *Brief for the United States as Amicus Curiae in Shelley v. Kramer, et al.*, 1947.

McGrath, J. Howard, and Philip B. Perlman. *Brief of the United States as Amicus Curiae on a Writ of Certiorari to the Supreme Court of the United States, Elmer Henderson, Petitioner*, October 1949.

National Association of Real Estate Boards. *Brief Amicus Curiae on Behalf of the National Association of Real Estate Boards in Shelley v. Kramer, et al.*, 1947.

Perlman, Philip B., and Philip Elman. *Brief of the United States as Amicus Curiae on a Writ of Certiorari to the Supreme Court of the United States, George W. McLaurin, Petitioner*, February 1950.

Wirin, A. L., Charles Horsky, and Ernest W. Jennes. *Brief for Petitioners on Writ of Certiorari to the Supreme Court of California, Fred Oyama and Kajiro Oyama, Petitioners, in the Supreme Court of the United States*, 1947.

U.S. Supreme Court and Lesser Court Cases

Abrams v. U.S., 250 U.S. 616.

Asakura v. Seattle, 265 U.S. 332.

Bolling v. Sharpe, 347 U.S. 497.

Joseph Burstyn, Inc. v. Wilson, 343 U.S. 495.
Cameron Septic Tank Co. v. Knoxville, 227 U.S. 39.
Chaplinsky v. New Hampshire, 315 U.S. 568.
The Cherokee Tobacco, 11 Wall. 616.
Dred Scott v. Sanford, 19 Howard 393.
Ex Parte Quirin, 317 U.S. 1.
Fairfax's Devisee v. Hunter's Lessee, 7 Cranch 603.
Foster & Elam v. Neilson, 2 Pet. 253.
Fox v. Washington, 236 U.S. 273.
Frohwerk v. United States, 249 U.S. 204.
Geofroy v. Riggs, 133 U.S. 258.
Giboney v. Empire Storage Co., 336 U.S. 490.
Hauenstein v. Lynham, 100 U.S. 483.
Henderson v. United States, 339 U.S. 816.
Holden v. Joy, 17 Wall. 211.
Missouri v. Holland, 252 U.S. 416.
Namba v. McCourt, 204 P.2nd 569 (Oregon).
New Orleans v. United States, 10 Pet. 662.
Over the Top, 5 F.2nd 838 (Connecticut).
Oyama v. California, 332 U.S. 633.
Perkins v. Elg, 307 U.S. 325.
Rice v. Sioux City Memorial Cemetery, Inc., 349 U.S. 70.
Schenck v. United States, 249 U.S. 52.
Shelley v. Kramer, 334 U.S. 1.
Sweatt v. Painter, 339 U.S. 629.
Takahashi v. Fish and Game Commission, 334 U.S. 410.
Terminiello v. Chicago, 337 U.S. 1.
United States ex rel. Jaegelar v. Carusi, 342 U.S. 347.
United States v. Arjona, 120 U.S. 479.
United States v. Curtiss-Wright Corp., 299 U.S. 304.
United States v. Ferreira, 54 U.S. 40.
United States v. Hudson, 11 U.S. 31.
United States v. Smith, 5 Wheat. 157.
Ware v. Hylton, 3 Dallas 199.
Zorach v. Clauson, 343 U.S. 306.

Articles and Books

Acheson, Dean. *Present at the Creation: My Years in the State Department*. New York: Norton, 1969.
American Law Institute. *Annual Report of William Draper Lewis, Director*. New York: American Law Institute, 1943.
Annan, Kofi. "In Larger Freedom: Report of the Secretary-General," A/59/2005, 21 March 2005.
Backus, Dana C. "Preserve Treaty Making Powers." *Foreign Policy Bulletin* 32 (15 May 1953): 4, 6.
Baldwin, Roger. *Human Rights: World Declaration and American Practice*. New York: Public Affairs Committee of the ACLU, 1950.

Ballew, Joseph H. "Assault on American Sovereignty." *The Freeman* 2 (24 March 1952): 397–400.

Barley, Mary F. "Do Americans Want the Genocide Convention Ratified?" *Daughters of the American Revolution Magazine* 85 (April 1951): 289–90.

Bigman, Stanley K. "The 'New Internationalism' Under Attack." *Public Opinion Quarterly* 14 (Summer 1950): 235–61.

Borchard, Edwin. "Historical Background of International Protection of Human Rights." *Annals of the American Academy of Political and Social Science* 243 (January 1946): 112–17.

"Bricker Amendment Treaty Debate." *Congressional Quarterly Almanac* 10 (1954): 254–62.

Bricker, John W. "The Application of Constitutional Restraints to the Treaty-Making Power." *Daughters of the American Revolution Magazine* 88 (March 1954): 233–34, 264.

———. "Making Treaties and Other International Agreements." *Annals of the American Academy* 289 (September 1953): 134–44.

———. "Safeguarding the Treaty Power." *Federal Bar Journal* 13 (December 1952): 77–98.

———. "UN Blueprint for Tyranny." *The Freeman* 2 (28 January 1952): 265–68.

Bricker, John W., and Charles H. Webb. "The Bricker Amendment: Treaty Law vs. Domestic Constitutional Law." *Notre Dame Lawyer* 29 (August 1954): 529–50.

Brown, Ben, Jr. "Congress and the Department of State." *Annals of the American Academy* 289 (September 1953): 100–107.

Carlston, Kenneth S. "The Genocide Convention: A Problem for the American Lawyer." *American Bar Association Journal* 36 (March 1950): 206–9.

Carroll, Mitchell B. "Further Action on the United Nations Charter." *American Bar Association Journal* 31 (September 1945): 457–58.

———. "State Department and the Bar Discuss World Organization." *American Bar Association Journal* 31 (March 1945): 124–25.

Chafee, Zechariah, Jr. "Stop Being Terrified of Treaties: Stop Being Scared of the Constitution." *American Bar Association Journal* 38 (September 1952): 731–34.

Churchill, Winston S. *The Second World War.* Vol. 3, *The Grand Alliance.* Boston: Houghton Mifflin, 1950.

Civil Rights Congress. *We Charge Genocide: The Historic Petition to the United Nations for Relief from a Crime of the United States Government Against the Negro People.* New York: International Publishers, 1970.

Commission to Study the Organization of Peace. *Fundamentals of the International Organization: General Statement* in *Building Peace: Reports of the Commission to Study the Organization of Peace.* Metuchen, NJ: Scarecrow Press, 1973.

———. *International Safeguard of Human Rights.* New York: Commission to Study the Organization of Peace, 1944.

———. *A Message from the National Study Conference on Churches and a Just and Durable Peace.* New York: Commission to Study the Bases of a Just and Durable Peace, 1942.

———. *Preliminary Report.* New York: Commission to Study the Organization of Peace, 1940.

———. *Strengthening the United Nations.* New York: Harper and Brothers, 1957.

———. *Toward Greater Freedom: Problems of War and Peace.* 3rd ed. New York: Commission to Study the Organization of Peace, 1944.

———. *Winning the War on the Spiritual Front.* New York: Commission to Study the Organization of Peace, 1943.

"Congress Takes a Careful Look at the UN's Genocide Treaty." *Congressional Digest* 29 (December 1950): 291–320.

Corbett, Percy. "Next Steps after the Charter: An Approach to the Enforcement of Human Rights." *Commentary* (November 1945): 23.

Council on Foreign Relations. "Problems of Postwar International Organization: A Tentative Outline." In *Studies of American Interests in the War and the Peace: Political Series.* New York: Council on Foreign Relations, 1942.

"Curbing the Treaty Power." *Congressional Digest* 31 (November 1952): 257–88.

Daniels, Jonathan, ed. *Complete Presidential Press Conferences of Franklin D. Roosevelt.* Vols. 15–16. New York: Da Capo Press, 1972.

Deutsch, Eberhard P. "The Need for a Treaty Amendment: A Restatement and a Reply." *American Bar Association Journal* 38 (September 1952): 735–38, 793–96.

Du Bois, W.E.B., ed. *An Appeal to the World: A Statement on the Denial of Human Rights to Minorities in the Case of Citizens of Negro Descent in the United States of America and an Appeal to the United Nations for Redress.* New York: National Association for the Advancement of Colored People, 1947.

Dulles, John Foster. *Long Range Peace Objectives.* New York: Commission to Study the Bases of a Just and Durable Peace, 1941.

———, ed. *A Righteous Faith for a Just and Durable Peace.* New York: Commission to Study the Bases of a Just and Durable Peace, 1942.

———. *War or Peace.* New York: Macmillan, 1950.

Eichelberger, Clark. *Organizing for Peace: A Personal History of the Founding of the United Nations.* New York: Harper & Row, 1977.

Eisenhower, Dwight D. *The White House Years: Mandate for Change, 1953–1956.* Garden City, NY: Doubleday, 1963.

Farmer, Fyke. "Now Is the Accepted Time." *American Bar Association Journal* 32 (May 1946): 267–71.

Finch, George. "Genocide Convention." *American Journal of International Law* 43 (October 1949): 732–38.

Fitzpatrick, William H. "Government by Treaty: What We Can Do About It." *New Orleans State* (19 December 1950): 633–35.

Fleming, William. "Danger to America: The Draft Covenant on Human Rights." *American Bar Association Journal* 37 (October 1951): 739–42, 794–99; (November 1951): 816–20, 855–60.

Garrett, Garet. "Nullification by Treaty." *The Freeman* 3 (4 May 1953): 549–50.

Gregory, Tappan. "International Legislation Without the Consent of Congress?" *American Bar Association* 34 (August 1948): 698–700.

Griffith, Ernest. "The Place of Congress in Foreign Relations." *Annals of the American Academy* 289 (September 1953): 11–21.

Hatch, Vernon. "The Treaty-Making Power: 'An Extraordinary Power Liable to Abuse.'" *American Bar Association Journal* 39 (September 1953): 808–11, 853–55.

Hatch, Vernon, George Finch, and Frank Ober. "The Treaty Power and the Constitution: The Case for Amendment." *American Bar Association Journal* 40 (March 1954): 207–10, 252–60.

Hendrick, James P. "An International Bill of Human Rights." *U.S. Department of State Bulletin* 18 (15 February 1948): 195–208.

———. "Progress Report on Human Rights." *U.S. Department of State Bulletin* 19 (8 August 1948): 159–72, 186.

Hinton, Harold C. "The Bricker Amendment." *Commonweal* 56 (15 August 1952): 458–60.

Hogan, Edward. "Limitations on the Secret Treaty Power." *Hastings Law Journal* 5 (Spring 1954): 118–32.

Holman, Frank E. *Achievements to Date in the Bricker Amendment Fight: 1956, the Year of Victory*. Seattle: Argus Press, 1955.

———. *The Dangers of Treaty Law: A Constitutional Amendment Is the Only Answer*. Yakima, WA: Veterans of Foreign Wars, 1952.

———. "The Greatest Threat to American Freedom." *Daughters of the American Revolution Magazine* 87 (August 1953): 981–88, 1005.

———. "An 'International Bill of Rights': Proposals Have Dangerous Implications for U.S." *American Bar Association Journal* 34 (November 1948): 984–86, 1078–81.

———. *The Life and Career of a Western Lawyer, 1886–1961*. Baltimore: Port City Press, 1963.

———. "1949 Regional Conference Solicitous for American System of Rights." *American Bar Association Journal* 35 (March 1949): 203–4.

———. "President Holman's Comments on Mr. Moskowitz's Reply." *American Bar Association Journal* 35 (April 1949): 288–90, 360–62.

———. "The President's Page." *American Bar Association Journal* 35 (March 1949): 201–3.

———. *State Department Half Truths and False Assurances Regarding the U.N. Charter, Genocide Convention, and Proposed Covenant on Human Rights*. Seattle: Argus Press, 1952.

———. *The Story of the "Bricker" Amendment (The First Phase)*. New York: Committee for Constitutional Government, 1954.

———. "Treaty Law-Making." *Washington Law Review and State Bar Journal* 25 (November 1950): 382–400.

———. "Treaty-Law Making: A Blank Check for Writing a New Constitution." *American Bar Association Journal* 36 (September 1950): 707–10, 787–90.

———. "'World Government' No Answer to America's Desire for Peace." *American Bar Association Journal* 32 (October 1946): 642–44, 718–21.

Hughes, Emmet John. *The Ordeal of Power: A Political Memoir of the Eisenhower Years*. New York: Atheneum, 1963.

Hula, Erich. "International Law and the Protection of Human Rights." In *Law and Politics in the World Community*, edited by George Lipsky, 162–90. Berkeley: University of California Press, 1953.

Hull, Cordell. *The Memoirs of Cordell Hull*. 2 vols. New York: Macmillan, 1948.

Humphrey, John P. *Human Rights and the United Nations: A Great Adventure*. Dobbs Ferry, NY: Transnational Publishers, 1984.

Inter-American Juridical Committee. *The Dumbarton Oaks Proposals: Preliminary Comments and Recommendations*. Washington, DC: Pan American Union, 1944.

Israel, Fred L., ed. *The War Diary of Breckinridge Long: Selections from the Years 1939–1944*. Lincoln: University of Nebraska Press, 1966.

Keck, Margaret E., and Kathryn Sikkink. *Activists Beyond Borders: Advocacy Networks in International Politics*. Ithaca: Cornell University Press, 1998.

Kennan, George F. *American Diplomacy, 1900–1950*. Chicago: University of Chicago Press, 1951.

Kimball, Warren F., ed. *Churchill and Roosevelt: The Complete Correspondence*. Vols. 2 and 3. Princeton: Princeton University Press, 1984.

Korey, William. *NGOs and the Universal Declaration of Human Rights: A Curious Grapevine*. New York: Palgrave, 1998.

Kuhn, A. K. "The Genocide Convention and States Rights." *American Journal of International Law* 43 (July 1949): 498–501.

Lemkin, Raphael. *Axis Rule in Occupied Europe: Laws of Occupation, Analysis of Government, Proposals for Redress.* Washington, DC: Carnegie Endowment for International Peace, 1944.

———. "Genocide." *American Scholar* 15 (April 1946): 227–30.

———. "Genocide as a Crime Under International Law." *The American Journal of International Law* 41 (January 1947): 145–51.

———. "Genocide as a Crime Under International Law." *United Nations Bulletin* 4 (15 January 1948): 70–71.

MacChesney, Brunson. "The Bricker Amendment: The Fallacies in the Case for the Amendment." *Notre Dame Lawyer* 29 (August 1954): 551–82.

———. "Should the United States Ratify the Covenants? A Question of Merits, Not of Constitutional Law." *American Journal of International Law* 62 (October 1968): 912–17.

MacChesney, Brunson, Myres McDougal, Robert E. Matthews, Covey T. Oliver, and F.D.G. Ribbie. "The Treaty Power and the Constitution: The Case Against the Amendment." *American Bar Association Journal* 40 (March 1954): 203–6, 248–52.

McDougal, Myres, and R. Arens. "Genocide Convention and the Constitution." *Vanderbilt Law Review* 3 (June 1950): 683–710.

McDougal, Myres, and Asher Lans. "Treaties and Congressional-Executive or Presidential Agreements: Interchangeable Instruments of National Policy." *Yale Law Journal* (March 1945): 181–351, 534–615.

Mathews, J. B. "Civil Liberties Upside Down." *American Mercury* 72 (March–April 1953): 34–49.

Michigan State Bar Association. "The Bricker Amendment." *Michigan State Bar Journal* 34 (July 1955): 20–37.

Molotov, V. M. *Speech Delivered at the Session of the United Nations Conference on International Organization in San Francisco on April 26, 1945.* San Francisco: American Russian Institute, 1945.

Morton, H. V. *Atlantic Meeting.* New York: Dodd, Mead and Company, 1943.

Nolde, O. Frederick. "Possible Functions of the Commission on Human Rights." *Annals of the American Academy of Political and Social Science* 243 (January 1946): 144–49.

Notter, Harley. *Postwar Foreign Policy Preparation, 1939–1945.* Washington, DC: U.S. Government Printing Office, 1950.

Ober, Frank. "The Treaty-Making and Amending Powers: Do They Protect Our Fundamental Rights?" *American Bar Association Journal* 36 (September 1950): 715–19, 793–96.

Patton, Marguerite, and Frances B. Lucas. "Bill of Rights." *Daughters of the American Revolution Magazine* 88 (December 1954): 1237–38.

———. "Covenant of Human Rights." *Daughters of the American Revolution Magazine* 88 (June 1954): 662.

———. "The Story of the Bricker Amendment." *Daughters of the American Revolution Magazine* 88 (September 1954): 936–38.

———. "The United Nations." *Daughters of the American Revolution Magazine* 87 (August 1953): 997–99.

Pearson, Theodore, and Dana Converse Backus. "Save the Peace Power: Don't Strait-Jacket Treaties." *American Bar Association Journal* 39 (September 1953): 804–8.

Philips, Draper W. "The Senate Must Recover Its Lost Powers in Treaty Making." *Saturday Evening Post* 223 (3 March 1951): 12.

Phillips, Orie L. "The Genocide Convention: Its Effect on Our Legal System." *American Bar Association Journal* 35 (August 1949): 623–25.

Ransom, William. "United Nations Will Proceed with Declaration and Covenant on Human Rights." *American Bar Association Journal* 34 (December 1948): 1091.

Reiff, Henry. *Transition from League of Nations to United Nations.* Washington, DC: U.S. Government Printing Office, 1946.

Reynolds, Katharine, and Frances Lucas. "International Criminal Court." *Daughters of the American Revolution Magazine* 87 (February 1953): 191–92.

———. "International Criminal Jurisdiction." *Daughters of the American Revolution Magazine* 86 (January 1952): 31.

———. "Let Us Be Thankful." *Daughters of the American Revolution Magazine* 84 (November 1950): 877.

———. "Mid-Century Appraisal." *Daughters of the American Revolution Magazine* 87 (June 1953): 767–69.

———. "A Proposed Constitutional Amendment." *Daughters of the American Revolution Magazine* 86 (May 1952): 609.

———. "Threats to Americanism." *Daughters of the American Revolution Magazine* 86 (December 1952): 1299–1304.

———. "Wake Up America." *Daughters of the American Revolution Magazine* 84 (December 1950): 939–42.

———. "We Take Our Stand." *Daughters of the American Revolution Magazine* 86 (June 1952): 733–37.

Rix, Carl B. "Human Rights and International Law: Effect of the Covenant Under Our Constitution." *American Bar Association Journal* 35 (July 1949): 551–54, 618–21.

Roosevelt, Eleanor. *The Autobiography of Eleanor Roosevelt.* New York: Harper & Brothers, 1958.

———. *On My Own: The Years Since the White House.* New York: Harper & Brothers, 1958.

———. "Progress Towards the Completion of a Human Rights Covenant." *U.S. Department of State Bulletin* 26 (30 June 1952): 1024–28.

———. "Reply to Attack on U.S. Attitude Toward Human Rights Covenant." *U.S. Department of State Bulletin* 26 (14 January 1952): 59–61.

———. *This I Remember.* New York: Harper Brothers, 1949.

Rosenman, Samuel I., ed. *Public Papers and Addresses of Franklin D. Roosevelt.* Vols. 11–13. New York: Harper and Brothers, 1948–1950.

Rovere, Richard. "A Letter from Washington." *New Yorker* 25 (11 February 1950): 50–58.

Sharp, Walter. "Basic American Interests." In *Studies of American Interests in the War and the Peace: Political Series.* New York: Council on Foreign Relations, 1941.

Sherwood, Robert E. *Roosevelt and Hopkins: An Intimate History.* New York: Harper and Brothers, 1948.

Simsarian, James. "Economic, Social, and Cultural Provisions in the Human Rights Covenant." *U.S. Department of State Bulletin* 24 (25 June 1951): 1003–14.

———. "Human Rights: Draft Covenant Revised at Fifth Session of Commission on Human Rights." *U.S. Department of State Bulletin* 21 (11 July 1949): 3–12.

———. "Proposed Human Rights Covenant." *U.S. Department of State Bulletin* 22 (12 June 1950): 945–54.

———. "United Nations Action on Human Rights in 1948." *U.S. Department of State Bulletin* 20 (2 January 1949): 18–23.

Sohn, Louis. "The Development of International Law: Drafting and Implementing an International Covenant on Human Rights." *American Bar Association Journal* 34 (March 1948): 200–201.

Stettinius, Edward. *Charter of the United Nations: Report to the President on the Results of the San Francisco Conference.* Washington, DC: U.S. Government Printing Office, 1945.

———. "The Commission on Human Rights." *Annals of the American Academy of Political and Social Science* 243 (January 1946): 1–3.

———. "United Nations Conference on International Organization: Provisions on Human Rights." *U.S. Department of State Bulletin* 12 (1945): 928–30.

Streit, Clarence K. *Union Now: A Proposal for a Federal Union of the Democracies of the North Atlantic.* New York: Harper & Brothers, 1939.

Summers, Robert E., ed. *Dumbarton Oaks.* New York: H. W. Wilson, 1945.

Sutherland, Arthur. "The Bricker Amendment, Executive Agreements, and Imported Potatoes." *Harvard Law Review* 67 (1953–1954): 281–92.

———. "Restricting the Treaty Power." *Harvard Law Review* 65 (1951–1952): 1305–38.

Tondel, Lyman M. "The Section on International Law: Its Work and Its Objectives." *American Bar Association Journal* 38 (November 1952): 928–31.

"Treaty Power (Bricker) Amendment." *Congressional Quarterly Almanac* 9 (1953): 233–37, 255–58.

Truman, Harry S. *Memoirs.* Vol. 1, *Year of Decisions.* Garden City, NY: Doubleday, 1955.

———. *Memoirs.* Vol. 2, *Years of Trial and Hope.* Garden City, NY: Doubleday, 1956.

———. *Report by the President to the Congress for the Year 1946.* United States and United Nations Report Series 7. Washington, DC: U.S. Government Printing Office, 1947.

Vandenberg, Arthur H., Jr., ed. *The Private Papers of Senator Vandenberg.* Boston: Houghton Mifflin, 1952.

Vasak, Karel, ed. *The International Dimensions of Human Rights.* Vol. 1. Paris: United Nations Economic and Social Council, 1982.

Wallace, Henry. *Democracy Reborn.* New York: Reynal & Hitchcock, 1944.

Welles, Sumner. *The Time for Decision.* New York: Harper & Brothers, 1944.

———. *Where Are We Heading?* New York: Harper & Brothers, 1946.

White, A. A. "Tomorrow One May Be Guilty of Genocide." *Texas Bar Journal* 12 (May 1949): 203–4, 225–29.

Whiteman, Marjorie M. "Mrs. Franklin D. Roosevelt and the Human Rights Commission." *American Journal of International Law* 62 (1968): 918–21.

Whitton, J. B., and J. E. Fowler. "Bricker Amendment Fallacies and Dangers." *American Journal of International Law* 48 (1954): 23–56.

Widener, Alice. "The UN's Pink Sisters." *The Freeman* 3 (29 December 1952): 233–36.

Wright, Quincy. "Human Rights and the World Order." *International Conciliation* 389 (April 1943): 238–62.

———. "National Courts and Human Rights: The Fujii Case." *American Journal of International Law* 45 (1951): 62–82.

Journals and Newspapers

American Bar Association Journal

Chicago Tribune

Christian Century
Christian Science Monitor
Commission on Human Rights Reports
Congressional Quarterly Almanac
Congressional Record
New York Times
Reports of the American Bar Association
United Nations News
United Nations Weekly Bulletin
U.S. Department of State Bulletin
Washington Post

Secondary Sources

Articles and Books

Abraham, Henry J. *Freedom and the Court: Civil Rights and Liberties in the United States.* New York: Oxford University Press, 1988.

Alcock, Antony. *A History of the International Labor Organization.* New York: Octagon Books, 1971.

Alexander, Stella. *The Triple Myth: A Life of Archbishop Alojzije Stepinac.* New York: Columbia University Press, 1987.

Alston, Philip. *The United Nations and Human Rights: A Critical Appraisal.* Oxford: Clarendon Press, 1992.

Amnesty International. *United States of America: Rights for All.* New York: Amnesty International, 1998.

Anderson, Carol. *Eyes off the Prize: The United Nations and the African American Struggle for Human Rights, 1944–1955.* Cambridge: Cambridge University Press, 2003.

———. "From Hope to Disillusion: African Americans, the United Nations, and the Struggle for Human Rights, 1944–1947." *Diplomatic History* 20 (Fall 1996): 531–63.

Asher, Robert, et al. *The United Nations and Promotion of the General Welfare.* Washington, DC: Brookings Institution, 1957.

Balakian, Peter. *The Burning Tigris: The Armenian Genocide and America's Response.* New York: Perennial, 2003.

Barton, Keith M. "The Dumbarton Oaks Conference." PhD diss., Florida State University, 1974.

Beisner, Robert. *Twelve Against Empire: The Anti-Imperialists, 1898–1900.* New York: McGraw-Hill, 1968.

Bendiner, Elmer. *A Time for Angels: The Tragicomic History of the League of Nations.* New York: Knopf, 1975.

Berger, Jason. *A New Deal for the World: Eleanor Roosevelt and American Foreign Policy.* New York: Social Science Monographs, 1981.

Berman, William C. *The Politics of Civil Rights in the Truman Administration.* Columbus: Ohio State University Press, 1970.

Biggs, Robert E. *Foreign Policy and US.* New York: Appleton-Century-Crofts, 1971.

Black, Allida. *Casting Her Own Shadow: Eleanor Roosevelt and the Shaping of Postwar Liberalism.* New York: Columbia University Press, 1996.

Boer, Nicholas. *Cardinal Mindszenty and the Implacable War of Communism Against Religion and the Spirit.* London: B. U. E., 1949.

Borgwardt, Elizabeth. *A New Deal for the World: America's Vision for Human Rights*. Cambridge, MA: Harvard University Press, 2005.

Borstelmann, Thomas. *Apartheid's Reluctant Uncle: The United States and Southern Africa in the Early Cold War*. New York: Oxford University Press, 1993.

Brands, H. W., Jr. *Cold Warriors: Eisenhower's Generation and American Foreign Policy*. New York: Columbia University Press, 1988.

Brinkley, Douglas, and David R. Facey-Crowther, eds. *The Atlantic Charter*. New York: St. Martin's Press, 1994.

Brown, Peter G., and Douglas MacLean. *Human Rights and U.S. Foreign Policy: Principles and Applications*. Lexington, MA: D. C. Heath and Company, 1979.

Buhite, Russell D., ed. *Calls to Arms: Presidential Speeches, Messages, and Declarations of War*. Wilmington, DE: Scholarly Resources, 2003.

Bunyon, Bryant, and Robert H. Jones. "The U.S. and the 1948 Genocide Convention." *Harvard International Law Journal* 16 (Summer 1975): 683–704.

Burns, James MacGregor. *Roosevelt: The Soldier of Freedom*. New York: Harcourt Brace Jovanovich, 1970.

Claude, Inis. *National Minorities: An International Problem*. Cambridge, MA: Harvard University Press, 1955.

Cooper, John. *Raphael Lemkin and the Struggle for the Genocide Convention*. New York: Palgrave Macmillan, 2008.

Cumings, Bruce. *The Origins of the Korean War*. Vol. 2, *The Roaring of the Cataract, 1947–1950*. Princeton: Princeton University Press, 1990.

Cushman, Robert. *Leading Constitutional Decisions*. New York: Appleton-Century-Crofts, 1966.

Dallek, Robert. *Franklin D. Roosevelt and American Foreign Policy, 1932–1945*. New York: Oxford University Press, 1979.

Davidson, Scott. *The Inter-American Human Rights System*. Aldershot, England: Dartmouth, 1997.

Davies, Peter, ed. *Human Rights*. London: Routledge, 1988.

Davies, Richard O. *Defender of the Old Guard: John Bricker and American Politics*. Columbus: Ohio State University Press, 1993.

Divine, Robert. *Roosevelt and World War II*. Baltimore: Johns Hopkins Press, 1969.

———. *Second Chance: The Triumph of Internationalism in America During World War II*. New York: Atheneum, 1967.

Donovan, Frank. *Mr. Roosevelt's Four Freedoms: The Story Behind the United Nations Charter*. New York: Dodd, Mead and Company, 1966.

Dorsey, Kurk. "Scientists, Citizens, and Statesmen." *Diplomatic History* 19 (Summer 1995): 407–29.

Dower, John W. *War Without Mercy: Race and Power in the Pacific War*. New York: Pantheon Books, 1986.

Dray, Philip. *At the Hands of Persons Unknown: The Lynching of Black America*. New York: Modern Library, 2002.

Du Bois, W.E.B. *The Souls of Black Folk*, in *Three Negro Classics*. New York: Avon Books, 1965.

Dudziak, Mary. *Cold War Civil Rights: Race and the Image of American Democracy*. Princeton: Princeton University Press, 2000.

———. "Desegregation as Cold War Imperative." *Stanford Law Review* 41 (November 1988): 61–120.

Egerton, John. *Speak Now Against the Day: The Generation Before the Civil Rights Movement in the South.* New York: Knopf, 1994.

Emblidge, David, ed. *Eleanor Roosevelt's My Day: Her Acclaimed Columns, 1945–1952.* Vol. 2, *The Post-War Years.* New York: Pharos Books, 1990.

Evans, Tony. *U.S. Hegemony and the Project of Universal Human Rights.* New York: St. Martin's Press, 1996.

Falk, Richard A. "Ideological Patterns in the United States Human Rights Debate: 1945–1978." In *The Dynamics of Human Rights in U.S. Foreign Policy*, edited by Natalie Kaufman Hevener, 29–51. New Brunswick, NJ: Transaction Books, 1981.

Fareed, Nabiel J. "The United Nations Commission on Human Rights and Its Work for Human Rights and Fundamental Freedoms." PhD diss., Washington State University, 1977.

Fine, Sidney. *Frank Murphy: The Washington Years.* Ann Arbor: University of Michigan Press, 1984.

Foner, Eric. *The Story of American Freedom.* New York: W. W. Norton, 1998.

Formicola, Jo Renee. *The Catholic Church and Human Rights: Its Role in the Formulation of U.S. Policy, 1945–1980.* New York: Garland Publishing, 1988.

Forsythe, David P. *Human Rights and U.S. Foreign Policy: Congress Reconsidered.* Gainesville: University of Florida Press, 1988.

Franklin, John Hope, and Alfred A. Moss, Jr. *From Slavery to Freedom: A History of Negro Americans.* New York: Alfred A. Knopf, 1988.

Friere, Paulo. *Pedagogy of the Oppressed.* New York: Continuum, 1990.

Gaddis, John Lewis. *The United States and the Origins of the Cold War, 1941–1947.* New York: Columbia University Press, 1972.

Gardner, Michael R. *Harry Truman and Civil Rights: Moral Courage and Political Risks.* Carbondale: Southern Illinois University Press, 2002.

Garrett, Steve. "Foreign Policy and the American Constitution: The Bricker Amendment in Contemporary Perspective." *International Studies Quarterly* 16 (June 1972): 187–220.

Gellman, Irwin F. *Secret Affairs: Franklin Roosevelt, Cordell Hull, and Sumner Welles.* Baltimore: Johns Hopkins University Press, 1995.

Gibney, Mark, ed. *World Justice? U.S. Courts and International Human Rights.* Boulder, CO: Westview Press, 1991.

Glendon, Mary Ann. *A World Made New: Eleanor Roosevelt and the Universal Declaration of Human Rights.* New York: Random House, 2001.

Green, James Frederick. *The United Nations and Human Rights.* Washington, DC: Brookings Institution, 1956.

Greenberg, Jack. *Crusaders in the Courts: How a Dedicated Band of Lawyers Fought for the Civil Rights Revolution.* New York: Basic Books, 1994.

Gurewitsch, David, ed. *Eleanor Roosevelt: Her Day.* New York: Interchange Foundation, 1973.

Gutman, Roy. *A Witness to Genocide.* New York: Macmillan, 1993.

Hall, Kermit, ed. *The Oxford Companion to the Supreme Court of the United States.* New York: Oxford University Press, 1992.

Hamilton, Alexander, James Madison, and John Jay. *The Federalist Papers.* New York: Mentor, 1961.

Hannum, Hurst, and Dana D. Fischer, eds. *U.S. Ratification of the International Covenants on Human Rights.* Irvington-on-Hudson, NY: Transnational Publications, 1993.

Henkin, Louis. *The Age of Rights*. New York: Columbia University Press, 1990.

———. *Foreign Affairs and the Constitution*. New York: W. W. Norton, 1972.

———. *The International Bill of Rights: The Covenant on Civil and Political Rights*. New York: Columbia University Press, 1981.

———. "U.S. Ratification of Human Rights Conventions: The Ghost of Senator Bricker." *American Journal of International Law* 89 (April 1995): 341–50.

Heros, Alfred. *The Southerner and World Affairs*. Baton Rouge: Louisiana State University Press, 1965.

Hietala, Thomas. *Manifest Design: Anxious Aggrandizement in Late Jacksonian America*. Ithaca: Cornell University Press, 1985.

Hilderbrand, Robert C. *Dumbarton Oaks: The Origins of the United Nations and the Search for Postwar Security*. Chapel Hill: University of North Carolina Press, 1990.

Hiltzik, Michael. *The New Deal: A Modern History*. New York: Free Press, 2011.

Hochschild, Adam. *King Leopold's Ghost: A Story of Greed, Terror, and Heroism in Colonial Africa*. London: Pan Books, 2002.

Hogan, Michael J. *The Marshall Plan: America, Britain, and the Reconstruction of Western Europe, 1947–1952*. Cambridge: Cambridge University Press, 1987.

Holborn, Louise W., ed. *War and Peace Aims of the United Nations*. 2 vols. Boston: World Peace Foundation, 1943–1948.

Holcombe, Arthur N. "The Covenant on Human Rights." *Law and Contemporary Problems* 14 (1949): 413–29.

Holloway, Kaye. *Modern Trends in Treaty Law: Constitutional Law, Reservations and the Three Modes of Legislation*. Dobbs Ferry, NY: Oceana, 1967.

Hoopes, Townsend, and Douglas Brinkley. *FDR and the Creation of the U.N.* New Haven: Yale University Press, 1997.

Hunt, Michael. *Ideology and U.S. Foreign Policy*. New Haven: Yale University Press, 1987.

Immerman, Richard H. *John Foster Dulles: Piety, Pragmatism, and Power in U.S. Foreign Policy*. Wilmington, DE: Scholarly Resources, 1999.

Iriye, Akira. *Across the Pacific: An Inner History of American–East Asian Relations*. New York: Harcourt Brace & World, 1967.

———. *Cultural Internationalism and World Order*. Baltimore: Johns Hopkins University Press, 1997.

Isaacson, Walter, and Evan Thomas. *The Wise Men: Six Friends and the World They Made*. New York: Simon and Schuster, 1986.

Ishay, Micheline R. *The Human Rights Reader: Major Political Writings, Essays, Speeches, and Documents from the Bible to the Present*. New York: Routledge, 1997.

Jacobs, Steven L. *Raphael Lemkin's Thoughts on Nazi Genocide: Not Guilty?* Lewiston, NY: Edwin Mellen Press, 1992.

James, Robert Rhodes. *Winston S. Churchill: His Complete Speeches, 1897–1963*. Vol. 6, *1935–1942*. New York: Chelsea House, 1974.

Johnson, M. Glen. "The Contributions of Eleanor and Franklin Roosevelt to the Development of International Protection for Human Rights." *Human Rights Quarterly* 9 (February 1987): 19–48.

Johnson, M. Glen, and Janusz Symonides. *The Universal Declaration of Human Rights: A History of Its Creation and Implementation, 1948–1998*. Paris: UNESCO, 1998.

Kangar, Helle. *Human Rights in the U.N. Declaration*. Uppsala: Acta Universitatis Upsaliensis, 1984.

Kaufman, Natalie Hevener. *Human Rights Treaties and the Senate: A History of Opposition.* Chapel Hill: University of North Carolina Press, 1990.

Kaufman, Natalie Hevener, and David Whiteman. "Opposition to Human Rights Treaties in the United States Senate: The Legacy of the Bricker Amendment." *Human Rights Quarterly* 10 (1988): 309–37.

Kendrick, Frank J. "The United States and the International Protection of Human Rights." Master's Thesis, University of Chicago, 1956.

Kennedy, Paul. *The Parliament of Man: The Past, Present, and Future of the United Nations* New York: Random House, 2006.

Kimball, Warren. *Franklin D. Roosevelt and World Crisis, 1937–1945.* Lexington, MA: D.C. Health, 1973.

Kinzer, Stephen. *Overthrow: America's Century of Regime Change from Hawaii to Iraq.* New York: Times Books, 2006.

Knock, Thomas J. *To End All Wars: Woodrow Wilson and the Quest for a New World Order.* Princeton: Princeton University Press, 1992.

Krenn, Michael L. *Black Diplomacy: African Americans and the State Department, 1945–1969.* Armonk, NY: M. E. Sharpe, 1999.

Kuper, Leo. *The Prevention of Genocide.* New Haven: Yale University Press, 1985.

Laqueur, Walter, and Barry Rubin, eds. *The Human Rights Reader.* New York: Meridian, 1979.

Lash, Joseph. *Eleanor and Franklin.* New York: New American Library, 1973.

———. *Eleanor: The Years Alone.* New York: W. W. Norton, 1972.

———, ed. *From the Diaries of Felix Frankfurter.* New York: W. W. Norton, 1975.

Lauren, Paul G. *The Evolution of International Human Rights: Visions Seen.* Philadelphia: University of Pennsylvania Press, 1998.

———. "First Principles of Racial Equality: History and the Politics and Diplomacy of Human Rights Provisions in the United Nations Charter." *Human Rights Quarterly* 5 (Winter 1983): 9–12.

———. "Human Rights in History: Diplomacy and Racial Equality at the Paris Peace Conference." *Journal of Diplomatic History* 2 (June 1978): 257–78.

Lauterpacht, Hersch. *International Law and Human Rights.* New York: Frederick A. Praeger, 1950.

LeBlanc, Lawrence. *The United States and the Genocide Convention.* Durham, NC: Duke University Press, 1991.

Leffler, Melvyn P. *A Preponderance of Power: National Security, the Truman Administration, and the Cold War.* Stanford: Stanford University Press, 1992.

Levin, N. Gordon, Jr. *Woodrow Wilson and World Politics: America's Response to War and Revolution.* London: Oxford University Press, 1968.

Lillich, Richard B. *Invoking International Human Rights Law in Domestic Courts.* Washington, DC: American Bar Association, 1985.

———, ed. *U.S. Ratification of the Human Rights Treaties: With or Without Reservations?* Charlottesville: University Press of Virginia, 1981.

Lilly, Edward P. "The Psychological Strategy Board and Its Predecessors, 1938–1953." In *Studies in Modern History*, edited by Gaetano L. Vincitorio. New York: St. John's University Press, 1968.

Lindley, William R. "The Atlantic Charter: Press Release or Historic Document?" *Journalism Quarterly* 41 (Summer 1964): 375–79, 394.

Locke, John. *Two Treatises of Government*. New York: Cambridge University Press, 1960.

Lockwood, Bert B. "The United Nations Charter and United States Civil Rights Litigation: 1946–1955." *Iowa Law Review* 69 (May 1984): 901–49.

Luard, Evan. *A History of the United Nations*. Vol. 1, *The Years of Western Domination, 1945–1955*. New York: St. Martin's Press, 1982.

Madison, James. *Notes of Debates in the Federal Convention of 1787*. New York: W. W. Norton, 1966.

Martin, James J. *The Man Who Invented "Genocide": The Public Career and Consequences of Raphael Lemkin*. Torrance, CA: Institute for Historical Review, 1984.

Mayer, Arno J. *Politics and Diplomacy of Peacemaking: Containment and Counterrevolution at Versailles, 1918–1919*. New York: Vintage Books, 1967.

McCormick, Thomas. *America's Half-Century: United States Foreign Policy in the Cold War*. Baltimore: Johns Hopkins University Press, 1989.

McDougal, Myres, Harold D. Lasswell, and Lung-Chu Chen. *Human Rights and World Public Order*. New Haven: Yale University Press, 1980.

McElvaine, Robert S. *The Great Depression: America, 1929–1941*. New York: Times Books, 1993.

Meisler, Stanley. *United Nations: The First Fifty Years*. New York: Atlantic Monthly Press, 1995.

Merin, K. D. *The Bricker Amendment: Limiting the Treaty Power by Constitutional Amendment*. Washington, DC: Library of Congress, Congressional Research Service, 1978.

Merk, Frederick. *Manifest Destiny and Mission in American History: A Reinterpretation*. New York: Vintage Books, 1963.

Mower, A. Glenn, Jr. *The United States, the United Nations, and Human Rights: The Eleanor Roosevelt and Jimmy Carter Eras*. Westport, CT: Greenwood Press, 1979.

Murray, Gilbert. *From the League to U.N.* London: Oxford University Press, 1948.

Neumann, William L. *Making the Peace, 1941–1945: The Diplomacy of the Wartime Conferences*. Washington, DC: Foundation for Foreign Affairs, 1950.

Newberg, Paula. *The Politics of Human Rights*. New York: New York University Press, 1982.

Newhouse, Wade J. "United Nations Convention on the Prevention and Punishment of Genocide: An Analysis of Its Legal Problems and Proposed Action for the United States." Seminar Paper, University of Michigan Law School, 1950.

Nolan, Cathal J. "The Last Hurrah of Conservative Isolationism: Eisenhower, Congress, and the Bricker Amendment." *Presidential Studies Quarterly* 22 (Spring 1992): 337–49.

Osgood, Kenneth. *Total Cold War: Eisenhower's Secret Propaganda Battle at Home and Abroad*. Lawrence: University Press of Kansas, 2006.

Ostrower, Gary B. *The League of Nations, 1919–1929*. Garden City Park, NY: Avery Publishing, 1996.

Pabst, William R., and Ray Dickens. *The United Nations Charter and U.N. General Assembly Resolutions as Basis for Jurisdiction in Federal Court*. [Houston, TX]: Center for the Independence of Judges and Lawyers of the United States, 1983.

Parson, Donald P. "The Individual Right to Petition: A Study of the Methods Used by International Organizations to Utilize the Individual as a Source of Information on the Violations of Human Rights." *Wayne Law Review* 13 (1967): 678–705.

Paterson, Thomas G., and J. Garry Clifford. *America Ascendant: U.S. Foreign Relations Since 1939*. Lexington, MA: D. C. Heath and Company, 1995.

Paton, Alan. *Cry, the Beloved Country*. New York: Charles Scribner's Sons, 1948.

Pauly, Karl B. *Bricker of Ohio: The Man and His Record*. New York: G. P. Putnam's Sons, 1944.

Pei-heng, Chiang. *Non-Governmental Organizations at the United Nations: Identity, Role, and Function*. New York: Praeger, 1981.

Persico, Joseph. *Nuremberg: Infamy on Trial*. New York: Penguin, 1994.

Plischke, Elmer. *U.S. Department of State: A Reference History*. Westport, CT: Greenwood Press, 1999.

Plokhy, S. M. *Yalta: The Price of Peace*. New York: Viking, 2010.

Plummer, Brenda Gayle. *Rising Wind: Black Americans and U.S. Foreign Affairs, 1935–1960*. Chapel Hill: University of North Carolina Press, 1996.

———. *Window on Freedom: Race, Civil Rights, and Foreign Affairs, 1945–1988*. Chapel Hill: University of North Carolina Press, 2003.

Polonsky, Anthony, ed. *The Great Powers and the Polish Question, 1941–1945*. London: London School of Economics and Political Science, 1976.

Porter, Jack Nusan, ed. *Genocide and Human Rights: A Global Anthology*. Washington, DC: University Press of America, 1982.

Pratt, Virginia A. *The Influence of Domestic Controversy on American Participation in the United Nations Commission on Human Rights, 1946–1953*. New York: Garland Publishing, 1986.

Pruden, Caroline. *Conditional Partners: Eisenhower, the United Nations, and the Search for a Permanent Peace*. Baton Rouge: Louisiana State University Press, 1998.

Pruessen, Ronald W. *John Foster Dulles: The Road to Power*. New York: Free Press, 1982.

Ramcharan, B. G., ed. *Human Rights: Thirty Years After the Universal Declaration*. The Hague: Martinus Nijhoff, 1979.

Randall, Kenneth C. *Federal Courts and the International Human Rights Paradigm*. Durham: Duke University Press, 1990.

Riggs, Robert E. *Foreign Policy and the US/UN International Organization*. New York: Appleton-Century-Crofts, 1971.

Robertson, A. H., ed. *Human Rights in National and International Law*. Dobbs Ferry, NY: Oceana, 1968.

———. *Human Rights in the World*. Manchester: Manchester University Press, 1972.

Robins, Dorothy B. *Experiment in Democracy: The Story of U.S. Citizen Organizations in Forging the Charter of the United Nations*. New York: Parkside Press, 1971.

Robinson, Jacob. *Human Rights and Fundamental Freedoms in the Charter of the United Nations: A Commentary*. New York: Institute of Jewish Affairs, 1946.

Robinson, Nehemiah. *The Genocide Convention: A Commentary*. New York: Institute of Jewish Affairs, 1960.

———. *The Universal Declaration of Human Rights: Its Origin, Significance, Application, and Interpretation*. New York: Institute of Jewish Affairs, 1958.

Rothman, Sheila M. *Woman's Proper Place: A History of Changing Ideals and Practices, 1870 to the Present*. New York: Basic Books, 1978.

Rubin, Barry M., and Elizabeth P. Spiro, eds. *Human Rights and U.S. Foreign Policy*. Boulder, CO: Westview Press, 1979.

Rupp, Leila J. *Worlds of Women: The Making of an International Women's Movement*. Princeton: Princeton University Press, 1997.

Russell, Ruth B. *A History of the United Nations Charter: The Role of the United States, 1940–1945*. Washington, DC: Brookings Institution, 1958.

Schabas, William. *The Abolition of the Death Penalty in International Law*. Cambridge: Cambridge University Press, 1997.

Schild, Georg. *Bretton Woods and Dumbarton Oaks: American Economic and Political Postwar Planning in the Summer of 1944*. New York: St. Martin's Press, 1995.

Schlesinger, Arthur, Jr. "Origins of the Cold War." *Foreign Affairs* 46 (October 1967): 23–52.

Schlesinger, Stephen C. *Act of Creation: The Founding of the United Nations*. Boulder, CO: Westview Press, 2003.

Schmidhauser, John, and Larry Berg. "The ABA and Human Rights Conventions: The Political Significance of Private Professional Associations." *Social Forces* 38 (1971): 362–410.

Schroeder, Oliver, Jr. *International Crime and the U.S. Constitution*. [Cleveland]: Western Reserve University Press, 1950.

Schulzinger, Robert. *The Wise Men of Foreign Affairs: The History of the Council on Foreign Relations*. New York: Columbia University Press, 1984.

Schwelb, Egon. *Human Rights and the International Community: The Roots and Growth of the Universal Declaration of Human Rights, 1948–1963*. Chicago: Quadrangle Books, 1964.

Scott, William A., and Stephen B. Whitney. *The United States and the United Nations: The Public View, 1945–1955*. New York: Manhattan Publishing Company, 1958.

Seary, Bill. "The Early History: From the Congress of Vienna to the San Francisco Conference." In *The Conscience of the World: The Influence of Non-Governmental Organisations in the UN System*, edited by Peter Willetts, 15–30. Washington, DC: Brookings Institution, 1996.

Sherry, Michael. *Preparing for the Next War: American Plans for Postwar Defense, 1941–1945*. New Haven: Yale University Press, 1977.

Shoup, Laurence H., and William Minter. *Imperial Brain Trust: The Council on Foreign Relations and United States Foreign Policy*. New York: Monthly Review Press, 1977.

Small, Melvin. *Democracy and Diplomacy: The Impact of Domestic Politics on U.S. Foreign Policy, 1789–1994*. Baltimore: Johns Hopkins University Press, 1996.

Southard, Jo L. "Human Rights Provisions of the U.N. Charter: The History in U.S. Courts." *International Law Students Association Journal of International and Comparative Law* 1 (Spring 1995): 41–65.

Stephanson, Anders. *Manifest Destiny: American Expansion and the Empire of Right*. New York: Hill and Wang, 1995.

Stewart, James Brewer. *Holy Warriors: The Abolitionists and American Slavery*. New York: Hill and Wang, 1996.

Stoler, Mark. "U.S. World War II Diplomacy." *Diplomatic History* 18 (Summer 1994): 375–403.

Stuart, Graham. *The Department of State: A History of Its Organization, Procedure, and Personnel*. New York: Macmillan Company, 1949.

Summers, Robert E., ed. *Dumbarton Oaks*. New York: H. W. Wilson Company, 1945.

Tananbaum, Duane. *The Bricker Amendment Controversy: A Test of Eisenhower's Political Leadership*. Ithaca: Cornell University Press, 1988.

Tolley, Howard, Jr. *The U.N. Commission on Human Rights*. Boulder, CO: Westview Press, 1987.

Toulouse, Mark G. *The Transformation of John Foster Dulles: From Prophet of Realism to Priest of Nationalism*. Macon, GA: Mercer University Press, 1985.

Tucker, Robert C., ed. *The Marx-Engels Reader*. New York: W. W. Norton, 1978.

Van Dyke, Vernon. *Human Rights, the United States, and World Community*. New York: Oxford University Press, 1970.

Vogelgesang, Sandy. *American Dream, Global Nightmare: The Dilemma of U.S. Human Rights Policy*. New York: W. W. Norton, 1980.

Walker, Richard L. *The American Secretaries of State and Their Diplomacy.* Vol. 14, *E. R. Stettinius, Jr.* Edited by Robert H. Ferrell and Samuel F. Bemis. New York: Cooper Square Publishers, 1965.

Westerfield, H. Bradford. *Foreign Policy and Party Politics: Pearl Harbor to Korea.* New Haven: Yale University Press, 1955.

Williams, William Appleman. *The Tragedy of American Diplomacy.* New York: W. W. Norton, 1972.

Wilson, Theodore. *The First Summit: Roosevelt and Churchill at Placentia Bay, 1941.* Lawrence: University Press of Kansas, 1991.

Wood, Gordon S. *The Radicalism of the American Revolution.* New York: Alfred A. Knopf, 1992.

Wrage, Stephen D. "Human Rights and the American National Myth." PhD diss., Johns Hopkins University, 1987.

Wyman, David S. *The Abandonment of the Jews: America and the Holocaust, 1941–1945.* New York: Pantheon Books, 1984.

Yahil, Leni. *The Holocaust: The Fate of European Jewry, 1932–1945.* New York: Oxford University Press, 1990.

Yergin, Daniel. *Shattered Peace: The Origins of the Cold War.* New York: Penguin, 1990.

Zimmerman, Warren. *First Great Triumph: How Five Americans Made Their Country a World Power.* New York: Farrar, Straus and Giroux, 2002.

Zuijdwijk, Ton J. M. *Petitioning the United Nations: A Study in Human Rights.* New York: St. Martin's Press, 1982.

Index

International Covenant on Civil and Political Rights (ICCPR), 253, 255
International Covenant on Economic, Social, and Cultural Rights (ICESCR), 253–55
International Criminal Court (ICC), 254, 259
International Labor Organization (ILO), 8, 9, 134
international law, 84; cited by Supreme Court, 254–55; genocide under, 172, 174–88, 198; human rights under, 15, 45, 87, 254; individuals under, 47, 66; international tribunals under, 34; powers of U.N. under, 63; on sovereignty, 6–7
International Law Commission (ILC), 177–78, 180, 181, 188
International League for the Rights of Man, 154, 155, 239–40
Irwin, Wallace, 244–45

Jackson, C. D., 241–43, 245
Jackson, Robert H., 174, 182
Japan, 9; Pearl Harbor attacked by, 23; WWII atrocities by, 172, 196
Jenks, C. Wilfred, 73
Jim Crow. *See* racial segregation and discrimination; racism
Justice, Department of (U.S.): first civil rights cases of, 120; on United Nations Charter, 139

Kafauver, Estes, 231
Kennan, George, 96
Koo, Wellington, 9, 78
Korean War: Chinese intervention in, 161; in election of 1952, 232; Genocide Convention and, 158, 196, 203–5; Truman's public approval during, 168
Koretsky, Vladimir, 110, 111
Kotschnig, Walter, 156, 223; prior to Dumbarton Oaks Conference, 58; on Genocide Convention, 181; on petitions submitted to UNCHR, 111, 155; State Dept. Subcommittee on Human Rights and Status of Women chaired by,

102–3, 108, 110, 117; on Stepinac issue, 105; on UNCHR, 120
Krock, Arthur, 40, 156

Labor, Department of (U.S.), 121
LaFollette, Robert M., Jr., 55, 71
Latin America, 67–68, 85; human rights courts and agreements in, 255; Mexico City Conference of nations of, 71–72, 81
Laugier, Henri, 73, 115, 154
Lauterpacht, Hersch, 107, 112
League of Nations, 8, 9, 43, 56, 205, 250
League of Nations Association, 17, 27
Leahy, William D., 61
Lehman, Herbert, 209
Lemkin, Raphael, 208; genocide defined and studied by, 173–76; Senate lobbied by, 194, 195, 203, 204; U.N. lobbied by, 187–90
Lend-Lease Act (1941), 14, 18–19, 23
Lewis, William Draper, 66, 73
Lie, Trygve, 167; Du Bois and, 115; on genocide, 177; on ratification of Genocide Convention, 205; U.S. blacks' attempt to meet with, 99
Ligue pour la Defense des Droits de l'Homme, 9
Lilly, Edward, 243
Litvinov, Maxim, 24
Lochard, Metz, 99
Lodge, Henry Cabot, Jr.: on Lord, 236; psychological warfare project of, 241–46; on segregation, 160; as Senator, 204; on South Africa, 161; as U.N. ambassador, 208–9, 211
Lodge Human Rights Project, 241–47
Logan, Rayford, 115
Lord, Mary Pillsbury, 236, 238–40
Lovett, Robert, 117, 135–38, 187

MacKay, John A., 45
Maisky, Ivan, 22
Maktos, John, 182–85, 188–89, 251
Malan, Daniel, 218
Malik, Charles, 122, 129; at first meeting of UNCHR, 104; Genocide Convention and, 187; Eleanor Roosevelt and,

on South Africa, 218–19; as UNCHR
chair, 96–98, 100, 103–6, 110–12,
117–20, 147–48, 153–55, 170, 251;
on UNCHR Declaration, 123–24; on
UNCHR Drafting Committee, 122–23;
on UNCHR powers, 151; at UNCHR
session of 1951, 165–68; on Universal
Declaration of Human Rights, 129–30,
226–27; on *We Charge Genocide*, 216
Roosevelt, Franklin D., 50; on Atlantic
Charter, 69–70; at Atlantic Charter
conference, 20–22; on crimes against
humanity, 172; death of, 77; on
Dumbarton Oaks Conference, 59, 63,
64; in election of 1944, 51; Four Freedoms speech of, 14–15, 28, 108, 261n1;
on German invasion of Poland, 16; on
human rights, 68, 249–50; on human
rights in U.N.Charter, 74; on Lend-
Lease Act, 18–19; New Deal programs
of, 10; on plans for United Nations,
52–55; on postwar human rights policies, 5; at Quebec Conference, 41–42;
on U.S. exceptionalism, 249; during
WWII, 248; at Yalta Conference, 70–71
Roosevelt administration, 88, 249
Rosenberg, James, 186–87, 195
Ross, John, 96
Ross, Robert, 105, 112
Rusk, Dean: on genocide, 178–80, 182;
on Genocide Convention, 199, 201–2;
on human rights violations, 135; on
opposition to U.N., 133; on petitioning
the U.N., 136; Eleanor Roosevelt's U.N.
speech and, 125; on Stepinac issue,
112–13; on UNCHR draft, 120
Rutledge, Wiley, 119

Sandifer, Durward, 55; at American Law
Institute, 36, 47; as chair of State Dept.
Working Group on Human Rights, 103,
105; on colonies of European nations,
143; after Dumbarton Oaks Conference, 66; on Genocide Convention, 187;
in human rights discussions, 42–43;
on Hungary, Bulgaria, and Romania,
159; in Mr. Pasvolsky's Committee, 69;

273n31; on opposition to U.N., 133; on
petitions submitted to UNCHR, 155;
Eleanor Roosevelt and, 95, 125, 157,
233, 240; on separation of economic
from political rights, 214; on South
Africa, 219; on Subcommittee on Politi-
cal Problems, 30–34, 37; in UNCHR
session of 1951, 165; on Universal Dec-
laration of Human Rights, 129, 153
San Francisco Conference (1945), 5, 51, 71,
72, 78–89, 250; planning for, 75–77
Santa Cruz, Hernan, 129
Schenck v. United States (U.S., 1919), 179
Schmidt, Petrus, 98, 99
Schweppe, Alfred, 169, 196, 197; ABA
Amendment and, 237; Bricker and,
220, 221; Genocide Convention opposed by, 252
Secretariat (U.N.). *See* United Nations
Secretariat
Section on International and Comparative
Law (ABA), 191, 193, 207, 222, 230
Security Council (U.N.): ad hoc criminal
tribunals created by, 259; Dumbarton
Oaks Conference on, 70; Holman on,
141; on Right to Protect doctrine,
256–57; veto in, 177
segregation. *See* racial segregation and
discrimination
Sei Fujii v. California (California, 1950),
156, 157, 169
self-determination: in Atlantic Charter, 70;
developing nations on, 252; General
Assembly on, 162–63, 218; UNCHR on,
225–26; U.S. opposition to, 217; Wilson
on, 249
Senate (U.S.): Bricker and ABA Amendments in, 222, 237, 240, 253; civil
rights legislation in, 148; Committee of
Eight in, 55–56; after election of 1950,
164; Foreign Relations Committee of,
157; Genocide Convention passed by
(1986), 253; Genocide Convention rejected by, 6, 12, 168, 172, 191, 194–209,
211, 212, 246, 251–52; hearings on U.S.
membership in U.N. by, 86–88; League
of Nations rejected by, 8; opposition to